Nonparametric Econometric Methods and Application

Nonparametric Econometric Methods and Application

Special Issue Editor

Thanasis Stengos

MDPI • Basel • Beijing • Wuhan • Barcelona • Belgrade

Special Issue Editor
Thanasis Stengos
University of Guelph
Canada

Editorial Office
MDPI
St. Alban-Anlage 66
4052 Basel, Switzerland

This is a reprint of articles from the Special Issue published online in the open access journal *Journal of Risk and Financial Management* (ISSN 1911-8074) from 2018 to 2019 (available at: https://www.mdpi.com/journal/jrfm/special_issues/nonparametric_econometric).

For citation purposes, cite each article independently as indicated on the article page online and as indicated below:

LastName, A.A.; LastName, B.B.; LastName, C.C. Article Title. *Journal Name* **Year**, *Article Number*, Page Range.

ISBN 978-3-03897-964-7 (Pbk)
ISBN 978-3-03897-965-4 (PDF)

Contents

About the Special Issue Editor

Thanasis Stengos is a member of the Department of Economics and Finance of the University of Guelph, Canada, where he has held a University Research Chair position since 2004. He received his B.Sc. and M.Sc. in Economics from the London School of Economics and his Ph.D. from Queen's University, Canada. He currently serves as an Associate Editor of the Journal of Applied Econometrics, Empirical Economics, and Economics Letters, he is a member of the editorial board of the Journal of Risk and Financial Management, and he is coeditor of the Review of Economic Analysis. His research has been published in journals including the *Review of Economic Studies, European Economic Review, International Economic Review, Economic Journal, Journal of Monetary Economics, Journal of Econometrics, Econometric Theory, The Review of Economic and Statistics, Journal of Applied Econometrics, Journal of Business and Economic Statistics,* and the *Journal of Economic Growth.*

Preface to "Nonparametric Econometric Methods and Application"

An area of very active research in econometrics over the last 30 years has been that of non- and semiparametric methods. These methods have provided ways to complement more traditional parametric approaches in terms of robust alternatives as well as preliminary data analysis. The field has expanded with important advances both in time series and cross-sectional frameworks and more recently in panel data settings, allowing for data-driven flexibility that has proved invaluable in applied research. The methodology has been enhanced by software developments that have made these methods easy to apply, which has opened up a variety of potentially important and relevant applications in all areas of economics: microeconomics, macroeconomics, economic growth, finance, and labor, etc. The present Special Issue collects a number of new contributions both at the theoretical level and in terms of applications.

The papers in the collection cover a number of different topics. Sun and Wu study the contemporaneous relationship between S&P 500 index returns and log increments of the market volatility index (VIX) via a nonparametric copula method, where they propose a conditional dependence index to investigate how the dependence between the two series varies across different segments of the market return distribution. Kalaitzidakis, Mamuneas and Stengos use a smooth coefficient semiparametric model to examine the effect of emissions, as measured by carbon dioxide (CO_2), on economic growth among a set of OECD countries during the period 1981–1998 and directly estimate the output elasticity of emissions. Yan and Li develop a nonparametric method to estimate a conditional quantile function for a panel data model with an additive individual fixed effects, a model that can be applied to a variety of circumstances. Tzeremes examines the effect of financial development on countries' production efficiency levels and develops robust (order-m) time-dependent conditional nonparametric frontier estimators in order to measure 87 countries' production efficiency levels over the period 1970–2014. Eroglu and Soybilgen apply wavelet methods in the popular augmented Dickey–Fuller and M types of unit root tests, and they perform an extensive comparison of the wavelet-based unit root tests, which also includes the recent contributions in the literature. Chen and Sun compare the finite sample performance of three nonparametric threshold estimators via the Monte Carlo method, and they find that the finite sample performance of the three estimators is not robust to the position of the threshold level along the distribution of the threshold variable, especially when a structural change occurs at the tail part of the distribution. Jensen and Maheu examine the presence of volatility feedback in the often-debated risk–return relationship by modeling the contemporaneous relationship between market excess returns and log-realized variances with a nonparametric, infinitely ordered, mixture representation of the observables' joint distribution. Luong and Dokuchaev address the forecasting of realized volatility for financial time series using the heterogeneous autoregressive model (HAR) and machine learning techniques, and they find that their proposed model offers improvements when applied to historical high-frequency data. Koroglu investigates the public debt and economic growth relationship using the semiparametric smooth coefficient approach that allows democracy to influence this relationship and parameter heterogeneity in the unknown functional form and addresses the endogeneity of variables. Reza and Rilstone extend Horowitz's smoothed maximum score estimator to discrete-time duration models. They derive both asymptotic properties and examine finite sample performance through Monte Carlo simulations. Finally, Melecky, Stanickova and Hanclova apply data envelopment analysis (DEA) methodology to compare the dynamic efficiency of European countries over the last decade.

All of the above papers cover many diverse applications and contributions of nonparametric methods that we hope will add to the already rich literature and become useful additions to applied and theoretical econometricians alike.

Thanasis Stengos
Special Issue Editor

Journal of
Risk and Financial Management

MDPI

Article

Leverage and Volatility Feedback Effects and Conditional Dependence Index: A Nonparametric Study

Yiguo Sun [1,*] and Ximing Wu [2]

1 Department of Economics and Finance, University of Guelph, Guelph, ON N1G2W1, Canada
2 Department of Agricultural Economics, Texas A&M University, College Station, TX 77843, USA; xwu@email.tamu.edu
* Correspondence: yisun@uoguelph.ca; Tel.: +1-519-824-4120

Received: 5 April 2018; Accepted: 4 June 2018; Published: 8 June 2018

Abstract: This paper studies the contemporaneous relationship between S&P 500 index returns and log-increments of the market volatility index (VIX) via a nonparametric copula method. Specifically, we propose a conditional dependence index to investigate how the dependence between the two series varies across different segments of the market return distribution. We find that: (a) the two series exhibit strong, negative, extreme tail dependence; (b) the negative dependence is stronger in extreme bearish markets than in extreme bullish markets; (c) the dependence gradually weakens as the market return moves toward the center of its distribution, or in quiet markets. The unique dependence structure supports the VIX as a barometer of markets' mood in general. Moreover, applying the proposed method to the S&P 500 returns and the implied variance (VIX^2), we find that the nonparametric leverage effect is much stronger than the nonparametric volatility feedback effect, although, in general, both effects are weaker than the dependence relation between the market returns and the log-increments of the VIX.

Keywords: conditional dependence index; Kendall's tau; leverage effect; nonparametric copula; tail dependence index; volatility feedback effect

JEL Classification: C13; C22; G1

---

1. Introduction

Investors witnessed severe downturn in the U.S. stock market in the second half of the year 2008 when the mood of the bearish market was often cited through an implied volatility index—the VIX, a trade mark held by the Chicago Board Options Exchange (CBOE). The VIX is designed to retrieve the market's estimate of average S&P 500 index volatility over the subsequent 22 trading days. As bearish markets frequently observed counter-movements between S&P 500 index prices and the VIX, the VIX earned itself a reputation of market barometer of investors' fear (see Figure 1).[1] Motivated by this observation, we join the traditional finance literature to study the leverage and volatility feedback effects via the nonparametric method, where the asymmetric GARCH-in-mean type of models are popularly used in such a study (see Bekaert and Wu (2000), and references therein).

---

1 "Fears Takes a Holiday: VIX at 7-Month Low". The Wall Street Journal, 4 December 2010.

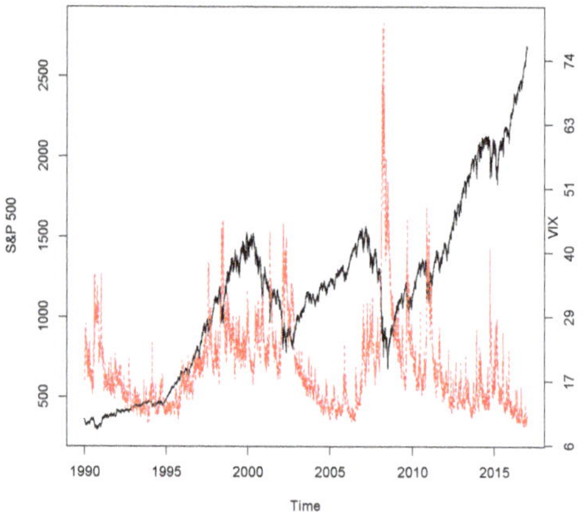

Figure 1. Raw Data Plot (01/02/1990–12/29/2017; black: S&P 500 Index; red: VIX).

To explain a stylized fact of stock markets—the asymmetric volatility: Volatility responds more to a drop in the value of a stock (index) than an increase of an equal amount in the value of the stock (index); two popular hypotheses have been put forward such as the leverage and volatility feedback effects hypotheses; see Black (1976); Bollerslev and Zhou (2006); Campbell and Hentschel (1992); Christie (1982); French et al. (1987), among many others. From the empirical financial econometrics point of view, the two hypotheses explain opposite causality between stock price movements and volatility. So, which direction of causality is stronger? The answer is inconclusive; see, Bekaert and Wu (2000); Bollerslev et al. (2006), among others. Moreover, there is no agreement on which data set shall be used. For example, the literature has seen volatility measured by historical volatility, conditional volatility, realized volatility and implied volatility. A noticeable research study has been made to learn the information content of the four different volatility measures; for example, Christensen and Prabhala (1998); Fleming (1998); Blair et al. (2001); Poon and Granger (2003); Becker et al. (2009); Jiang and Tian (2005), among many others.

In this paper, we use the VIX as the measure of volatility. The VIX is published by the CBOE almost continuously each trading day such that it is public information available to all investors. Therefore, it will be a public interest to learn more about how the two publicly observable series, the S&P 500 index and its implied volatility index (or VIX), interact with each other. In addition, in empirical finance literature, the relationships between VIX (or the VIX changes) and market returns are popularly studied in semiparametric or parametric regression framework, which can potentially suffer model misspecification problem. For example, Bollerslev and Zhou (2006) and Bekiros et al. (2017) estimate the leverage and volatility feedback effects from several competitive parametric models and notice that the magnitude of these effects is very sensitive to the underlying model used for the analysis. In this paper, we therefore introduce a model-free approach to reinvestigate the causality between the implied variance (or the changes in VIX) and the market returns, by estimating the joint density functions of the two variables of interest. Specifically, we apply the nonparametric copula technique developed by Wu (2010) to estimate the joint density functions.

The current paper contributes to the existing literature in two folds: a new methodology and new empirical findings. In the aspect of a new methodology in studying the leverage and volatility feedback effects, we attach both effects to market specific conditions by proposing a nonparametric conditional dependence index (see Section 4). Take the leverage effect as an example. It is a common practice in the traditional finance literature that volatility asymmetry is linked to the sign of market returns (or the sign of market return innovations) in asymmetric GARCH-type models, where a negative leverage parameter is seen as an evidence supporting the leverage hypothesis. Our proposed method, however, can be used to uncover the strength of the leverage effects across different market conditions, as we directly measure the dependence of the implied variances on S&P 500 index returns given that S&P 500 returns fall into different segments of the return distribution. Consequently, our results enable investors to understand under what circumstances they should pay particular attention to the leverage effect of the market returns on the market expected future volatility. Here, the concept of the *leverage effect* is extended to the impact of the (contemporaneous and lagged) S&P 500 index returns on the implied variances.

One advantage of our research is that we attach the leverage effect with the performance of S&P 500 index, while traditional research, using asymmetric GARCH-type models to study the leverage effect, tends to define the leverage effect with respect to a predetermined reference point, usually zero.[2] Interestingly, we find that the leverage effects exhibit a W shape across different segments of S&P 500 index return distribution. To our knowledge, this is an interesting new finding that has not been documented in the finance literature: When studying the leverage effects of market returns, one needs to look beyond how market volatility reacts to positive or negative market returns.

The volatility feedback effect documented states that market returns are positively correlated with market volatility, and the returns are high (low) if the anticipated volatility increases (decreases). GARCH-in-mean type of models are usually used to test the volatility feedback effect (e.g., Poterba and Summers (1986); French et al. (1987); Campbell and Hentschel (1992); Glosten et al. (1993)), where the coefficient for volatility effect is assumed to be a positive constant. Bekaert and Wu (2000) did allow market volatility to bear a varying risk premium when modeling excess stock (index) returns of Japanese market by assuming a conditional version of the CAPM based on the riskless debt model; however, the volatility feedback effect is difficult to be estimated accurately as stated in their paper. In this paper, the conditional dependence index proposed in Section 4 is a model-free measure of the volatility feedback effect. We find that the volatility feedback effect is a U-shape curve as the squared VIX moves across different segment of its distribution. In contrast to Bekaert and Wu's (2000) finding, but consistent with Engle and Ng (1993) and references in Bollerslev et al. (2006), we find that the volatility feedback effect is generally smaller than the leverage effect.

Most researchers agree that the implied variance, VIX^2, has a long-memory of its past, while S&P 500 market returns have a very short memory of its past. We therefore decompose the logarithm of the implied variance into two components: its previous day value and its daily increment (named *rvix* in this paper). We show that the log-increment of the VIX has very short memory comparable with the market return. Since the relation between market returns and the implied variance is a balanced or net outcome of the relation of the market returns with each component of the implied variance, we then explore the instantaneous relation between the short-memory component of the implied variance and the market returns. That is, we investigate not only the leverage and volatility feedback effects along the line of the traditional finance literature, but also study the relation between the log-increments of the VIX and the market returns. Our empirical findings are consistent with our intuition: we observe considerable contemporaneous dependence between S&P 500 index returns and the logarithm changes of the VIX, which is bigger than both the leverage and volatility feedback effects in terms of magnitude in general.

The strong daily, negative, asymmetric relation between the market returns and the increments of the market volatility is also found in Giot (2005) and Hibbert et al. (2008) in a simple linear regression model framework and Bekiros et al. (2017) in a linear quantile regression setup. Our analysis provides several additional noteworthy results: (a) the two series exhibit strong, negative, extreme tail

---

2 As an exception, Wu and Xiao (2002) studied the asymmetry of the volatility response curve via a generalized partially linear regression model of the VIX on S&P 100 index, which is a semiparametric approach.

dependency; (b) the negative dependency is stronger in extreme downturn markets than in extreme bullish markets; (c) the dependency gradually weakens as the market return moves toward the center of its distribution, or in quiet markets. These results imply that the simple linear regression model with a dummy variable to account for positive or negative market returns may not be sufficient to capture the extreme tail relation between the log-increments of the VIX and the S&P 500 index returns and that the average relation implied by the linear regression model may understate the relation of the two series in extreme market conditions.

The rest of the paper is organized as follows. Section 2 presents the data and summary statistics. Section 3 discusses the nonparametric estimation of copula joint densities and presents the tail dependence indexes of interest. In Section 4, we propose a conditional dependence index to study the leverage and volatility feedback effects and the relation between market returns and the log-increments of the VIX. To check on the robustness of the results, we conduct subsample analysis by splitting the data into four subsample periods. We conclude in Section 5.

2. Data and Descriptive Statistics

We downloaded daily S&P 500 index prices from DataStream and daily implied volatility (or VIX) from the CBOE. The data span from 2 January 1990 (the first date that the VIX is available) to 29 December 2017. The VIX is designed to provide a benchmark market volatility index measuring the market's aggregate view of the average market volatility over the subsequent 22 trading days, calculated from both at-the-money and out-of-the-money S&P 500 option contracts satisfying some volume conditions (Whaley 1993, 2000) via a model-free method developed by Demeterfi et al. (1999) and originated from the seminal work of Breeden and Litzenberger (1978). Detailed information about the VIX can be found at http://www.cboe.com.

The VIX is frequently cited as a barometer of investors' fear, and this view of the implied volatility has found strong popularity among the investor community. A high VIX beyond 40 is usually linked to a severe bear market while a low VIX value to a market with more confidence. The first time that the VIX surpassed the value of 40 was on 31 August 1998, a year marked by Russia's currency devaluation and national debt moratorium and the collapse of the Long Term Capital Management in the U.S.A. The number of transaction days with the VIX value exceeding 40 is 15, 4, 10, 63, 61, 3, 11, and 1 in the year of 1998, 2001, 2002, 2008, 2009, 2010, 2011, and 2015, respectively. On 20 November 2008, the VIX reached its record high of 80.86, marking an unprecedented financial crisis faced by global financial markets.

We plot the two data series in Figure 1. For the data period under consideration, the two indexes moved in opposite directions in 77.68 percent of the total transaction days. Splitting the data according to the directions of the S&P 500 index price movements, we observe this: of 77.08 percent of the total 3285 transaction days that the S&P 500 index fell, the VIX gained; of 78.30 percent of the total 3765 transaction days that the S&P 500 index gained, the VIX fell. We also see a significant increase in counter-movements between the two indexes during extremely bearish market periods; for example, the two series move in opposite directions 84.92%, 88.93%, and 80.15% of the transaction days in the year of 1998, 2008, and 2009, respectively.

Let P_t and VIX_t^2 be the S&P 500 index price and the *implied variance* at date t, respectively.[3] We construct the daily S&P 500 index return and the log-increment of the VIX as follows:

$$rsp_t = 100 \times \ln\left(P_t/P_{t-1}\right) \text{ and } rvix_t = 100 \times \ln\left(VIX_t/VIX_{t-1}\right). \quad (1)$$

[3] The VIX is the implied standard deviation of near future average market index volatility. Therefore, the implied variance equals the squared value of the VIX.

Table 1 reports the summary statistics of the implied variance, S&P 500 index returns, and log-changes of the VIX. It is noted that $rvix_t$ has a slightly lower average but significantly higher variation than rsp_t during the sample period. We then split the data according to the sign of rsp_t and calculate the upside and downside averages and sample standard deviations for both rsp_t and $rvix_t$. Interestingly, we observe that both series exhibit stronger volatility in the downturn markets than in the upturn markets. In the downturn markets, the market index performed considerably worse than in the upturn markets, and the opposite holds true for the VIX index. In addition, the implied variance, VIX_t^2, is on average lower and less volatile when the S&P 500 index prices went up than when the S&P 500 index prices came down.[4]

Table 1. Summary Statistics (01/02/1990–12/29/2017).

Variable	$\bar{x}$	$\bar{x}_-$	$\bar{x}_+$	$\hat{\sigma}$	$\hat{\sigma}_-$	$\hat{\sigma}_+$
VIX^2	450.178	492.787	412.208	479.277	538.629	415.808
$rvix$	0.018	3.410	−3.010	5.888	5.432	4.454
rsp	0.019	−0.791	0.742	1.137	0.882	0.802
	$\rho\,(1)$	$\rho\,(2)$	$\rho\,(3)$	$\rho\,(4)$	$\rho\,(5)$	$\rho\,(6)$
VIX^2	0.971	0.947	0.933	0.916	0.908	0.896
$rvix$	−0.091	−0.081	−0.033	−0.034	−0.014	−0.030
rsp	−0.049	−0.069	0.024	−0.025	−0.035	0.005

a. $\bar{x}$ = average return, $\bar{x}_-$ = downside average return over times when $rsp < 0$, $\bar{x}_+$ = upside average return over times when rsp ≥ 0; b. $\hat{\sigma}$ = sample standard deviation, $\hat{\sigma}_-$ = downside sample standard deviation over times when $rsp < 0$, $\hat{\sigma}_+$ = upside sample standard deviation over times when $rsp \geq 0$. c. $\hat{\rho}\,(h)$ is the sample autocorrelation of lag h and the 5% critical value equals 0.023. Also, the Ljung-Box statistics with six lags are $Q_{rsp}(6) = 45.58$, $Q_{rvix}(6) = 110.72$, and $Q_{VIX^2}(6) = 36769$, where the 1% critical value equals 16.811.

Next, we use three dependence measures between rsp and $rvix$ to examine the counter-movements between the S&P 500 index prices and the VIX values, including Pearson's correlation coefficient, Kendall's tau,[5] and $\lambda = \Pr(rsp_t \times rvix_t < 0)$. Kendall's tau reveals a strong negative (or positive) association between the two series if it is close to negative (or positive) one, and a weak association if it is close to zero. Kendall's tau equals zero, if the two series are independent, but it may not hold true vice versa. As for $\lambda \in [0,1]$, the probability that the two series move in opposite directions, the closer λ is to one, the stronger is the negative association between rsp_t and $rvix_t$. We report our estimates in the fourth to sixth columns in Table 2. The sample correlation between $rvix_t$ and rsp_t ranges from −0.878 in 2015 to −0.450 in 1995 and Kendall's tau ranges from −0.727 in 2015 to −0.295 in 1995. The negative dependence was more prominent in the past 18 years of the 21th century than in the 1990s. For the entire sample period under consideration, there is a 77.7 percent chance that the S&P 500 index prices and the VIX values moved in opposite directions, and this number peaked at 88.9 percent in 2008 and bottomed at 63.9 percent in 1995. Roughly speaking, the worse the market is, the stronger is the negative dependence.

---

4 Some results are studied but not reported in the main text for brevity. We constructed two optimal portfolios of S&P 500 index and VIX based on minimum variance criterion and maximum Sharpe ratio criterion. The results show that the optimal portfolios enjoy much smaller volatility than the market index, but little improvement on average returns. In addition, the optimal portfolios allocate a higher percentage of investment to the VIX in bearish markets than in bullish markets.

5 Kendall's tau is given by

$$\begin{aligned}\tau &= \Pr[(X_1 - X_2)(Y_1 - Y_2) > 0] - \Pr[(X_1 - X_2)(Y_1 - Y_2) < 0] \\ &= 2\Pr[(X_1 - X_2)(Y_1 - Y_2) > 0] - 1,\end{aligned}$$

where (X_1, Y_1) and (X_2, Y_2) are continuous random vectors drawn from the same joint cumulative distribution $F(x,y)$; see Nelsen (1999, chp. 5).

Table 2. Sample Correlation, Kendall's τ, λ, Average Compound Return of the S&P 500 Index, and Average VIX.

Year	Sample Correlation	Kendall's τ	Sample Correlation	Kendall's τ	λ	Average S&P 500 Return	Average VIX
	(VIX^2, rsp)		$(rvix, rsp)$				
ALL	−0.135	−0.065	−0.707	−0.539	0.777	0.028	19.37
1990	−0.19	−0.109	−0.537	−0.353	0.71	−0.034	23.09
1991	−0.051	−0.066	−0.557	−0.362	0.727	0.092	18.38
1992	−0.164	−0.084	−0.547	−0.351	0.673	0.017	15.45
1993	−0.182	−0.099	−0.51	−0.362	0.672	0.027	12.69
1994	−0.29	−0.17	−0.724	−0.496	0.75	−0.006	13.93
1995	−0.3	−0.212	−0.45	−0.295	0.639	0.116	12.39
1996	−0.316	−0.193	−0.687	−0.457	0.713	0.073	16.44
1997	−0.117	−0.154	−0.701	−0.53	0.771	0.107	22.38
1998	−0.183	−0.106	−0.819	−0.641	0.849	0.094	25.60
1999	−0.28	−0.18	−0.799	−0.6	0.829	0.071	24.37
2000	−0.247	−0.134	−0.784	−0.571	0.81	−0.042	23.32
2001	−0.159	−0.044	−0.82	−0.6	0.794	−0.056	25.75
2002	−0.129	−0.09	−0.818	−0.646	0.81	−0.106	27.29
2003	−0.111	−0.081	−0.642	−0.462	0.746	0.093	21.98
2004	−0.25	−0.136	−0.759	−0.539	0.806	0.034	15.48
2005	−0.253	−0.163	−0.831	−0.621	0.813	0.012	12.81
2006	−0.262	−0.179	−0.822	−0.564	0.737	0.051	12.81
2007	−0.195	−0.093	−0.85	−0.672	0.813	0.014	17.54
2008	−0.141	−0.109	−0.847	−0.69	0.889	−0.192	32.69
2009	−0.19	−0.08	−0.755	−0.556	0.802	0.084	31.48
2010	−0.3	−0.171	−0.848	−0.604	0.813	0.048	22.55
2011	−0.189	−0.085	−0.867	−0.664	0.821	0.000	24.20
2012	−0.223	−0.139	−0.761	−0.548	0.764	0.050	17.80
2013	−0.322	−0.147	−0.83	−0.603	0.798	0.103	14.23
2014	−0.269	−0.139	−0.853	−0.644	0.817	0.043	14.18
2015	−0.251	−0.113	−0.878	−0.727	0.865	−0.003	16.67
2016	−0.246	−0.122	−0.813	−0.624	0.774	0.036	15.83
2017	−0.334	−0.196	−0.746	−0.476	0.745	0.071	11.09

The compound return of the S&P500 index is the log-difference of market indexes observed at the ending and starting date of the period under consideration multiplied by 100; λ gives the relative frequency that the market index and market volatility index moved to opposite directions for the period of time under consideration.

The second and third columns of Table 2 report the sample correlation and Kendall's tau of (VIX_t^2, rsp_t), which give an overall measure of the relation between the expected near future market aggregate risk and current market aggregate return. All these statistics are negative and significantly different from zero at the 5% level, but less prominent than those between $rvix_t$ and rsp_t. The overall lower negative relation between rsp_t and VIX_t^2 is not a surprise, given the fact that the VIX_t^2 is a long-memory process while the rsp_t has a very short serial correlation with itself; see Table 1.

To sum up, Table 2 indicates a significant negative relation between the market returns and the log-increments of the VIX (and market implied variance). At the same time, we also notice that the negative relation is stronger when the market index performs poorly than when the market index performs well. It implies that an overall negative association between the two series cannot tell the full story of how the two series relate. This observation motivates us to examine the joint distribution of the two series in the next section.

3. Copula Function and Tail-Dependence Index

To further our understanding of the dependence relationship between the S&P 500 returns and the log-increments of the VIX and between the S&P 500 returns and the VIX^2, we use the device of copula to decompose their joint probability density functions (or p.d.f.'s). According to the Skalar's theorem, the joint density of two continuous random variables X and Y can be written as

$$f(x, y) = f_X(x) f_Y(y) c(F_X(x), F_Y(y)), \tag{2}$$

where X has a marginal p.d.f. $f_X(x)$ and a cumulative distribution function (or c.d.f., hereafter) $F_X(x)$, and Y has a marginal p.d.f. $f_Y(y)$ and a c.d.f. $F_Y(y)$. As a function of the c.d.f.'s of X and Y, the *copula density function*, $c\left(F_X\left(x\right), F_Y\left(y\right)\right)$, captures completely the dependence structure between X and Y. We refer interested readers to Nelsen (1999) for a thorough treatment of the copula method and Cherubino et al. (2004) for applications in finance.

As a powerful tool to measure extreme co-movement across different international stock markets and different assets, copulas have been widely used in empirical finance literature to explore nonlinear tail dependence; e.g., Chollete et al. (2011); Liu et al. (2017) and references therein. However, it is common practice for researchers to assume a certain parametric copula function in their analysis, which can create a model misspecification problem. The commonly used parametric copula families (e.g., Gaussian copula, Student's t copula, and Fréchet copula) implicitly impose a specific dependence structure between X and Y, which may not be supported by empirical data. For example, Gaussian copula density assumes that the two variables have a constant correlation regardless of whether X and Y are around the median or tails of their respective distributions. This dependence structure imposed by Gaussian copula evidently is not consistent with the fact documented in the preceding section that the dependence between the S&P 500 index returns and the implied variance is stronger during severe bearish market periods, which is featured with unusually high implied variance and low S&P 500 index returns, than during quiet market periods with relatively low implied variance. Therefore, in this paper, to avoid misspecifying the dependence structure of (rsp_t, VIX_t^2) and of $(rsp_t, rvix_t)$, we shall adopt a nonparametric copula method proposed by Wu (2010) to estimate their copula density functions. Allowing the data to speak out their true relation, Wu (2010) proposes an exponential series copula density estimator (henceforth, ESE) without preassuming the parametric form of dependence structure between two series of interest.

Below, we briefly explain the ESE estimator, denoting $u = F_X\left(x\right)$ and $v = F_Y\left(y\right)$ to simplify our notation. Firstly, to guarantee a positive copula density function, we approximate it by

$$c\left(u,v;\theta\right) = \exp\left(\sum_{0<i+j\leq m} \theta_{ij} u^i v^j + \theta_0\right), 0 \leq u,v \leq 1, \tag{3}$$

where m is a positive integer, and $\theta_0 = -\ln \int_0^1 \int_0^1 \exp\left(\sum_{0<i+j\leq m} \theta_{ij} u^i v^j\right) dudv$ is a constant to ensure that $c(u,v;\theta)$ integrates to unity. The ESE can be viewed as a series approximation of the log density, and the functional form of $c\left(u,v;\theta\right)$ is determined by m, which is the order of polynomials of the log copula density.

Secondly, to estimate the parameters, $\theta = \left(\theta_0, \left\{\theta_{i,j} : 1 \leq i+j \leq m\right\}\right)$, in (3), we apply Jaynes' (1957) famous Maximum Entropy (ME) Principle, which minimizes Shannon's information entropy

$$\max_{\theta} - \int_0^1 \int_0^1 c(u,v;\theta) \log c(u,v;\theta) dudv \tag{4}$$

subject to the following integration-to-unity condition and m moment conditions

$$\int_0^1 \int_0^1 c(u,v;\theta) dudv = 1 \tag{5}$$

$$\int_0^1 \int_0^1 u^i v^j c(u,v;\theta) dudv = E\left(u^i v^j\right), \; 0 < i+j \leq m. \tag{6}$$

Finally, in practice, letting the number of moments increase with sample size at an appropriate rate and replacing the population moments in (6) with their corresponding sample moments, one obtains a consistent nonparametric estimator of the underlying copula density function. The sample moments are sufficient statistics of the underlying distribution, and the MLE estimator of the ME density can be shown to be asymptotically efficient (Crain 1974).

Jaynes' (1957) ME Principle suggests that one can use a number of sufficient statistics that depict the copula density function. For example, if X and Y are drawn from a bivariate normal distribution, it is well-known that knowing the mean and variance suffice to identify the Gaussian copula density function; i.e., m will be two. As one does not know the true copula density function in practice, an incorrectly selected set of sufficient statistics would lead to misleading inference on the dependence relation between variables of interest. How does the choice of the set of sufficient statistics affect our estimation of the copula density function? The intuition is this: a smaller set of sufficient statistics may omit important, relevant information associated with some missing sufficient statistics, which will evidently lead to biased inference on the true dependence structure between the two variables of interest; on the other hand, a larger than necessary set of sufficient statistics will incorporate redundant information associated with the inclusion of some non-useful extra moments, inflating the variation in the estimation of θ's because of the loss of degree of freedoms. Therefore, the set of sufficient statistics, or more precisely, the order of m of polynomial in the exponent of Equation (3) shall be selected carefully. In fact, one can view m as a *smoothing parameter* in the framework of nonparametric density estimation. In this paper, m is selected in a data-driven manner according to the Akaike Information Criterion (AIC), an information criterion balances the trade off between accuracy and complexity in model construction.[6]

Now, let the marginal cumulative distribution functions of $rvix_t$, VIX_t^2 and rsp_t denoted by $u_{rvix,t} \equiv F_{rvix}(x)$, $u_{VIX^2,t} \equiv F_{VIX^2}(x)$, and $v_t \equiv F_{rsp}(x)$, respectively.[7] Since these quantities are usually unknown, we replace them by their frequency estimates, i.e., $\hat{F}_{rvix}(x) = 1/T \sum_{t=1}^{T} I(rvix_t \leq x)$, $\hat{F}_{VIX^2}(x) = 1/T \sum_{t=1}^{T} I(VIX_t^2 \leq x)$, and $\hat{F}_{rsp} = 1/T \sum_{t=1}^{T} I(rsp_t \leq x)$, respectively. Several benefits could result from the one-to-one transformation of the variable of interest via its cumulative distribution function: (a) it can effectively mitigate potential outlier problems in the nonparametric estimation; (b) as a measure of the likelihood of the occurrence of an event, probability provides a more direct way of capturing market relative status than the raw data value does across time, which is of the upmost important in our study of the relationship between the two indexes in a quick-changing market environment. Furthermore, the study of the transformed data (v, u_{rvix}) and (v, u_{VIX^2}), instead of the raw data, provides a key tool to consolidate historical study of similar situations so that we can discuss the relation between two series according to event probabilities. This point will be illustrated in the next section where we discuss the full sample and subsample results.

In Figure 2, we plot the estimated copula density functions for (v, u_{rvix}) with $m = 5$ and for (v, u_{VIX^2}) with $m = 7$, where m's are selected to minimize the AIC. The preliminary results in Section 2 indicate a strong negative association between rsp_t and $rvix_t$ without identifying the sources of the observed relation. The left panel in Figure 2 suggests that the negative dependence between the S&P 500 index returns and the log-increments of the VIX is largely driven by the counter-movements at the two tails, since the bulk of the copula density is along the anti-diagonal line and spikes up at the two corners. In other words, the co-movements of the opposite tails of the two marginal distributions contribute significantly to the negative dependence between the S&P 500 index returns and the log-increments of the VIX. In addition, the density at the upper left corner in this graph, corresponding to the case of low market index returns and high VIX changes, is larger than its counterpart associated with high market index returns and low VIX changes. Except for the two tails along the anti-diagonal line in the $[0,1]^2$ unit square, the copula density appears to be rather symmetric.

---

6 Of course, one can also apply other nonparametric methods to estimate $c(u, v)$. For example, one can use a kernel estimator or an empirical distribution based estimator. We choose to use the ESE estimator as Wu (2010) suggests that the ESE estimator suffers less bias than the kernel estimator when (u, v) taking values near the boundary of the space of unit square $[0,1]^2$. In addition, the empirical distribution based estimator may be less smooth than the ESE estimate.

7 To simplify our notation, we will drop the subscript t from $u_{rvix,t}$, $u_{VIX^2,t}$, and v_t when we detract no confusion resulting from its omission.

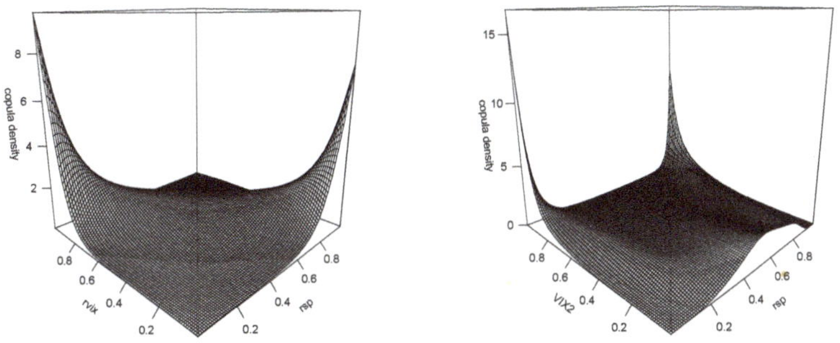

Figure 2. Joint Copula Density Functions Estimated by Nonparametric Copula Method (**Left**: $rvix_t$ and rsp_t; **Right**: VIX_t^2 and rsp_t).

The right panel in Figure 2 plots the estimated copula density for (v, u_{VIX^2}), where we observe that the S&P 500 index returns and the VIX^2 are strongly dependent when the implied variance is extremely high or its c.d.f. is close to one. The dependence is stronger when the market returns are extremely low and the implied variance is very high than when both the market returns and implied variance are extremely high. Or, put in other words, the estimated copula density indicates that the S&P 500 index returns and the VIX^2 is highly dependent during high volatile markets and the dependency is stronger in a panic triggered high volatile market than an exhilarated high volatile market. On the other hand, we observed that the dependence between the two variables flattens out when the implied variance locates between its 10th percentile to its 80th percentile. We also note that the estimated copula density humps up a bit when the implied variance locates to its left tail.

To sum up, the two joint copula densities consistently show that in a low volatility market environment, which usually accompanies limited movements in the changes of the VIX level, the dependencies between S&P 500 index returns and implied variance and between the market returns and log-increments of the VIX is less noticeable.

3.1. Tail Dependence Index Between rsp and rvix

The joint copula density of $(rsp, rvix)$ in Figure 2 clearly exhibits the left-right and right-left tail dependence between the S&P 500 index returns and log-increments of the VIX. To quantify the prominent tail dependence between the two series, one naturally wants to investigate the probability with which $rvix$ lies to the lower or upper tail area when rsp resides in the opposite tail area.[8] As the dependence occurs at the tails, such probability is usually called *tail dependence index* (or TDI, henceforth). This idea is not new and has been studied in different fields. For example, Poon et al. (2004) studied one particular tail index using extreme value theory, although they focus on the limited cases; that is, $\text{TDI}(\alpha) = \Pr\left(Y < F_Y^{-1}(\alpha) \,|\, X < F_X^{-1}(\alpha)\right)$ when $\alpha \to 1$ or $\alpha \to 0$, where $F_X^{-1}(\alpha)$ and $F_Y^{-1}(\alpha)$ are the $(100 \times \alpha)$th percentile of X and Y, respectively. Taking clues from the

8 We also calculated the tail dependence index on the conditional probability that rsp lies to its tail area given that $rvix$ resides in the opposite tail area. As this mirror relation to the one reported in the paper does not bring extra light to our findings, we choose not to report the result, although the results are available upon request from the authors.

estimated copula density seen in the left panel of Figure 2, we focus on the following two TDIs that capture the co-movements of opposite tails of $(rsp, rvix)$:

$$\mathrm{TDI}_1(\alpha) = \Pr\left(rvix < rvix_\alpha | rsp > rsp_{1-\alpha}\right) = \Pr\left(u_{rvix} < \alpha | v > 1-\alpha\right), \tag{7}$$

$$\mathrm{TDI}_2(\alpha) = \Pr\left(rvix > rvix_{1-\alpha} | rsp < rsp_\alpha\right) = \Pr\left(u_{rvix} > 1-\alpha | v < \alpha\right), \tag{8}$$

where $rvix_\alpha$ and rsp_α are the $(100 \times \alpha)$th percentile of the return series $rvix$ and rsp, respectively.

Taking $\alpha = 0.01$ and $\alpha = 0.05$ respectively, we obtain $\mathrm{TDI}_1(0.01) = 0.078$, $\mathrm{TDI}_2(0.01) = 0.101$, $\mathrm{TDI}_1(0.05) = 0.285$, and $\mathrm{TDI}_2(0.05) = 0.354$ from the estimated copula density exhibited in Figure 2. If the two series were independent, we would obtain $\mathrm{TDI}_j(\alpha) = \alpha$ for $j = 1, 2$. Therefore, the fact that $\mathrm{TDI}_j(\alpha)$ is substantially higher than α indicates strong negative tail dependence between rsp and $rvix$ series. In particular, our results suggest that extreme movements in the S&P 500 index are associated with extreme movements of the VIX to the opposite direction with high probabilities.

In addition, the fact that $\mathrm{TDI}_1(\alpha) < \mathrm{TDI}_2(\alpha)$ for both $\alpha = 0.01$ and $\alpha = 0.05$ reveals that the VIX asymmetrically responds to extreme movement of the S&P 500 index prices. The probability that the VIX increases abruptly when the market index faces free-fall is much higher than the probability that the VIX falls back when the market index price enjoys strong rebound. The asymmetry is consistent with the stylized fact frequently documented in the finance literature that the market tends to respond more to bad news than to good news of equal magnitude, although this stylized fact is described from our point view of tail dependence indexes.

The fact that the tail dependence is more pronounced when the market is in turmoil explains why the VIX is dubbed as the Investor Fear Gauge.

3.2. Tail Dependence Index Between rsp and VIX^2

As the right panel of Figure 2 exhibits a prominent dependence between the S&P 500 index returns and implied variances when the latter reside at the right tail of its distribution, we introduce the following four TDIs:

$$\widetilde{\mathrm{TDI}}_1(\alpha) = \Pr\left(rsp > rsp_{1-\alpha} | VIX^2 > VIX^2_{1-\alpha}\right) = \Pr\left(v > 1-\alpha | u_{VIX^2} > 1-\alpha\right) \tag{9}$$

$$\widetilde{\mathrm{TDI}}_2(\alpha) = \Pr\left(rsp < rsp_\alpha | VIX^2 > VIX^2_{1-\alpha}\right) = \Pr\left(v < \alpha | u_{VIX^2} > 1-\alpha\right) \tag{10}$$

$$\widetilde{\mathrm{TDI}}_3(\alpha) = \Pr\left(VIX^2 > VIX^2_{1-\alpha} | rsp > rsp_{1-\alpha}\right) = \Pr\left(u_{VIX^2} > 1-\alpha | v > 1-\alpha\right) \tag{11}$$

$$\widetilde{\mathrm{TDI}}_4(\alpha) = \Pr\left(VIX^2 > VIX^2_{1-\alpha} | rsp < rsp_\alpha\right) = \Pr\left(u_{VIX^2} > 1-\alpha | v < \alpha\right) \tag{12}$$

where VIX^2_α is the $(100 \times \alpha)$th percentile of the VIX^2 series. We use $\alpha = 0.01$ to illustrate the meaning of each index. First, $\widetilde{\mathrm{TDI}}_1(0.01)$ and $\widetilde{\mathrm{TDI}}_2(0.01)$ measure the probabilities that the S&P 500 returns reside to the respective right and left 1% tail of the return distribution in an extremely volatile market condition. Second, $\widetilde{\mathrm{TDI}}_3(\alpha)$ and $\widetilde{\mathrm{TDI}}_4(\alpha)$ give the probabilities that the market sees extremely high volatility with the implied variance falling to its upper 1% tail of its distribution in an extremely high and low market return periods.

By construction, $\widetilde{\mathrm{TDI}}_1(\alpha)$ and $\widetilde{\mathrm{TDI}}_2(\alpha)$ reflect the *volatility feedback effect* of market volatility on market returns at extreme situation, while $\widetilde{\mathrm{TDI}}_3(\alpha)$ and $\widetilde{\mathrm{TDI}}_4(\alpha)$ reflect the *leverage effect* of market returns on market volatility at extreme situations. Of course, the leverage and volatility feedback effects referred to here are extended from the traditional meaning of the two effects.

Again, we take $\alpha = 0.01$ and 0.05. From the estimated copula density function shown in Figure 2, we calculate $\widetilde{\mathrm{TDI}}_1(0.01) = 0.089$, $\widetilde{\mathrm{TDI}}_2(0.01) = 0.137$, $\widetilde{\mathrm{TDI}}_1(0.05) = 0.198$, $\widetilde{\mathrm{TDI}}_2(0.05) = 0.307$, $\widetilde{\mathrm{TDI}}_3(0.01) = 0.076$, $\widetilde{\mathrm{TDI}}_4(0.01) = 0.119$, $\widetilde{\mathrm{TDI}}_3(0.05) = 0.199$, and $\widetilde{\mathrm{TDI}}_4(0.05) = 0.308$. As $\widetilde{\mathrm{TDI}}_j(\alpha) > \alpha$ for all the cases studied, we see apparent tail dependence between the market returns and market implied variances, although the tail dependence of the implied variances on the market returns is generally weaker than that of the changes of VIX on the market returns. In addition, $\widetilde{\text{TDI}}_1(\alpha) < \widetilde{\text{TDI}}_2(\alpha)$ and $\widetilde{\text{TDI}}_3(\alpha) < \widetilde{\text{TDI}}_4(\alpha)$ for both $\alpha = 0.01$ and $\alpha = 0.05$, indicating asymmetric tail dependence between the market returns and implied variances; i.e., the TDIs are stronger when the market returns lie to the left tail of rather than to the right tail of the return distribution.

3.3. Contemporaneous and Lagged Conditional Distributions

The tail dependence index only describes the probability of the occurrence of one rare event given that of another rare event. In this section, we aim to extract more information from the data by estimating the conditional cumulative distribution (or c.d.f., henceforth) functions via the nonparametric copula method. Specifically, let A be a subset of $[0,1]$. We are interested in estimating the conditional c.d.f.'s listed in Table 3.

Table 3. The List of Conditional Cumulative Distributions of Interest.

Case	Conditiondal c.d.f.	Description
C1	$F\left(u_{rvix,t} \mid v_{t-h} \in A\right)$	the conditional c.d.f. of $u_{rvix,t}$ given $v_{t-h} \in A$
C2	$F\left(v_t \mid u_{rvix,t-h} \in A\right)$	the conditional c.d.f. of v_t given $u_{vix,t-h} \in A$
C3	$F\left(u_{VIX^2,t} \mid v_{t-h} \in A\right)$	the conditional c.d.f. of $u_{VIX^2,t}$ given $v_{t-h} \in A$
C4	$F\left(v_t \mid u_{VIX^2,t-h} \in A\right)$	the conditional c.d.f. of v_t given $u_{VIX^2,t-h} \in A$
Note: $h = 0$ and 1; $A = [0, 0.05]$, $[0.45, 0.55]$, and $[0.95, 1]$		

Figure 3 plots the estimated conditional c.d.f.'s for cases C1 and C2, while Figure 4 for cases C3 and C4, wherein the results for $h = 0$ and $h = 1$ are in color blue and red respectively. Taking $A = [0, 0.05]$, $[0.95, 1]$, and $[0.45, 0.55]$, we aim to study the behavior of the conditional c.d.f.'s under extreme and moderate market conditions. If each pair of variables among v, u_{rvix} and u_{VIX^2} were drawn from a bivariate normal distribution, one would expect the conditional c.d.f. invariant with respect to the choice of A. In addition, the choice of $h = 0$ or 1 is used to measure the strength of contemporaneous relation relative to lag-one relation. Examining Figures 3 and 4, we aim to visually test two hypotheses summarized in Table 4.

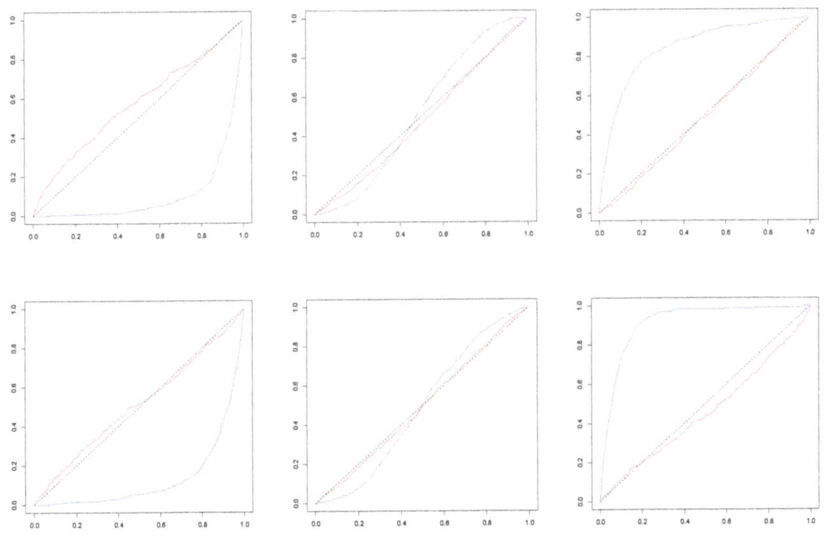

Figure 3. Conditional Ccumulative Distribution Function Estimates (blue: $h = 0$; red: $h = 1$) (**Upper row**: rvix|rsp; **Lower row**: rsp|rvix. **Left**: A = (0, 0.05]; **Middle**: A = [0.45, 0.55]; **Right**: A = [0.95, 1)).

Table 4. The Hypotheses of Interest.

The Null Hypothesis on $F(y_t \| x_{t-h} \in A)$	Implication
H_0^1: $F(y_t \| x_{t-h} \in A)$ coincides with the 45-degree line	y_t is independent of x_{t-h} when $x_{t-h} \in A$
H_0^2: $F(y_t \| x_{t-h} \in A)$ does not vary with A	(x_{t-h}, y_t) are jointly normally distributed
Note: $(x_t, y_{t-h}) = (u_{rvix,t}, v_{t-h})$, $(v_t, u_{rvix,t-h})$, $(u_{VIX^2,t}, v_{t-h})$, or $(v_t, u_{VIX^2,t-h})$; $h = 0, 1$; $A = [0, 0.05], [0.45, 0.55]$, and $[0.95, 1]$	

Reading Figure 3, we observe that both the hypotheses H_0^1 and H_0^2 fail to hold for all the contemporaneous c.c.d.f.'s. Evident deviations of the c.c.d.f.'s from the 45-degree line result from strong tail dependence between the log-increments of the VIX and the market returns. On the other hand, the inter-dependence between the two series are rather mild during quiet market periods. Evidently, the results in Figure 3 support the varying dependence relation between the two series across different market conditions, which suggests the inadequacy of fitting the data with bivariate normal distribution with a constant correlation. When $h = 1$, the hypothesis H_0^1 holds roughly true for all the lag-one conditional c.d.f.'s (or l.c.c.d.f.'s, hereafter), as they are all close to the 45-degree line. Combining our observations, we see strong daily contemporaneous dependence between the market returns and log-increments of the VIX and very weak if nothing at all one-day lag dependence. Actually, when we push h up to 20, we did not see significant lag dependences between the two series.

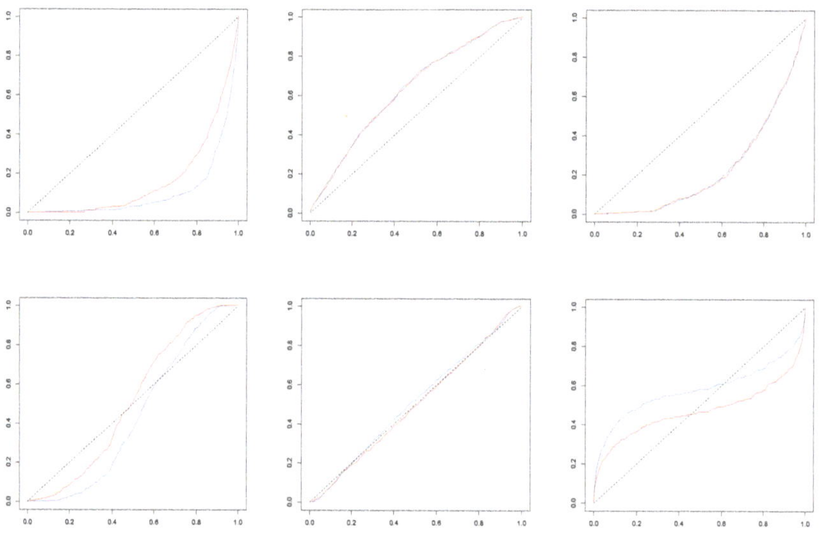

Figure 4. Conditional Cumulative Distribution Function Estimates (blue: $h = 0$; red: $h = 1$) (**Upper row**: VIX^2 |rsp; **Lower row**: rsp|VIX^2; **Left**: A = (0, 0.05]; **Middle**: A = [0.45, 0.55]; **Right**: A = [0.95, 1)).

Let us next look at Figure 4. Different from Figure 3, the c.c.d.f.'s and l.c.c.d.f.'s are very close to each other, which is especially true for the conditional c.d.f.'s of $u_{VIX^2,t}$ given $v_{t-h} \in A$ (in the first row of Figure 4), implying a strong persistent dependence of the implied variance (VIX^2) on the current and one-day lagged S&P 500 index returns. Again, as in Figure 3, Figure 4 rejects the hypothesis H_0^2 for all the cases. The hypothesis H_0^1 seems to hold only for the c.c.d.f.'s and l.c.c.d.f.'s of v_t given $u_{VIX^2,t-h} \in [0.45, 0.55]$. Overall, the c.c.d.f.'s and l.c.c.d.f.'s of $u_{VIX^2,t}$ given $v_{t-h} \in A$ deviate from the 45-degree line more than those of v_t given $u_{VIX^2,t-h} \in A$.

To sum up, we observe strong contemporaneous left-right and right-left tail dependence between rsp and $rvix$, significant contemporaneous and lagged tail dependence of the VIX^2 on the market returns, and mild tail dependence of the market returns on the VIX^2. Although useful, these qualitative assessments are largely based on smoothing and visualization of data. In the next section, we propose a conditional dependence index to formally quantify the conditional dependence between each pair of series of interest among the market returns, the log-increments of the VIX, and the VIX^2.

4. Conditional Dependence Index

As we discuss above, Figures 3 and 4 plot several estimated conditional distribution functions of u given $v \in A$, where A is a nonempty subinterval of the interval $[0,1]$. If u and v are independent of each other when $v \in A$, we have $F(u|v \in A) = F(u)$ for all $u \in [0,1]$ so that knowing the information $\{v \in A\}$ does not help us make better predictions about u. On the other hand, the further is the conditional c.d.f. away from the 45-degree line, the higher is the dependency between u and $v \in A$. Therefore, it is natural to use the area between the conditional c.d.f. and the 45-degree line as a proxy of the predictive power of $v \in A$ on u. In doing so, we are able to learn under what circumstances u and v are most dependent as v moves across its distribution function. Consequently, we can make inference on the relation between the pair of variables of interest conditional across different market status.

Hence, we propose a conditional dependence index (or CDI, henceforth) which equals twice of the area between a conditional c.d.f. and the 45-degree line, given the fact of $v \in A$. Thus, the index is defined as a functional of A:

$$G(A) = 2\int_0^1 |F(u|v \in A) - u|\, du = 2E\left[|F(u|v \in A) - u|\right]. \tag{13}$$

Evidently, for any given sub-interval $A \subset [0,1]$, $0 \le G(A) \le 1$, where $G(A) = 0$ means independence between u and v given $v \in A$, and the dependence of u on $v \in A$ grows as $G(A)$ gets closer to the unity. Partitioning the $[0,1]$ interval into 20 equal-width intervals, we calculate $G(A)$ for each interval and report the results in Table 5 for both $h = 0$ and $h = 1$.

Table 5. Conditional Dependence Indexes.

A	$rvix_t\|rsp_t$	$VIX_t^2\|rsp_t$	$rsp_t\|VIX_t^2$	$rvix_t\|rsp_{t-1}$	$VIX_t^2\|rsp_{t-1}$	$rsp_t\|VIX_{t-1}^2$
$(0, 0.05)$	0.787	0.686	0.213	0.138	0.669	0.179
$[0.05, 0.1)$	0.671	0.383	0.191	0.108	0.364	0.174
$[0.1, 0.15)$	0.555	0.197	0.143	0.087	0.194	0.129
$[0.15, 0.2)$	0.450	0.094	0.142	0.039 *	0.089	0.136
$[0.2, 0.25)$	0.359	0.045 *	0.124	0.053 *	0.043 *	0.096
$[0.25, 0.3)$	0.285	0.108	0.085	0.052 *	0.109	0.107
$[0.3, 0.35)$	0.233	0.141	0.080	0.042 *	0.143	0.052 *
$[0.35, 0.4)$	0.202	0.201	0.045 *	0.045 *	0.194	0.057 *
$[0.4, 0.45)$	0.171	0.229	0.053 *	0.025 *	0.225	0.039 *
$[0.45, 0.5)$	0.158	0.241	0.041 *	0.025 *	0.243	0.045 *
$[0.5, 0.55)$	0.158	0.278	0.025 *	0.090	0.268	0.018 *
$[0.55, 0.6)$	0.206	0.276	0.065	0.047 *	0.273	0.033 *
$[0.6, 0.65)$	0.217	0.205	0.039 *	0.087	0.189	0.048 *
$[0.65, 0.7)$	0.278	0.164	0.070	0.088	0.153	0.071
$[0.7, 0.75)$	0.307	0.146	0.081	0.032 *	0.146	0.070
$[0.75, 0.8)$	0.362	0.080 *	0.101	0.046 *	0.081 *	0.087
$[0.8, 0.85)$	0.424	0.052 *	0.124	0.025 *	0.051 *	0.109
$[0.85, 0.9)$	0.480	0.046 *	0.169	0.028 *	0.046 *	0.146
$[0.9, 0.95)$	0.611	0.195	0.197	0.022 *	0.201	0.190
$[0.95, 1)$	0.680	0.537	0.297	0.027 *	0.539	0.284

'*' marks the CDIs that are insignificant at the 5% level.

Now, we illustrate the estimation method and the test for $G(A) = 0$ for the case that $G(A) = 2E[|F(u_{rvix,t}|v_{t-h} \in A) - u_{rvix,t}|]$, the CDI of the log-increments of the VIX on the market returns. (The method is also applied to the other cases). We denote the estimator of $G(A)$ by $\hat{G}(A)$, which is given by

$$\hat{G}(A) = \frac{2}{n} \sum_{t=h+1}^{n} \left|\hat{F}(u_t|v_{t-h} \in A) - u_t\right|, \tag{14}$$

where we replace the unknown conditional c.d.f. $F(u_t|v_{t-h} \in A) = \Pr(u_{rvix,t} \le u_t, v_{t-h} \in A) / \Pr(v_{t-h} \in A)$ by its empirical conditional distribution,

$$\begin{aligned}\hat{F}(u_t|v_{t-h} \in A) &= \frac{n^{-1}\sum_{t=1}^{n} I(u_{rvix,t} \le u_t, v_{t-h} \in A)}{n^{-1}\sum_{t=1}^{n} I(v_{t-h} \in A)} \\ &= \frac{n^{-1}\sum_{t=1}^{n} I\left(rvix_t \le F_{rvix,t}^{-1}(u_t), rsp_{t-h} \in F_{rsp_{t-h}}^{-1}(A)\right)}{n^{-1}\sum_{t=1}^{n} I\left(rsp_{t-h} \in F_{rsp_{t-h}}^{-1}(A)\right)},\end{aligned} \tag{15}$$

with the total sample size, $n = 7055$, $I(\cdot)$ being the indicator function, and $F_{rvix,t}(\cdot)$ and $F_{rsp_{t-h}}(\cdot)$ being the unconditional c.d.f.'s of $rvix_t$ and rsp_{t-h}, respectively.

$\hat{G}(A)$ is a consistent estimator of $G(A)$ as $\sup_{u\in[0,1]} \left|F(u|v \in A) - \hat{F}(u|v \in A)\right| = o_p(1)$ and the sample mean is a consistent estimator of a population mean, given the fact that both series are stationary. Actually, $\hat{G}(A) = G(A) + O_p\left(n^{-1/2}\right)$.

Next, we are interested in testing the null hypothesis of $G(A) = 0$ against the alternative hypothesis of $G(A) > 0$. If the null hypothesis holds true, we can show that $\sqrt{n}\left(\hat{F}(u|v \in A) - u\right)$ converges to a normal random variable with zero mean and finite variance. Under the alternative hypothesis, we expect $\sqrt{n}\left(\hat{F}(u|v \in A) - u\right) = O_p\left(\sqrt{n}\right)$. Therefore, we expect $\sqrt{n}\hat{G}(A) = O_p(1)$ under the null hypothesis and $\sqrt{n}\hat{G}(A) = O_p\left(\sqrt{n}\right)$ under the alternative hypothesis. However, to conduct the test, we need to obtain proper critical values. As the distribution of $\hat{G}(A)$ under the null hypothesis does not have a simple formula, we propose to use bootstrap critical values.

Bootstrap critical values. Should the alternative hypothesis hold true, the realization of the log-increment of the VIX is affected by the realization of the market return. Therefore, the temporal ordering of the market return matters in the calculation of $\hat{G}(A)$. However, should the null hypothesis hold true, we have $\hat{F}(u|v \in A) = n^{-1}\sum_{t=1}^{n} I\left(rvix_t \le F_{rvix,t}^{-1}(u)\right)$, the empirical c.d.f. of $rvix_t$, which does not depend on the realization of the market returns, nor does $\hat{G}(A)$. Therefore, the temporal ordering of the market returns should not matter in the calculation of $\hat{G}(A)$, should the null hypothesis hold true. Based on these observations, we propose to obtain bootstrap samples by randomly shuffling the market returns while keeping the order of the log-increments of the VIX. As a result, the bootstrap sample contains the raw data on $rvix$ and the randomly shuffled market return data, rsp^*, and the bootstrap sample size is the same as the original sample size, n = 7055. To obtain the bootstrap critical value at the significance level of 5% for example, we repeat 500 bootstrap procedures and use the 95th percentile of the 500 bootstrap statistics, $\hat{G}^*(A)$, to approximate the critical value, where $\hat{G}^*(A)$ is the bootstrap estimate of $G(A)$ using (15).

In Table 5, we report $\hat{G}(A)$ for six cases: the CDIs of $rvix_t$ given rsp_{t-h}, VIX_t^2 given rsp_{t-h}, rsp_t given VIX_{t-h}^2 for $h = 0$ (capturing contemporaneous dependence) and for $h = 1$ (capturing one day lagged dependence).[9] We divide the interval $[0, 1]$ into 20 intervals with equal increments of 0.05. In Table 5, we marked the insignificant CDI estimates at the 5% level with an asterisk. The fifth column of Table 5 indicates little dependence of the log-increments of the VIX on the previous day's market

9 We calculated but decided not to report the CDIs of rsp_t given $rvix_{t-h}$ as the extra results do not add more information to the relation of the market returns and the log-increments of the VIX, and the intuition of which can be seen from Figure 3. However, these results can be obtained from the authors upon request.

index performance. Combining the second and fifth columns, we see close contemporaneous but less noticeable lagged relation between the changes of the VIX and the market returns. In contrast, the relation between implied variance and market returns are rather persistent but become weaker in general over time, where the persistent relation may result from the long-memory properties of the implied variance.

To enhance the readability of the results given in Table 5, we plot the contemporaneous CDIs in Figure 5. The black line shows how the distribution of the log-increments of the VIX depends on the market return as the market return moves from its lower 5% tail, (0.05, 0.10], (0.10, 0.15,], ..., to its upper 5% tail, where each probability interval contains equally 5% of the data. It shows a general U-shape curve, bottoming at the interval of (0.45, 0.50]—around the median of the market returns. The dependence of the distribution of the log-increments of the VIX on the market returns grows as market returns go farther away from its median, although the dependences grow faster with steeper slope when the market return falls below its median value than when the market return grows above its median value (for the full sample, the daily market average return is 0.04584%). At the extreme market cases, the CDI of the log-increments of the VIX takes the highest value .787 when the market return falls below its lower 5% tail, which is higher than .680 when the market return grows beyond its upper 5% tail. The finding reflects the market's asymmetric attitude toward an extreme down market and an extreme upper market: investors in general feel more nervous in the former than the latter situation.

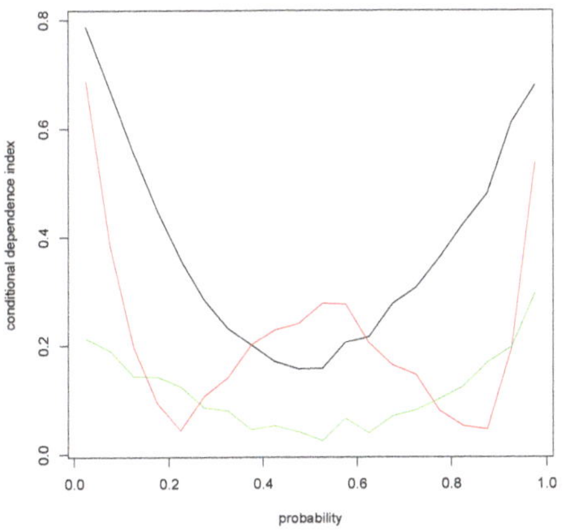

Figure 5. Full Sample Conditional Dependence Index Estimates (black: rvix|rsp; red: VIX^2|rsp; green: rsp|VIX^2).

Below, we will link our empirical results found in this section to the traditional findings on the leverage and volatility feedback effects. Here, we refer to the *leverage effect* as the dependence of the implied variance on the market returns at lag one and the *volatility feedback effect* as the dependence of the market returns on the implied variance at lag one.

The leverage effect. The red line in Figure 5 shows how the distribution of the VIX_t^2 depends on rsp_{t-1} as the market returns move from the lower 5% tail to the upper 5% tail of the return distribution. Surprisingly, we observe that the CDIs exhibit a W shape. The leverage effect is strongest when the market return falls below its 5% lower tail. If we call the volatility resulting from the market's expectation of a bright and a dismal future as good volatility and bad volatility, respectively, our results indicate that the dependence of the good volatility on market return is evidently lower than that of the bad volatility. This is consistent with the "asymmetric volatility" phenomenon documented in the literature (e.g., Aboura and Wagner 2016). We also observe strong leverage effect over the probability intervals, [0.4, 0.45), [0.45, 0.5), [0.5, 0.55), and [0.55, 0.6), and the noteworthy leverage effect when the market return falls into its [0.5, 0.55] probability interval dominates the relation of the log-increments of the VIX on the market return in the same probability interval. As the middle segment of the market return distribution symbolizes a very quiet market state; during which period, the market participants have the most uncertainty over the prediction of the direction of future market returns. Our conjecture is this: The uncertainty over future market direction may cause variance premium to dominate the conditional variance of market returns as the latter can be relatively accurately estimated during quiet market periods, where the implied variance equals the sum of variance premium and the conditional variance of market returns as defined in Bekaert and Hoerova (2014) who found that the variance premium is a component of the implied variance to predict future market returns.

The volatility feedback effect. The green line in Figure 5 shows how the distribution of rsp_t depends on VIX^2_{t-1}, where we see a much flatter convex curve than the black curve. The right most column of Table 5 shows that the volatility feedback effects are insignificant at the 5% significance level when the market return falls into the probability interval of [0.3, 0.35) to [0.6, 0.65). This means that we would not find a noticeable volatility feedback effect if we fit the data with a mean regression model. This result may be used to explain why empirical works cannot find volatility feedback effects with GARCH-in-mean model; e.g., Campbell and Hentschel (1992).

Comparing the three curves, we find noticeably higher dependence between the market returns and log-increments of the VIX than the leverage and volatility feedback effects, except for a higher leverage effect when the market return is moving around its medium value. This result encourages the econometric modeling of the market returns and log-changes of the VIX besides the leverage and volatility feedback effects. In addition, the volatility feedback effect is weaker than the leverage effect with some exceptions. This result may support the findings in Christie (1982) and Bekaert and Wu (2000) that neither the leverage effect nor the volatility feedback effect can be the sole explanation of the volatility asymmetry observed from stock markets.

To sum up, we find strong dependence between *rvix* and *rsp* and the dependence is stronger in volatile market periods than in relatively quiet market periods. As the VIX reveals market's expectation on the future 30-day volatility, our results indicate that investors make sharp revision on their belief of market risks during extreme volatile market periods, and that the revision is less noticeable during tranquil market periods. This again confirms that the negative association between the S&P 500 index prices and the VIX mainly come from tail events.

To check on how robust our findings are, we also conduct subsample analysis, where we split the sample period into five subperiods: 2 January 1990 to 31 December 1994; 1 January 1995 to 31 December 1999; 1 January 2000 to 31 December 2004; 1 January 2005 to 31 December 2009; 1 January 2010 to 31 December 2017.[10] Figure 6 plots the estimated CDIs for the four subsample periods. In general, the subsample results are similar to the full sample results shown in Figure 5, except for the first subperiod.

---

[10] Readers can certainly split the whole data period differently from ours.

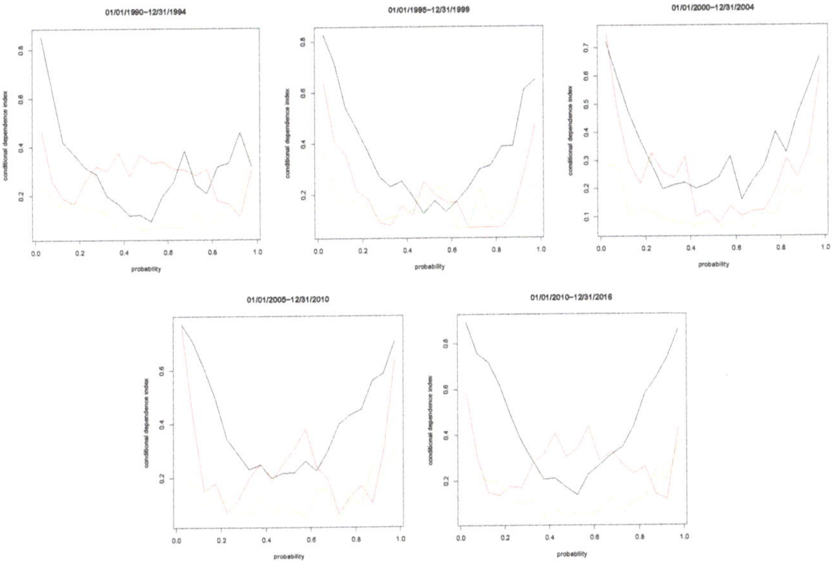

Figure 6. Subsample Conditional Dependence Index Estimates (black: rvix|rsp; red: VIX^2|rsp; green: rsp|VIX^2).

5. Concluding Remarks

Both leverage and volatility feedback hypotheses are developed to explain the stylized fact that volatility reacts asymmetrically to positive and negative stock returns. We re-examine the relationship between daily S&P 500 index returns and implied variance via the nonparametric method. By proposing a nonparametric conditional dependence index, we document three findings. First, the nonparametric leverage effect exhibits a W-shape curve as the implied variance moves from the left to the right tail of its distribution. Second, nonparametric volatility feedback exhibits a U-shape curve as the S&P 500 index returns moves across the return distribution. Third, the nonparametric leverage effect in general is higher than the nonparametric volatility feedback effect, except in relatively quiet market conditions.

The VIX index squared, as a risk-neutral measure of market volatility, is the market's best estimate of average future realized volatility over the ensuing 22 trading days plus a *volatility risk premium*, as documented by Todorov (2009); Bollerslev and Zhou (2006), among many others for other implied volatility indexes than S&P 500 implied volatility. Bakshi and Madan (2006) provide a theoretical model to explain that the VIX squared (or the implied variance) depends on historical skewness and kurtosis of return distributions and market risk aversions. Therefore, the log-increments of the VIX may reflect the market's revision on risk aversion and average future realized volatility as the S&P 500 index price changes. The empirical results in this paper indicate that the contemporaneous dependence between the market's revision on risk aversion and average future realized volatility and the market returns are stronger than the leverage and the volatility feedback effects when the market's movement deviates from its medium range.

Applying Wu's (2010) ESE nonparametric copula estimator in Section 3, we find strong tail dependency among the market returns, log-increments of the VIX and the VIX^2. From Figures 3 and 4, we get an impression that the dependence relations among each pair of the three series vary with market conditions and are strongest during extreme bearish markets.

We focus on the discovery of some noteworthy asymmetric and dynamic features between the stock returns and VIX in this study. The scope of investigation in this study is certainly limited. There are alternative nonparametric methods that can be used to conduct the analysis in this study. For example, Racine (2015) and Ho et al. (2016) study kernel-based estimation of copula models. This method is also used by Ho et al. (2018) in an in-depth analysis of tail dependence and co-movements of crude oil price. Bhatti and Nguyen (2012); Chaturvedi et al. (2012); Nguyen and Bhatti (2012); Nguyen et al. (2016); Al Rahahleh and Bhatti (2017), and Al Rahahleh et al. (2017) study the international equity market using a variety of copula-based models, with particular attention to tail dependence and extreme values. Validation and comparisons of our results with these alternative methods might provide new insight into the stock return and VIX relationship. This can be a possible topic for future research.

Author Contributions: The two authors both contributed to the formulation and execution of the investigation, and the preparation of the manuscript.

Acknowledgments: We thank two anonymous referees for helpful and constructive comments.

Conflicts of Interest: The authors declare no conflict of interest.

References

Aboura, Sofiane, and Niklas Wagner. 2016. Extreme asymmetric volatility: Stress and aggregateasset prices. *Journal of International Financial Markets, Institutions & Money* 41: 47–59.

Al Rahahleh, Naseem, and M. Ishaq Bhatti. 2017. Co-movement measure of information transmission on international equity markets. *Physica A: Statistical Mechanics and Its Applications* 470: 119–31. [CrossRef]

Al Rahahleh, Naseem, M. Ishaq Bhatti, and Iman Adeinat. 2017. Tail dependence and information flow: Evidence from international equity markets. *Physica A: Statistical Mechanics and Its Applications* 474: 319–29. [CrossRef]

Bakshi, Gurdip, and Dilip Madan. 2006. A theory of volatility spreads. *Management Science* 52: 1945–56. [CrossRef]

Becker, Ralf, Adam E. Clements, and Andrew McClelland. 2009. The jump component of S&P 500 volatility and the VIX index. *Journal of Banking & Finance* 33: 1033–38.

Bekaert, Geert, and Guojun Wu. 2000. Asymmetric volatility and risk in equity markets. *The Review of Financial Studies* 13: 1–42. [CrossRef]

Bekaert, Geert, and Marie Hoerova. 2014. The VIX, the variance premium and stock market volatility. *Journal of Econometrics* 183: 181–92. [CrossRef]

Bekiros, Stelios, Mouna Jlassi, Kamel Naoui, and Gazi Salah Uddin. 2017. The asymmetric relationship between returns and implied volatility: Evidence from global stock markets. *Journal of Financial Stability* 30: 156–74. [CrossRef]

Bhatti, M. Ishaq, and Cuong C. Nguyen. 2012. Diversification Evidence from International Equity Markets using Extreme Values and Stochastic Copulas. *Journal of International Financial Markets, Institutions & Money* 22: 622–46.

Black, Fischer. 1976. Studies of stock market volatility changes. In *Proceedings of the American Statistical Association, Business and Economics Statistics Section*. Alexandria: American Statistical Association, pp. 177–81.

Blair, Bevan J., Ser-Huang Poon, and Stephen J. Taylor. 2001. Forecasting S&P 100 volatility: The incremental information content of implied volatilities and high-frequency index returns. *Journal of Econometrics* 105: 5–26.

Bollerslev, Tim, Julia Litvinova, and George Tauchen. 2006. Leverage and volatility feedback effects in high-frequency data. *Journal of Financial Econometrics* 4: 353–84. [CrossRef]

Bollerslev, Tim, and Hao Zhou. 2006. Volatility puzzles: A simple framework for gauging return-volatility regressions. *Journal of Econometrics* 131: 123–50. [CrossRef]

Breeden, Douglas T., and Robert H. Litzenberger. 1978. Prices of state contingent claims implicit in option prices. *Journal of Business* 51: 621–51. [CrossRef]

Campbell, John Y., and Ludger Hentschel. 1992. No news is good news: An asymmetric model of changing volatility in stock returns. *Journal of Financial Economics* 31: 281–318. [CrossRef]

Chaturvedi, Anoop, Suchita Gupta, and M. Ishaq Bhatti. 2012. Confidence Ellipsoids based on a General Family of Shrinkage Estimators for a Linear Model with Non-spherical Disturbances. *Journal of Multivariate Analysis* 104: 140–58. [CrossRef]

Cherubini, Umberto, Elisa Luciano, and Walter Vecchiato. 2004. *Copula Methods in Finance*. Hoboken: John Wiley & Sons, Ltd.

Chollete, Lorán, Victor de la Peña, and Ching-Chih Lu. 2011. International diversification: A copula approach. *Journal of Banking & Finance* 35: 403–17.

Christie, Andrew A. 1982. The stochastic behavior of common stock variances-value, leverage and interest rate effects. *Journal of Financial Economics* 10: 407–32. [CrossRef]

Christensen, Bent J., and Nagpurnanand R. Prabhala. 1998. The relation between implied and realized volatility. *Journal of Financial Economics* 50: 125–50. [CrossRef]

Crain, Bradford R. 1974. Estimation of distributions using orthogonal expansions. *Annals of Statistics* 16: 454–63. [CrossRef]

Demeterfi, Kresimir, Emanuel Derman, Michael Kamal, and Joseph Zou. 1999. More than you ever wanted to know about volatility swaps. In *Quantitative Strategies Research Notes*. New York: Goldman Sachs.

Engle, Robert F., and Victor K. Ng. 1993. Measuring and testing the impact of news on volatility. *Journal of Finance* 48: 1749–78. [CrossRef]

Fleming, Jeff. 1998. The quality of market volatility forecasts implied by S&P 100 index option prices. *Journal of Empirical Finance* 5: 317–45.

French, Kenneth R., G. William Schwert, and Robert F. Stambaugh. 1987. Expected stock returns and volatility. *Journal of Financial Economics* 19: 3–29. [CrossRef]

Giot, Pierre. 2005. Relationships between implied volatility indexes and stock index returns. *The Journal of Portfolio Management* 31: 92–100. [CrossRef]

Glosten, Lawrence R., Ravi Jagannathan, and David E. Runkle. 1993. On the relation between the expected value and the volatility of the nominal excess return on stocks. *Journal of Finance* 48: 1779–801. [CrossRef]

Hibbert, Ann Marie, Robert T. Daigler, and Brice Dupoyet. 2008. A behavioral explanation for the negative asymmetric return-volatility relation. *Journal of Banking & Finance* 32: 2254–66.

Ho, Anson T. Y., Kim P. Huynh, and David T. Jacho-Chavez. 2016. Flexible Estimation of Copulas: An Application to the US Housing Crisis. *Journal of Applied Econometrics* 31: 603–10. [CrossRef]

Ho, Anson T. Y., Kim P. Huynh, and David T. Jacho-Chávez. 2018. Using Nonparametric Copulas to Measure Crude Oil Price Co-movements. *Energy Economics*. doi:10.1016/j.eneco.2018.05.022. [CrossRef]

Jaynes, Edwin T. 1957. Information theory and statistical mechanics. *Physics Review* 106: 620–30. [CrossRef]

Jiang, George J., and Yisong S. Tian. 2005. The model-free implied volatility and its information content. *The Review of Financial Studies* 18: 1305–41. [CrossRef]

Liu, Bing-Yue, Qiang Ji, and Ying Fan. 2017. A new time-varying optimal copula model identifying the dependence across markets. *Quantitative Finance* 17: 437–53. [CrossRef]

Nguyen, Cuong C., and M. Ishaq Bhatti. 2012. Copula Modelling Dependency Between oil prices and stock markets: Evidence from China and Vietnam. *Journal of International Financial Markets, Institutions & Money* 22: 758–73.

Nguyen, Cuong, M. Ishaq Bhatti, Magda Komorníková, and Jozef Komorník. 2016. Gold price and stock markets nexus under mixed-copulas. *Economic Modelling* 58: 283–92. [CrossRef]

Nelsen, Roger B. 1999. *An Introduction to Copulas*. New York: Springer.

Poon, Ser-Huang, and Clive W. J. Granger. 2003. Forecasting volatility in financial markets: A review. *Journal of Economic Literature* 41: 478–539. [CrossRef]

Poon, Ser-Huang, Michael Rockinger, and Jonathan Tawn. 2004. Extreme value dependence in financial markets: Diagnostics, models and financial implications. *The Review of Financial Studies* 17: 581–610. [CrossRef]

Poterba, James M., and Lawrence H. Summers. 1986. The persistence of volatility and stock market fluctuations. *American Economic Review* 76: 1142–51.

Racine, Jeffrey S. 2015. Mixed Data Kernel Copulas. *Empirical Economics* 48: 37–59. [CrossRef]

Todorov, Viktor. 2009. Variance risk-premium dynamics: The role of jumps. *The Review of Financial Studies* 23: 345–83. [CrossRef]

Whaley, Robert E. 1993. Derivatives on Market Volatility: Hedging Tools Long Overdue. *Journal of Derivatives* 1: 71–84. [CrossRef]

Whaley, Robert E. 2000. The Investor Fear Gauge. *Journal of Portfolio Management* 26: 12–17. [CrossRef]

Wu, Guojun, and Zhijie Xiao. 2002. A generalized partially linear model of asymmetric volatility. *Journal of Empirical Finance* 9: 287–319. [CrossRef]

Wu, Ximing. 2010. Exponential Series Estimator for Multivariate Densities. *Journal of Econometrics* 156: 354–66. [CrossRef]

Journal of
Risk and Financial Management

MDPI

Article

Greenhouse Emissions and Productivity Growth

Pantelis Kalaitzidakis [1], Theofanis P. Mamuneas [2] and Thanasis Stengos [3,*]

1 Department of Economics, University of Crete, Rethymno 74100, Greece; kalaitz@econ.soc.uoc.gr
2 Department of Economics, University of Cyprus, P.O. Box 20537, Nicosia 1678, Cyprus; tmamuneas@ucy.ac.cy
3 Department of Economics and Finance, University of Guelph, Guelph, ON N1G 2W1, Canada
* Correspondence: tstengos@uoguelph.ca; Tel.: +1-529-824-4120 (ext. 53917)

Received: 4 June 2018; Accepted: 3 July 2018; Published: 9 July 2018

Abstract: In this paper, we examine the effect of emissions, as measured by carbon dioxide (CO_2), on economic growth among a set of OECD countries during the period 1981–1998. We examine the relationship between total factor productivity (TFP) growth and emissions using a semiparametric smooth coefficient model that allow us to directly estimate the output elasticity of emissions. The results indicate that there exists a monotonically-increasing relationship between emissions and TFP growth. The output elasticity of CO_2 emissions is small with an average sample value of 0.07. In addition, we find an average contribution of CO_2 emissions to productivity growth of about 0.063 percent for the period 1981–1998.

Keywords: TFP growth; emissions; materials balance condition; semiparametric estimation

1. Introduction

The natural environment and natural resources unambiguously constitute important factors of the growth process, the shortage of which may impose a limit to growth. This limit to growth may arise either from the finite amounts of certain natural resources such as raw materials or by nature's limited ability to absorb human waste. The emphasis of the theoretical work in this area has concentrated on building growth models to study how economic policy and technological change may overcome the limits to growth imposed by the extensive use of the environment and still generate a positive long-run growth rate' see Bovenberg and Smulder (1995), Pittel (2002) and an extensive review of the literature by Brock and Taylor (2005).

Recently, more attention has been given to the growth effects of the deterioration in the quality of the environment due to increased accumulation of emissions. Emissions, which are usually modelled as a side product of the production process (see Anderson (1987)), may affect growth through two channels. If the natural environment is considered to be an input into the production function, then emissions represent the use of environmental capital, implying a positive effect of emissions on growth. If environmental quality enters the production function as an input, then emissions exert negative effects on growth by lowering the quality of the natural environment. In both cases, any abatement efforts by society reduce the available resources for production and may harm growth.

The empirical literature on the growth-emissions debate has mainly focused on investigating the famous environmental Kuznets curve (EKC). This voluminous literature studies the empirical relationship between real per capita income and polluting emissions per unit of output; see Schmalense et al. (1998), List et al. (2003) and Azomahou et al. (2006) for some recent studies that use flexible econometric methods to study this relationship. The main result of this literature is that polluting emissions' intensity initially rises with per capita income (at the early stages of economic development), but eventually falls as per capita income rises beyond some threshold level, at least for the case of developed economies; see Selten and Song (1994), Grossman and Krueger (1995),

List and Gallet (1999) and Stern and Common (2001), among others. However, there is evidence that this relationship may not be robust for a number of emission pollutants; see Harbaugh et al. (2002) and List et al. (2003).

The evidence gathered so far is rather mixed for carbon dioxide (CO_2) emissions. Making use of panel data, Holtz-Eakin and Selden (1995) and Heil and Selden (2001) employed parametric models with pooled data and obtained a U-shaped EKC for CO_2 per capita emissions. The works in Harbaugh et al. (2002), Bertinelli and Strobl (2005) and Azomahou et al. (2006) estimated non- or semi-parametric pooled regressions and nonlinear increasing shapes. Univariate approaches inspired from the income convergence literature have also been employed to explore the convergence of CO_2 per capita emissions between countries and regions. The works in List et al. (2003), Barassi et al. (2008) and Westerlund and Basher (2008) used unit root tests to investigate stochastic convergence for different sets of countries. The results are not conclusive, but the bulk of the evidence points towards convergence. The work in Taylor and Brock (2004) estimated growth regressions for per capita CO_2 emissions based on their Green–Solow model. The model is tested for OECD countries over the period 1960–1998, and the results suggest that most of the explanatory power comes from the initial level of CO_2 emissions.

In terms of econometric methodology, nonparametric estimation has recently gained popularity in this literature. Among the papers that use nonparametric estimation techniques is that of Harbaugh et al. (2002), where they use a nonparametric pooled regression to examine the relationship between a CO_2 environmental efficiency index and GDP per capita for a panel of countries. Their results indicate a U-shaped relationship followed by an inverted U relationship. The work in Bertinelli and Strobl (2005) employed a partially linear model in a cross-country context and found that a linear relationship between per capita income and SO_2 and CO_2 emissions cannot be rejected. The work in Azomahou et al. (2006) examined the relationship between CO_2 emissions per capita and GDP per capita using a pooled country-fixed effects nonparametric regression, and their results indicated a monotonically-increasing relationship. The work in Bertinelli et al. (2012) investigated the CO_2 emissions per capita-GDP per capita relationship by applying a kernel regression estimator to a panel of countries. They found that for some developed countries, the relationship between output and pollution after 1960 has been heterogeneous (for some rising, for some falling and for others flat). For almost all the developing countries in their sample, they found that the relationship was always upward sloping.

In Murdoch et al. (1997), Ansuategi (2003), Maddison (2006, 2007), another dimension was added to the empirical EKC literature, that of pollution spillovers between a set of EU countries (the dataset of Maddison (2006) is for a set of 135 countries). The empirical papers that account for transboundary pollution examine the implications of strategic interaction between countries, if any. The work in Murdoch et al. (1997) accounted for the spatial dispersion of sulphur and NOx emissions when empirically investigating the emissions reductions required by the Helsinki protocol in 25 European countries. They found that the demand for emissions reduction was higher the higher the deposition from neighbouring countries. Their model worked well for sulphur, but their results were less satisfying for NOx. The work in Ansuategi (2003) examined whether accounting for transboundary pollution affects the emissions-income relationship. He categorized countries into four groups according to their emissions and the amount of pollution they receive from other countries and estimated EKCs for each group. He found different results for different groups. The work in Helland and Whitford (2003) found that emissions releases are higher where it is likely that emissions cross state borders. On the contrary, Rupasingha et al. (2004) when examining the EKC hypothesis using U.S. county data for toxic releases, it was concluded that the EKC relationship they found was unaffected when they accounted for spatial dependence. U.S. data were also used in a study on water pollution by Sigman (2005); she used state-level data for water quality in state rivers and found evidence that states free ride. Finally, Maddison (2007) found that the quantity of transboundary imports of sulphur was statistically insignificant. However, he found that countries follow the environmental quality (per capita emissions) of their neighbours (see Maddison (2006, 2007)).

Less attention, however, has been given to the empirical investigation of the role of emissions in the production process and of the effects of emissions on economic growth. Recent studies by Tzouvelekas et al. (2006) and Vouvaki and Xepapadeas (2008) also tried to estimate the contribution of CO_2 emissions to the growth of real per capita output. Our work differs from theirs in that we employ a technique that allows us to estimate a general production function without imposing any restrictions on its functional form. Following a different line of research, Chimeli and Braden (2005) tried to derive a link between total factor productivity (TFP) and the environmental Kuznets curve. They derived a U-shaped response of environmental quality to variations in TFP.

Polluting emissions were modelled either as an input (see, e.g., Baumol and Oates (1988)) or as an (another) output of the production process; see Fare et al. (2001). Modelling polluting emissions as an output captures the idea that good output cannot be produced unless polluting emissions (bad output) are also produced; see Fare et al. (1993), Ball et al. (1994) and Fernandez et al. (2005). In this context, emissions are a by-product of the production of goods. Those who model polluting emissions as an input argue that trying to reduce them involves diverting some of the traditional inputs into the abatement effort, something that results in fewer inputs available in the production of goods. In other words, it is argued that by reducing emissions, output is reduced, and in this sense, emissions can be treated as an input to production; see Laffont (1988), Cropper and Oates (1992), Koo (1998) and Reinhar et al. (1999). Another argument in favour of the use of polluting emissions as an input is that the latter represent the extractive use of the natural environment. That is, emissions are treated as a proxy for the use of environmental resources; see Bovenberg and Smulder (1995), Brock and Taylor (2005).

However, a number of authors argue that some of these approaches are inconsistent with the materials' balance condition, a fundamental imperative of physical science, as well as common sense; see Murty and Russell (2002) and Murty et al. (2011). The materials' balance approach was first introduced by Ayres and Kneese (1969), and it was only recently that it has gained attention in the modelling of emissions or production residuals in the production process; see Murty and Russell (2002), Murty et al. (2011), Pethig (2003), Pethig (2006), Førsund (2009) and Lauwers (2009). The materials' balance condition implies that the generation of residuals inevitably arises in the process of consumption and production. The work in Murty and Russell (2002) accounted for this condition by defining a residual generating mechanism that relates the generation of production residuals to the use of polluting inputs. These polluting inputs (or material inputs as defined by others like Pethig (2003, 2006) are used in the production of the output, but are also responsible for the generation of a by-product; polluting emissions. Therefore, the link between output and polluting emissions comes through the use of the polluting generating inputs.

Although the literature on the relationship between pollution and economic growth is extensive, it ignores the role of emissions in the production process. In this paper, we investigate the empirical relationship between emissions and productivity growth using nonparametric econometric methods to uncover possible nonlinearities in the data. Proper modelling of emissions must take into account the materials' balance condition, which further results in the intuitively desirable positive correlation between the production residuals and output. To this end, this study models the relationship between output and emissions in a manner that is consistent with the residual generation mechanism. In particular, we examine the effect of CO_2 emissions, on economic growth among the advanced industrialized countries[1]. We construct a total factor productivity (TFP) index of the standard inputs, capital and labour, using the methodology that was adopted in Mamuneas et al. (2006). We then examine the relationship between TFP growth and CO_2 emissions using a semiparametric smooth

[1] Even though as mentioned above, studies that examine the EKC have used different pollutants besides CO_2, we concentrate on CO_2 as it best captures the use of energy in a production function setting that underlies our TFP approach.

coefficient model that allows us to directly estimate the elasticity of pollution. The data covers the period from 1981–1998, for a range of OECD countries, and the results indicate that there exists a nonlinear monotonically increasing relationship between polluting emissions and economic growth as captured by TFP. This is consistent with the materials' balance condition, which further results in the intuitively desirable positive correlation between the production residuals and output.

The paper is organized as follows. In the next section, we present the model specification and the data description. We proceed to discuss the empirical findings, and in the last section, we offer concluding remarks. In the Appendix, we present details about the econometric methodology of the smooth coefficient semiparametric model that we use and a test of linearity that we perform.

2. Methodology and Data Sources

2.1. Specification

Consider a general production function at time t as:

$$Y_t = F(X_t, E_t, t) \tag{1}$$

where Y is the total output, X is a vector of traditional inputs like physical capital K and labour inputs L, E is the energy input and t is a technology index measured by time trend. Based on the materials' balance approach, it is assumed that emissions are generated by the usage of energy, and it is a by-product of the production process. The emissions function is defined by:

$$P_t = g(E_t), \tag{2}$$

where P is the emissions variable, which is related to energy usage though the function g. This function is assumed to be an increasing monotonic function as it is specified by the laws of thermodynamics, that is $g' > 0$. Inverting Equation (2), we have:

$$E_t = g^{-1}(P_t) = \phi(P_t) \tag{3}$$

and substituting (3) in (1), we establish the link between output production and emissions; see Murty and Russell (2002) and Murty et al. (2011),

$$Y_t = F(X_t, \phi(P_t), t) = G(X_t, P_t, t)$$

To determine the effect of emissions in the production process, we follow an approach based on Mamuneas et al. (2006), who analysed the effect of human capital on TFP growth. Total differentiation of (1) with respect to time and division by Y yields:

$$\hat{Y}_t = \hat{A} + \varepsilon_K \widehat{K}_t + \varepsilon_L \widehat{L}_t + \varepsilon_E \widehat{E}_t \tag{4}$$

where (^) denotes a growth rate, $\hat{A} = \frac{(\partial F/\partial t)}{Y}$ is the exogenous rate of technological change and $\varepsilon_i = \frac{\partial \ln F}{\partial \ln Q_i}, (Qi = K, L, E)$ denotes output elasticity. Total differentiation of (3) with respect to time and division by E yields in growth form:

$$\widehat{E}_t = \eta \widehat{P}_t \tag{5}$$

where $\eta = \frac{\partial \ln \phi}{\partial \ln P} = \phi' \frac{P}{E} > 0$, is the energy elasticity with respect to emissions, and it is expected to be positive from the laws of thermodynamics.

Substituting Equation (5) in (4) and subtracting from both sides of Equation (4), the contribution of traditional inputs to the output growth, we get:

$$\hat{Y}_t - \varepsilon_K \widehat{K}_t - \varepsilon_L \widehat{L}_t = \hat{A} + \varepsilon_E \eta_P \widehat{P}_t \tag{6}$$

Note that the left-hand side of Equation (3) is directly observed from the data, if we assume a perfectly competitive environment. The output elasticities of labour and physical capital are equal to the observed output shares of labour, s_L, and physical capital, s_K. Therefore, we can define a TFP index based on the observable data, which discretely approximates the left-hand side of Equation (6). This index allows for the contribution of each input to differ across country and time and to be dictated by the data. We define the Tornqvist index of TFP growth for country i in year t as follows:

$$T\hat{F}P_{it} = \hat{Y}_{it} - w_{Lit}\hat{L}_{it} - w_{Kit}\hat{K}_{it} \tag{7}$$

where $w_{Qit} = 0.5(s_{Qit} + s_{Qit-1}), (Q_i = L, K)$ are the weighted average income shares of labour and physical capital and $\hat{Q}_{it} = \ln Q_{it} - \ln Q_{it-1}, (Q = Y, L, K)$. This measure of TFP contains the components of output growth that cannot be explained by the growth of the inputs (K, L) in Equation (6).

On the right-hand side of (6), the unobserved contribution of emissions to output growth is assumed to be an unknown function of the level of emissions i.e., $\theta(P_{it}) = \varepsilon_E \eta$. Note that the function θ captures the effect of emissions on productivity growth, and it can be only positive since it captures the combined effects of energy and emissions. Hence, putting all together, in a discrete form, Equation (6) can be written as:

$$T\hat{F}P_{it} = \hat{A}_{it} + \theta(P_{it})\widehat{P}_{it} \tag{8}$$

where Equation (8) can be estimated using semiparametric methods. It allows emissions to influence TFP growth in a nonlinear fashion. In the equation above, $\hat{A}_{it}$ can be considered as a function of country- and year-specific dummy variables. Country specific dummies, D_i, capture idiosyncratic exogenous technological change, and time specific dummies, D_t, capture procyclical behaviour of TFP growth. The equation of interest now becomes:

$$T\hat{F}P_{it} = \alpha_0 + \sum_{i=1}^{N-1} \alpha_i D_i + \sum_{t=1}^{T-1} \alpha_t D_t + \theta(P_{it})\widehat{P}_{it} + u_{it}$$

If we let $W_{it}^T = (D_i, D_t,)$ and $V_{it} = \{P_{it}, \Omega_{it}\}$ where Ω_{it} can be any other variable included in the smooth coefficient function, the model can be written more compactly as:

$$T\hat{F}P_{it} = W_{it}^T\beta + \theta(V_{it})\widehat{P}_{it} + u_{it} \tag{9}$$

For proper estimation, we assume that $\mathcal{E}(u_{it}|W_{it}, V_{it}, \widehat{P}_{it}) = 0$, where $\mathcal{E}(.)$ denotes the expectations operator.

We proceed to estimate the model of Equation (9) using a smooth varying coefficient semiparametric estimator. A smooth coefficient semiparametric model is considered to be a useful and flexible specification for studying a general regression relationship with varying coefficients. It is a special form of varying coefficient models, and it is based on polynomial regression; see Fan (1992), Fan and Zhang (1999), Li et al. (2002) and Mamuneas et al. (2006), among others. A semiparametric varying coefficient model imposes no assumption on the functional form of the coefficients, and the coefficients are allowed to vary as smooth functions of other variables. Specifically, varying coefficient models are linear in the regressors, but their coefficients are allowed to change smoothly with the value of other variables. In the Appendix, we present the mechanics of the method in more detail.

2.2. Data Sources

In order to investigate the empirical relationship between emissions and aggregate output, we collected data from the World Bank and the OECD databases covering a wide range of countries over the period 1981–1998. The countries chosen were based on the availability of pollution data, as well as physical capital and emissions data. The countries included in this analysis are: Australia, Austria, Belgium, Canada, Denmark, Finland, France, Greece, Ireland, Italy, Korea, the Netherlands, Portugal, Spain, Sweden, the U.K. and the USA.

The OECD databases provide data on GDP, employment and capital formation. All data are in millions of Euros, and the base year is 2000. Since energy is introduced as a paid input of production, which generates an unpaid by-product, emissions, the aggregate output measure has to be adjusted to include the contribution of energy. In other words, if energy is to be added on the right-hand side of the aggregate production function, then output would need to be adjusted, as well. Hence, the value of output used is a gross output measure, which consists of the value added in current prices plus the value of energy consumption. Output, Y, is defined then by deflating the above gross output measure by the GDP deflator. Labour input, L, is defined as the total man-hours (total number of workers times hours worked), and the capital stock, K, was constructed by accumulating gross investment in constant prices, using the perpetual inventory method, with a depreciation rate of 4%. Finally, the energy input, E, is constructed by dividing the value of energy consumption by the GDP deflator. The consumption of energy has been obtained from the EU KLEMS Growth and Productivity Accounts database[2]. As a proxy for emission flow, P, we used CO_2 emissions, obtained from the 2002 World Development Indicators. According to the World Bank definition, CO_2 emissions (kilotons (kt)) are those stemming from the burning of fossil fuels and the manufacture of cement. They include contributions to the carbon dioxide produced during consumption of solid, liquid and gas fuels and gas flaring.

As a proxy for pollution flow, we used CO_2 emissions, obtained from the 2002 World Development Indicators. According to the World Bank definition, CO_2 (carbon dioxide) emissions (kt) are those stemming from the burning of fossil fuels and the manufacture of cement. They include contributions to the carbon dioxide produced during consumption of solid, liquid and gas fuels and gas flaring. CO_2 is a stable gas, which is not transformed chemically in the atmosphere. However, some CO_2 is removed from the atmosphere by a natural process that includes the effect of vegetation, soils and oceans. Moreover, human activities such as reforestation, deforestation or land management may increase or decrease the amount of CO_2 removed from the atmosphere. This degree of atmospheric removal because of combined natural and human activities corresponds to a depreciation rate that is used to construct the total "stock" of accumulated pollution. The global natural CO_2 removal rate for the set of countries that we examine has been estimated to be around 60 percent for the period 1980–1989 and 52 percent for the 1989–1998 period; see IPCC (2000). If one adds the human-induced changes in land use and forestry, we derive country-specific values on the basis of CO_2 emission data provided on the website of the United Nations Framework Convention on Climate Change (UNFCCC)[3]. As part of their obligation, countries report to the UNFCCC their annual emissions of greenhouse gases, with data currently spanning the period 1990–2004. For all countries in our sample, emissions are provided with and without taking into account CO_2 removal resulting from direct human-induced land use, land use change and forestry (LULUCF). The ratio of emissions with LULUCF over emissions without LULUCF gives the rate of CO_2 removal because of human activities. The overall removal rate (depreciation rate) from both human activities and natural processes for the countries in our sample over the period that we examine is around seventy percent, which is what we use in our estimation to construct the total "stock" of accumulated pollution.

To express emissions in concentration terms, which is a more appropriate measure of pollution (see Brock and Taylor (2005)), we divide total emissions with the surface of each country so that our pollution variable, P, measures CO_2 emissions in kilotons per square kilometre. This is a measure of pollution intensity, and it is closely related to pollution concentration, which is emissions measured as

2 The site for the data is: www.euklems.net/eukdata.shtml.
3 See http://unfccc.int/ghg_emissions_data/predifined_qeuries/items/3814.php.

milligrams per cubic meter. The implication of this new pollution intensity concentration variable for our empirical specification is that the damage caused by CO_2 emission to the environment depends on the size of the natural environment[4].

3. Empirical Findings

We estimate the model of Equation (9) using a smooth coefficient semiparametric estimator. In Equation (9), the variables of interest are expressed in growth terms, and they are all $I(0)$. Our approach is different from univariate approaches inspired by the income convergence literature that have also been employed to explore the convergence of CO_2 per capita emissions between countries and regions using data in levels. The works in List et al. (2003), Barassi et al. (2008) and Westerlund and Basher (2008) used unit root tests to investigate stochastic convergence for different sets of countries. In our paper, we are particularly interested in the unknown coefficient function $\theta(P)$. The results are presented in Figure 1. The effect of polluting emissions on growth is positive and monotonically increasing. This result is consistent with the materials' balance condition where the generation of emission residuals inevitably arises in the production process. Our overall finding is that the effect of pollution emissions on growth is positive and nonlinear. This implies that the productivity effect dominates any negative externality effects. It is nearly constant up to a certain level of pollution intensity, and then, it appears to accelerate at higher levels. The presence of such a threshold effect is consistent with the presence of newer pollution abatement technologies "cleaner technologies" that kick in at higher levels of pollution and are responsible for increasing productivity gains. These productivity gains might also come from a reduction of negative pollution externalities due to abatement. It is interesting to note that the above finding can be also given an EKC interpretation as it would correspond to the second half of the U relationship that has been found in the literature, and given that our dataset consists of developed countries, this is consistent with the EKC evidence. This is consistent, for instance, with the evidence found in Stern and Common (2001) for another pollutant, sulphur, for the group of developed economies similar to the ones we examine.

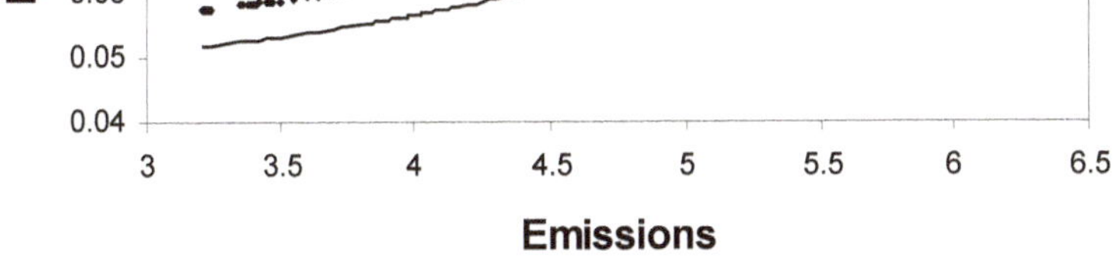

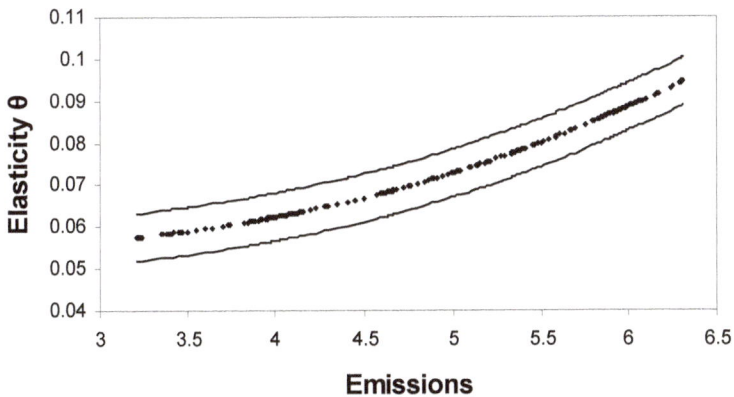

Figure 1. Output elasticity of emissions.

We proceed to test the specification of our model. First, we test that the model that generated the data in the graphs of Figure 1 is linear. In the Appendix, we present the mechanics of the linearity

---

[4] In the science of economic growth, it is customary to express variables in a per capita basis. However, in the environmental engineering literature, it is the concentration of pollution that is of interest. In our case, the elasticity of pollution intensity that we estimate is the same as that of pollution concentration, and as such, it is the appropriate concept to use. Another possible standardization, division by total GDP, is likely to introduce endogeneity issues.

test that we employ. We strongly reject the null hypothesis of linearity with a p-value less than 0.001 for the test statistic that we obtained. Next, we proceed to investigate the robustness of our findings. We first check for possible endogeneity in the model by following Cai et al. (2006), who propose an Intrumental Variables (IV) methodology for smooth coefficient models based on local linear methods. We obtain fitted values of current emissions and emission growth as functions of past output and emissions as instruments, which we then use in the second stage, as suggested by Cai et al. (2006). We tried different sets of past values, but the results were fairly robust, and the shape of the graph in Figure 1 was left essentially intact, irrespective of the different instruments used[5].

Finally, since the estimates of elasticities $\theta(P)$ depends on two unknown elasticities, the elasticity of output with respect to energy, ε_E, and the inverse elasticity of emissions with respect to energy, η, we have estimated two alternative specifications. Firstly, it is assumed that the output elasticity of energy is given by the observed energy share, and therefore, the unknown parameter to be estimated is $\eta(P)$, i.e., $\theta(P) = \eta(P)s_E$. Secondly, the inverse marginal effect of energy on emissions, $\phi'(P)$ is directly estimated observing that $\theta(P) = \phi'(P)\frac{P}{E}s_E$. The graphs of these specifications are presented in Figures 2 and 3, respectively. It is apparent that the total elasticity and the shape of the graph in Figure 1 remain unchanged irrespective of the parameter restrictions imposed.

To examine the effect per country, we have calculated the average output elasticity of emissions per country, and the results are presented in the first column of Table 1. The results indicate that the average elasticity of emission for all countries is 0.07 and significantly different from zero. This implies that a 1% increase of emissions increases on average the output by only 0.07%. In addition, it is clear from the table that the average elasticity of emissions per country varies according to the country's emission levels. It is interesting to note that the most industrialized countries have also the highest output elasticities, like the USA, Canada and the U.K. The second column of Table 1 provides the average contribution of CO_2 emissions growth on total factor productivity (TFP) growth. The results vary by country, depending on the output elasticity of emissions and the emissions growth rate. These results indicate that the effect of emissions on TFP growth and hence output growth is significant, but rather small for most countries of the sample For the period of consideration (1981–1998) emissions contributed positively to TFP growth in most of the countries that we consider, while they contributed negatively in some countries like Belgium, Sweden and the U.K., for example, due to the decline of their CO_2 emissions.

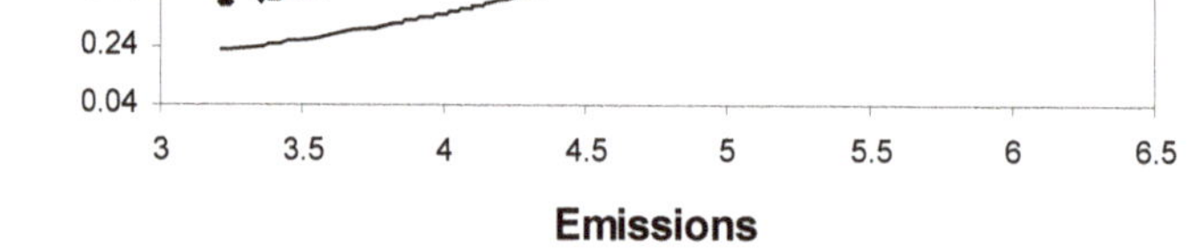

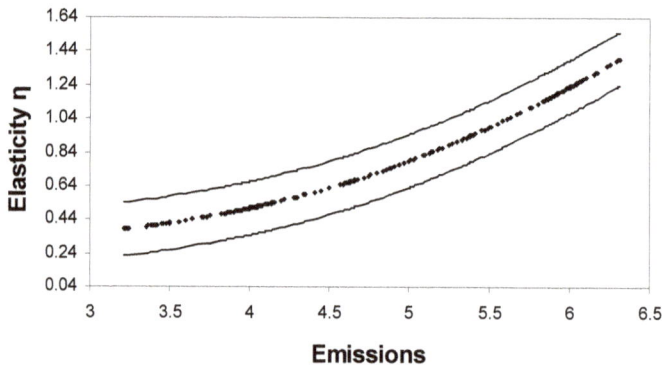

Figure 2. Elasticity of emissions.

[5] However, we should note that our model is more complicated than Cai et al. (2006) as endogeneity enters both the variable in the unknown coefficient function, as well as the regressor. In this case, the asymptotic variance component will be different than theirs. However, deriving the correct asymptotic variance for a functional coefficient of this model goes beyond the scope of the present paper.

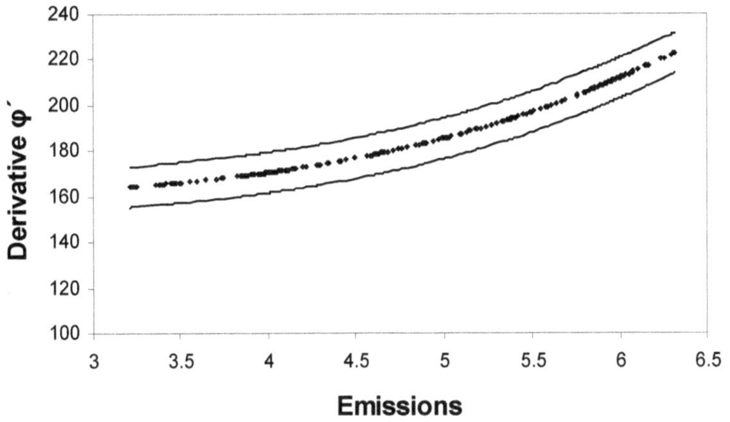

Figure 3. Marginal effect of emissions.

Table 1. Output elasticity of emissions.

CONTRIBUTION TO TFP GROWTH Average 1981–1998 (Stand. Error)		
Country	*Elasticity* $\theta(P)$	*TFP Contribution* $\theta(P) \times \widehat{P}$
Australia	0.0721 (0.0001)	0.00198 (0.00012)
Austria	0.0553 (0.0001)	0.00061 (0.00012)
Belgium	0.0607 (0.0001)	−0.00086 (0.00012)
Canada	0.0804 (0.0001)	0.00047 (0.00011)
Denmark	0.0555 (0.0001)	−0.00051 (0.00011)
Finland	0.0546 (0.0001)	−0.00018 (0.00001)
France	0.0778 (0.0001)	−0.00112 (0.00025)
Greece	0.0568 (0.0001)	0.00157 (0.00014)
Ireland	0.0515 (0.0001)	0.00121 (0.00009)
Italy	0.0784 (0.0001)	0.00048 (0.00008)
Korea	0.0711 (0.0001)	0.00415 (0.00012)
The Netherlands	0.0642 (0.0001)	0.00028 (0.00005)
Portugal	0.0529 (0.0001)	0.00208 (0.00009)
Spain	0.0690 (0.0001)	0.00084 (0.00006)
Sweden	0.0551 (0.0001)	−0.00116 (0.00007)
U.K.	0.0849 (0.0001)	−0.00032 (0.00003)
USA	0.1266 (0.0001)	0.00116 (0.00009)
Average	0.0686 (0.0001)	0.00063 (0.00003)

4. Conclusions

In this paper, we have studied the effect of emissions, as measured by CO_2, on economic growth among the advanced industrialized countries. We construct a TFP growth index by subtracting from the output growth the weighted growth of physical capital and labour inputs, using the observed income shares of physical capital and labour as weights. The TFP index based on the observable data allows for the contribution of each input to differ across country and time and to be dictated by the data. We then examine the relationship between TFP growth and emissions using a semiparametric smooth coefficient model that allows us to directly estimate the elasticity of emissions.

Our results indicate that there exists a robust nonlinear relationship between CO_2 and economic growth as captured by TFP growth. We find that the CO_2 emissions effect varies depending on a country's emissions level. In addition, we find a monotonically-increasing relationship between emissions and output, a result that is consistent with the materials' balance condition. Overall, emission elasticities vary among different countries with an average elasticity (for all countries) of 0.07. Finally, we find that CO_2 emissions contribute on average about 0.063% to productivity growth in the countries of our sample for the period 1981–1998.

Author Contributions: All authors have contributed equally.

Funding: This research was funded by Social Science and Humanities Research Council of Canada, grant number 4301.

Acknowledgments: We would like to thank Theodoros Zachariades for helpful comments. The third author would like to acknowledge financial support from Social Science and Humanities Council of Canada.

Conflicts of Interest: The authors declare no conflict of interest.

Appendix A. Econometric Estimation: A Smooth Coefficient Semiparametric Approach

A semiparametric varying coefficient model imposes no assumption on the functional form of the coefficients, and the coefficients are allowed to vary as smooth functions of other variables. Specifically, varying coefficient models are linear in the regressors, but their coefficients are allowed to change smoothly with the value of other variables. One way of estimating the coefficient functions is by using a local least squares method with a kernel weight function. A semiparametric smooth coefficient model is given by:

$$y_i = \alpha(z_i) + x_i'\beta(z_i) + u_i \tag{A1}$$

where y_i denotes the dependent variable (the TFP index as discussed earlier), x_i denotes a $p \times 1$ vector of variables of interest (in the case of Equation (6), $\widehat{E}_{it}$ and $\widehat{H}_{it}$), z_i denotes a $q \times 1$ vector of other exogenous variables (the $V_{it} = \{E_{it}, \Omega_{it}\}$ from Equation (5) above) and $\beta(z_i)$ is a vector of unspecified smooth functions of z_i ($\theta(.)$ in Equation (6)). To simplify the exposition, we ignore the partially linear nature of Equation (6), by suppressing for now the vector of the w's. Based on Li et al. (2002), the above semiparametric model has the advantage that it allows more flexibility in functional form than a parametric linear model or a semiparametric partially linear specification. Furthermore, the sample size required to obtain a reliable semiparametric estimation is not as large as that required for estimating a fully nonparametric model. It should be noted that when the dimension of z_i is greater than one, this model also suffers from the "curse of dimensionality", although to a lesser extent than a purely nonparametric model where both z_i and x_i enter nonparametrically. The work in Fan and Zhang (1999) suggested that the appeal of the varying coefficient model is that by allowing coefficients to depend on other variables, the modelling bias can significantly be reduced, and the curse of dimensionality can be avoided. Equation (6) above can be rewritten as:

$$y_i = \alpha(z_i) + x_i^T\beta(z_i) + \varepsilon_i = (1, x_i^T)\begin{pmatrix}\alpha(z_i)\\ \beta(z_i)\end{pmatrix} + \varepsilon_i \tag{A2}$$

$$y_i = X_i^T\delta(z_i) + \varepsilon_i$$

where $\delta(z_i) = (\alpha(z_i), \beta(z_i)^T)^T$ is a smooth but unknown function of z. One can estimate $\delta(z)$ using a local least squares approach, where:

$$\widehat{\delta}(z) = [(nh^q)^{-1}\sum_{j=1}^{n} X_jX_j^T K(\frac{z_j - z}{h})]^{-1}\{(nh^q)^{-1}\sum_{j=1}^{n} X_jy_jK(\frac{z_j - z}{h})\}$$

$$= [D_n(z)]^{-1}A_n(z)$$

$D_n(z) = (nh^q)^{-1}\sum_{j=1}^{n} X_jX_j^T K$, $A_n(z) = (nh^q)^{-1}\sum_{j=1}^{n} X_jy_jK$, $K = K(\frac{z_j - z}{h})$ is a kernel function, and $h = h_n$ is the smoothing parameter for sample size n. The intuition behind the above local least squares estimator is straightforward. Let us assume that z is a scalar and $K(.)$ is a uniform kernel. In this case, the expression for $\widehat{\delta}(z)$ becomes:

$$\widehat{\delta}(z) = [\sum_{|z_j - z| \leq h} X_j X_j^T]^{-1} \sum_{|z_j - z| \leq h} X_j y_j$$

In this case, $\widehat{\delta}(z)$ is simply a least squares estimator obtained by regressing y_j on X_j using the observations of (X_j, y_j) that their corresponding z_j is close to z ($|z_j - z| \leq h$). Since $\delta(z)$ is a smooth function of z, $|\delta(z_j) - \delta(z)|$ is small when $|z_j - z|$ is small. The condition that nh^q is large ensures that we have sufficient observations within the interval $|z_j - z| \leq h$ when $\delta(z_j)$ is close to $\delta(z)$. Therefore, under the conditions that $h \to 0$ and $nh^q \to \infty$, one can show that the local least squares regression of y_j on X_j provides a consistent estimate of $\delta(z)$. In general, it can be shown that:

$$\sqrt{nh^q}(\widehat{\delta}(z) - \delta(z)) \to N(0, \Omega) \text{ in distribution}$$

where Ω can be consistently estimated. The estimate of Ω can be used to construct confidence bands for $\widehat{\delta}(z)$. We use a standard multivariate kernel density estimator with a Gaussian kernel and cross-validation to choose the bandwidth.

An interesting special case of Equation (A2) is when the w's from Equation (6) are taken into account. In that case, some of the coefficients in Equation (A2) are constants (independent of z). In that case, Equation (A2) can be rewritten as:

$$y_i = W_i^T \alpha + X_i^T \delta(z_i) + \varepsilon_i \tag{A3}$$

where W_i is the i-th observation on a $(q \times 1)$ vector of additional regressors that enter the regression function linearly (in our case where W, the country specific and time dummies $(D_i, D_t,)$). The estimation of this model requires some special treatment as the partially-linear structure may allow for efficiency gains, since the linear part can be estimated at a much faster rate, namely $\sqrt{n}$.

The partially-linear model in Equation (A3) has been studied by Zhang et al. (2002) and Ahmad et al. (2005). The work in Zhang et al. (2002) suggests a two-step procedure where the coefficients of the linear part are estimated in the first step using polynomial fitting with an initial small bandwidth using cross-validation; see Hoover et al. (1998). In other words, the approach is based on undersmoothing in the first stage. Then, these estimates are averaged to yield the final first step linear part estimates, which are then used to redefine the dependent variable and return to the environment of Equation (A1) where local smoothers can be applied as described above.

Appendix B. Linearity Test

We will present below a test statistic that was used by Li et al. (2002). In our implementation, we will use a bootstrap version of this test. Let y_i denote the dependent variable, and let x_i be $p \times 1$ and z_i be $q \times 1$ vectors of exogenous variables. Consider the following linear model:

$$y_i = \alpha_0(z_i) + x_i^T \beta_0(z_i) + \varepsilon_i = (1, x_i^T) \begin{pmatrix} \alpha_0(z_i) \\ \beta_0(z_i) \end{pmatrix} + \varepsilon_i \tag{A4}$$

$$y_i = X_i^T \delta_0(z_i) + \varepsilon_i$$

where $\delta_0(z_i) = (\alpha_0(z_i), \beta_0(z_i)^T)^T$ is a smooth known function of z. For example, in the context of Equation (2), ignoring for the moment the presence of the w's, we have $\alpha_0(z_i) = \alpha + z_i\theta$ and $\beta_0(z_i) = \beta$. Similarly, Equation (A1) captures the case of the augmented version of (2) to allow for the simple interactions of the x's with z, where $\alpha_0(z_i) = \alpha + z_i\theta$ and $\beta_0(z_i) = \beta_1 + \beta_2 z_i$.

We can test the adequacy of (A1), H_0, against the semiparametric alternative (1) using the following test statistic.

$$\begin{aligned} \widehat{I}_n &= \frac{1}{n^2h^q}\sum_i\sum_{j\neq i} X_i^T(y_i - X_i^T\widehat{\delta}_0(z_i))X_j(y_j - X_j^T\widehat{\delta}_0(z_j))K(\frac{z_j - z_i}{h}) \\ &= \frac{1}{n^2h^q}\sum_i\sum_{j\neq i} X_i^T X_j\widehat{\varepsilon}_i\widehat{\varepsilon}_j K(\frac{z_j - z_i}{h}) \end{aligned}$$

where $\widehat{\varepsilon}_i$ denotes the residual from parametric estimation (under H_0). It can be shown that under H_0, $J_n = nh^{q/2}\widehat{I}_n/\widehat{\sigma}_0 \longrightarrow N(0,1)$, where $\widehat{\sigma}_0^2$ is a consistent estimator of the variance of $nh^{q/2}\widehat{I}_n$; see Li et al. (2002). It can be shown that the test statistic is a consistent test for testing H_0 (Equation (3)) against H_1 (Equation (1)). We use a bootstrap version of the above test statistic, since bootstrapping improves the size performance of kernel-based tests for the functional form; see Zheng (1996) and Li and Wang (1998).

References

Ahmad, Ibrahim, Sittisak Leelahanon, and Qi Li. 2005. Efficient estimation of a semiparametric partially varying linear model. *Annals of Statistics* 33: 258–83. [CrossRef]

Anderson, Curt L. 1987. The production process: Inputs and wastes. *Journal of Environmental Economics and Management* 14: 1–12. [CrossRef]

Ansuategi, Alberto. 2003. Economic growth and transboundary pollution in Europe: An empirical analysis. *Environmental and Resource Economics* 26: 305–28. [CrossRef]

Ayres, Robert U., and Allen V. Kneese. 1969. Production, Consumption, and Externalities. *American Economic Review* 59: 282–97.

Azomahou, Theophile, François Laisney, and Phu Nguyen Van. 2006. Economic development and CO_2 emissions: A nonparametric panel approach. *Journal of Public Economics* 90: 1347–63. [CrossRef]

Ball, V. Eldon, Ca Knox Lovell, Richard Nehring, and Agapi Somwaru. 1994. Incorporating Undesirable Outputs into Models of Production: An Application to US Agricultural. *Cahiers d'Economique et Sociologie Rurales* 31: 59–73.

Barassi, Marco R., Matthew A. Cole, and Robert J. R. Elliott. 2008. Stochastic divergence or convergence of per capita carbon dioxide emissions: Re-examining the evidence. *Environmental and Resource Economics* 40: 121–37. [CrossRef]

Baumol, William J., and Wallace E. Oates. 1988. *The Theory of Environmental Policy*, 2nd ed. Cambridge: Cambridge U. Press.

Bertinelli, Luisito, and Eric Strobl. 2005. The Environmental Kuznets Curve semi-parametrically revisited. *Economics Letters* 88: 350–57. [CrossRef]

Bertinelli, Luisito, Eric Strobl, and Benteng Zou. 2012. Sustainable economic development and the environment: Theory and evidence. *Energy Economics* 34: 1105–14. [CrossRef]

Bovenberg, A. Lans, and Sjak Smulder. 1995. Environmental quality and pollution-augmenting technological change in a two-sector endogenous growth model. *Journal of Public Economics* 57: 369–91. [CrossRef]

Brock, William A., and M. Scott Taylor. 2005. Economic growth and the environment: A review of theory and empirics. In *Handbook of Economic Growth II*. Edited by Aghion Philippe and Durlauf Steven. New York: Elsevier, Chp. 28, pp. 1749–821.

Cai, Zongwu, Mitali Das, Huaiyu Xiong, and Xizhi Wu. 2006. Functional coefficient instrumental variable models. *Journal of Econometrics* 133: 207–41. [CrossRef]

Chimeli, Ariaster B., and John B. Braden. 2005. Total factor productivity and the environmental Kuznets curve. *Journal of Environmental Economics and Management* 49: 366–80. [CrossRef]

Cropper, Maureen L., and Wallace E. Oates. 1992. Environmental Economics: A survey. *Journal of Economic Literature* 30: 675–740.

Fan, Jianqing. 1992. Design-adaptive nonparametric regression. *Journal of the American Statistical Association* 87: 998–1004. [CrossRef]

Fan, Jianqing, and Wenyang Zhang 1999. Statistical estimation in varying-coefficient models. *Annals of Statistics* 27: 1491–518.

Fare, Rolf, Shawna Grosskopf, C. A. Knox Lovell, and Suthathip Yaisawarng. 1993. Derivation of shadow prices for undesirable outputs: A distance function approach. *Review of Economics and Statistics* 75: 375–80. [CrossRef]

Fare, Rolf, Shawna Grosskopf, and Carl A. Pasurka, Jr. 2001. Accounting for air pollution emissions in measures of state manufacturing productivity growth. *Journal of Regional Science* 41: 381–409. [CrossRef]

Fernandez, Carmen, Gary Koop, and Mark F. J. Steel. 2005. Alternative efficiency measures for multiple-output production. *Journal of Econometrics* 126: 411–44. [CrossRef]

Førsund, Finn R. 2009. Good Modelling of Bad Outputs: Pollution and Multiple-Output Production. *International Review of Environmental & Recourse Economics* 3: 1–38.

Grossman, Gene M., and Alan B. Krueger. 1995. Economic growth and the environment. *Quarterly Journal of Economics* 110: 353–77. [CrossRef]

Harbaugh, William T., Arik Levinson, and David Molloy Wilson. 2002. Reexamining the empirical evidence for an environmental Kuznets curve. *Review of Economics and Statistics* 84: 541–51. [CrossRef]

Heil, Mark T., and Thomas M. Selden. 2001. Carbon emissions and economic development: Future trajectories based on historical experience. *Environment and Development Economics* 6: 63–83. [CrossRef]

Helland, Eric, and Andrew B. Whitford. 2003. Pollution incidence and political jurisdiction: Evidence from TRI. *Journal of Environmental Economics and Management* 46: 403–24. [CrossRef]

Holtz-Eakin, Douglas, and Thomas M. Selden. 1995. Stocking the fires? CO_2 emissions and economic growth. *Journal of Public Economics* 57: 85–101. [CrossRef]

Hoover, Donald R., John A. Rice, Colin O. Wu, and Li-Ping Yang, 1998, Nonparametric Smoothing Estimates of Time-Varying Coefficient Models with Longtitudinal Data. *Biometrica* 85: 809–22. [CrossRef]

IPCC. 2000. *IPCC Special Report on Land Use Change and Forestry-Summary for Policymakers*. Geneva: Intergovernmental Panel on Climate Change. Available online: https://www.ipcc.ch/pdf/special-reports/spm/srl-en.pdf (accessed on 5 July 2018).

Koop, Gary. 1998. Carbon Dioxide emissions and economic growth: A structural approach. *Journal of Applied Statistics* 25: 489–515. [CrossRef]

Laffont, Jean-Jacque. 1988. *Fundamentals of Public Economics*. Cambridge: MIT Press.

Lauwers, Ludwig. 2009. Justifying the incorporation of the materials balance principle into frontier-based eco-efficiency models. *Ecological Economics* 68: 1605–14. [CrossRef]

Li, Qi, Cliff J. Huang, Dong Li, and Tsu-Tan Fu. 2002. Semiparametric smooth coefficient models. *Journal of Business Econom* 20: 412–22. [CrossRef]

Li, Qi, and Suojin Wang. 1998. A Simple Consistent Bootstrap Test for a Parametric Regression Functional Form. *Journal of Econometrics* 87: 145–65. [CrossRef]

List, John A., and Craig A. Gallet. 1999. The environmental Kuznets curve: Does one size fit all? *Ecological Economics* 31: 409–23. [CrossRef]

Millimet, Daniel L., John A. List, and Thanasis Stengos. 2003. The environmental Kuznets curve: Real progress or misspecified models? *Review of Economics and Statistics* 85: 1038–47. [CrossRef]

Maddison, David. 2006. Environmental Kuznets Curves: A spatial econometric approach. *Journal of Environmental Economics and Management* 51: 218–30. [CrossRef]

Maddison, David. 2007. Modelling sulphur in Europe: A spatial econometric approach. *Oxford Economics Paper* 59: 726–43. [CrossRef]

Mamuneas, Theofanis P., Andreas Savvides, and Thanasis Stengos. 2006. Economic development and the return to human capital: A smooth coefficient semiparametric approach. *Journal of Applied Econometrics* 21: 111–32. [CrossRef]

Murdoch, James C., Tod Sandler, and Keith Sargent. 1997. A tale of two collectives: Sulphur versus nitrogen oxide emission reduction in Europe. *Economica* 64: 281–301. [CrossRef]

Murty, Sushama, and R. Robert Russell. 2002. *On Modelling Pollution-Generating Technologies*. Riversid: Department of Economics, University of Californiae.

Murty, Sushama, R. Robert Russell, and Steven B. Levkoff. 2011. *On Modelling Pollution-Generating Technologies*. Discussion Paper 11/1. Exeter: Department of Economics, University of Exeter, ISSN 1473-3307.

Pethig, Rüdiger. 2003. *The 'Materials Balance Approach' to Pollution: Its Origin, Implications and Acceptance*. Economics Discussion Paper No. 105-03. Siegen: University of Siegen.

Pethig, Rüdiger. 2006. Nonlinear Production, Abatement, Pollution and Materials Balance Reconsidered. *Journal of Environmental Economics and Management* 51: 185–204. [CrossRef]

Pittel, Karen 2002. *Sustainability and Economic Growth*. Cheltenham: Edward Elgar.

Reinhard, Stijn, C. A. Knox Lovell, and Geert Thijssen. 1999. Econometric Estimation of Technical and Environmental Efficiency: An Application to Dutch Dairy Farms. *American Journal of Agricultural Economics* 81: 44–60. [CrossRef]

Rupasingha, Anil, Stephan J. Goetz, David L. Debertin, and Angelos Pagoulatos. 2004. The environmental Kuznets curve for US counties: A spatial econometric analysis with extensions. *Papers in Regional Science* 83: 407–24. [CrossRef]

Schmalensee, Richard, Thomas M. Stoker, and Ruth A. Judson. 1998. World Carbon Dioxide Emissions: 1950–2050. *The Review of Economics and Statistics* 80: 15–27. [CrossRef]

Selden, Thomas M., and Daqing Song. 1994. Environmental quality and development: Is there a Kuznets curve for air pollution emission? *Journal of Environmental Economics and Management* 27: 147–62. [CrossRef]

Sigman, Hilary. 2005. Transboundary spillovers and decentralization of environmental policies. *Journal of Environmental Economics and Management* 50: 82–101. [CrossRef]

Stern, David I., and Michael S. Common. 2001. Is there an Environmental Kuznets curve for sulphur? *Journal of Environmental Economics and Management* 41: 162–78. [CrossRef]

Taylor, M. Scott, and William A. Brock. 2004. The Green Solow Model. NBER Working Paper 10557. Calgary, AB, Canada: University of Calgary.

Tzouvelekas, Vangelis, Dimitra Vouvaki, and Anastasios Xepapadeas. 2006. *Total Factor Productivity and the Environment: A Case for Green Growth Accounting*. Crete: University of Crete.

Vouvaki, Dimitra, and Anastasios Xepapadeas. 2008. *Total Factor Productivity Growth when Factors of Production Generate Environmental Externalities*. MPRA Paper 10237. Munich: University of Munich.

Westerlund, Joakim, and Syed A. Basher. 2008. Testing the convergence in carbon dioxide emissions using a century of panel data. *Environmental and Resource Economics* 40: 109–20. [CrossRef]

Zhang, Wenyang, Sik-Yum Lee, and Xinyuan Song. 2002. Local polynomial fitting in semivarying coefficient model. *Journal of Multivariate Analysis* 82: 166–88. [CrossRef]

Zheng, John Xu. 1996. A Consistent Test of Functional Form via Nonparametric Estimation Techniques. *Journal of Econometrics* 75: 263–89. [CrossRef]

Journal of
Risk and Financial Management

Article

Nonparametric Estimation of a Conditional Quantile Function in a Fixed Effects Panel Data Model

Karen X. Yan [1] and Qi Li [1,2,*]

1 Department of Economics, Texas A&M University, College Station, TX 77845, USA; yanxueqing@tamu.edu
2 International School of Economics and Management (ISEM), Capital University of Economics and Business, Beijing 100070, China
* Correspondence: qi-li@tamu.edu

Received: 11 July 2018; Accepted: 1 August 2018; Published: 3 August 2018

Abstract: This paper develops a nonparametric method to estimate a conditional quantile function for a panel data model with an additive individual fixed effects. The proposed method is easy to implement, it does not require numerical optimization and automatically ensures quantile monotonicity by construction. Monte Carlo simulations show that the proposed estimator performs well in finite samples.

Keywords: nonparametric method; conditional quantile function; panel data

JEL Classification: C14; C21

1. Introduction

Using nonparametric techniques to estimate econometric models has received increasing attention among econometricians in recent decades (see, for example, Pagan and Ullah (1999); Hall et al. (2007); Belloni et al. (2016); Lin et al. (2015); Li et al. (2013); Firpo et al. (2009) and Firpo et al. (2018) for the literature of nonparametric methods and applications). The most popular nonparametric model is the conditional mean regression model. However, compared with a conditional mean function, a conditional quantile regression function, when evaluated at different quantiles, can reveal an entire distributional relationship between the covariates and the response variable. Quantile regression therefore has many useful applications in economics and finance. For example, in risk and financial management, researchers are more concerned about the uncertainty or the risk of an asset, which can be characterized by its left tail behavior (corresponding to the lower quantiles) (see Al Rahahleh and Bhatti (2017); Al Rahahleh et al. (2017); Nguyen and Bhatti (2015); Al Rahahleh et al. (2016); Bartram et al. (2018); Al Shubiri and Jamil (2018) for the literature on idiosyncratic risk), and quantile regression can play an important role in this line of research.

The existing work on nonparametric estimation of quantile functions mostly focuses on cross-sectional data, or weakly dependent stationary data processes. Nonparametric estimation of conditional quantile functions with panel data is more difficult when there exists fixed effects term that is correlated with covariates. In this paper, we consider the following nonparametric panel data model with individual fixed effects:

$$Y_{it} = \alpha_i + m(X_{it}) + \epsilon_{it}, \quad i = 1, \cdots, N; \; t = 1, \cdots, T, \tag{1}$$

where Y_{it} is the outcome variable, X_{it} is a scalar[1], α_i is the individual fixed effect, it has zero mean and is allowed to be correlated with X_{it} in an unknown correlation form, $m(\cdot)$ is smooth but otherwise unspecified function, the idiosyncratic error ϵ_{it} is *i.i.d* with zero mean and a finite variance. Given that $\alpha_i + \epsilon_{it}$ has a zero mean, we have from Equation (1) that $E(Y_{it}) = E[m(X_{it})]$. Without loss of generality, we assume that $E\left[m(X_{it})\right] = 0$.[2]

A key attractive feature of panel data for empirical researchers is that it controls for the unobserved heterogeneity. Equation (1) has been discussed in Henderson et al. (2008), with a focus on the nonparametric estimation and testing of the conditional mean function. Our interest lies in estimating the conditional quantile function of $Y_{it} - \alpha_i = m(X_{it}) + \epsilon_{it}$ given $X_{it} = x$. The application of quantile regression to panel data framework has been a challenging task (see, for example, Koenker (2004); Abrevaya and Dahl (2008); Kato et al. (2012); Harding and Lamarche (2014)). The check-function method and inverse-CDF method are the two main methods in quantile regression analysis, with the former most widely used in literature. One main challenge with the check-function method is that the objective criterion function is non-differentiable and therefore numerical optimization is required. This creates a computational burden. Another drawback of the check-function method is the lack of monotonicity, also known as the quantile crossing problem (see Bassett and Koenker (1982) and He (1997)). Researchers often need to impose shape restrictions or use monotone rearrangement to address the quantile crossing problem (Chernozhukov et al. (2010); Qu and Yoon (2015)).

This paper develops a new quantile regression method for the nonparametric panel data Equation (1) in the spirit of Fang et al. (2018)[3]. The new method exploits the location-scale structure of Equation (1). Note that the conditional τ-th quantile function of $Y_{it} - \alpha_i$ given $X_{it} = x$, denoted by $q_\tau(x)$, takes a particularly simple closed-form structure:

$$q_\tau(x) = m(x) + Q_\epsilon(\tau)\,, \tag{2}$$

for all $\tau \in (0,1)$, where $Q_\epsilon(\tau)$ is the τ-th quantile of ϵ_{it}[4]. Thus, if $\hat{m}(x)$ is the estimator of $m(x)$, then $q_\tau(x)$ can be estimated by

$$\hat{q}_\tau(x) = \hat{m}(x) + \hat{Q}_\epsilon(\tau)\,, \tag{3}$$

where $\hat{Q}_\epsilon(\tau)$ is the empirical quantile function of the (normalized) regression residuals.

For estimation, we first use the first-difference transformation to get rid of the individual fixed effect α_i and estimate the the unknown function $m(\cdot)$ by the series method, we then use deconvolution method to back up the distribution of error term $\{\epsilon_{it}\}$, therefore the quantile estimator of ϵ. Finally, we exploit the location-scale structure of the first-differenced model to derive the quantile estimator of $Y_{it} - \alpha_i$, which is given in Equation (3). The deconvolution step closely relates to the papers by Horowitz and Markatou (1996) and Evdokimov (2010) for the application of the deconvolution method to recover the density of panel data error term. Our approach does not require numerical optimization, is computationally easy to implement, and automatically ensures quantile monotonicity by construction. For asymptotic property of the conditional quantile estimator, as long as the series estimator $\hat{m}(x)$ and $\hat{Q}_\epsilon(\tau)$ are consistent [5], the conditional quantile estimator $\hat{q}_\tau(x)$ is also consistent by

---

1. For ease of exposition, we assume X_{it} is univariate, the extension to multivariate case can be carried over straightforwardly.
2. This can be achieved by using de-mean data for the dependent variable, i.e., replacing Y_{it} by $Y_{it} - (NT)^{-1}\sum_{j=1}^{N}\sum_{s=1}^{T} Y_{js}$ in Equation (1). For notational simplicity, we still use Y_{it} to denote the dependent variable although it is actually the de-mean version of it.
3. Recently, Fang et al. (2018) proposes a new nonparametric method for estimating a conditional quantile function with cross-sectional data. We refer readers to Fang et al. (2018) for a detailed discussion.
4. For ease of exposition, we drop the subscript *it* in $Q_{\epsilon_{it}}(\tau)$ and use $Q_\epsilon(\tau)$ to denote the τ-th quantile of ϵ_{it} in general, since ϵ_{it} is an *i.i.d.* sequence.
5. The consistency can be straightforwardly shown using similar arguments as in Fang et al. (2018) and Horowitz and Markatou (1996).

Equation (3) and the continuous mapping theorem. While we do not provide theoretical underpinnings for the proposed quantile estimator, Monte Carlo simulation results show that the estimator performs well in finite samples.

The remainder of the paper is organized as follows. Section 2 gives a detailed description of the methodology. Section 3 presents a Monte Carlo simulation to examine the finite-sample performance of the proposed quantile estimator. Section 4 considers an extension where the error is heteroskedastic. Section 5 concludes the paper.

2. Methodology

In this section, we describe the three-step procedure to estimate the conditional quantile function $q_\tau(x)$.

STEP 1. Use the first-difference to get rid of individual fixed effects and estimate $m(\cdot)$ by the nonparametric series method.

First differencing Equation (1), we have that

$$Y_{it} - Y_{i,t-1} = m(X_{it}) - m(X_{i,t-1}) + \epsilon_{it} - \epsilon_{i,t-1}, \quad i = 1, \cdots, N; t = 2, \cdots, T. \tag{4}$$

Note that despite if one uses a de-mean dependent variable or not, it leads to the same first-differenced Equation (4) because any additive constant will be wiped out by first-difference transformation.

Let $P^K(X_{it}) = [\xi_1(X_{it}), \xi_2(X_{it}), ..., \xi_K(X_{it})]'$ denote the $K \times 1$ dimensional basis functions, where K is the number of basis functions. For example, we may choose power series base function so that $[\xi_1(X_{it}), \xi_2(X_{it}), ..., \xi_K(X_{it})]' = [X_{it}, X_{it}^2, \cdots, X_{it}^K]'$, or we can choose spline base function. By the approximation property of series basis function, there exists an $K \times 1$ vector of constants β such that $\sup_{x \in S} |P^K(x)'\beta - m(x)| \to 0$ as $K \to \infty$, where $S \in \mathcal{R}$ is a compact support of X_{it}. In practice, one can estimate β by the least squares method based on

$$\begin{aligned} \Delta Y_{it} &= Y_{it} - Y_{i,t-1} \\ &= \left[P^K(X_{it})' - P^K(X_{i,t-1})'\right]\beta + v_{it} \\ &= \Delta P_{it} + v_{it}, \end{aligned} \tag{5}$$

where $v_{it} = \epsilon_{it} - \epsilon_{i,t-1} + m(X_{it}) - m(X_{i,t-1}) - \left[P^K(X_{it})' - P^K(X_{i,t-1})'\right]\beta$, $\Delta Y_{it} \equiv Y_{it} - Y_{i,t-1}$, $\Delta P_{it} \equiv P^K(X_{it}) - P^K(X_{i,t-1})$, and $v_{it} = \epsilon_{it} - \epsilon_{i,t-1} + m(X_{it}) - m(X_{i,t-1}) - \left[P^K(X_{it})' - P^K(X_{i,t-1})'\right]\beta$.

We estimate β by applying the OLS to Equation (5), yielding that

$$\hat{\beta} = (\Delta P'\Delta P)^{-1}\Delta P'\Delta Y,$$

where $\Delta P = [\Delta P_2', \cdots, \Delta P_N']'$ is an $N(T-1) \times K$ matrix of base functions, $\Delta P_i = [\Delta P_{i2}, \cdots, \Delta P_{iT}]'$ is an $(T-1) \times K$ matrix, $\Delta Y = [\Delta Y_2', \cdots, \Delta Y_N']'$ is an $N(T-1) \times 1$ vector of outcome variables, and $\Delta Y_i = [\Delta Y_{i2}, \cdots, \Delta Y_{iT}]'$ is an $(T-1) \times 1$ vector.

We therefore obtain the series estimator of $m(X_{it})$:

$$\hat{m}(X_{it}) = P^K(X_{it})'\hat{\beta}, \quad i = 1, \cdots, N; t = 1, \cdots, T.$$

STEP 2. Let $f_\epsilon(\cdot)$ denote the density of ϵ_{it}. In this step, we use the deconvolution method to recover $f_\epsilon(\cdot)$.

From Step 1, one can obtain the estimator of $u_{it} = \epsilon_{it} - \epsilon_{i,t-1}$ by $\hat{u}_{it} \equiv Y_{it} - Y_{i,t-1} - \hat{m}(x_{it}) - \hat{m}(x_{i,t-1}) = \hat{\epsilon}_{it} - \hat{\epsilon}_{i,t-1}$.

To see how the density of ϵ_{it} can be estimated, let $\phi_u(t) = E(e^{\iota t u_{it}})$ and $\phi_\epsilon = E(e^{\iota t \epsilon_{it}})$ denote the characteristic functions of u_{it} and ϵ_{it}, respectively, where $\iota = \sqrt{-1}$. Assume that the distribution of ϵ_{it} is such that ϕ_ϵ is real and positive for all $t \in \mathcal{R}$. Then, it is easy to see that

$$\begin{aligned} \phi_u(t) &= E(e^{\iota t u_{it}}) \\ &= E(e^{\iota t \epsilon_{it} - \iota t \epsilon_{i,t-1}}) \\ &= E(e^{\iota t \epsilon_{it}})E(e^{-\iota t \epsilon_{i,t-1}}) \\ &= E(e^{\iota t \epsilon_{it}})E(e^{\iota t \epsilon_{i,t-1}}) \\ &= [E(e^{\iota t \epsilon_{it}})]^2 \\ &\equiv [\phi_\epsilon(t)]^2, \end{aligned}$$

where in the third equality we use the independence of ϵ_{it} and $\epsilon_{i,t-1}$, and the fourth equality uses the symmetry of $\eta_{i,t-1}$.

Therefore,

$$\phi_\epsilon(t) = \sqrt{\phi_u(t)}. \tag{6}$$

We propose the following steps to obtain the density estimate of ϵ_{it}:

(1) Estimate $\phi_u(t)$ by

$$\hat{\phi}_u(t) = \frac{1}{NT}\sum_{i=1}^{N}\sum_{s=1}^{T} e^{\iota t \hat{u}_{is}}. \tag{7}$$

(2) By Equations (6) and (7), we estimate $\phi_\epsilon(t)$ by

$$\hat{\phi}_\epsilon(t) = \sqrt{\hat{\phi}_u(t)}.$$

(3) By the deconvolution method, we estimate $f_\epsilon(\cdot)$ by

$$\hat{f}_\epsilon(z) = \frac{1}{2\pi}\int_{-\infty}^{\infty} e^{-\iota t z}\Phi_k\left(\frac{t}{T_n}\right)\hat{\phi}_\epsilon(t)dt, \quad z \in \mathcal{R}, \tag{8}$$

where $\Phi_k(\frac{t}{T_n})$ is the Fourier transform of the kernel function $k(x) = \frac{\sin \pi x}{\pi x}$ with bandwidth $\frac{1}{T_n}$, and

$$\Phi_k(t) = \begin{cases} 0, & |t| \geq \frac{1}{2}, \\ \frac{1}{2}, & |t| = \frac{1}{2}, \\ 1, & |t| \leq \frac{1}{2}. \end{cases}$$

STEP 3. We estimate $Q_\epsilon(\tau)$ by $\hat{Q}_\epsilon(\tau)$ such that for $\tau \in (0,1)$, $\hat{Q}_\epsilon(\tau)$ satisfies the following condition:

$$\tau = \int_{-\infty}^{\hat{Q}_\epsilon(\tau)} \hat{f}_\epsilon(x)dx.$$

Therefore, for $\tau \in (0,1)$, the τ-th conditional quantile estimator of $Y_{it} - \alpha_i$, given $X_{it} = x$, is estimated by

$$\hat{q}_\tau(x) = \hat{m}(x) + \hat{Q}_\epsilon(\tau),$$

where $\hat{m}(x)$ and $\hat{Q}_\epsilon(\tau)$ are estimated in Steps 1 and 2, respectively.

Remark 1. *In Step 1, the consistency estimation of $m(x)$ requires that as $NT \to \infty$, $K \to \infty$ and $K/(NT) \to 0$. In series estimation, $K/(NT)$ plays a role similar to the bandwidth h in kernel methods. In practice, one can use Mallows's C_L or leave-one-out cross-validation method to determine the series term K. We refer readers to Li and Racine (2007) for details.*

Remark 2. *Note that, in Step 2, assuming $\phi_\epsilon(t)$ is real and is equivalent to assuming that the density of ϵ_{it} is symmetric around 0. We are using the assumption that $\phi_{\epsilon_{it}}$ is positive in deriving Equation (6).*

Remark 3. *In Step 2, the smoothing parameter T_n depends on the sample size $n = NT$. To guarantee that $\hat{\phi}_\epsilon(t)$ uniformly converges to $\phi_\epsilon(t)$ over $[-T_n, T_n]$ at a geometric rate with respect to the sample size n, Hu and Ridder (2010) suggests that we can choose T_n such that*

$$T_n = c\left(\frac{n}{log(n)}\right)^{\gamma}, \qquad \gamma \in \left(0, \frac{1}{2}\right),$$

where $c > 0$ is a constant.

Remark 4. *For inference, we recommend using a residual bootstrap method similar to Fang et al. (2018). We leave the proof of validity of such a bootstrap procedure to a future research topic.*

3. Monte Carlo Simulation

In this section, we conduct Monte Carlo simulations to assess the performance of the proposed conditional quantile estimator.

We consider the following data generating process (DGP):

$$Y_{it} = \alpha_i + 2sin(X_{it}) + X_{it} + \epsilon_{it},$$

where $X_{it} = 0.4\alpha_i + \xi_{it}$, where ξ_{it} is *i.i.d.* $\sim uniform[-1, 1]$, α_i is *i.i.d.* $\sim uniform[-1, 1]$. We consider two distributions for ϵ_{it}: (i) ϵ_{it} is *i.i.d.* $\sim N(0, 1)$; (ii) ϵ_{it} is *i.i.d.* $\sim t(3)$ (a *t*-distribution with degree of freedom 3).

We conduct 2000 Monte Carlo replications for samples of size $N = 100, 200, 400$ with $T = 10$. We report mean squared error (MSE) of three estimators: (1) the series estimator $\hat{m}(x)$ with $MSE(\hat{m}) = (NT)^{-1}\sum_{i=1}^{N}\sum_{t=1}^{T}\left(\hat{m}(X_{it}) - m(X_{it})\right)^2$, (2) the quantile estimator $\hat{Q}_\tau(\epsilon)$ with $MSE(\hat{Q}_\epsilon(\tau)) = \left[\hat{Q}_\epsilon(\tau) - Q_\epsilon(\tau)\right]^2$, and (3) the conditional quantile estimator $\hat{q}_\tau(x)$ with $MSE(\hat{q}_\tau) = (NT)^{-1}\sum_{i=1}^{N}\sum_{t=1}^{T}\left(\hat{q}_\tau(X_{it}) - q_\tau(X_{it})\right)^2$. For each of the three quantities above, we average them over the 2000 replications.

We first examine the performance of the deconvolution method for recovering the density of error terms. As an illustration, we only present the result (Figure 1) for the case of $\epsilon_{it} \sim N(0, 1)$, with sample size $N = 100, T = 10$. We examine the sensitivity of the estimated density to the choice of different bandwidths. We set $c = 1$, and $\gamma = \frac{1}{8}, \frac{3}{16}, \frac{1}{4}, \frac{3}{8}$. It can be seen from Figure 1 that the performance of the deconvolution method can be somewhat sensitive to the choice of bandwidth. This is a well known problem of the deconvolution method, not a particular problem to our approach. When γ is small, say $\gamma = \frac{1}{8}$, the estimated density is flatter than the true density. However, generally, the estimated density tracks the true density[6].

Tables 1 and 2 report the Mean MSE of $\hat{m}$, $\hat{Q}_\epsilon(\tau)$ and $\hat{q}_\tau$. It can be seen that, as sample size doubles, MSEs of $\hat{m}$, $\hat{Q}_\epsilon(\tau)$, and $\hat{q}_\tau$ decrease by about $\frac{1}{2}$, which indicates that the proposed estimator behaves well.

---

[6] There is no rule-of-thumb to choose the optimal bandwidth in the deconvolution method. In practice, researchers can try different bandwidths as a robust check to see how results vary across the different bandwidths.

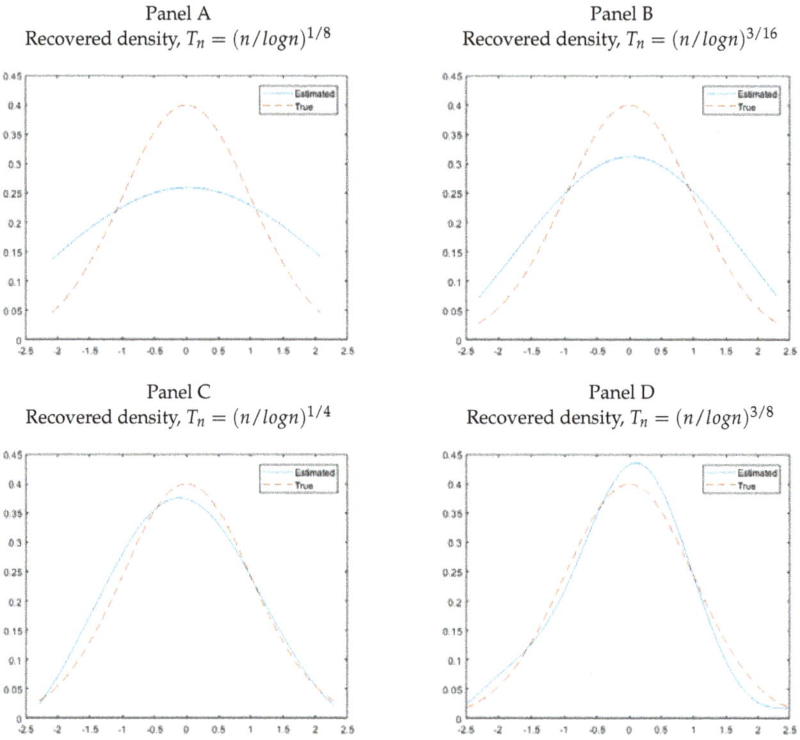

Panel A
Recovered density, $T_n = (n/logn)^{1/8}$
Panel B
Recovered density, $T_n = (n/logn)^{3/16}$
Panel C
Recovered density, $T_n = (n/logn)^{1/4}$
Panel D
Recovered density, $T_n = (n/logn)^{3/8}$
Estimated
True

Figure 1. Recovered densities across different bandwidths and homoskedastic symmetric normal errors.

Table 1. Mean MSE ($\times 100$), $N(0,1)$ Errors.

Sample Size (N,T)	Estimators						
	$MSE(\hat{m})$	$MSE(\hat{Q}_\epsilon(\tau))$			$MSE(\hat{q}_\tau)$		
		$\tau = 0.2$	$\tau = 0.3$	$\tau = 0.4$	$\tau = 0.2$	$\tau = 0.3$	$\tau = 0.4$
(100, 10)	0.0149	0.0037	0.0022	0.0006	0.0204	0.0185	0.0163
(200, 10)	0.0092	0.0012	0.0007	0.0002	0.0107	0.0102	0.0096
(400, 10)	0.0048	0.00051	0.00028	0.000082	0.0052	0.0050	0.0048

Table 2. Mean MSE ($\times 100$), $t(3)$ Errors.

Sample Size (N,T)	Estimators						
	$MSE(\hat{m})$	$MSE(\hat{Q}_\epsilon(\tau))$			$MSE(\hat{q}_\tau)$		
		$\tau = 0.2$	$\tau = 0.3$	$\tau = 0.4$	$\tau = 0.2$	$\tau = 0.3$	$\tau = 0.4$
(100, 10)	0.0139	0.0423	0.0235	0.0065	0.0642	0.0433	0.0235
(200, 10)	0.0094	0.0210	0.0128	0.0036	0.0304	0.0222	0.0130
(400, 10)	0.0048	0.0091	0.0063	0.0019	0.0104	0.0112	0.0067

4. Extension: Conditional Heteroskedastistic Error Case

In this section, we consider an extension where the error term is conditional heteroskedastic. Specifically, we generalize Equation (1) to the following case[7]:

$$Y_{it} = \alpha_i + m(X_{it}) + \sigma(X_{it})\eta_{it}, \quad i = 1, \cdots, N; \; t = 1, \cdots, T, \tag{9}$$

where $\sigma(X_{it}) > 0$ is an unknown function, η_{it} is assumed to be *i.i.d* with zero mean, unit variance and independent of $\{X_{js}\}_{j=1,\ldots,N; s=1,\ldots,T}$. Without loss of generality, we assume that $E[m(X_{it})] = 0$ (similar to the conditional homoskedasticity case).

Define $\epsilon_{it} \equiv \sigma(X_{it})\eta_{it}$. The conditional τ-th quantile function of $Y_{it} - \alpha_i$ given $X_{it} = x$, denoted by $q_\tau(x)$, takes the following closed-form structure:

$$q_\tau(x) = m(x) + Q_{\epsilon|X=x}(\tau) = m(x) + \sigma(x)Q_\eta(\tau), \tag{10}$$

for all $\tau \in (0, 1)$, where $Q_{\epsilon|X=x}(\tau) = \sigma(x)Q_\eta(\tau)$, and $Q_\eta(\tau)$ is the (un-conditional) τ-th quantile of η_{it}.

Remark 5. *In deriving Equation (10), we use the fact that $Q_{\epsilon|X=x}(\tau) = \sigma(x)Q_\eta(\tau)$ because $\sigma(x) > 0$ and X_{it} and η_{it} are independent with each other.*

Remark 6. *Noting that, due to the independence between X_{it} and ϵ_{js}, we have that $\epsilon_{it}|_{X_{it}=x} = \epsilon_{it}|_{X_{it}=X_{i,t-1}=x} = \sigma(x)\eta_{it}$, and this implies that $f_{\epsilon_{it}|X_{it},X_{i,t-1}}(u) = f_{\epsilon_{it}|X_{it}}(u)$ (conditional independence property).*

We propose the following three-step procedure to estimate the conditional quantile function of $Y_{it} - \alpha_i = m(X_{it}) + \sigma(X_{it})\eta_{it}$ given $X_{it} = x$.

STEP 1. We obtain $\hat{m}(X_{it}) = P^K(X_{it})'\hat{\beta}$ by exactly the same procedure as in Step 1 of the conditional homoskedastic error case.

STEP 2. We use the deconvolution method to estimate $f_{\epsilon_{it}|X_{it}=x}(\cdot)$, the conditional density of ϵ_{it} given $X_{it} = x$. Define $\Delta Y_{it} \equiv Y_{it} - Y_{it-1}$. Assuming that the density of η_{it} is symmetric around zero,[8] and note that $[m(X_{it}) - m(X_{i,t-1})]_{X_{it}=x, X_{i,t-1}=x} = m(x) - m(x) = 0$, we have

$$\begin{aligned}
\phi_{\Delta Y_{it}}(s|x) &\equiv E[exp(\iota s \Delta Y_{it})|X_{it} = X_{it-1} = x] \\
&= E[exp[\iota s(\epsilon_{it} - \epsilon_{it-1})|X_{it} = X_{it-1} = x] \\
&= \Big\{E[exp(\iota s \epsilon_{it})|X_{it} = x]\Big\}\Big\{E[exp(-\iota s \epsilon_{it-1})|X_{it-1} = x]\Big\} \\
&= \Big\{E[exp(\iota s \epsilon_{it})|X_{it} = x]\Big\}\Big\{E[exp(\iota s \epsilon_{it-1})|X_{it-1} = x]\Big\} \\
&= \Big\{E[exp(\iota s \epsilon_{it})|X_{it} = x]\Big\}^2 \\
&\equiv \phi^2_{\epsilon_{it}}(s|x),
\end{aligned} \tag{11}$$

where $\iota = \sqrt{-1}$, the third equality uses the conditional independence property as described in Remark 6, and in the fourth equality we use the symmetry of $\epsilon_{i,t-1}|X_{i,t-1} = x = \sigma(x)\eta_{i,t-1}$, and $\eta_{i,t-1}$ is symmetric around zero.

---

7 Fang et al. (2018) also considers the same form of heteroskedastic error as described here.

8 This implies the conditional density of ϵ_{it} given $X_{it} = x$ is symmetric, since, given that $\epsilon_{it}|_{X_{it}=x} = \sigma(x)\eta_{it}$, the symmetry of η_{it} is equivalent to the symmetry of ϵ_{it}.

Under the assumption that $\phi_\epsilon(s|x)$ is positive, the above equation implies that $\phi_{\epsilon_{it}}(s|x) = \sqrt{\phi_{\Delta Y_{it}}(s|x)}$. The left-hand side of Equation (11) can be estimated from data:

$$\hat{\phi}_{\Delta Y_{it}}(s|x) = \frac{\sum_{i=1}^{N}\sum_{t=2}^{T} exp\left[\iota s(Y_{it} - Y_{i,t-1})\right] K(\frac{X_{it}-x}{h_1}) K(\frac{X_{i,t-1}-x}{h_2})}{\sum_{i=1}^{N}\sum_{t=2}^{T} K(\frac{X_{it}-x}{h_1}) K(\frac{X_{i,t-1}-x}{h_2})}.$$

Therefore, we estimate $\phi_{\epsilon_{it}}(s|x)$ by $\hat{\phi}_{\epsilon_{it}}(s|x) = \sqrt{\hat{\phi}_{\Delta Y_{it}}(s|x)}$. Let $f_{\epsilon_{it}|X_{it}=x}(\cdot)$ denote the conditional density of $\epsilon_{it} = \sigma(X_{it})\eta_{it}$ given $X_{it} = x$. Then, using the deconvolution method as in the homoskedastic case, one can recover $\hat{f}_{\epsilon_{it}|X_{it}=x}(\cdot)$ using $\hat{\phi}_{\epsilon_{it}}(s|x)$ as in Equation (8). We use $\hat{f}_{\epsilon_{it}|X_{it}=x}(\cdot)$ to denote the resulting estimator of $f_{\epsilon_{it}|X_{it}=x}(\cdot)$.

STEP 3. Let $\hat{Q}_{\epsilon|X=x}(\tau)$ denote the estimate of $Q_{\epsilon|X=x}(\tau)$, $\tau \in (0,1)$. The following identity

$$\tau = \int_{-\infty}^{Q_{\epsilon|X=x}(\tau)} f_{\epsilon|X=x}(z)dz$$

suggests that we can obtain $\hat{Q}_{\epsilon|X=x}(\tau)$ based on the following equation:

$$\tau = \int_{-\infty}^{\hat{Q}_{\epsilon|X=x}(\tau)} \hat{f}_{\epsilon|X=x}(z)dz,$$

where $\hat{f}_{\epsilon|X=x}(z)$ is estimated from Step 2.

By Equation (10), the τ-th conditional quantile estimator of $Y_{it} - \alpha_i$, given $X_{it} = x$, is estimated by

$$\hat{q}_\tau(x) = \hat{m}(x) + \hat{Q}_{\epsilon|X=x}(\tau), \qquad \tau \in (0,1),$$

where $\hat{m}(x) = P^K(x)'\hat{\beta}$ is obtained in Step 1, and $\hat{Q}_{\epsilon|X=x}(\tau)$ is obtained in Step 3.

Remark 7. *Note that, in the last step, we estimate the τ-th quantile of $\epsilon_{it} \equiv \sigma(X_{it})\eta_{it}$ directly, instead of estimating the unknown function $\sigma(\cdot)$ and $Q_\eta(\tau)$ separately (e.g., Fang et al. (2018)).*

5. Conclusions

In this paper, we propose an easy-to-implement nonparametric method to estimate conditional quantile functions in a fixed effects panel data model. There are many directions that one can extend the results of this paper to more general settings. For example, one can allow for panel non-stationary data as considered in Chen and Khan (2008) or allow for the covariate X_{it} to be endogenous. We leave these as possible future research topics.

Author Contributions: The two authors both contribute to the project formulation and paper preparation.

Funding: This research received no external funding.

Acknowledgments: We thank three anonymous referees for helpful and constructive comments.

Conflicts of Interest: The authors declare no conflict of interest.

References

Abrevaya, Jason, and Christian M. Dahl. 2008. The effects of birth inputs on birthweight. *Journal of Business & Economic Statistics* 26: 379–97.

Al Rahahleh, Naseem, Iman Adeinat, and M. Ishaq Bhatti. 2016. On ethnicity of idiosyncratic risk and stock returns puzzle. *Humanomics* 32: 48–68. [CrossRef]

Al Rahahleh, Naseem, and M. Ishaq Bhatti. 2017. Co-movement measure of information transmission on international equity markets. *Physica A: Statistical Mechanics and its Applications* 470: 119–31. [CrossRef]

Al Rahahleh, Naseem, M. Ishaq Bhatti, and Iman Adeinat. 2017. Tail dependence and information flow: Evidence from international equity markets. *Physica A: Statistical Mechanics and its Applications* 474: 319–29. [CrossRef]

Al Shubiri, Faris Nasif, and Syed Ashsan Jamil. 2018. The impact of idiosyncratic risk of banking sector on oil, stock market, and fiscal indicators of Sultanate of Oman. *International Journal of Engineering Business Management* 10: doi:10.1177/1847979017749043. [CrossRef]

Bartram, Söhnke M., Gregory W. Brown, and René M. Stulz. 2018. *Why Has Idiosyncratic Risk Been Historically Low in Recent Years?* National Bureau of Economic Research Working Paper NO. 24270, Cambridge, MA, USA: National Bureau of Economic Research, January.

Bassett, Gilbert, Jr., and Roger Koenker. 1982. An empirical quantile function for linear models with iid errors. *Journal of the American Statistical Association* 77: 407–15. [CrossRef]

Belloni, Alexandre, Victor Chernozhukov, and Ivan Fernández-Val. 2016. Conditional quantile processes based on series and many regressors. *arXiv*, arXiv:1105.6154.

Chen, Songnian, and Shakeeb Khan. 2008. Semiparametric estimation of nonstationary censored panel data models with time varying factor loads. *Econometric Theory* 24: 1149–73. [CrossRef]

Chernozhukov, Victor, Iván Fernández-Val, and Alfred Galichon. 2010. Quantile and probability curves without crossing. *Econometrica* 78: 1093–25.

Evdokimov, Kirill. 2010. *Indentification and Estimation of a Nonparametric Panel Data Model with Unobserved Heterogeneity*. Working Paper, Princeton, NJ, USA: Princeton University.

Fang, Zheng, Qi Li, and Karen Yan. 2018. *A Simple Nonparametric Method for Estimation and Inference of Conditional Quantile Functions*. Working Paper. Available online: https://ssrn.com/abstract=3223015 (accessed on 3 August 2018).

Firpo, Sergio, Nicole M. Fortin, and Thomas Lemieux. 2009. Unconditional quantile regressions. *Econometrica* 77: 953–73.

Firpo, Sergio P., Nicole M. Fortin, and Thomas Lemieux. 2018. Decomposing wage distributions using recentered influence function regressions. *Econometrics* 6: 28. [CrossRef]

Hall, Peter, Qi Li, and Jeffrey S. Racine. 2007. Nonparametric estimation of regression functions in the presence of irrelevant regressors. *The Review of Economics and Statistics* 89: 784–89. [CrossRef]

Harding, Matthew, and Carlos Lamarche. 2014. Estimating and testing a quantile regression model with interactive effects. *Journal of Econometrics* 178: 101–13. [CrossRef]

He, Xuming. 1997. Quantile curves without crossing. *The American Statistician* 51: 186–92.

Henderson, Daniel J., Raymond J. Carroll, and Qi Li. 2008. Nonparametric estimation and testing of fixed effects panel data models. *Journal of Econometrics* 144: 257–75. [CrossRef] [PubMed]

Horowitz, Joel L., and Marianthi Markatou. 1996. Semiparametric estimation of regression models for panel data. *The Review of Economic Studies* 63: 145–68. [CrossRef]

Hu, Yingyao, and Geert Ridder. 2010. On deconvolution as a first stage nonparametric estimator. *Econometric Reviews* 29: 365–96. [CrossRef]

Kato, Kengo, Antonio F. Galvao, and Gabriel V. Montes-Rojas. 2012. Asymptotics for panel quantile regression models with individual effects. *Journal of Econometrics* 170: 76–91. [CrossRef]

Koenker, Roger. 2004. Quantile regression for longitudinal data. *Journal of Multivariate Analysis* 91: 74–89. [CrossRef]

Li, Qi, Juan Lin, and Jeffrey S. Racine. 2013. Optimal bandwidth selection for nonparametric conditional distribution and quantile functions. *Journal of Business & Economic Statistics* 31: 57–65.

Li, Qi, and Jeffrey Scott Racine. 2007. *Nonparametric Econometrics: Theory and Practice*. Princeton: Princeton University Press.

Lin, Wei, Zongwu Cai, Zheng Li, and Li Su. 2015. Optimal smoothing in nonparametric conditional quantile derivative function estimation. *Journal of Econometrics* 188: 502–13. [CrossRef]

Nguyen, Cuong, and M. Ishaq Bhatti. 2015. Investor sentiment and idiosyncratic volatility puzzle: Evidence from the chinese stock market. *Journal of Stock and Forex Trading* 4: 2.

Pagan, Adrian, and Aman Ullah. 1999. *Nonparametric Econometrics*. Cambridge: Cambridge University Press.
Qu, Zhongjun, and Jungmo Yoon. 2015. Nonparametric estimation and inference on conditional quantile processes. *Journal of Econometrics* 185: 1–19. [CrossRef]

Journal of
Risk and Financial Management

MDPI

Article

Financial Development and Countries' Production Efficiency: A Nonparametric Analysis

Nickolaos G. Tzeremes

Laboratory of Economic Policy and Strategic Planning, Department of Economics, University of Thessaly, 38333 Volos, Greece; bus9nt@econ.uth.gr; Tel.: +30-2421-074911

Received: 16 July 2018; Accepted: 6 August 2018; Published: 7 August 2018

Abstract: This paper examines the effect of financial development on countries' production efficiency levels. By applying a probabilistic framework it develops robust (Order-m) time-dependent conditional nonparametric frontier estimators in order to measure 87 countries' production efficiency levels over the period 1970–2014. In order to examine the effect of time and domestic credit on countries' production efficiency levels, a second-stage nonparametric econometric analysis is performed. Specifically, generalized additive models with tensor products and cubic spline penalties are applied in order to investigate the potential nonlinear behavior of financial development on countries' production efficiency levels. The results reveal that the effect of financial development on production efficiency is nonlinear. Specifically, the effect is positive up to a certain credit level after which it becomes negative. Finally, the evidence suggests that the effect is influenced by a country's financial system, institutional, and development characteristics.

Keywords: financial development; production efficiency; nonparametric frontiers; generalized additive models; tensor products; cubic spline penalty

---

1. Introduction

The empirical evidence on countries' economic growth paths emphasize the existence of nonlinear trends which are of great importance for policy implications and for further investigation (Liu and Stengos 1999; Kalaitzidakis et al. 2001; Maasoumi et al. 2007). Such a nonlinear trend is also evident when examining the impact of financial development on countries' economic growth levels (Rousseau and Wachtel 2011; Arcand et al. 2015). Since countries' different development, institutional and financial system arrangements differentiate the way financial development impacts countries' growth levels (Arestis and Demetriades 1997), asymmetric phenomena can arise, which in turn, are worth the investigation using nonparametric econometric tools. Shen (2013) provides evidence of such nonlinear effects among financial development and economic growth, whereas, Beck et al. (2014) suggests that the provision of credit has a positive influence on the output growth only up to a point, after which the influence becomes negative. On the other hand, Ang (2011) provides evidence of a positive effect of financial development on innovation. Mallick et al. (2016) using a probabilistic framework of directional distance functions, provide evidence of a nonlinear effect of financial development on countries' technological change and technological catch-up levels. Based on this stream of research, this study further examines the effect of financial development on countries' growth levels, by investigating in a robust nonparametric frontier setting its effect on countries' production efficiency levels.

Specifically, by using Order-m (robust) frontier estimators (Cazals et al. 2002) and the recent developments on the probabilistic approach of nonparametric frontier analysis (Daraio and Simar 2005, 2007a, 2007b; Bădin et al. 2010, 2012, 2014), we develop in a first-stage analysis robust time-dependent conditional measures (Mastromarco and Simar 2015). By doing so, we evaluate 87 countries' production efficiency levels under the effect of both time and financial development over the period 1970–2014. As has been asserted by Daraio et al. (2018), the adopted approach does not assume that the restrictive "separability" assumption between the financial development, time and the input/output set holds. A vast majority of nonparametric efficiency and productivity studies in different research fields (i.e., production economics, environmental economics, banking/finance, hospitality, transport, etc.) estimate in a first-stage analysis different efficiency scores. Then, in a second-stage analysis the estimated efficiency scores are regressed on some environmental/exogenous factors[1] using different parametric/nonparametric regression approaches. However, these studies wrongly assume that the 'separability' assumption among the environmental/exogenous factors and the frontier of the attainable set holds. This assumption has been proven by Simar and Wilson (2007, 2011) that in the majority of times it is unrealistic since it implies that these factors do not influence: 'neither the shape nor the level of the boundary of the attainable set' but they affect only the distribution of the estimated inefficiencies (Daraio et al. 2018). Simar and Wilson (2011) assert that the studies which do not account properly for the 'separability' assumption, are applying questionably defined statistical models describing the data-generating process (DGP). As a result, the absence of inference does not lead to meaningful efficiency measurements. The lack of a coherent statistical model on such measurements leads to "unknown" estimations which are meaningless both for evaluating factors affecting DMUs' performance levels, but also for managerial and policy implications (Simar and Wilson 2011, p. 206). Following those arguments, the applied conditional probabilistic approach does not assume that the 'separability' assumption holds. Specifically, in a second-stage analysis we investigate the effect of financial development and time on the estimated time-dependent conditional Order-m efficiencies. We apply a generalized additive model (Hastie and Tibshirani 1990) with smooth functions (tensor products with cubic spline penalties) as has been analyzed by Wood (2002, 2003, 2004, 2006, 2017). As such the adoption of robust nonparametric frontier methods alongside the nonparametric econometric advances will enable us to reveal potential nonlinear phenomena of the examined relationship. The remainder of the paper is as follows: Section 2 describes the data and the methodologies adopted, whereas, Section 3 provides the findings of our analysis. Finally, the last Section concludes our paper.

2. Materials and Methods

2.1. Probabilistic Approach of Countries' Production Frontier

Based on the activity analysis by Debreu (1951), countries' production function can be characterized by a set of inputs $x \in \mathbb{R}^p_+$ and by a set of outputs $y \in \mathbb{R}^q_+$. In our case the inputs are: Capital stock at current PPPs (in mil. 2011 US dollars) and the number of total labor force (in millions), whereas, the output is the output-side real GDP at current PPPs (in mil. 2011 US dollars). The data are covering 87 countries[2] over the period 1970-2014 and have been extracted from the latest version of Penn World Tables-PWT v9.0 (Feenstra et al. 2015).[3] We argue that countries' production process can be affected by the different levels of domestic credit to the private sector (% of GDP),

---

1 The environmental/exogenous factors are referring to those factors which are not under (or partially under) the control of the decision maker.

2 OECD countries (20): Australia, Canada, Chile, Denmark, Finland, Iceland, Ireland, Israel, Italy, Japan, Mexico, Netherlands, New Zealand, Norway, Republic of Korea, Sweden, Switzerland, Turkey, United Kingdom and United States. Non-OECD countries (67): Argentina, Bahamas, Benin, Bolivia, Botswana, Brazil, Burkina Faso, Burundi, Cameroon, Central African Republic, Chad, Colombia, Congo, Costa Rica, Côte d'Ivoire, D.R. of the Congo, Dominican Republic, Ecuador, Egypt, El Salvador, Fiji, Gabon, Gambia, Ghana, Guatemala, Honduras, India, Iran, Jamaica, Jordan, Kenya, Kuwait, Madagascar, Malawi, Malaysia, Mali, Malta, Mauritius, Morocco, Nepal, Niger, Nigeria, Oman, Pakistan, Panama, Paraguay, Peru, Philippines, Qatar, Saudi Arabia, Senegal, Sierra Leone, Singapore, South Africa, Sri Lanka, Sudan, Suriname, Swaziland, Syrian Arab Republic, Thailand, Togo, Trinidad and Tobago, Tunisia, Uganda, Uruguay, Venezuela and Zambia.

3 The codenames of the variables which have been extracted from PWT v9.0 are: "ck", "emp" (inputs) and "cgdpo" (output).

which is used as a proxy of financial development.[4] Then the vector of domestic credit to private sector (PCR) can be noted as $C \in \mathcal{C} \subset \mathbb{R}^r$, and the production attainable set can be represented as:

$$\Omega = \{ (x, y) | x \text{ can produce } y \}, \quad (1)$$

whereas, the conditional attainable set (i.e., under the effect of domestic credit to private sector) can be presented as:

$$\Omega^c = \{ (x, y) | C = c, \ x \text{ can produce } y \}. \quad (2)$$

Based on Daraio and Simar (2005, 2007a, 2007b), we have $\Omega = \bigcup_{c \in \mathcal{C}} \Omega^c$ so that we can have for all $C \in \mathcal{C}$, $\Omega^c \subseteq \Omega$.

According to the work of Farrell (1957) and Shephard (1970), countries' output-oriented efficiency at (x_0, y_0) level can be defined as:

$$\psi(x_0, y_0) = sup\{ \psi > 0 | (x_0, \psi y_0) \in \Omega \}. \quad (3)$$

As has been shown by Cazals et al. (2002), countries' production process can be characterized by the probability function (x, y) as:

$$(x, y) = Prob(X \leq x, Y \geq y). \quad (4)$$

As a result, the output oriented efficiency measure in (3) can be presented as:

$$\psi(x_0, y_0) = sup\{ \psi | (x_0, \psi y_0) > 0 \}. \quad (5)$$

Following Daraio and Simar (2005), (x, y) can be decomposed as:

$$(x, y) = P(Y \geq y | X \leq x) P(X \leq x) = \Gamma_{Y|X}(y|x) F_x(x). \quad (6)$$

Then countries' output-oriented efficiency measure at point $(x_0, y_0) \in \Omega$ can be defined by the support of the survival function $\Gamma_{Y|X}(y_0|x_0) = Prob(Y \geq y_0 | X \leq x_0)$ as:

$$\psi(x_0, y_0) = sup\left\{ \psi | \Gamma_{Y|X}(\psi y_0 | x_0) > 0 \right\}. \quad (7)$$

As a result, in the presence of domestic credit to the private sector, the conditional distribution can be defined as:

$$(x, y|c) = Prob(X \leq x, Y \geq y | C = c), \quad (8)$$

which signifies the probability of a country operating at level (x, y) to be dominated by countries having the same domestic credit conditions. Then we can have an additional decomposition of (8) as:

$$(x, y|c) = Prob(Y \geq y | X \leq x, \ C = c) Prob(X \leq x | C = c) = \Gamma_{Y|X,C}(y|x, c) F_{X|C}(x|c), \quad (9)$$

Then by following the relative literature (Bădin et al. 2010, 2012, 2014) a country's conditional efficiency measure operating at level (x_0, y_0) under the domestic credit conditions $C = c_0$, can be expressed as:

$$\begin{aligned} \psi(x_0, y_0 | c_0) = & \ sup\{ \psi > 0 | (x_0, \psi y_0) \in \Omega^{c_0} \} \\ & = sup\left\{ \psi > 0 | \Gamma_{Y|X,C}(\psi y_0 | X \leq x_0, \ C = c_0) > 0 \right\}.^5 \end{aligned} \quad (10)$$

[4] The data for domestic credit to the private sector (% of GDP) has been extracted from World Development Indicators.

Recently, Mastromarco and Simar (2015) considered the above output-oriented efficiency measure in a time-dependent framework by considering time T as an additional conditional variable alongside with C. As a result the conditional probability will take the form:

$$\Gamma^t_{X,Y|C}(x,y|c) = Prob(Y \geq y|X \leq x, C = c,\ T = t), \tag{11}$$

and a country's conditional efficiency measure operating at level $(x_0,\ y_0)$ under the domestic credit conditions $C = c_0$ and at a period $T = t_0$, can be expressed as:

$$\psi_t(x_0,\ y_0|c_0) = sup\{\psi > 0|(x_0, \psi y_0) \in \Omega_t^{c_0}\} = sup\{\psi > 0|\Gamma^t_{X,Y|C}(\psi y_0|X \leq x_0,\ C = c_0,\ T = t_0) > 0\}. \tag{12}$$

As has been proposed by the relative literature (Daraio and Simar 2005, 2007a, 2007b; Bădin et al. 2010, 2012, 2014), smoothing techniques via kernel-based methods need to be applied in order to estimate $\Gamma^t_{X,Y|C}(x,y|c)$ conditioning on $X \leq x$, both time $T = t$ and domestic credit $C = c$. Using the techniques by Hall et al. (2004) and Li and Racine (2007) we can estimate $\Gamma^t_{X,Y|C}(x,y|c)$ as:

$$\hat{\Gamma}^t_{X,Y|C}(x,y|c) = \frac{\sum_{s=(i,v)} I(x_s \leq x,\ y_s \geq y) K_{h_c}(c_s - c) K_{h_t}(v - t)}{\sum_{s=(i,v)} I(x_s \leq x) K_{h_c}(c_s - c) K_{h_t}(v - t)}. \tag{13}$$

In Equation (13) $I(\cdot)$ is an indicator function and $K(\cdot)$ represents kernels with compact support (in our case we have use Epanechnikov kernels). Finally, optimal bandwidths (h) are selected using the least squares cross-validation (LSCV) criterion (Li and Racine 2007).[6] It must be noted that the time-dependent conditional full frontier efficiency measure in (12) is a Free disposal hull (FDH) estimator which is not robust (Deprins et al. 1984) and can be obtained by plugging into its formula the nonparametric estimator presented in (13). Another point that needs to be emphasized is the treatment of time in Equation (13). Obviously time is a discrete variable and discrete kernels can be used (De Witte and Kortelainen 2013). However, as indicated by Li and Racine (2007) and Mastromarco and Simar (2015, p. 830), continuous kernels are more appropriate when the discrete variables take many different values. In our case, T takes the values from 1 to 45 (i.e., from 1970 to 2014) and, therefore, continuous kernels have been applied. Another point that needs to be considered is the *i.i.d.* structure of our data. The independence of observations cannot be assumed in our case (especially with the time variable). However, as has been analyzed by Hart (1996), if the kernel used has the support on $[-1,\ 1]$, then the estimator uses only the observations determined by the bandwidth window. Therefore the dependency is deteriorated among the small 'window' and makes the data in that window "essentially independent" from the rest of the data. This is what Hart (1996, p. 117) refers to as the principle of "whitening by windowing".

2.2. Robust (Order-m) Conditional Frontiers

The Order-m (robust) estimators were first introduced by Cazals et al. (2002) and were further developed by Daraio and Simar (2005, 2006, 2007a, 2007b). In our paper we apply these estimators since they are less sensitive to outliers/extreme values producing, therefore, robust production efficiency estimates. For a given level of countries' inputs x in the interior of the support of X, let us consider m, *i.i.d.* random variables $Y_i,\ i = 1, \ldots, m$ which have been generated by the conditional $q-variate$ distribution function $\Gamma_{Y|X}(y|x_0) = Prob(Y \leq y_0|X \leq x_0)$. Then a random set can be defined as:

$$\Omega_m(x_0) = \left\{ (x\acute{,}y) \in \mathbb{R}_+^{p+q} \middle| \acute{x} \leq x_0, y \leq Y_i,\ i = 1, \ldots, m \right\}, \tag{14}$$

---

6 For computational details see Bădin et al. (2010, p. 640).

whereas similar to (3) we can define:

$$\widetilde{\psi}_m(x_0, y_0) = sup\{\psi > 0|(x_0, \psi y) \in \Omega_m(x_0)\} = \max_{i=1,\ldots,m}\left\{\min_{j=1,\ldots,q}\frac{Y_i^j}{y_0^j}\right\}. \tag{15}$$

Then countries' robust output-oriented production efficiency measure can be presented as:

$$\psi_m(x_0, y_0) = \mathbb{E}(\widetilde{\psi}_m(x_0, y_0)|X \leq x_0). \tag{16}$$

Moreover, the original $\psi_m(x_0, y_0)$ and the time-dependent conditional efficiency measures $\psi_{t,m}(x_0, y_0|c_0)$ can be estimated as:

$$\hat{\psi}_m(x_0, y_0) = \int_0^\infty\left[1 - \left(1 - \hat{\Gamma}_{Y|X}(uy_0|X \leq x_0)\right)^m\right]du = \hat{\psi}(x_0, y_0) - \int_0^{\hat{\psi}(x_0, y_0)} \left(1 - \hat{\Gamma}_{Y|X}(uy_0|X \leq x_0)\right)^m du, \tag{17}$$

$$\hat{\psi}_{t,m}(x_0, y_0|c_0) = \int_0^\infty\left[1 - \left(1 - \hat{\Gamma}^t_{X,Y|C}(uy_0|X \leq x_0, C = c_0, T = t_0)\right)^m\right]du = \hat{\psi}_t(x_0, y_0|c_0) - \int_0^{\hat{\psi}_t(x_0, y_0|c_0)} \left(1 - \hat{\Gamma}^t_{X,Y|C}(uy_0|X \leq x_0, C = c_0, T = t_0)\right)^m du. \tag{18}$$

Both the unconditional (17) and the time-dependent conditional (18) robust frontiers take as benchmark the expectation of best performing countries (among m countries) drawn randomly from the population of countries using less input factors of production than x_0. Finally, as proven by Cazals et al. (2002), both $\hat{\psi}_m(x_0, y_0)$ and $\hat{\psi}_{t,m}(x_0, y_0|c_0)$ are $\sqrt{n} - consistent$ estimators[8], which means that the they convergence to the true values similar to the parametric estimators, whereas, they do not suffer from the curse of dimensionality in comparison to the standard DEA and FDH estimators.

2.3. *Analysing the Effect of Domestic Credit*

By using time-dependent conditional efficiency estimates in a second-stage nonparametric regression analysis we evaluate the effect of both time and domestic credit on countries' production efficiency levels (Bădin et al. 2012; Daraio et al. 2015). Relevant studies using a second-stage nonparametric regression analysis used either a local constant and/or a local linear estimator in order to reveal nonlinear phenomena (Daraio and Simar 2005; Jeong et al. 2010). According to Stone (1985), the fundamental properties of such statistical models are their ability: To provide accurate data fits (flexibility), to minimize the increase of variance due to an increase in dimensionality (curse of dimensionality), and finally, to effectively reveal the underlying structure (interpretability). Compared to the local linear and local constant estimators, generalized additive models (GAM) appear to cope better with the problem of dimensionality since they use a sum of nonparametric functions over the components (Carroll et al. 1997). Moreover, since the Order-m estimators do not suffer from the curse of dimensionality (relative to the FDH and the DEA estimators), it appears that GAM models are suited most to our analysis. Therefore, we apply a generalized additive model as was initially introduced by Hastie and Tibshirani (1990) and was further developed by Wood (2002, 2003, 2004, 2017). In its general form the model can be expressed as:

$$g(\varphi_i) = X_i^*\vartheta + f_1(C_i) + u_i \; i = 1, \ldots, n \tag{19}$$

where $\varphi_i \equiv \mathbb{E}(\psi_{t,m,i})$.

---

[8] The Data Envelopment Analysis (DEA) and the FDH estimators are $n^{2/(p+q+1)}$ and $n^{1/(p+q)}$ respectively- consistent estimators (Daraio and Simar 2006).

In Equation (19), $\psi_{t,m,i}$ is the depended variable, whereas, X_i^* represents the parametric part of the model with their parameters defined by ϑ. The $f(\cdot)$ are the smooth functions of the associated C_i. In our case the smooth functions are tensor products which are invariant to linear rescaling of covariates (Wood 2006).

In order to illustrate the smooth functions applied, let us assume a situation where we have three covariates x_1, x_2 and x_3 and their low-rank bases of smooth functions in their general form can be represented as:

$$\int_{x_1}(x_1)=\sum_{i=1}^{I}\alpha_i b_{1i}(x_1),\ \int_{x_2}(x_2)=\sum_{j=1}^{J}\beta_j b_{2j}(x_2),\text{ and }\int_{x_3}(x_3)=\sum_{k=1}^{K}\gamma_k b_{3k}(x_3) \tag{20}$$

and $b_{1i}(x_1)$, $b_{2j}(x_2)$ and $b_{3k}(x_3)$ are the basis functions, whereas α_i, β_j, γ_k are the parameters. Then x_1 can be converted to smooth functions x_1, x_2 as:

$\alpha_i(x_2) = \sum_{j=1}^{J}\beta_{ij}b_{2j}(x_2)$ which results in $\int_{x_1x_2}(x_1,x_2) = \sum_{i=1}^{I}\sum_{j=1}^{J}\beta_{ij}b_{2j}(x_2)b_{1i}(x_1)$. Similarly, the tensor product of the three covariates can be represented as:

$$\int_{x_1x_2x_3}(x_1,x_2,x_3) = \sum_{i=1}^{I}\sum_{j=1}^{J}\sum_{k=1}^{K}\gamma_{ijk}b_{3k}(x_3)b_{2j}(x_2)b_{1i}(x_1). \tag{21}$$

Now let $\Theta.$ matrices contain the coefficients and let α,β and γ represent the coefficients of the marginal smooths. As a result, the quadratic form of the wiggliness function can be respectively presented as:

$$J_{x_1}(f_{x_1}) = \alpha^{\mathrm{T}}\Theta_{x_1}\alpha,\ J_{x_2}(f_{x_2}) = \beta^{\mathrm{T}}\Theta_{x_2}\beta,\ J_{x_3}(f_{x_3}) = \gamma^{\mathrm{T}}\Theta_{x_3}\gamma \tag{22}$$

Then the cubic spline penalty can be defined as:

$$J_{x_1}(f_{x_1}) = \int\left(\partial^2 f_{x_1}/\partial {x_1}^2\right)^2 dx_1.$$

Finally, the wiggliness of $f_{x_1x_2x_3}$ can be presented as:

$$\begin{aligned} J(f_{x_1x_2x_3}) = \delta_{x_1}\int_{x_2,x_3} J_{x_1}(f_{x_1}|x_2,x_3)d_{x_2}d_{x_3} + \delta_{x_2}\int_{x_1,x_3} J_{x_2}(f_{x_2}|x_1,x_3)d_{x_1}d_{x_3} + \\ \delta_{x_3}\int_{x_1,x_2} J_{x_3}(f_{x_3}|x_1,x_2)d_{x_1}d_{x_2} \end{aligned} \tag{23}$$

whereas $\delta.$ represents the smoothing parameters allowing the invariance of the penalty to the rescaling of the covariates.

3. Results

Before we analyze the effect of domestic credit and time on countries' production performance levels, we analyze the efficiency distributions as derived from the free disposal hull (FDH) estimators (Deprins et al. 1984). Figure 1 presents the density plots from the efficiencies derived from Equation (7). In our setting, efficiency is indicated with values equal to 1. However, values greater than one suggest inefficiency. It must be noted that in this setting (i.e., FDH frontiers) we envelope all countries and the estimates are derived by comparing countries of different size, development stage, institutional arrangements, etc. As has been expected, OECD countries have higher production efficiency levels compared to the non-OECD countries. In Figure 1 the red dotted line indicates countries' average efficiency levels. It is evident that OECD countries' average efficiency score is placed nearer to unity in comparison to the non-OECD countries. Furthermore, the results suggest that the larger mass of OECD countries' production efficiency estimates are located near to unity, whereas, for the non-OECD countries the larger mass of the estimates is located to the left of the unity, suggesting higher production inefficiencies.

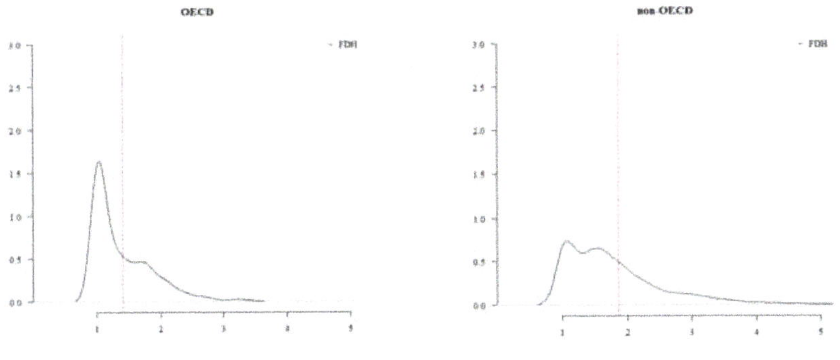

(a)

(b)

Figure 1. Density plots of unconditional countries' production efficiency levels derived from the FDH estimator: (**a**) FDH production efficiencies of OECD countries; (**b**) FDH production efficiencies of the non-OECD countries.

In contrast to the FDH analysis, Figure 2 presents our findings which have been derived from the Order-m model (Equation (17)). According to Cazals et al. (2002) and Daraio and Simar (2007a), partial frontiers (i.e., Order-m) are less sensitive to outliers. If a country is performing superior compared to the randomly drawn m countries with $X \leq x$ (in our case $m = 20$)[8], then it is said to be a super-efficient country. In such cases, the estimated Order-m output efficiency score would take values less than one. Let us now consider a paradigm in which a country has an Order-m production efficiency score equal to 1.25. Then this score indicates that if this country would perform as efficient as the m best practice countries (with $X \leq x$), then its GDP levels could increase on average by 25%. Figure 2 presents diachronically the robust estimates for 1970, 1980, 1990, 2000, 2010 and 2014. The results suggest that on average terms countries have performed better during 1970, 1980, 1990 and 2000. For the years 2010 and 2014 greater production inefficiencies are reported which may be attributed to the negative effects of the Global Financial Crisis (Gourinchas and Obstfeld 2012). It must be highlighted that the output-oriented Order-m frontier compares each country with the m-peer countries which are using input levels $\leq x$. As has been emphasized by Daraio and Simar (2006, p. 523): "*The benchmark, in fact, is not made against the most efficient units in the group, but against an appropriate measure drawn from a large number of random samples of size m within the group*". In fact this property of the Order-m estimator is very appealing in our case since it will not allow the effect of domestic credit to be masked over by different country sizes (in terms of their input levels). In contrast, the benchmark of the FDH analysis is made against the most efficient units of the entire group assuming that all countries (regardless their input levels) constitute the technology set, and as a result all countries are compared to each other.

8 The value of m has been chosen following Daraio and Simar (2005), suggesting that we select a value of m in which the number of super-efficient DMUs (in our case countries) stabilize. However, different m values have also been tested (i.e., 40, 50 and 80). When we increase the m parameter the results converge to the FDH estimator. All results which have been estimated with different m values are available upon request.

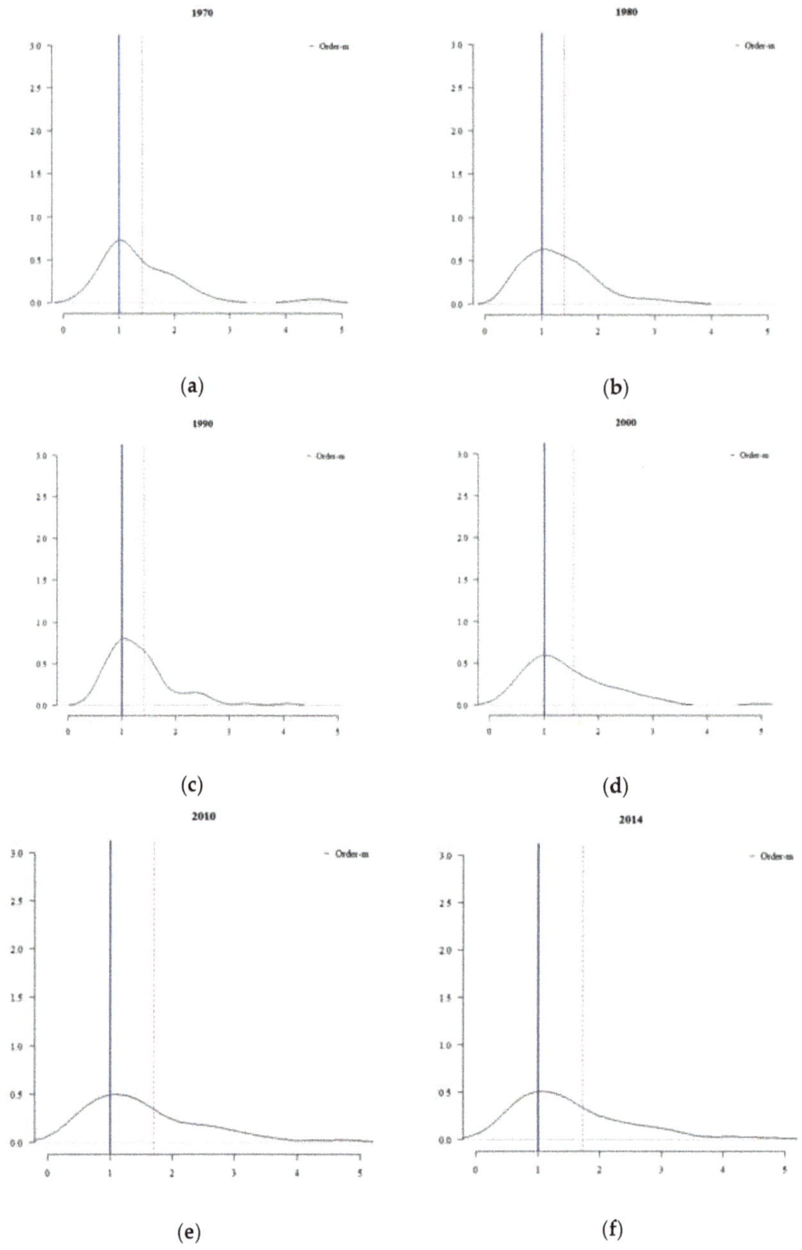

Figure 2. A diachronic representation of unconditional countries' production efficiency levels derived from the Order-m estimator. Note: The red dotted line indicates the average Order-m value; The blue solid line indicates unity.

Then we apply a second-stage analysis as described in the relevant literature (Daraio and Simar 2006, 2014; Bădin et al. 2012; De Witte and Kortelainen 2013; Tzeremes 2014; Bădin et al. 2014; Daraio et al. 2015). Moreover, we regress the estimated time-dependent conditional Order-m production efficiencies on the domestic credit levels and time using the generalized additive model using tensor products as smooth factors with cubic regression splines (Wood 2006; Wood 2017). In our setting, a decreasing fitted additive nonparametric line indicates a positive effect of domestic credit and time on countries' production efficiency. From the other hand, an increasing fitted additive nonparametric regression line indicates a negative effect.[9] Figure 3 presents graphically the results from the examined effects from the entire sample. The results suggest that the effect both of domestic credit and time on countries' production efficiencies is nonlinear. It is also evident that when the domestic credit increases, the effect on countries' production efficiency levels is positive up to a certain level. After that level the effect becomes negatively indicated by an increasing nonparametric regression line. Moreover, the effect of time is also nonlinear, signifying a positive effect on countries' productive efficiencies from the 70s to 90s. However, after that period the effect becomes negative. Furthermore we check the robustness of our findings analyzing separately the effects for the OECD and the non-OECD countries. Specifically, Figure 4 in a similar manner like Figure 3 presents both the effect of domestic credit to the private sector and time on OECD countries' production efficiency levels.

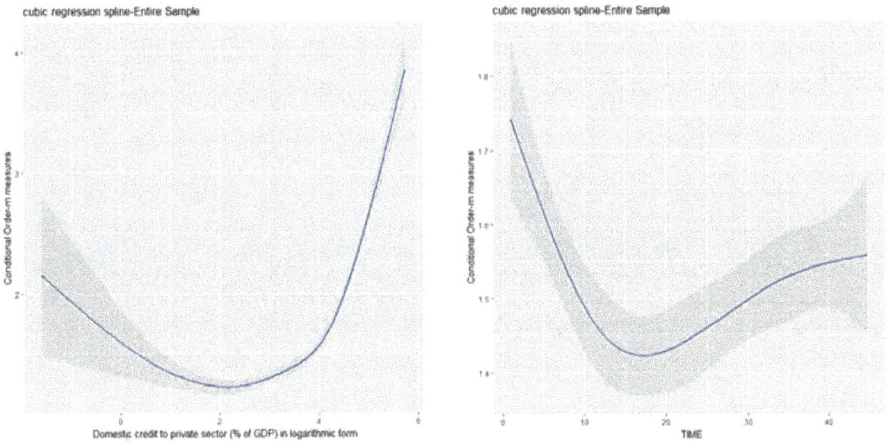

(a) (b)

Figure 3. The effect of domestic credit and time on countries production efficiencies (entire sample): (**a**) The effect of domestic credit to private sector (entire sample); (**b**) the effect of time (entire sample).

The effect of domestic credit to the private sector has a similar trend as the one presented for the case of our entire sample. However, it must be highlighted that the turning point in which the effect turns from positive to negative is higher. The contradictive finding (compared to Figure 3) is for the effect of time on countries' production efficiency levels which is positive throughout the entire period, presented by a decreasing additive nonparametric regression line.

Finally, when examining the effects for the non-OECD countries (Figure 5), we observe a different picture of the examined relationship. For the case of time the effect is similar to our initial finding (Figure 3), suggesting a positive effect on non-OECD countries' production efficiencies up to the mid-90s. After that point again the effect turns to negative indicated by an increasing additive nonparametric regression line. The effect of domestic credit on countries' efficiency levels is highly nonlinear. The graphical evidence suggests that for the largest part of domestic credit the effect is

[9] As presented previously, in the output oriented case Order-m efficiency values greater than unity indicate higher production inefficiency levels.

positively signified by a decreasing additive nonparametric regression line. However, for a certain domestic credit range (i.e., from 3 to 4) the effect becomes negative, but after that point the effect turns again to positive. Therefore, our findings which are provided by the adopted nonparametric econometric methods, suggest that even though in principle the overall effect of domestic credit is highly nonlinear, it is also attributed by countries' different stages of development, financial stability and institutional levels (Arestis and Demetriades 1997).

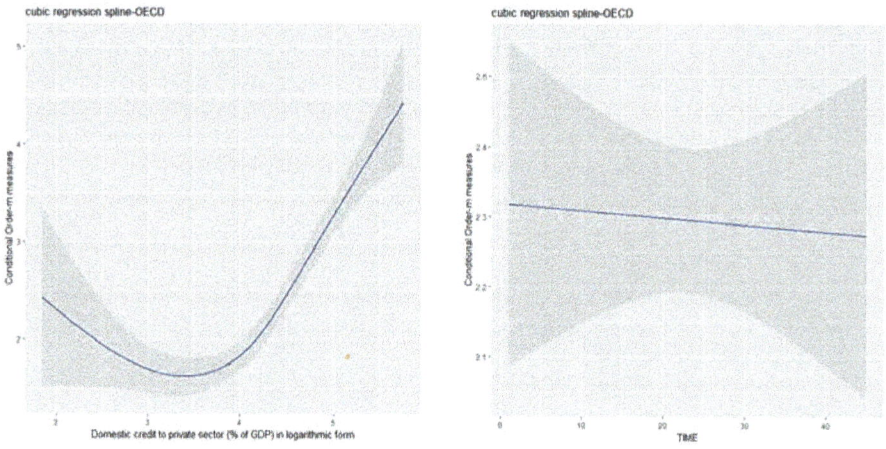

(a) (b)

Figure 4. The effect of domestic credit and time on countries' production efficiencies (OECD countries): (**a**) The effect of domestic credit to private sector (OECD countries); (**b**) the effect of time (OECD countries).

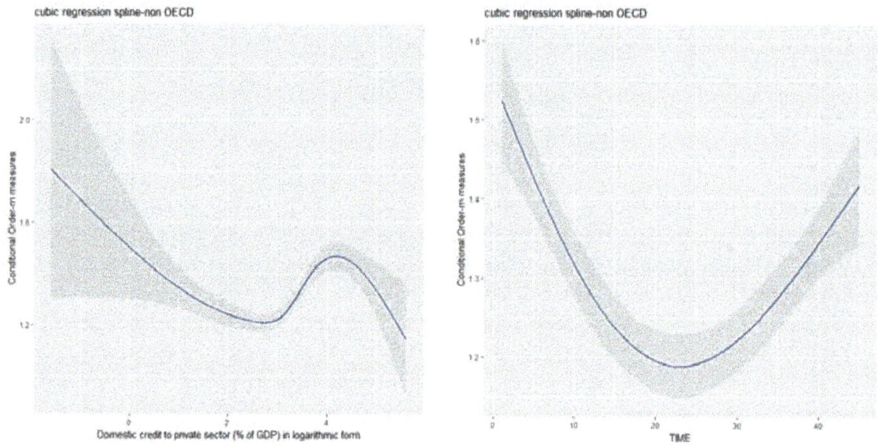

(a) (b)

Figure 5. The effect of domestic credit and time on countries' production efficiencies (non-OECD countries): (**a**) The effect of domestic credit to the private sector (non-OECD countries); (**b**) the effect of time (non-OECD countries).

4. Conclusions

This paper investigates the effect of financial development on countries' production efficiency levels using different nonparametric statistical and econometric methods. Specifically, in a first stage analysis using different smoothing techniques and specific procedures for bandwidth selection (Bădin et al. 2010, 2012, 2014), we apply a probabilistic approach of nonparametric frontier analysis on estimating 87 countries' production efficiency levels over the period 1970–2014. For the purpose of our analysis we apply time-dependent conditional Order-m estimators incorporating in the efficiency measurement the effect both of time and countries' financial development levels. Then in a second-stage analysis, generalized additive models (Hastie and Tibshirani 1990) using tensor products with cubic spline penalties (Wood 2002, 2003, 2004, 2006, 2017) are applied.

Our findings reveal a nonlinear effect of financial development on countries' production efficiency levels. The results also suggest that the effect of financial development is positive on countries' production efficiency levels up to a certain threshold level. After that point the effect becomes negative. Our evidence is consistent with the "vanishing effect" point of view described by Rousseau and Wachtel (2011). Under this view the negative effect of financial deepening on economic growth is attributed to financial crises and to domestic banking incidences. Arcand et al. (2015) verifies empirically the "vanishing effect" and provides evidence under which the financial deepening starts having a negative effect when credit to the private sector reaches 100% of GDP. In our case, the negative effect on countries' production efficiencies starts when the level of domestic credit to the private sector reaches 50% of GDP. However, according to Arcand et al. (2015), another possible explanation of financial development's negative effect on countries' production efficiency levels may be attributed to misallocation of resources. This is apparent in the case where the cost of maintaining countries' financial stability overcomes the returns of financial development.

Overall our findings support those studies providing evidence of a nonlinear behavior among financial development and economic growth (Shen 2013; Beck et al. 2014; Arcand et al. 2015). Finally, as explained in the early study by Arestis and Demetriades (1997), the evidence suggests that this effect can be shaped also by countries' different institutional, development and financial system conditions.

Funding: This research received no external funding.

Acknowledgments: The author is grateful to Thanasis Stengos and the anonymous referees for their valuable remarks.

Conflicts of Interest: The author declares no conflict of interest.

References

Ang, James B. 2011. Financial Development, Liberalization and Technological Deepening. *European Economic Review* 55: 688–701. [CrossRef]

Arcand, Jean Louis, Enrico Berkes, and Ugo Panizza. 2015. Too Much Finance? *Journal of Economic Growth* 20: 105–48. [CrossRef]

Arestis, Philip, and Panicos Demetriades. 1997. Financial Development and Economic Growth: Assessing the Evidence. *Economic Journal* 107: 783–99. [CrossRef]

Bădin, Luiza, Cinzia Daraio, and Léopold Simar. 2010. Optimal Bandwidth Selection for Conditional Efficiency Measures: A Data-Driven Approach. *European Journal of Operational Research* 201: 633–40. [CrossRef]

Bădin, Luiza, Cinzia Daraio, and Léopold Simar. 2012. How to Measure the Impact of Environmental Factors in a Nonparametric Production Model. *European Journal of Operational Research* 223: 818–33. [CrossRef]

Bădin, Luiza, Cinzia Daraio, and Léopold Simar. 2014. Explaining Inefficiency in Nonparametric Production Models: The State of the Art. *Annals of Operations Research* 214: 5–30. [CrossRef]

Beck, Roland, Georgios Georgiadis, and Roland Straub. 2014. The Finance and Growth Nexus Revisited. *Economics Letters* 124: 382–85. [CrossRef]

Carroll, Raymond J., Jianqing Fan, Irene Gijbels, and Matt P. Wand. 1997. Generalized Partially Linear Single-Index Models. *Journal of the American Statistical Association* 92: 477–89. [CrossRef]

Cazals, Catherine, Jean-Pierre Florens, and Léopold Simar. 2002. Nonparametric Frontier Estimation: A Robust Approach. *Journal of Econometrics* 106: 1–25. [CrossRef]

Daraio, Cinzia, and Léopold Simar. 2005. Introducing Environmental Variables in Nonparametric Frontier Models: A Probabilistic Approach. *Journal of Productivity Analysis* 24: 93–121. [CrossRef]

Daraio, Cinzia, and Léopold Simar. 2006. A Robust Nonparametric Approach to Evaluate and Explain the Performance of Mutual Funds. *European Journal of Operational Research* 175: 516–42. [CrossRef]

Daraio, Cinzia, and Léopold Simar. 2007a. *Advanced Robust and Nonparametric Methods in Efficiency Analysis: Methodology and Applications*. Berlin: Springer Science & Business Media.

Daraio, Cinzia, and Léopold Simar. 2007b. Conditional Nonparametric Frontier Models for Convex and Nonconvex Technologies: A Unifying Approach. *Journal of Productivity Analysis* 28: 13–32. [CrossRef]

Daraio, Cinzia, and Léopold Simar. 2014. Directional Distances and Their Robust Versions: Computational and Testing Issues. *European Journal of Operational Research* 237: 358–69. [CrossRef]

Daraio, Cinzia, Andrea Bonaccorsi, and Léopold Simar. 2015. Rankings and University Performance: A Conditional Multidimensional Approach. *European Journal of Operational Research* 244: 918–30. [CrossRef]

Daraio, Cinzia, Léopold Simar, and Paul W. Wilson. 2018. Central Limit Theorems for Conditional Efficiency Measures and Tests of the 'Separability' condition in Non-Parametric, Two-Stage Models of Production. *Econometrics Journal*. [CrossRef]

De Witte, Kristof, and Mika Kortelainen. 2013. What Explains the Performance of Students in a Heterogeneous Environment? Conditional Efficiency Estimation with Continuous and Discrete Environmental Variables. *Applied Economics* 45: 2401–12. [CrossRef]

Debreu, Gerard. 1951. The Coefficient of Resource Utilization. *Econometrica* 19: 273–92. [CrossRef]

Deprins, Dominique, Léopold Simar, and Henry Tulkens. 1984. Measuring Labor Inefficiency in Post Offices. In *The Performance of Public Enterprises: Concepts and Measurements*. Edited by Maurice Marchand, Pierre Pestieau and Henry Tulkens. Amsterdam: Elsevier Science Ltd., pp. 243–67.

Farrell, Michael J. 1957. The Measurement of the Productive Efficiency. *Journal of the Royal Statistical Society. Series A* 120: 253–29. [CrossRef]

Feenstra, Robert C., Robert Inklaar, and Marcel P. Timmer. 2015. The Next Generation of the Penn World Table. *American Economic Review* 105: 3150–82. [CrossRef]

Gourinchas, Pierre-Olivier, and Maurice Obstfeld. 2012. Stories of the Twentieth Century for the Twenty-First. *American Economic Journal: Macroeconomics* 4: 226–65. [CrossRef]

Hall, Peter, Jeff Racine, and Qi Li. 2004. Cross-Validation and the Estimation of Conditional Probability Densities. *Journal of the American Statistical Association* 99: 1015–26. [CrossRef]

Hart, Jeffrey D. 1996. Some Automated Methods of Smoothing Time-Dependent Data. *Journal of Nonparametric Statistics* 6: 115–42. [CrossRef]

Hastie, Trevor J., and Robert J. Tibshirani. 1990. Generalized Additive Models. In *Monographs on Statistics and Applied Probability*. London: Chapman & Hall, vol. 43.

Jeong, Seok-Oh, Byeong U. Park, and Léopold Simar. 2010. Nonparametric Conditional Efficiency Measures: Asymptotic Properties. *Annals of Operations Research* 173: 105–22. [CrossRef]

Kalaitzidakis, Pantelis, Theofanis P. Mamuneas, Andreas Savvides, and Thanasis Stengos. 2001. Measures of Human Capital and Nonlinearities in Economic Growth. *Journal of Economic Growth* 6: 229–54. [CrossRef]

Li, Qi, and Jeffrey Scott Racine. 2007. *Nonparametric Econometrics: Theory and Practice*. Princeton: Princeton University Press.

Liu, Zhenjuan, and Thanasis Stengos. 1999. Non-Linearities in Cross-Country Growth Regressions: A Semiparametric Approach. *Journal of Applied Econometrics* 14: 527–38. [CrossRef]

Maasoumi, Esfandiar, Jeff Racine, and Thanasis Stengos. 2007. Growth and Convergence: A Profile of Distribution Dynamics and Mobility. *Journal of Econometrics* 136: 483–508. [CrossRef]

Mallick, Sushanta, Roman Matousek, and Nickolaos G Tzeremes. 2016. Financial Development and Productive Inefficiency: A Robust Conditional Directional Distance Function Approach. *Economics Letters* 145: 196–201. [CrossRef]

Mastromarco, Camilla, and Léopold Simar. 2015. Effect of FDI and Time on Catching Up: New Insights from a Conditional Nonparametric Frontier Analysis. *Journal of Applied Econometrics* 30: 826–47. [CrossRef]

Rousseau, Peter L., and Paul Wachtel. 2011. What Is Happening to the Impact of Financial Deepening on Economic Growth? *Economic Inquiry* 49: 276–88. [CrossRef]

Shen, Leilei. 2013. Financial Dependence and Growth: Diminishing Returns to Improvement in Financial Development. *Economics Letters* 120: 215–19. [CrossRef]

Shephard, Ronald W. 1970. *Theory of Cost and Production Functions*. Princeton: Princeton University Press.

Simar, Leopold, and Paul W. Wilson. 2007. Estimation and Inference in Two-Stage, Semi-Parametric Models of Production Processes. *Journal of Econometrics* 136: 31–64. [CrossRef]

Simar, Léopold, and Paul W. Wilson. 2011. Two-Stage Dea: Caveat Emptor. *Journal of Productivity Analysis* 36: 205–18. [CrossRef]

Stone, Charles J. 1985. Additive Regression and Other Nonparametric Models. *The Annals of Statistics* 13: 689–705. [CrossRef]

Tzeremes, Nickolaos G. 2014. The Effect of Human Capital on Countries' Economic Efficiency. *Economics Letters* 124: 127–31. [CrossRef]

Wood, Simon N. 2002. Modelling and Smoothing Parameter Estimation with Multiple Quadratic Penalties. *Journal of the Royal Statistical Society: Series B* 62: 413–28. [CrossRef]

Wood, Simon N. 2003. Thin Plate Regression Splines. *Journal of the Royal Statistical Society: Series B* 65: 95–114. [CrossRef]

Wood, Simon N. 2004. Stable and Efficient Multiple Smoothing Parameter Estimation for Generalized Additive Models. *Journal of the American Statistical Association* 99: 673–86. [CrossRef]

Wood, Simon N. 2006. Low-Rank Scale-Invariant Tensor Product Smooths for Generalized Additive Mixed Models. *Biometrics* 62: 1025–36. [CrossRef] [PubMed]

Wood, Simon N. 2017. *Generalized Additive Models: An Introduction with R*. Boca Raton: Chapman and Hall/CRC.

Journal of
Risk and Financial Management

MDPI

Article

On the Performance of Wavelet Based Unit Root Tests

Burak Alparslan Eroğlu [1,*] **and Barış Soybilgen** [2]

[1] Department of Economics, Istanbul Bilgi University, Istanbul 34060, Turkey

[2] Institute of Graduate Programs, Istanbul Bilgi University, Istanbul 34060, Turkey; baris.soybilgen@bilgi.edu.tr

* Correspondence: burak.eroglu@bilgi.edu.tr; Tel.: +90-505-587-5014

Received: 21 June 2018; Accepted: 8 August 2018; Published: 13 August 2018

Abstract: In this paper, we apply the wavelet methods in the popular Augmented Dickey-Fuller and M types of unit root tests. Moreover, we provide an extensive comparison of the wavelet based unit root tests which also includes the recent contributions in the literature. Moreover, we derive the asymptotic properties of the wavelet based unit root tests under generalized least squares detrending mechanism. We demonstrate that the wavelet based M tests exhibit better size performance even in problematic cases such as the presence of negative moving average innovations. However, the power performances of the wavelet based unit root tests are quite similar to each other.

Keywords: unit root testing; wavelet; GLS detrending

---

1. Introduction

It is well known that many financial and economic time series exhibit non-stationary characteristics. Without treatment of these non-stationary characteristics, both univariate and multivariate analysis on these kinds of series may yield incorrect conclusions. Therefore, in numerous studies both in economy and finance, testing the unit root of time series is usually the first step before conducting the econometric analysis. The unit root testing procedure is first introduced by Dickey and Fuller (1979) and Dickey and Fuller (1981). Afterwards, many different unit root tests have been devised in the literature. Except for a few studies, overwhelmingly these unit root tests are constructed in the time domain. However, conclusions drawn from these tests remain controversial in many cases due to the low power of tests in near unit root cases and severe size distortions, especially in the case of the large negative moving average (MA) root.

Even before the introduction of the unit root testing, Granger (1966) points out that most economic time series have a spectral density characterized by the significant power in low frequencies followed by exponential decline at higher frequencies, especially in trending series. This observation implies that the variance of a unit root process is mostly originated from the low frequencies. Capitalizing on this notion, Fan and Gencay (2010) developed a wavelet based unit root testing procedure. Using a wavelet spectrum, the contribution of the variance to the overall variance at each frequency can be decomposed, and therefore it is straightforward to construct a wavelet based unit root testing procedure. Fan and Gencay (2010) rely on the discrete wavelet transformation (DWT) to extract the most persistent component of time series called the scaling (approximation) coefficients and use these coefficients, particularly the ratio of the variance from the unit scale to the total variance of the time series to build their test statistics. Even though Fan and Gencay's (2010) unit root test enjoys considerable power, their test suffers from the size distortions when the MA error part has large negative unit roots. Trokić (2016) improves upon Fan and Gencay's (2010) unit root test by constructing a nonparametric testing procedure and shows that size distortions can be treated by using a bootstrap-like procedure called wavestrapping. These two tests are the only wavelet based unit root tests in the literature currently.

Following the same logic behind Fan and Gencay (2010) and Trokić (2016) unit root testing procedures, we propose the wavelet based versions of Dickey and Fuller (1981) and Ng and Perron (2001) tests. We use a generalized least squares (GLS) detrending to get rid of the deterministic components in the observed data. As wavelet filtering doesn't alter the nature of linear time series process, our wavelet based tests share the same asymptotic distributions of the original tests. Using Monte Carlo simulations, we evaluate size and power properties of our tests against Fan and Gencay (2010) and Trokić (2016). In these simulations, we consider Daubechies and Symlet filter families since the developed methodology is compatible with compactly supported wavelets. From these filters, Daubechies are the compactly supported filters that have a maximum amount of vanishing moments. Furthermore, Symlet filters are obtained by increasing the symmetry of Daubechies filters.

Our results show that the new proposed unit tests have less size distortions in sample without relying on a bootstrap routine compared to Fan and Gencay (2010) and Trokić (2016). The power performance of the tests indicates there is no single dominating test. Moreover, in medium length filters (filter length of 2 or 4), type of wavelet does not alter the results drastically.

The rest of the paper is as follows. Section 2 introduces the wavelet theory. Section 3 explains our wavelet based tests as well as Fan and Gencay (2010) and Trokić's (2016) methods. Section 4 presents Monte Carlo simulation results and Section 5 provides the conclusions and the Appendix A presents proofs of the theorems and the lemmas. All limits in the paper are as $T \to \infty$, $\to$ denotes the weak convergence in distribution and $\lfloor x \rfloor$ denotes the closest integer to x.

2. Wavelet Transform

Recently, the wavelet filters have become frequently used tools in unit root and cointegration studies. In these studies, the authors utilize the fact that wavelet filters can operate in both time and frequency domain. This feature helps the wavelets capture the nonstationarity across a wide range of frequencies (Fan and Gencay (2010)). This makes the wavelet transform a proper instrument for unit root and cointegration testing. Accordingly, for the construction of the new unit test, we utilize the wavelet methods. First, we briefly introduce the wavelet transformation. This section and the notation used in this paper mostly follow Fan and Gencay (2010) and Eroğlu (2018).

A wavelet, $\psi(t)$, is a real-valued function oscillating in a finite domain with the following basic properties:

$$\int_{-\infty}^{\infty} \psi(t)dt = 0 \text{ and } \int_{-\infty}^{\infty} \psi(t)^2 dt = 1.$$

The first property implies that a wavelet function must take a non-zero value in a finite time period and the second property indicates that all the departures from zero should be cancelled out Gençay et al. (2001). Using the function $\psi(t)$, we can design the continuous time wavelet transform (CWT) of a time series x_t as it follows:

$$W(u,s) = \int_{-\infty}^{\infty} x_t \psi_{u,s}(t)dt,$$

where $\psi_{u,s}(t) = \frac{1}{\sqrt{s}}\psi\left(\frac{t-u}{s}\right)$ is translated by u and dilated by s. Note that $W(u,s)$ is called the wavelet coefficient in this transfigurations. Additionally, the parameter $s \in \mathbb{R}^+$ allows wavelets to work under different frequencies. However, the CWT has an important shortcoming: it is almost impossible to analyse all wavelet coefficients for all frequencies. Furthermore, in the CWT, the wavelet coefficients are redundant transformation for time series data. Hence, the CWT is not very appropriate in unit root testing. Nevertheless, the wavelet theory equipped with many other transformations that can solve the problems of the CWT such as the DWT, the maximum overlap discrete wavelet transform, and the discrete wavelet packet transform, etc. From these techniques, the DWT that shares the fundamental properties of the CWT creates a non-redundant decomposition with a finite number of frequencies. Consequently, the DWT is a more suitable instrument for our study.

The DWT can be defined with two separate filters. The first filter $h = (h_0, h_1, \ldots, h_{L-1})$ is called the discrete wavelet (or high pass) filter with a finite length L where h_l corresponds to a filter coefficient for all $l = 0, \ldots, L-1$. The high pass filters satisfy the zero sum condition, $\sum_{l=0}^{L-1} h_l = 0$ and these filters have unit energy, $\sum_{l=0}^{L-1} h_l^2 = 1$ as do the CWT filters. The high pass filter does not provide the full analysis of the observed series. However, we also have an complementary filter g (low pass filter). The low pass filter g can be obtained by the quadrature mirror relationship[1]. Unlike the high pass filter, the low pass filters sum to $\sqrt{2}$, $\sum_{l=0}^{L-1} g_l = \sqrt{2}$, but they also have unit energy, $\sum_{l=0}^{L-1} g_l^2 = 1$.

Using the convolution on the observed series and the filters defined above, we transform the time series process into its high frequency and low frequency components. Let $\{x_t\}_{t=1}^{T}$ be the observed time series process with dyadic length $T = 2^J$ for some integer J. Then, the matrix of the DWT coefficients can be defined as $\mathcal{W}^L = \left[\mathbf{W}_1^L, \mathbf{W}_2^L, \ldots, \mathbf{W}_J^L, \mathbf{V}_J^L\right]'$, where, for $j = 1, 2, \ldots, J$, $\mathbf{W}_j^L$ is the column vector of j-th level wavelet coefficients and $\mathbf{V}_J^L$ is the column vector of J-th level scaling (approximation) coefficients. In this decomposition, the approximation coefficients $\mathbf{V}_J^L$ explain the fluctuations of x_t on the scale 2^J (the largest scale among the all coefficients) and the wavelet coefficients $\mathbf{W}_j^L$ are associated with the changes on the scale 2^{j-1}. Note that scale and frequency are inversely proportional. As a result, $\mathbf{V}_J^L$ captures the lowest frequency and $\mathbf{W}_1^L$ captures the highest frequency components of the transformed series. Additionally, the approximation coefficient $\mathbf{V}_J^L$ has a length of $T/2^J$ and $\mathbf{W}_j^L$ has a length of $T/2^j$ for each $j = 1, 2, \ldots, J$.

In practice, the wavelet and the approximation coefficients for the levels higher than 1 can be obtained by the pyramid algorithm, which is firstly proposed by Mallat (1989). However, in this study, we focus on the first level wavelet transformation. We can obtain this transformation as the following:

$$V_{1,t}^L = \sum_{l=0}^{L-1} g_l x_{2t-l \bmod T}, \qquad \textit{and} \qquad W_{1,t}^L = \sum_{l=0}^{L-1} h_l x_{2t-l \bmod T} \quad \textit{for all } t = 1, 2, \ldots, T, \tag{1}$$

where the filtering is carried out by the convolution of the observed series with the high pass and low filters. In the construction of our test statistic, we only use the first level approximation coefficients of the observed time series processes, $V_{1,t}^L$. Notice that $V_{1,t}^L$ corresponds to lowest frequency data in level 1 decomposition. In this regard, we separate the data from the high frequency components that contain short term fluctuations. As indicated (Fan and Gencay, 2010), Trokić (2016) and Eroğlu (2018), this separation also filters out the short run problematic dynamics in the process such as the innovations of the observed series with highly negative MA roots. Accordingly, the wavelet transform helps us to remove some problematic issues before the testing stage. In the literature, there are other variants of wavelet transformation such as the maximum overlap discrete wavelet transform and the discrete wavelet packet transform. In simulations, we also utilize the maximum overlap discrete wavelet transform; however, DWT has better performance overall so we drop the maximum overlap discrete wavelet transform for brevity.[2] Another issue worth considering is the performance of higher level wavelet transformations. For instance, Trokić (2016) utilizes higher level transformations upto 3rd level, but he achieves the best results by means of power with the first level DWT while the higher level DWT has slight size improvements in the testing.

---

1 The quadrature mirror relationship can be characterized by: $g_l = (-1)^{l+1} h_{L-1-l}$ for $l = 0, \ldots, L-1$ (Fan and Gencay 2010).
2 The results for the maximum overlap discrete wavelet transform are available upon request.

3. Regression Based Wavelet Unit Root Tests

We consider a basic unit root model:

$$x_t = \gamma' \mu_t + y_t, \tag{2}$$

$$(1 - \rho B) y_t = u_t = \phi(B) \epsilon_t, \tag{3}$$

where μ_t captures the deterministic component, y_t is the stochastic part of the observed series, B denotes the back-shift or lag operator and the parameter ρ governs the unit root process where we assume $|\rho| \leq 1$. For brevity, we only consider two scenarios for the deterministic component. We index these cases with the letter j. $j = 0$ indicates no deterministic component in the observed series, thus $\mu_t = 0$ for all t. When $j = 1$, we assume a mean, i.e., $\mu_t = 1$ for all t and, when $j = 2$, we assume a mean and trend such that $\mu_t = \begin{bmatrix} 1 & t \end{bmatrix}$. As in the classical unit root testing, we first need to remove the deterministic trends from the observed series. Otherwise, these components introduce nuisance parameters in the asymptotic distribution of the test statistics. In order to eliminate these nuisance parameters, we apply a GLS detrending algorithm to the observed series. To obtain the GLS detrended series, we first employ quasi-differencing on the observed series x_t and μ_t with some positive constant $\bar{c}$, which is a quasi-differencing parameter. The quasi-differencing algorithm can be seen as follows:

$$x_{\bar{c},t} = x_t - (1 - \bar{c}/T) x_{t-1} \quad \forall t = 1, \cdots, T,$$

$$\mu_{\bar{x},t} = \mu_t - (1 - \bar{c}/T) \mu_{t-1} \quad \forall t = 1, \cdots, T,$$

where $x_{\bar{c},0} = x_0$ and $\mu_{\bar{c},0} = \mu_0$. Nielsen (2009) demonstrates the GLS detrended series as:

$$\hat{x}_{\bar{c},t} = x_t - \hat{\gamma}_{GLS} \mu_t,$$

where

$$\hat{\gamma}_{GLS} = \arg\min_{\gamma} \sum_{t=1}^{T} \left(x_{\bar{c},t} - \gamma' \mu_{\bar{c},t} \right)^2.$$

After obtaining the GLS detrended series, we apply the first level wavelet transform with filter length L to these series:

$$\hat{V}^{L}_{\bar{c},1,t} = G(B) \hat{x}_{\bar{c},2t}. \tag{4}$$

For simplicity, we first assume $\mu_t = 0$. Notice that we can apply Equation (1) on y_t to obtain as follows:

$$V^{L}_{\bar{c},1,t} = G(B) y_{2t},$$

where we drop mod T and L notation for brevity and $G(B) = g_0 + g_l B + \cdots + g_{L-1} B^{L-1}$. Now, consider $y_{2t} = \rho^2 y_{2t-2} + u_{2t} + \rho\, u_{2t-1} = \rho^2 y_{2t-2} + (1 + \rho B) u_{2t}$. Using this result, we can write:

$$V_{\bar{c},1,t} = G(B) y_{2t} = \rho^2 G(B) y_{2t-2} + G(B)(1 + \rho B) u_{2t} = \rho^2 G(B) y_{2t-2} + v_t.$$

In addition, note that $V_{\bar{c},1,t-1} = G(B) y_{2t-2}$; then, we can conclude that $V_{\bar{c},1,t} = \rho^2 V_{\bar{c},1,t-1} + G(B)(1 + \rho B) u_{2t}$. This result implies that, if y_t follows a unit root process, then $V_{\bar{c},1,t}$ also follows a unit root process, but the innovation structure of the wavelet transformed series carries further MA roots. However, these additional MA roots do not alter the stationarity of the innovation terms. Accordingly, we can claim that v_t admits a stationary Wold decomposition: $v_t = \sum_{j=0}^{\infty} \phi_j^* \epsilon_t^*$, where ϵ_t^* is an i.i.d random variable. From Chang and Park (2002), we can approximate v_t as a finite order autoregressive (AR) process:

$$v_t = \alpha_1 v_{t-1} + \alpha_2 v_{t-1} + \cdots + \alpha_p v_{t-p} + \epsilon^*_{p,t},$$

where $\epsilon^*_{p,t} = \epsilon^*_t + \sum_{k=p+1}^{\infty} \alpha_k u_{t-k}$. We can use the following assumption from Chang and Park (2002) for the new innovations:

Assumption 1. *Let* (ϵ_t, F_t) *be a martingale difference sequence, with some filtration* (F_t)*, such that a.* $\mathbb{E}\left(\epsilon_t^2|F_{t-1}\right) = \sigma^2$ *and b.* $\mathbb{E}\left|\epsilon_t\right|^r < K$ *with* $r \geq 4$*, where K is a constant depending only on r.*

Remark 1. *Assumption 1 indicates that the innovation process* ϵ_t *admits a stationary Wold decomposition. On the other hand, with simple algebra, it is possible to show that the innovations of the filtered* y_t*, say* ϵ^*_t*, also follow a stationary Wold decomposition. Accordingly, we can rewrite Assumption 1 for* ϵ^*_t*as:*

Assumption 1': *Let* (ϵ^*_t, F^*_t) *be a martingale difference sequence, with some filtration* (F^*_t)*, such that a.* $\mathbb{E}\left(\epsilon_t^{*2}|F^*_{t-1}\right) = \sigma^{*2}$ *and b.* $\mathbb{E}\left|\epsilon^*_t\right|^r < K$ *with* $r \geq 4$*, where K is a constant depending only on r.*

Assumption 2. *Let* $\alpha(z) \neq 0$ *for all* $|z| \leq 1$*, and* $\sum_{k=0}^{\infty} |k|^s |\alpha_k| < \infty$ *for some* $s \geq 1$*.*

Before presenting our theoretical results on a wavelet based unit root test, we review the recent methods that also deal with the unit root problem by utilizing wavelet theory. These recent methods include contributions of Fan and Gencay (2010) and Trokić (2016). First, Fan and Gencay (2010) propose a unit root test based on the notion of Granger (1981) who argues that generally time series after detrending has a peak in power spectra at low frequencies and exponential decline at higher frequencies. Fan and Gencay (2010) decompose variance of the observed series into low and high frequency components via DWT to test for unit root. More specifically, their unit root test is based on the ratio of the variance from the low pass filtered series and the variance of observed series.

Fan and Gencay's (2010) unit root test statistics are defined as follows:

$$FG_1 = \frac{T\hat{\lambda}_u^2}{\hat{\lambda}_0} \frac{\sum_{t=1}^{T/2}(\hat{V}_{\tilde{c},1,t})^2}{\sum_{t=1}^{T}(\hat{x}_{\tilde{c},t})^2}, \tag{5}$$

where $\hat{\lambda}_v^2 = 4\hat{\omega}^2$ and $\hat{\omega}^2$ is the long run variance of u_t in Equation (3), and $\hat{\lambda}_0$ is the estimate of the variance of ϵ_t. These parameters can be estimated by applying a nonparametric kernel estimation with Barlett kernel to the residuals obtained after applying a detrending procedure on x_t. We consider GLS detrending for this test in this study.

Trokić (2016) argues that, even though Fan and Gencay (2010) enjoy high statistical power, their test suffers from violent size distortions in the presence of errors with negative MA roots and follow a parametric way to correct the long run variance of the observed series. In this regard, Trokić (2016) tries to improve the Fan and Gencay (2010) test by devising a parameter free unit root test that is more robust to size distortions. Trokić's (2016) test is based on the variance of the scaling coefficients and the variance of its fractionally differenced transform series with some order $d > 0$. The test statistics of Trokić's (2016) unit root test are as follows:

$$\tau^*(d) = T_1^{2d} \frac{\sum_{t=1}^{T_1} \hat{V}^2_{\tilde{c},1,t}}{\sum_{t=1}^{T_1} \tilde{\hat{V}}^2_{\tilde{c},1,t}}, \tag{6}$$

where $\tilde{\hat{V}}_{\bar{c},1,t} = \Delta_+^{-d}\hat{V}_{\bar{c},1,t}$ is the fractional transform of $\hat{V}_{\bar{c},1,t}$ and Δ_+^{-d} is the fractional differencing operator that can be written for some time series process $\{v_t\}_{t=1}^T$ as:

$$\Delta_+^{-d} v_t = \sum_{j=0}^{t} \frac{\Gamma(j+d)}{\Gamma(j+1)\Gamma(d)} v_{t-j} \qquad \forall t = 1, 2, \cdots, T.$$

Note that this operator does not include the prehistoric observation of the time series process v_t and $T_1 = T/2$, since every time we apply wavelet filters to the observed series, we lose half of the sample. Additionally, Trokić (2016) and Nielsen (2009) suggest that the parameter d can be chosen from the inverval $(0, 1)$ by the practitioner. While Nielsen (2009) sets $d = 0.1$ to obtain the best power performance, Trokić (2016) picks $d = 0.05$.

The asymptotic distribution of Fan and Gencay's (2010) and Trokić's (2016) tests can be summarized as the following:

$$FG_1 \to -\frac{1}{\int_0^1 W_{j,\bar{c}}(s)^2},$$

$$\tau^*(d) \to \frac{\int_0^1 W_{j,\bar{c}}(s)^2}{\int_0^1 W_{j,1+d,\bar{c}}(s)^2},$$

where $W_{j,\bar{c}}(s)$ is defined in Theorem 1 and $W_{j,1+d,\bar{c}}(s)$ is the fractional Brownian motion that is demonstrated in Nielsen (2009). However, although Trokić (2016) and Fan and Gencay (2010) do not explicitly derive the asymptotic results for GLS detrending series, following Nielsen (2009), Fan and Gencay (2010), and Trokić (2016), one can easily reach the outcome.[3]

Now, we can illustrate our theoretical contribution on wavelet based unit root tests. Under Assumptions 1 and 2, the approximation error is small as p becomes large (Chang and Park 2002). As a result, we can use the following augmented regression for unit root testing:

$$\Delta\hat{V}_{\bar{c},1,t} = \delta\hat{V}_{\bar{c},1,t-1} + \sum_{k=1}^{p} \alpha_k \Delta\hat{V}_{\bar{c},1,t-k} + \epsilon_{p,t}^*. \tag{7}$$

Note that when $\delta = 0$, $\hat{V}_{\bar{c},1,t}$ is a unit root process and if $\delta < 0$, then $\hat{V}_{\bar{c},1,t}$ is a stationary process. We base our unit root test on Equation (7). This equation is similar to the conventional Augmented Dickey-Fuller (ADF) regression, thus we can use a similar procedure. Suppose that we estimate the model in Equation (7) with OLS and obtain the estimates $\hat{\delta}$, $\hat{\alpha}_1, \cdots, \hat{\alpha}_{p-1}$ and $\hat{\alpha}_p$. We construct the null hypothesis of a unit root in x_t as $H_0 : \delta = 0$. This hypothesis can be tested with two different t statistics:

$$ADF_t^* = \frac{\hat{\delta}}{se\left(\hat{\delta}\right)}, \tag{8}$$

$$ADF_\alpha^* = T_1 \frac{\hat{\delta}}{\hat{\alpha}(1)}, \tag{9}$$

where $se\left(\hat{\delta}\right)$ is the standard deviation of the OLS estimator of δ and $\hat{\alpha}(1) = 1 - \sum_{k=1}^{p} \hat{\alpha}_k$ in the Equation (7). Additionally, we can also construct modified wavelet based Phillips and Perron (1988) tests. These are given as:

3 Similar to the results observed in the literature, we observe that GLS detrending generates better power performance than the ordinary least squares (OLS) detrending mechanism, so we use GLS detrending in this study. Results for OLS detrending are available upon request.

$$MZ_{\alpha}^{*} = \frac{T_1^{-1}\hat{V}_{\bar{c},1,T_1}^2 - T_1^{-1}\hat{V}_{\bar{c},1,,0}^2 - s_{AR}^{*2}(p)}{2T_1^{-2}\sum_{t=1}^{T_1}\hat{V}_{\bar{c},1,t-1}^2/s_{AR}^{*2}(p)}, \tag{10}$$

$$MSB^{*} = \left(T_1^{-2}\sum_{t=1}^{T_1}\hat{V}_{\bar{c},1,t-1}^2/s_{AR}^{*2}(p)\right)^{0.5}, \tag{11}$$

$$MZ_t^{*} = MSB^{*} \times MZ_{\alpha}^{*}, \tag{12}$$

where $s_{AR}^{*2}(p) = \hat{\sigma}^2/\hat{\alpha}(1)^2$ is the spectral AR estimate of long run variance from ADF regression in Equation (7). Note that both ADF and M type tests require the selection of lag length p. We can apply an information criteria based method to select the optimal lag length.

Theorem 1. *Let Assumptions 1 and 2 hold, then*

$$ADF_{\alpha}^{*}, MZ_{\alpha}^{*} \to 0.5\frac{W_{j,\bar{c}}(1)^2 - W_{j,\bar{c}}(0)^2 - 1}{\int_0^1 W_{j,\bar{c}}(s)^2 ds},$$

$$MSB^{*} \to \left(\int_0^1 W_{j,\bar{c}}(s)^2 ds\right)^{1/2},$$

$$ADF_t^{*}, MZ_t^{*} \to 0.5\frac{W_{j,\bar{c}}(1)^2 - W_{j,\bar{c}}(0)^2 - 1}{\left(\int_0^1 W_{j,\bar{c}}(s)^2 ds\right)^{1/2}},$$

where $W_{j,\bar{c}}(s)$ is defined as:

$$W_{1,\bar{c}}(s) = W(s) \quad \text{if } j = 1,$$

$$W_{2,\bar{c}}(s) = W(s) - \left(\frac{1+\bar{c}}{1+\bar{c}+\bar{c}^2/3}W(1) + \frac{\bar{c}^2}{1+\bar{c}+\bar{c}^2/3}\int_0^1 rW(r)dr\right)s \quad \text{if } j = 2,$$

and $W(s)$ is the standard Brownian Motion.

Theorem 1 shows that the wavelet based tests share the same asymptotic distribution as the classical tests. This result is expected since wavelet filtering does not alter the nature of the linear time series process. Moreover, these results provide two new contributions in the wavelet based unit root testing literature. First, we derive the theoretical results for the GLS detrending mechanism in wavelet based unit root tests. Second, we modify the ADF and Ng and Perron's (2001) tests by utilizing the wavelet theory.

4. Small Sample Properties

In this section, we evaluate the performance of different wavelet based unit root tests by Monte Carlo simulations. In these simulations, we consider five different wavelets, namely, *Haar*, *Db*2, *Db*4, *sym*2, and *sym*4. We can categorise these wavelets into two main groups. The first group consists of Daubechies wavelets which are characterized by a maximal number of vanishing moments. In our exercise, we consider Daubechies wavelets *Db*2 and *Db*4 with lengths 4 and 8, respectively. The second group is called *Symlet* which are modified version of Daubechies wavelets with increased symmetry.[4] The lengths of Symlet wavelets *sym*2 and *sym*4 are 4 and 8, respectively. Finally, *Haar* wavelet, which has length of 2, is a special type of filter that can be placed in Daubechies and Symlet at the same time.

[4] We also consider Daubechies and Symlet wavelets with different lengths, but they exhibit similar performance by means of size and size-adjusted power.

For simulations, we consider the following data generation process:

$$x_t = \gamma' \mu_t + y_t, \tag{13}$$
$$y_t = \rho y_{t-1} + \epsilon_t, \tag{14}$$
$$\epsilon_t = e_t + \theta e_t, \tag{15}$$

where e_t is i.i.d standard normal random variables. Since the coefficient γ is asymptotically irrelevant, we set $\gamma = 0$ for all cases. Furthermore, for the size exercise, we set $\rho = 1$ and for the power exercise we use $\rho = 0.99$ and 0.9[5].

As we discussed in the previous sections, we compare three different families of wavelet based unit root test statistics. These are Trokić's (2016) variance ratio statistic, Fan and Gencay's (2010) statistic and the wavelet version of Ng and Perron's (2001) test statistics. To evaluate the small sample and large sample properties, we use sample size $T = 100$ and $T = 1000$. Moreover, we examine three types of deterministic component adjustments. These are no deterministic component, only mean, and mean and trend cases.

The newly proposed wavelet based M type and ADF tests require optimal lag length selection to remove the present serial correlation innovation process. In this study, we utilize modified Akaike information criteria (MAIC) information criteria proposed by Ng and Perron (2001). Other information criterion can be considered; however, in our simulation studies, we observe the best results can be obtained with MAIC. Moreover, we also consider the modification of Perron and Qu (2007) for the lag selection procedure. Following Perron and Qu (2007), we utilize OLS instead of GLS detrended data to calculate MAIC, but use GLS detrended data in the testing phase.

As mentioned in Section 3, $\bar{c}$ is used for GLS detrending. This parameter is chosen, for each test, as at the local alternative $\rho = 1 - \bar{c}/T$, the test obtains 50% power with the critical values generated by the same value of $\bar{c}$. This value for each test statistic can be find by running an expensive grid search. We present the values of this parameter in Table 1:[6]

Table 1. The values of $\bar{c}$ and the associated critical values of the wavelet based tests at a 5% significance level.

μ_t	$\bar{c}$	$ADF^*_\alpha, MZ^*_\alpha$	ADF^*_t, MZ^*_t	MSB^*
1	9.8	−16.94	−2.83	0.17
$[1, t]$	18.8	−7.91	−1.92	0.23

4.1. The Size Performance of the Wavelet Based Tests

First, we evaluate the size performance of the wavelet based tests with simulated data. In these simulations, we focus on MA(1) innovations for brevity. The MA(1) coefficient θ in Equation (15) is chosen from $\{0.8, 0, -0.8\}$[7]. The results of the size exercise can be found in Tables 2 and 3 for sample sizes 100 and 1000, respectively.

First, we discuss about the over-size problem with negative MA innovations when $T = 100$. Almost every test statistic in Table 2 exhibits severe size distortions under this scenario. However, M type of unit root tests can eliminate the problem successfully, while ADF tests also demonstrate smaller size distortion relative to Trokić's (2016) and Fan and Gencay's (2010) statistics. Additionally, Fan and Gencay's (2010) test statistic seems to suffer the severest size distortion among all statistics.

5 The results for other intermediate values of ρ are available upon request.

6 In the simulation, we observe that, for all tests, the optimal $\bar{c}$ is very close. As a result, we use the same $\bar{c}$ for all tests. A similar approach is adopted by Ng and Perron (2001). The values of critical values with other significant levels are available upon request.

7 The simulations can be conducted under different ARMA innovations. These results are available upon request. Since they do not alter the findings, we skip them for brevity.

These features also persist in larger samples (see Table 3). When $T = 1000$, we observe size distortions, but slightly less than observed in small samples. Another important observation in these table is that the size distortion problem becomes more severe when we consider deterministic component adjustments, especially in detrending cases. Nonetheless, M type of tests still provide satisfactory size correction even after the detrending procedure.

Table 2. The empirical size of wavelet based tests with sample size = 100.

μ_t	θ	Wavelet	τ^*	FG	MZ_α^*	MZ_t^*	MSB^*	ADF_α^*	ADF_t^*
		Haar	0.212	0.729	0.040	0.046	0.034	0.085	0.067
		Db2	0.212	0.729	0.041	0.049	0.035	0.084	0.066
	−0.8	*Db4*	0.220	0.729	0.038	0.047	0.034	0.086	0.067
		sym2	0.214	0.727	0.041	0.049	0.035	0.085	0.066
		sym4	0.207	0.723	0.040	0.046	0.033	0.084	0.065
		Haar	0.040	0.046	0.028	0.030	0.028	0.031	0.031
		Db2	0.041	0.045	0.029	0.030	0.030	0.031	0.031
0	0	*Db4*	0.045	0.047	0.033	0.036	0.031	0.035	0.036
		sym2	0.044	0.046	0.030	0.031	0.030	0.033	0.032
		sym4	0.040	0.043	0.028	0.029	0.027	0.032	0.031
		Haar	0.037	0.020	0.040	0.040	0.040	0.043	0.039
		Db2	0.039	0.020	0.040	0.040	0.041	0.042	0.036
	0.8	*Db4*	0.042	0.020	0.040	0.043	0.040	0.040	0.036
		sym2	0.039	0.019	0.040	0.040	0.041	0.042	0.037
		sym4	0.038	0.018	0.036	0.037	0.034	0.039	0.034
		Haar	0.227	0.803	0.035	0.039	0.031	0.088	0.074
		Db2	0.228	0.804	0.035	0.037	0.034	0.087	0.071
	−0.8	*Db4*	0.241	0.806	0.043	0.056	0.034	0.091	0.073
		sym2	0.232	0.804	0.034	0.036	0.032	0.087	0.071
		sym4	0.229	0.802	0.039	0.046	0.033	0.089	0.073
		Haar	0.048	0.054	0.033	0.033	0.033	0.036	0.035
		Db2	0.050	0.053	0.033	0.033	0.035	0.037	0.035
1	0	*Db4*	0.053	0.055	0.040	0.042	0.037	0.042	0.042
		sym2	0.051	0.054	0.034	0.035	0.035	0.038	0.037
		sym4	0.051	0.053	0.035	0.036	0.032	0.038	0.038
		Haar	0.045	0.022	0.046	0.046	0.048	0.049	0.044
		Db2	0.045	0.022	0.046	0.046	0.047	0.049	0.042
	0.8	*Db4*	0.050	0.024	0.050	0.053	0.048	0.050	0.044
		sym2	0.048	0.022	0.046	0.047	0.048	0.049	0.042
		sym4	0.048	0.022	0.045	0.046	0.042	0.048	0.042
		Haar	0.498	0.999	0.030	0.032	0.028	0.113	0.072
		Db2	0.501	0.999	0.031	0.032	0.030	0.113	0.069
	−0.8	*Db4*	0.519	0.999	0.033	0.040	0.029	0.116	0.068
		sym2	0.502	0.999	0.031	0.032	0.030	0.116	0.071
		sym4	0.513	0.999	0.032	0.034	0.030	0.116	0.069
		Haar	0.051	0.038	0.010	0.011	0.011	0.017	0.020
		Db2	0.058	0.039	0.012	0.012	0.012	0.017*	0.021
$[1, t]$	0	*Db4*	0.064	0.040	0.015	0.017	0.014	0.023	0.029
		sym2	0.055	0.037	0.012	0.012	0.012	0.018	0.021
		sym4	0.065	0.041	0.013	0.014	0.013	0.021	0.024
		Haar	0.045	0.021	0.025	0.026	0.026	0.032	0.027
		Db2	0.049	0.022	0.025	0.025	0.026	0.032	0.024
	0.8	*Db4*	0.056	0.024	0.027	0.028	0.026	0.032	0.026
		sym2	0.048	0.022	0.026	0.026	0.027	0.032	0.025
		sym4	0.056	0.023	0.022	0.023	0.022	0.030	0.024

Table 3. The empirical size of wavelet based tests with sample size = 1000.

μ_t	θ	Wavelet	τ^*	FG	MZ_α^*	MZ_t^*	MSB^*	ADF_α^*	ADF_t^*
		Haar	0.113	0.636	0.051	0.053	0.047	0.067	0.06
		Db2	0.114	0.637	0.053	0.056	0.049	0.069	0.062
	−0.8	*Db4*	0.118	0.638	0.052	0.055	0.05	0.068	0.062
		sym2	0.115	0.638	0.053	0.056	0.051	0.069	0.062
		sym4	0.115	0.635	0.054	0.057	0.05	0.069	0.063
		Haar	0.046	0.049	0.047	0.047	0.047	0.048	0.047
		Db2	0.048	0.05	0.049	0.048	0.048	0.049	0.047
0	0	*Db4*	0.05	0.049	0.048	0.047	0.047	0.048	0.045
		sym2	0.048	0.049	0.048	0.048	0.048	0.048	0.047
		sym4	0.047	0.048	0.046	0.046	0.045	0.046	0.045
		Haar	0.045	0.04	0.044	0.045	0.045	0.045	0.044
		Db2	0.048	0.041	0.046	0.047	0.046	0.047	0.045
	0.8	*Db4*	0.05	0.041	0.048	0.048	0.047	0.048	0.045
		sym2	0.047	0.04	0.045	0.045	0.046	0.046	0.044
		sym4	0.047	0.041	0.046	0.047	0.046	0.047	0.045
		Haar	0.112	0.651	0.049	0.051	0.047	0.067	0.062
		Db2	0.114	0.651	0.046	0.048	0.046	0.067	0.061
	−0.8	*Db4*	0.112	0.652	0.052	0.056	0.048	0.068	0.062
		sym2	0.108	0.652	0.047	0.048	0.045	0.066	0.061
		sym4	0.111	0.652	0.049	0.051	0.046	0.065	0.06
		Haar	0.047	0.049	0.048	0.048	0.048	0.049	0.048
		Db2	0.048	0.048	0.047	0.047	0.047	0.047	0.046
1	0	*Db4*	0.048	0.051	0.048	0.05	0.048	0.049	0.047
		sym2	0.047	0.05	0.049	0.048	0.048	0.049	0.047
		sym4	0.048	0.05	0.047	0.047	0.047	0.047	0.046
		Haar	0.046	0.041	0.046	0.046	0.046	0.046	0.044
		Db2	0.048	0.041	0.045	0.046	0.046	0.046	0.044
	0.8	*Db4*	0.047	0.041	0.047	0.048	0.047	0.047	0.044
		sym2	0.047	0.041	0.046	0.046	0.046	0.047	0.044
		sym4	0.047	0.041	0.046	0.046	0.046	0.047	0.044
		Haar	0.268	0.994	0.031	0.032	0.029	0.074	0.056
		Db2	0.267	0.994	0.03	0.031	0.03	0.074	0.056
	−0.8	*Db4*	0.27	0.994	0.033	0.038	0.03	0.075	0.056
		sym2	0.267	0.994	0.032	0.033	0.031	0.075	0.058
		sym4	0.272	0.994	0.032	0.034	0.03	0.073	0.056
		Haar	0.062	0.048	0.041	0.041	0.041	0.044	0.042
		Db2	0.063	0.049	0.043	0.043	0.043	0.046	0.042
$[1, t]$	0	*Db4*	0.065	0.049	0.043	0.044	0.043	0.045	0.041
		sym2	0.063	0.049	0.043	0.043	0.043	0.046	0.042
		sym4	0.068	0.051	0.044	0.044	0.043	0.046	0.042
		Haar	0.06	0.028	0.041	0.042	0.042	0.044	0.039
		Db2	0.06	0.028	0.04	0.041	0.04	0.043	0.037
	0.8	*Db4*	0.065	0.028	0.042	0.043	0.042	0.043	0.036
		sym2	0.06	0.028	0.041	0.041	0.041	0.044	0.038
		sym4	0.065	0.029	0.042	0.043	0.041	0.045	0.038

For no serial correlation ($\theta = 0$) and positive MA innovation case ($\theta = 0.8$), we observe all wavelet based tests are either correctly sized or slightly undersized. For instance, Fan and Gencay's (2010) test is undersized by 0.03% when $\theta = 0.8$ for all deterministic component cases. On the other hand, when $\theta = 0.8$ and we have trend and mean as the deterministic component, M tests show 0.02% size distortion. Finally, Trokić's (2016) test is the least affected by detrending algorithms by means of size distortion. Again, these findings are also valid for large sample size ($T = 1000$), but with slight improvement as expected.

In another exercise, we compare the size performances of standard and wavelet based tests. In this exercise, we only consider GLS demeaned statistics with sample sizes $T = 100$ and 1000 for brevity and space constraints. Moreover, we utilize the same serial correlation scenarios as in the previous exercises. The results for this exercise can be found in Table 4. In this table, when $T = 100$ and $\theta = -0.8$, standard tests are undersized and the wavelet based tests are oversized, but the size distortions are almost the same. However, when $\theta = 0.8$, the wavelet based tests are much more successful than the standard tests. Although this result seems controversial, we know that Ng and Perron's (2001) M tests are quite successful without further modification. Additionally, the wavelet modification engenders better results against standard ADF tests, especially ADF_α. In the large sample case, all tests are performing similarly as expected. As a result, there is no single winner in the size contest for the small samples. Moreover, we can attribute the difference appeared in standard and wavelet M tests to the fact that wavelet based tests effectively utilize half of the sample. We expect this difference would be eliminated in the moderate sample sizes.

In the current literature, GLS is generally preferred to OLS for demeaning and detrending series. Therefore, we also use GLS demeaning and detrending in our study. However, we also conduct a small simulation to compare results of GLS and OLS in the case of demeaning with sample size $T = 100$. We use *Haar*, *Db*2, and *sym*2 as they usually perform quite well in our simulations. The results of this simulation are shown in Table 5. For $\theta = 0$ and 0.8, tests based on OLS demeaning are significantly undersized and are clearly worse than their GLS demeaning based counterparts. For a negative MA root case, the tests are oversized except Trokić's (2016) test and tests based on GLS demeaning have slightly better sizes than those based on OLS demeaning except Trokić's (2016) test and ADF_t^* test.

Finally, we present size properties of tests when different lengths of wavelets are selected. For the case of $T = 100$ and GLS demeaning, Figure 1 shows sizes of tests with wavelet length between 2 and 16 for $\theta = -0.8, 0,$ and $0,8$, respectively. Results clearly show that, for $\theta = 0$ and 0.8 when the wavelength increases over 8, tests become significantly oversized. For $\theta = -0.8$, sizes of tests don't change much with the wavelet length. These results show that tests based on smaller wavelet lengths show better size properties.

Table 4. The size comparison of the standard and wavelet based unit root tests under GLS demeaning.

				Wavelet Based Tests				
T	θ	τ^*	MZ_α^*	MZ_t^*	MSB^*	ADF_α^*	ADF_t^*
	−0.8	0.315	0.066	0.068	0.064	0.150	0.121
100	0	0.053	0.037	0.036	0.036	0.042	0.043
	0.8	0.048	0.046	0.046	0.049	0.048	0.040
	−0.8	0.113	0.047	0.048	0.047	0.067	0.062
1000	0	0.048	0.050	0.048	0.048	0.049	0.047
	0.8	0.045	0.039	0.044	0.045	0.045	0.043
				Standard Tests			
T	θ	τ	MZ_α	MZ_t	MSB	ADF_α	ADF_t
	−0.8	0.582	0.037	0.039	0.035	0.162	0.119
100	0	0.069	0.047	0.048	0.047	0.054	0.056
	0.8	0.054	0.071	0.070	0.072	0.072	0.043
	−0.8	0.186	0.041	0.042	0.039	0.080	0.074
1000	0	0.050	0.048	0.048	0.049	0.049	0.049
	0.8	0.047	0.053	0.053	0.053	0.054	0.048

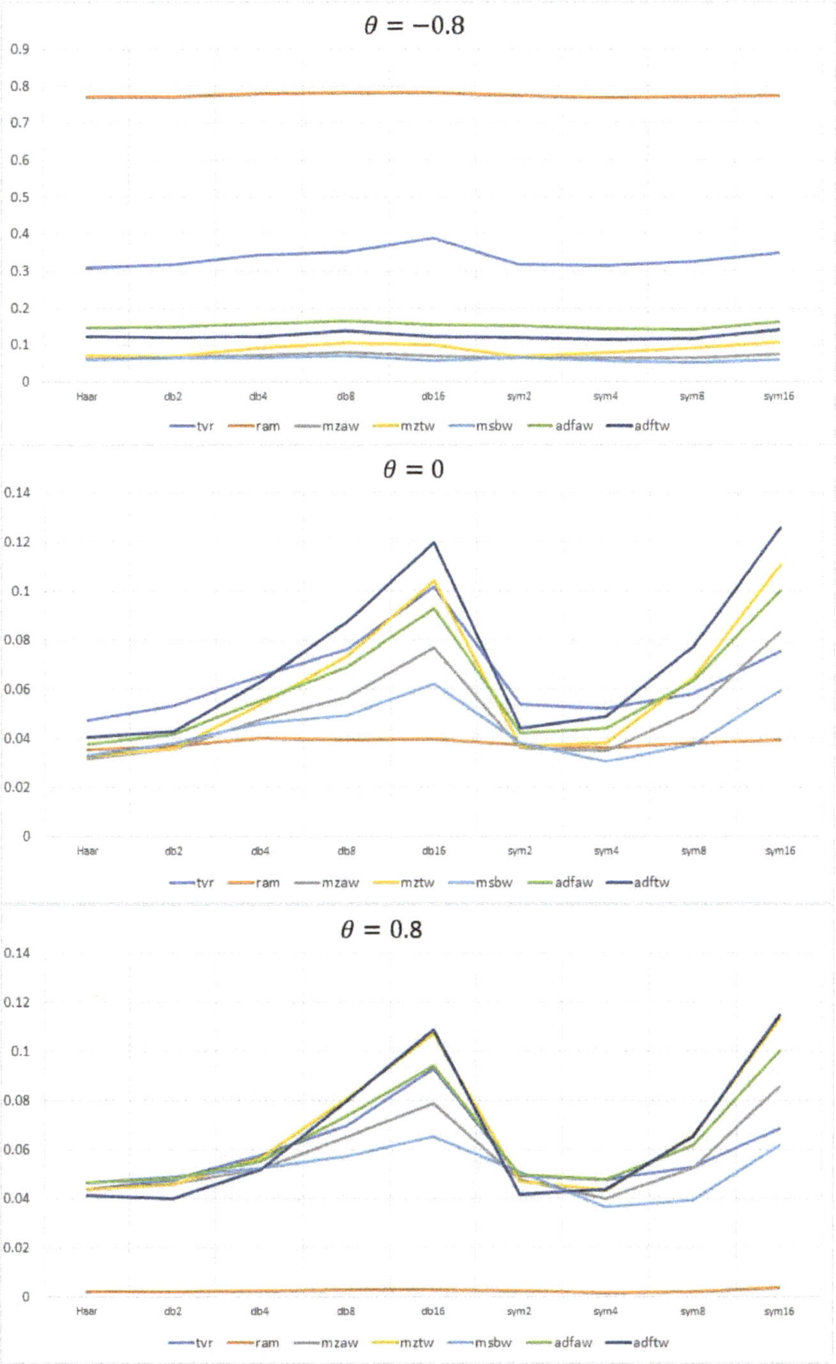

Figure 1. The size comparison of tests with various wavelet lengths with sample size $T = 100$. Note: tvr, ram, mzaw, mztv, msbw, adfaw and adftw correspond to τ^*, FG, MZ_{α}^*, MZ_t^*, MSB^*, ADF_{α}^*, and ADF_t^*, respectively.

Table 5. The size comparison of the OLS and GLS demeaning with sample size $T = 100$.

GLS Demeaning									
Wavelet	θ	τ^*	FG	MZ_α^*	MZ_t^*	MSB^*	ADF_α^*	ADF_t^*
Haar	−0.8	0.307	0.771	0.065	0.071	0.059	0.147	0.123
	0	0.047	0.035	0.032	0.033	0.033	0.038	0.041
	0.8	0.044	0.002	0.044	0.044	0.047	0.047	0.041
db2	−0.8	0.315	0.771	0.066	0.068	0.064	0.150	0.121
	0	0.053	0.037	0.036	0.036	0.038	0.042	0.043
	0.8	0.048	0.002	0.046	0.046	0.049	0.048	0.040
sym2	−0.8	0.317	0.772	0.065	0.067	0.064	0.151	0.120
	0	0.054	0.037	0.036	0.037	0.038	0.042	0.044
	0.8	0.049	0.002	0.048	0.047	0.051	0.050	0.042
OLS demeaning								
Wavelet	θ	τ^*	FG	MZ_α^*	MZ_t^*	MSB^*	ADF_α^*	ADF_t^*
Haar	−0.8	0.423	0.999	0.073	0.063	0.077	0.184	0.105
	0	0.017	0.020	0.011	0.021	0.013	0.017	0.033
	0.8	0.013	0.000	0.015	0.023	0.019	0.020	0.029
db2	−0.8	0.423	0.999	0.077	0.068	0.081	0.190	0.119
	0	0.018	0.018	0.010	0.014	0.013	0.016	0.028
	0.8	0.014	0.000	0.014	0.018	0.020	0.019	0.026
sym2	−0.8	0.432	0.999	0.078	0.069	0.081	0.192	0.119
	0	0.019	0.019	0.010	0.015	0.014	0.017	0.031
	0.8	0.015	0.000	0.015	0.018	0.021	0.020	0.028

4.2. The Size-Adjusted Power Performance of the Wavelet Based Tests

In this part, we investigate the size-adjusted power properties of the wavelet based tests. We use the model in Equations (13)–(15). As in the size exercise, we utilize the same data generation and detrending algorithms, but we set ρ as 0.99 and 0.9. The results for the size-adjusted power performance of wavelet based unit root tests are summarized in Tables 6–8.

These tables demonstrate a few interesting findings. First, Fan and Gencay's (2010) test suffers extreme power loss when $\theta = -0.8$ and $T = 100$. We cannot observe conventional power curve for this test since the power is decreasing with increasing values of ρ. This result is surprising in unit root literature. The detrending or demeaning algorithm does not alter this conclusion, but larger sample size approximately corrects this distortion. On the other hand, other tests still maintain conventional power performance. Second, detrending or demeaning slightly reduce the power of the tests for both small and large samples. Third, the tests show similar power performance in the no serial correlation case. However, we observe slightly worse power for Trokić's (2016) test when $\theta = 0.8$ than the other tests. Finally, when we compare M tests and ADF tests, ADF tests exhibit better performance than M tests in almost all cases.

These findings imply that there is no single dominant test by means of size and size-adjusted power. While M and ADF tests engender better size correction in problematic cases, Trokić (2016) generates more stable power properties. Moreover, the type of wavelet filter (being from the family of Daubechies or Symlets) does not matter by means of size or size-adjusted power.

Table 6. The size-adjusted power of wavelet based tests.

T	μ_t	θ	Wavelet	ρ	τ^*	FG	MZ_α^*	MZ_t^*	MSB^*	ADF_α^*	ADF_t^*
100	0	−0.8	Haar	0.99	0.109	0.104	0.109	0.111	0.104	0.111	0.111
				0.9	0.988	0.073	0.523	0.537	0.507	0.769	0.640
			Db2	0.99	0.115	0.105	0.108	0.109	0.105	0.113	0.113
				0.9	0.989	0.073	0.520	0.535	0.505	0.772	0.643
			Db4	0.99	0.113	0.104	0.110	0.111	0.106	0.115	0.115
				0.9	0.989	0.072	0.516	0.521	0.508	0.781	0.655
			sym2	0.99	0.114	0.107	0.109	0.111	0.104	0.112	0.113
				0.9	0.989	0.075	0.524	0.539	0.507	0.773	0.645
			sym4	0.99	0.117	0.109	0.111	0.109	0.109	0.114	0.114
				0.9	0.991	0.078	0.522	0.530	0.512	0.776	0.641
		0	Haar	0.99	0.101	0.110	0.110	0.112	0.101	0.111	0.115
				0.9	0.884	0.980	0.859	0.859	0.843	0.903	0.870
			Db2	0.99	0.103	0.113	0.110	0.114	0.104	0.113	0.115
				0.9	0.889	0.982	0.853	0.854	0.839	0.901	0.866
			Db4	0.99	0.101	0.112	0.114	0.116	0.106	0.114	0.118
				0.9	0.889	0.981	0.854	0.856	0.837	0.896	0.856
			sym2	0.99	0.102	0.112	0.112	0.113	0.105	0.113	0.116
				0.9	0.883	0.979	0.853	0.854	0.838	0.900	0.865
			sym4	0.99	0.106	0.115	0.117	0.118	0.111	0.117	0.120
				0.9	0.898	0.982	0.852	0.851	0.844	0.897	0.857
		0.8	Haar	0.99	0.105	0.114	0.113	0.115	0.108	0.115	0.117
				0.9	0.873	0.952	0.789	0.790	0.767	0.844	0.811
			Db2	0.99	0.103	0.111	0.111	0.112	0.105	0.113	0.114
				0.9	0.875	0.950	0.790	0.791	0.771	0.851	0.817
			Db4	0.99	0.103	0.113	0.113	0.115	0.107	0.115	0.118
				0.9	0.879	0.951	0.805	0.808	0.781	0.860	0.824
			sym2	0.99	0.104	0.114	0.111	0.113	0.106	0.115	0.115
				0.9	0.878	0.951	0.791	0.791	0.770	0.851	0.818
			sym4	0.99	0.106	0.115	0.113	0.115	0.109	0.114	0.115
				0.9	0.886	0.954	0.801	0.797	0.790	0.855	0.813
	1	−0.8	Haar	0.99	0.093	0.087	0.091	0.091	0.088	0.093	0.090
				0.9	0.371	0.017	0.148	0.151	0.143	0.237	0.189
			Db2	0.99	0.094	0.086	0.090	0.090	0.086	0.095	0.092
				0.9	0.377	0.016	0.148	0.149	0.145	0.240	0.193
			Db4	0.99	0.092	0.086	0.086	0.086	0.086	0.090	0.088
				0.9	0.373	0.016	0.147	0.156	0.144	0.242	0.197
			sym2	0.99	0.095	0.087	0.092	0.093	0.089	0.094	0.093
				0.9	0.374	0.017	0.149	0.149	0.146	0.238	0.193
			sym4	0.99	0.095	0.087	0.091	0.089	0.089	0.093	0.090
				0.9	0.377	0.017	0.152	0.154	0.149	0.243	0.194
		0	Haar	0.99	0.101	0.111	0.108	0.110	0.102	0.110	0.114
				0.9	0.728	0.895	0.776	0.775	0.756	0.820	0.791
			Db2	0.99	0.100	0.114	0.111	0.113	0.104	0.112	0.116
				0.9	0.735	0.900	0.775	0.774	0.754	0.819	0.787
			Db4	0.99	0.104	0.113	0.109	0.111	0.103	0.111	0.114
				0.9	0.747	0.899	0.775	0.779	0.754	0.818	0.776
			sym2	0.99	0.103	0.112	0.108	0.110	0.102	0.109	0.112
				0.9	0.737	0.898	0.771	0.771	0.751	0.818	0.785
			sym4	0.99	0.107	0.115	0.112	0.113	0.108	0.114	0.114
				0.9	0.747	0.900	0.765	0.761	0.756	0.812	0.768
		0.8	Haar	0.99	0.102	0.111	0.110	0.112	0.103	0.112	0.114
				0.9	0.839	0.927	0.746	0.749	0.718	0.806	0.778
			Db2	0.99	0.104	0.112	0.110	0.112	0.107	0.113	0.112
				0.9	0.847	0.928	0.751	0.752	0.730	0.814	0.782
			Db4	0.99	0.103	0.111	0.110	0.111	0.105	0.113	0.114
				0.9	0.854	0.928	0.773	0.776	0.745	0.829	0.793
			sym2	0.99	0.102	0.112	0.112	0.114	0.104	0.114	0.118
				0.9	0.845	0.927	0.753	0.754	0.724	0.814	0.786
			sym4	0.99	0.103	0.110	0.108	0.110	0.106	0.110	0.112
				0.9	0.858	0.930	0.763	0.759	0.754	0.819	0.779

Table 7. The size-adjusted power of wavelet based unit root tests, continued.

T	μ_t	θ	Wavelet	ρ	τ^*	FG	MZ_α^*	MZ_t^*	MSB^*	ADF_α^*	ADF_t^*
			Haar	0.99	0.058	0.055	0.057	0.057	0.057	0.058	0.057
				0.9	0.400	0.026	0.162	0.163	0.161	0.229	0.182
			Db2	0.99	0.060	0.053	0.057	0.058	0.058	0.058	0.058
				0.9	0.411	0.024	0.161	0.161	0.160	0.229	0.184
		−0.8	*Db4*	0.99	0.060	0.054	0.055	0.055	0.055	0.057	0.056
				0.9	0.405	0.024	0.159	0.162	0.158	0.229	0.184
			sym2	0.99	0.058	0.054	0.056	0.056	0.055	0.056	0.056
				0.9	0.401	0.024	0.160	0.161	0.159	0.225	0.180
			sym4	0.99	0.057	0.053	0.056	0.056	0.057	0.058	0.057
				0.9	0.407	0.024	0.165	0.164	0.165	0.233	0.186
			Haar	0.99	0.061	0.061	0.059	0.059	0.058	0.060	0.061
				0.9	0.646	0.805	0.611	0.613	0.595	0.648	0.648
			Db2	0.99	0.060	0.061	0.061	0.061	0.061	0.061	0.062
				0.9	0.640	0.800	0.612	0.616	0.599	0.649	0.646
100	$[1,t]$	0	*Db4*	0.99	0.059	0.060	0.059	0.059	0.058	0.060	0.060
				0.9	0.648	0.804	0.627	0.628	0.613	0.662	0.636
			sym2	0.99	0.061	0.062	0.060	0.061	0.059	0.061	0.060
				0.9	0.644	0.804	0.611	0.616	0.597	0.650	0.644
			sym4	0.99	0.060	0.060	0.059	0.059	0.059	0.060	0.060
				0.9	0.650	0.802	0.617	0.614	0.613	0.652	0.631
			Haar	0.99	0.059	0.059	0.058	0.058	0.058	0.059	0.058
				0.9	0.670	0.672	0.365	0.373	0.345	0.430	0.476
			Db2	0.99	0.060	0.060	0.058	0.059	0.058	0.060	0.060
				0.9	0.676	0.667	0.398	0.407	0.381	0.471	0.515
		0.8	*Db4*	0.99	0.058	0.058	0.058	0.058	0.058	0.059	0.060
				0.9	0.679	0.665	0.446	0.459	0.423	0.517	0.552
			sym2	0.99	0.059	0.058	0.054	0.055	0.053	0.055	0.057
				0.9	0.678	0.668	0.391	0.401	0.374	0.463	0.513
			sym4	0.99	0.060	0.060	0.058	0.059	0.058	0.059	0.059
				0.9	0.678	0.675	0.452	0.454	0.444	0.510	0.531
			Haar	0.99	0.621	0.699	0.650	0.654	0.625	0.677	0.675
				0.9	1.000	1.000	0.978	0.979	0.973	1.000	0.999
			Db2	0.99	0.626	0.696	0.650	0.652	0.629	0.680	0.674
				0.9	1.000	0.999	0.977	0.977	0.973	1.000	0.999
		−0.8	*Db4*	0.99	0.627	0.703	0.650	0.647	0.631	0.683	0.677
				0.9	1.000	1.000	0.974	0.971	0.972	1.000	0.999
			sym2	0.99	0.622	0.697	0.645	0.645	0.620	0.676	0.670
				0.9	1.000	0.999	0.977	0.977	0.972	1.000	0.999
			sym4	0.99	0.626	0.699	0.641	0.645	0.623	0.671	0.664
				0.9	1.000	1.000	0.976	0.976	0.972	1.000	0.999
			Haar	0.99	0.523	0.704	0.707	0.711	0.680	0.711	0.711
				0.9	1.000	1.000	0.999	0.998	0.999	1.000	0.999
			Db2	0.99	0.526	0.707	0.707	0.707	0.684	0.709	0.707
				0.9	1.000	1.000	0.999	0.999	0.999	1.000	0.999
1000	0	0	*Db4*	0.99	0.528	0.711	0.712	0.718	0.686	0.715	0.717
				0.9	1.000	1.000	0.999	0.999	0.999	1.000	0.999
			sym2	0.99	0.523	0.711	0.711	0.712	0.682	0.714	0.712
				0.9	1.000	1.000	0.999	0.998	0.999	1.000	0.999
			sym4	0.99	0.533	0.716	0.714	0.714	0.690	0.717	0.715
				0.9	1.000	1.000	0.999	0.999	0.999	1.000	0.999
			Haar	0.99	0.527	0.703	0.705	0.707	0.679	0.708	0.708
				0.9	1.000	1.000	0.999	0.999	0.999	1.000	0.999
			Db2	0.99	0.524	0.704	0.701	0.703	0.674	0.704	0.704
				0.9	1.000	1.000	0.999	0.999	0.999	1.000	0.999
		0.8	*Db4*	0.99	0.519	0.697	0.689	0.695	0.665	0.694	0.697
				0.9	1.000	1.000	0.999	0.999	0.999	1.000	0.999
			sym2	0.99	0.522	0.709	0.706	0.710	0.678	0.709	0.711
				0.9	1.000	1.000	0.999	0.999	0.999	1.000	0.999
			sym4	0.99	0.525	0.702	0.694	0.694	0.668	0.696	0.696
				0.9	1.000	1.000	0.999	0.998	0.999	1.000	0.999

Table 8. The size-adjusted power of wavelet based unit root tests, continued.

T	μ_t	θ	Wavelet	ρ	τ^*	FG	MZ_α^*	MZ_t^*	MSB^*	ADF_α^*	ADF_t^*
1000	1	−0.8	*Haar*	0.99	0.391	0.447	0.454	0.456	0.438	0.474	0.471
				0.9	0.551	0.429	0.248	0.255	0.238	0.433	0.413
			Db2	0.99	0.387	0.444	0.455	0.457	0.436	0.473	0.469
				0.9	0.554	0.429	0.245	0.248	0.238	0.434	0.414
			Db4	0.99	0.393	0.448	0.455	0.454	0.439	0.477	0.472
				0.9	0.554	0.430	0.250	0.266	0.238	0.435	0.416
			sym2	0.99	0.397	0.455	0.461	0.460	0.443	0.479	0.474
				0.9	0.557	0.437	0.246	0.249	0.240	0.436	0.416
			sym4	0.99	0.395	0.452	0.456	0.458	0.440	0.474	0.467
				0.9	0.556	0.435	0.254	0.264	0.242	0.437	0.416
		0	*Haar*	0.99	0.514	0.698	0.694	0.694	0.668	0.697	0.694
				0.9	0.950	1.000	0.948	0.948	0.942	0.982	0.972
			Db2	0.99	0.521	0.702	0.699	0.699	0.673	0.703	0.699
				0.9	0.954	0.999	0.951	0.950	0.945	0.983	0.974
			Db4	0.99	0.519	0.694	0.697	0.699	0.670	0.701	0.697
				0.9	0.953	0.999	0.953	0.954	0.945	0.983	0.973
			sym2	0.99	0.518	0.690	0.691	0.696	0.666	0.695	0.695
				0.9	0.952	0.999	0.948	0.948	0.942	0.982	0.972
			sym4	0.99	0.516	0.693	0.692	0.695	0.668	0.695	0.694
				0.9	0.953	1.000	0.950	0.951	0.945	0.983	0.973
		0.8	*Haar*	0.99	0.529	0.699	0.704	0.706	0.673	0.707	0.706
				0.9	0.998	1.000	0.993	0.992	0.991	0.999	0.998
			Db2	0.99	0.526	0.697	0.696	0.697	0.667	0.700	0.700
				0.9	0.998	1.000	0.992	0.992	0.991	0.999	0.998
			Db4	0.99	0.530	0.699	0.694	0.697	0.665	0.698	0.699
				0.9	0.998	1.000	0.994	0.994	0.992	0.999	0.998
			sym2	0.99	0.526	0.698	0.696	0.701	0.669	0.700	0.702
				0.9	0.998	1.000	0.993	0.992	0.991	0.999	0.998
			sym4	0.99	0.529	0.695	0.689	0.689	0.665	0.691	0.690
				0.9	0.998	1.000	0.993	0.993	0.993	0.999	0.998
	$[1, t]$	−0.8	*Haar*	0.99	0.246	0.255	0.218	0.220	0.215	0.234	0.228
				0.9	0.796	0.607	0.261	0.264	0.257	0.549	0.483
			Db2	0.99	0.242	0.250	0.213	0.214	0.211	0.231	0.224
				0.9	0.793	0.604	0.257	0.259	0.255	0.546	0.479
			Db4	0.99	0.240	0.256	0.214	0.215	0.212	0.232	0.225
				0.9	0.792	0.609	0.257	0.267	0.253	0.543	0.478
			sym2	0.99	0.235	0.248	0.208	0.210	0.207	0.225	0.221
				0.9	0.793	0.599	0.255	0.257	0.253	0.542	0.475
			sym4	0.99	0.238	0.256	0.218	0.218	0.214	0.235	0.228
				0.9	0.794	0.613	0.261	0.263	0.258	0.550	0.485
		0	*Haar*	0.99	0.269	0.302	0.291	0.293	0.286	0.293	0.293
				0.9	0.997	1.000	0.941	0.942	0.940	0.992	0.968
			Db2	0.99	0.260	0.293	0.278	0.281	0.274	0.280	0.282
				0.9	0.997	1.000	0.938	0.938	0.937	0.991	0.966
			Db4	0.99	0.266	0.292	0.280	0.283	0.276	0.281	0.283
				0.9	0.998	1.000	0.943	0.945	0.940	0.991	0.968
			sym2	0.99	0.262	0.292	0.281	0.281	0.275	0.283	0.283
				0.9	0.998	1.000	0.938	0.938	0.937	0.992	0.967
			sym4	0.99	0.259	0.290	0.275	0.278	0.269	0.277	0.277
				0.9	0.997	1.000	0.941	0.941	0.939	0.992	0.967
		0.8	*Haar*	0.99	0.267	0.292	0.281	0.285	0.276	0.283	0.284
				0.9	0.999	1.000	0.970	0.970	0.970	0.998	0.987
			Db2	0.99	0.266	0.289	0.280	0.280	0.273	0.283	0.283
				0.9	0.999	1.000	0.971	0.970	0.971	0.998	0.988
			Db4	0.99	0.262	0.285	0.277	0.279	0.271	0.279	0.282
				0.9	0.999	1.000	0.971	0.972	0.970	0.998	0.989
			sym2	0.99	0.260	0.281	0.275	0.279	0.268	0.277	0.278
				0.9	0.999	1.000	0.971	0.970	0.970	0.998	0.989
			sym4	0.99	0.261	0.283	0.271	0.273	0.268	0.275	0.274
				0.9	1.000	1.000	0.972	0.971	0.971	0.998	0.987

In the last two Monte Carlo exercises, we evaluate the large sample properties of the wavelet based and standard unit root tests under GLS demeaning[8]. First, we examine the asymptotic behaviour of the wavelet based test with different wavelet filters and lengths. In this exercise, we only consider the asymptotic power properties of the MZ_{α}^{*} test and seven different wavelet filters, namely *Haar*, *Db*2, *Db*4, *Db*8, *sym*2, *sym*4 and *sym*8. These results, which are generated under no serial correlation and sample size 1000, are presented in Figure 2. From this figure, it is clear that wavelet type and length do not matter asymptotically.

In another exercise, we compare the asymptotic power curves of the GLS demeaned standard and wavelet based tests. From these tests, we consider τ^{*}, FG, MZ_{α}^{*} and MZ_{t}^{*}, as the wavelet based tests, andτ, MZ_{α} and MZ_{t} as standard unit root tests. The results of the simulations, which are run with no serial correlation and sample size 1000, are given in Figure 3. The findings are twofold: (1) Nielsen's (2009) test and its wavelet version are almost asymptotically equivalent; and (2) there are very slight deviations in other tests. However, increasing the sample size further may eliminate the difference further. On the other hand, the figure illustrates that the most powerful tests are M tests, the second rank belongs to Fan and Gencay's (2010) test and the least powerful tests are Nielsen's (2009) test.

8 We also consider GLS detrending, but, for the space considerations, we do not present them. If requested, they are available from the authors.

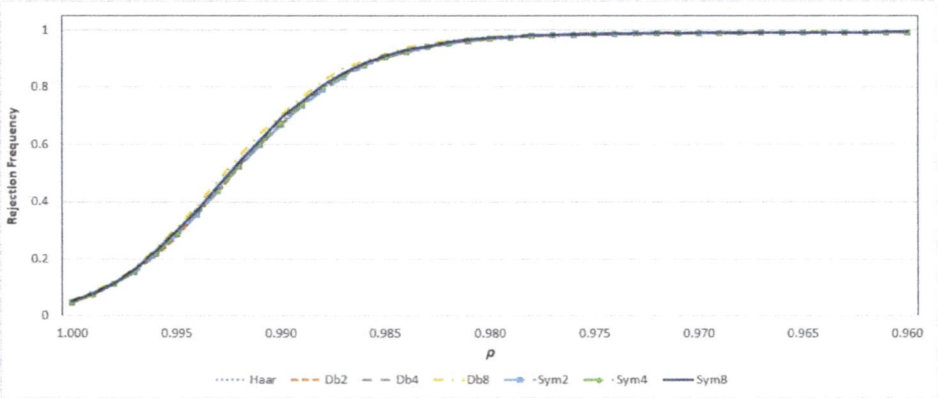

Figure 2. Asymptotic power curves of the wavelet based MZ_α with different wavelet filters under GLS demeaning. Note: Filters are defined in the text.

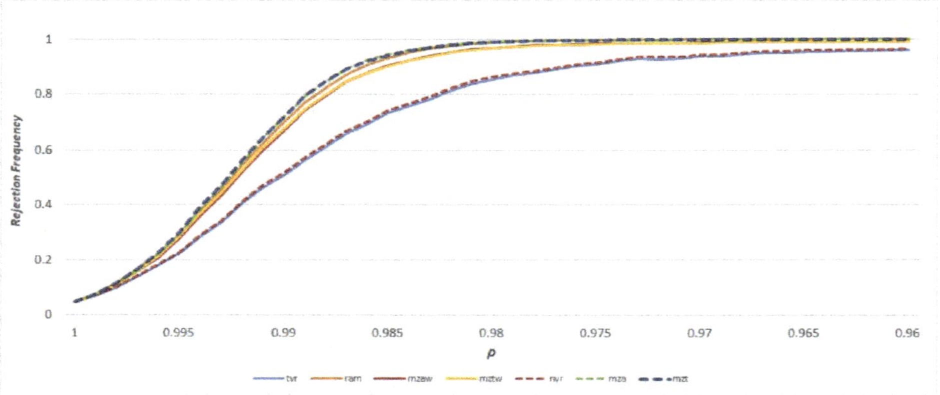

Figure 3. Asymptotic power curves of the wavelet based and standard unit root tests under GLS demeaning. Note: $tvr, ram, mzaw$ and $mztw$ correspond to τ^*, FG, MZ_α^* and MZ_t^*, respectively. nvr, mza and mzt correspond to τ, MZ_α and MZ_t which are standard unit root tests without the wavelet application, respectively.

5. Conclusions

In this study, we extend the results of Fan and Gencay (2010) in Ng and Perron's (2001) framework and we provide an analysis of the application of GLS detrending in the wavelet framework.

As a result of our comparison exercise, relative to existing wavelet based unit roots, the newly proposed tests seem to be more robust to problematic innovation structures such as negative MA roots. Although all tests suffer size distortion from the presence of the negative MA innovations, in particular, M type tests are almost correctly sized. Furthermore, our tests also exhibit local power, while there is no single test that dominates the power performance contest.

We also show that the wavelet type does not matter in unit root testing. However, using higher length filters may distort the performance of wavelet based tests. Nonetheless, we can suggest length 2 or 4 wavelets for wavelet based unit root tests.

For the future work, we also consider wavelet based Johansen cointegration test using similar methodology. Recently, Eroğlu (2018) combine the Fan and Gencay (2010) and Trokić's (2016) results with a Nielsen (2010) cointegration test. Utilizing wavelet based techniques in a Johansen cointegration test may engender a fruitful comparison. Finally, one can also consider the evaluation of the wavestrapping or other bootstrapping techniques for the wavelet based unit root tests.

Author Contributions: Both authors contributed equally to this manuscript.

Funding: This research received no external funding.

Conflicts of Interest: The authors declare no conflict of interest.

Appendix A. Proofs of the Theorems and the Lemmas

Lemma A1. *Suppose that Assumptions 1 and 2 hold and define $V_{1,t} = G(B)y_{2t}$. Under the null hypothesis of $\rho = 1$,*

$$T_1^{-1/2}V_{1,T_1}(t) = T_1^{-1/2}\sum_{s=1}^{\lfloor tT_1 \rfloor} V_{1,s} \to 2\sigma\phi(1)W(t) \qquad \forall t \in [0,1],$$

where $W(t)$ is a standard Brownian motion and $\phi(1)$ is the long run variance of u_t.

The proof of this lemma can found in Trokić (2016) and Fan and Gencay (2010).

Lemma A2. *Suppose that Assumptions 1–2 hold and x_t is generated by Equations (2) and (3). Let $V_{1,\bar{c},t}$ be defined in Equation (4). The partial sum process of $\hat{V}_{1,\bar{c},t}$ satisfies the following properties:*

$$T_1^{-1/2}\hat{V}_{1,\bar{c},T_1}(t) = T_1^{-1/2}\sum_{s=1}^{\lfloor tT_1 \rfloor} \hat{V}_{1,\bar{c},s} \to 2\sigma\phi(1)W_{j,\bar{c}}(t),$$

where $W_{j,\bar{c}}(s)$ is demonstrated in Theorem 1.

Proof of Lemma 2. First, we decompose $\hat{x}_{\bar{c},t}$ as $\hat{x}_{\bar{c},t} = y_t - (\hat{\gamma}_{GLS,0} - \gamma_0) - (\hat{\gamma}_{GLS,1} - \gamma_1)t$ where $\hat{\gamma}_{GLS} = \begin{bmatrix}\hat{\gamma}_{0,GLS} & \hat{\gamma}_{1,GLS}\end{bmatrix}$ when $j = 2$ and $\hat{x}_{\bar{c},t} = y_t - (\hat{\gamma}_{GLS,0} - \gamma_0)$ where $\hat{\gamma}_{GLS} = \begin{bmatrix}\hat{\gamma}_{0,GLS}\end{bmatrix}$ when $j = 1$. Now, we write

$$\hat{V}_{1,\bar{c},t} = G(B)\hat{x}_{\bar{c},2t} = V_{1,t} - G(1)(\hat{\gamma}_{GLS,0} - \gamma_0) - (\hat{\gamma}_{GLS,1} - \gamma_1)G(B)2t \quad \text{if } j = 2,$$
$$\hat{V}_{1,\bar{c},t} = G(B)\hat{x}_{\bar{c},2t} = V_{1,t} - G(1)(\hat{\gamma}_{GLS,0} - \gamma_0) \quad \text{if } j = 1.$$

Note that $G(B)y_{2t} = V_{1,t}$. This result implies that

$$T_1^{-1/2}\hat{V}_{1,\bar{c},T_1}(t) = T_1^{-1/2}V_{1,T_1} - T_1^{-1/2}G(1)(\hat{\gamma}_{GLS,0} - \gamma_0) - T_1^{-1/2}(\hat{\gamma}_{GLS,1} - \gamma_1)G(B)2\lfloor tT_1 \rfloor \quad if\, j = 2, \tag{A1}$$

$$T_1^{-1/2}\hat{V}_{1,\bar{c},t} = T_1^{-1/2}V_{1,t} - T_1^{-1/2}G(1)(\hat{\gamma}_{GLS,0} - \gamma_0) \quad if\, j = 1. \tag{A2}$$

Elliott et al. (1996) $(\hat{\gamma}_{GLS,0}) = O_p(1)$ as a result $T_1^{-1/2}G(1)(\hat{\gamma}_{GLS,0} - \gamma_0)$ converges to zero in the limit, and the convergence of the second deterministic term is shown as

$$T^{1/2}(\hat{\gamma}_{GLS,1} - \gamma_1) \to \sigma\phi(1)\left(\frac{1+\bar{c}}{1+\bar{c}+\bar{c}^2/3}W(1) + \frac{\bar{c}^2}{1+\bar{c}+\bar{c}^2/3}\int_0^1 rW(r)dr\right).$$

Using these results, we can rewrite Equations (A1) and (A2) as:

$$T_1^{-1/2}\hat{V}_{1,\bar{c},T_1} = T_1^{-1/2}V_{1,T_1} - T_1^{-1/2}G(1)(\hat{\gamma}_{GLS,0} - \gamma_0) \tag{A3}$$

$$- T_1^{1/2}(\hat{\gamma}_{GLS,1} - \gamma_1)G(B)2\lfloor tT_1 \rfloor / T_1 \quad if\, j = 2, \tag{A4}$$

$$T_1^{-1/2}\hat{V}_{1,\bar{c},t} = T^{-1/2}V_{1,t} - T^{-1/2}G(1)(\hat{\gamma}_{GLS,0} - \gamma_0) \quad if\, j = 1. \tag{A5}$$

Note that $G(1) = \sqrt{2}$ and $2G(B)t/T = 2G(1)\lfloor tT_1 \rfloor / T_1 - 2\sum_{l=0} lg_l / T_1$. The second term can be written as $2G(B)\lfloor tT_1 \rfloor / T = \sqrt{2}t/T$ in the limit since $2\sum_{l=0} lg_l / T_1 = o_p(1)$. Finally, we can show,

$$T_1^{-1/2}\hat{V}_{1,\bar{c},T_1}(t) \to T_1^{-1/2}V_{1,T_1}(t) - \sqrt{2}T_1^{1/2}(\hat{\gamma}_{GLS,1} - \gamma_1)t/T \tag{A6}$$

$$\to T_1^{-1/2}V_{1,T_1}(t) - 2T^{1/2}(\hat{\gamma}_{GLS,1} - \gamma_1)t/T \tag{A7}$$

$$\to 2\sigma\phi(1)W(t) \tag{A8}$$

$$- 2\sigma\phi(1)\left(\frac{1+\bar{c}}{1+\bar{c}+\bar{c}^2/3}W(1) + \frac{\bar{c}^2}{1+\bar{c}+\bar{c}^2/3}\int_0^1 rW(r)dr\right)t \tag{A9}$$

$$= 2\sigma\phi(1)W_{2,\bar{c}}(s) \quad if\, j = 2, \tag{A10}$$

$$T_1^{-1/2}\hat{V}_{1,\bar{c},t}(t) \to T^{-1/2}V_{1,t}(t) \to 2\sigma\phi(1)W(t) = 2\sigma\phi(1)W_{2,\bar{c}}(s) \quad if\, j = 1, \tag{A11}$$

where Equation (A7) follows from the fact that $T_1^{1/2} = \sqrt{2}T^{1/2}$. □

Lemma A3. *Let assumptions of Theorem 1 hold, then* $s_{AR}^{*2}(p) \to 2\sigma\phi(1)$.

Proof of Lemma 3. The proof of this lemma can be obtained from the consistency of $\hat{\alpha}(1)$, which is demonstrated in Lemma 3.5 of Chang and Park (2002) and the results of Lemma A1. First, note that $\hat{\alpha}(1) \to \alpha(1)$, thus $1/\hat{\alpha}(1) \to 1/\alpha(1)$. Additionally, $\hat{\sigma}$ is a consistent estimator of the variance of $\epsilon_{p,t}^*$. However, from Fan and Gencay (2010) and Trokić (2016), we know the long run variance of v_t is given as $2\sigma\phi(1)$, and then we obtain the result from Continuous Mapping Theorem (CMT) since we also have $\hat{\sigma} \to \sigma^{*2}$. □

Proof of Theorem 1. The proof of results for the ADF test based on wavelet transformed series directly follows Chang and Park (2002). Note that the wavelet based augmented regression satisfies the same conditions as the classical ADF regression. As a result, we can use Lemmas A2 and A3 to obtain the results. The proof is the same as in Chang and Park (2002), and thus we skip the details.

The results for the wavelet based M tests follow from Lemmas A2 and A3. We simply apply CMT to reach the desired outcome. □

References

Chang, Yoosoon, and Joon Y. Park. 2002. On the asymptotics of ADF tests for unit roots. *Econometric Reviews* 21: 431–47. [CrossRef]

Dickey, David A., and Wayne A. Fuller. 1979. Distribution of the estimators for autoregressive time series with a unit root. *Journal of the American Statistical Association* 74: 427–31.

Dickey, David A., and Wayne A. Fuller. 1981. Likelihood ratio statistics for autoregressive time series with a unit root. *Econometrica* 49: 1057–72. [CrossRef]

Elliott, Graham, Thomas J. Rothenberg, and James H. Stock. 1996. Efficient Tests for an Autoregressive Unit Root. *Econometrica* 64: 813–36. [CrossRef]

Eroğu, Burak. 2018. *Wavelet Variance Ratio Test And Wavestrapping for the Determination of the Cointegration Rank*. CEFIS Working Paper Series November 2017; Frankfurt am Main, Germany: The Center for Financial Studies.

Fan, Yanqin, and Ramazan Gencay. 2010. Unit Root Tests with Wavelets. *Econometric Theory* 5: 1305–31. [CrossRef]

Gençay, Ramazan, Faruk Selçuk, and Brandon J. Whitcher. 2001. *An Introduction to Wavelets and Other Filtering Methods in Finance and Economics*. Cambridge, MA, USA: Academic Press.

Granger, Clive W. J. 1966. The typical spectral shape of an economic variable. *Econometrica* 34: 150–61. [CrossRef]

Granger, Clive W. J. 1981. Some Properties of Time Series Data and Their Use in Econometric Model Specification. *Journal of Econometrics* 16: 121–30. [CrossRef]

Mallat, Stephane G. 1989. A Theory for Multiresolution Signal Decomposition: The Wavelet Representation. Pattern Analysis and Machine Intelligence. *IEEE Transactions* 11: 674–93.

Ng, Serena, and Pierre Perron. 2001. Lag length selection and the construction of unit root tests with good size and power. *Econometrica* 69: 1519–54. [CrossRef]

Nielsen, Morten Ørregaard. 2009. A powerful Test of the Autoregressive Unit Root Hypothesis Based on a Tuning Parameter Free Statistic. *Econometric Theory* 25: 1515–44. [CrossRef]

Nielsen, Morten Ørregaard. 2010. Nonparametric Cointegration Analysis of Fractional Systems with Unknown Integration Orders. *Journal of Econometrics* 155: 170–87. [CrossRef]

Perron, Pierre, and Zhongjun Qu. 2007. A simple modification to improve the finite sample properties of Ng and Perron's unit root tests. *Economics Letters* 94: 12–19. [CrossRef]

Phillips, Peter C. B., and Pierre Perron. 1988. Testing for a Unit Root in Time Series Regression. *Biometrika* 75: 335–46. [CrossRef]

Trokic, Mirza. 2016. Wavelet Energy Ratio Unit Root Tests. *Econometric Reviews*, 1–19. [CrossRef]

Journal of
Risk and Financial Management

Article

Monte Carlo Comparison for Nonparametric Threshold Estimators

Chaoyi Chen * and Yiguo Sun

Department of Economics and Finance, University of Guelph, Guelph, ON N1G 2W1, Canada; yisun@uoguelph.ca
* Correspondence: chaoyi@uoguelph.ca

Received: 17 July 2018; Accepted: 15 August 2018; Published: 17 August 2018

Abstract: This paper compares the finite sample performance of three non-parametric threshold estimators via the Monte Carlo method. Our results indicate that the finite sample performance of the three estimators is not robust to the position of the threshold level along the distribution of the threshold variable, especially when a structural change occurs at the tail part of the distribution.

Keywords: difference kernel estimator; integrated difference kernel estimator; M-estimation; Monte Carlo; nonparametric threshold regression

JEL Classification: C14; C21

---

1. Introduction

Popularly used to describe structural changes in economic relationships, threshold models have seen many applications, especially in macro fields (e.g., Hansen 2011; Potter 1995). Typical examples include the nonlinearity in public debt to GDP ratio (e.g., Afonso and Jalles 2013; Caner et al. 2010; Cecchetti et al. 2011). A number of threshold estimators for threshold models have been proposed in the literature, and the asymptotic results of these estimators can be categorized into two groups based on different assumptions. The first group is based on the "fixed threshold effect" assumption. The second group imposes a "diminishing threshold effect" assumption introduced by Hansen (2000). For example, it is well known that, for the least-squares estimator, the threshold estimator is super-consistent with the convergence rate n under the "fixed threshold effect" assumption and $n^{1-2\alpha}$ under the "diminishing threshold effect" assumption, respectively, where α measures the diminishing rate of the threshold effect.

The asymptotic theory and statistical inference have been well developed for the least-squares estimator exogenous regressors and exogenous threshold variable (e.g., Chan 1993; Hansen 2000; Seo and Linton 2007). Recently, there has been a growing interest in studying threshold models with endogenous regressors and/or a threshold variable. Extending the framework of Hansen (2000), Caner and Hansen (2004) applied the two-step least-squares method to estimate threshold models with endogenous slope regressors. In the spirit of the sample selection technique of Heckman (1979), imposing the joint normality assumption, Kourtellos et al. (2016) explored the case that both the threshold variable and slope regressors are endogenous. The work in Seo and Shin (2016) proposed a two-step GMM estimator for a dynamic panel threshold model with fixed effects, which allows endogeneity in both the slope regressors and threshold variable. It is worth noticing that the GMM method allows both a fixed and diminishing threshold effect, and the convergence rate for the GMM threshold estimator is not super-consistent. By relaxing the joint normality assumption of Kourtellos et al. (2016, 2017), a two-step least square estimator based on a nonparametric control function approach to correct the threshold endogeneity was proposed. The semiparametric threshold model separates the threshold effect into two parts, namely the exogenous threshold effect and endogenous threshold bias-correction term. Therefore, with a "small threshold" effect, the convergence rate for the threshold variable depends on diminishing rates of the threshold effect and the bias-correction term.

However, few studies have worked on the estimation and statistical inference of threshold estimators based on nonparametric estimation methods, which do not rely on the least square method. The work in Delgado and Hidalgo (2000) suggested a difference kernel estimator (or DKE), which depends on a chosen point. The convergence rate of Delgado and Hidalgo (2000) DKE is nh^{d-1}, which depends on both the bandwidth, h, and the dimensionality of regressors in their threshold model, $d \geq 1$. Built upon the method of Delgado and Hidalgo (2000), Yu et al. (2018) introduced an integrated difference kernel estimator (or IDKE). The work in Yu et al. (2018) argued that the IDKE can be applied to the case with the endogenous threshold variable. The convergence rate of the IDKE is not related to either the bandwidth or the dimensionality of regressors and is super-consistent with the rate n. Using recently-developed discrete smoothing methods, Henderson et al. (2017) introduced a semiparametric M-estimator of a nonparametric threshold regression model. The threshold estimator of Henderson et al. (2017) can be estimated at the rate $\sqrt{n/h}$ (h is the bandwidth), which is faster than the parametric convergence rate of $\sqrt{n}$. One may notice that the aforementioned convergence rate is the same as that of the smoothed least squares estimator in Seo and Linton (2007). However, they are entirely different. The work in Henderson et al. (2017) focussed on the nonparametric threshold model, and their proposed estimator was based on a non-smooth objective function. On the contrary, Seo and Linton (2007) worked on a linear threshold model, and the proposed estimator was based on a smooth objective function with the indicator function replaced by a CDF-type smooth function.

With many applications and simulations available for comparing the parametric threshold estimators in the literature, little guidance is available for researchers to apply as to the choice of nonparametric threshold estimators. Moreover, to avoid the boundary effect of the threshold estimator, most simulations are designed deliberately with the true threshold level chosen at the middle point of the threshold variable distribution, which can be highly doubted in reality. Therefore, the purpose of this paper is to carefully compare the three nonparametric threshold estimators mentioned above using the Monte Carlo method. More importantly, we consider the case that the true threshold level is not only at the middle, but also at the two tails of the threshold variable distribution.

The rest of the paper is organized as follows. In Section 2, we briefly review the estimation procedure of three nonparametric threshold estimators such as DKE, IDKE and the M-estimator, where threshold models have exogenous regressors and a threshold variable. In Section 3, we illustrate the possible theoretical reason for the conjecture of the poor finite sample performance of the difference kernel-type estimators. Section 4 presents the design of the Monte Carlo simulations. Section 5 reports the finite sample performance. Section 6 concludes.

2. Three Nonparametric Threshold Estimators

In this paper, we aim to compare the finite sample performance of three nonparametric threshold estimators: Henderson et al. (2017) the semiparametric M-estimator, Delgado and Hidalgo (2000) the difference kernel estimator (DKE) and Yu et al. (2018) the integrated difference kernel estimator (IDKE).

Following Henderson et al. (2017), we consider a generalized threshold regression model:

$$y_i = \alpha_0(X_i) + \beta_0 I\{q_i > \gamma_0\} + \varepsilon_i, \quad (1)$$

for $i = 1, ..., n$, where $\alpha_0(\cdot)$ is an unknown smooth function, X_i is a vector of d regressors, q_i is the threshold variable, γ_0 is the threshold level, $I(\cdot)$ is the indicator function and β_0 measures the jump size of the regression function at $q > \gamma$. Furthermore, X_i and q_i are both exogenous and may have a common variable.

2.1. Semiparametric M-Estimator

If γ_0 is known a priori, Model (1) is known as a partially linear model. The conventional method to estimate the unknown γ_0 is minimizing the sum of squared errors, which can be iterated by the grid search. Therefore, Henderson et al. (2017) suggested the semi-parametric M-estimator of the nonparametric threshold model, which can be obtained in three steps.

In Step 1, given (β, γ), Model (1) becomes a standard nonparametric model. Therefore, we can obtain the Nadaraya–Watson (NW) estimator of $\alpha_0(x)$ at an interior point, x, i.e.,

$$\hat{\alpha}(x;\beta,\gamma) = arg\min_{\alpha\in\Theta_\alpha} n^{-1}\sum_{i=1}^{n}[y_i - \alpha - \beta I\{q_i > \gamma\}]^2 K_h(X_i - x), \tag{2}$$

where $K_h(X_i - x) = h^{-d}\prod_{j=1}^{d} k(\frac{X_{ij}-x_j}{h})$, $X_i = [X_{i,1}, ..., X_{i,d}]'$, $x = [x_1, ..., x_d]'$, $k(\cdot)$ is a second order kernel function, h is the bandwidth and d is the dimension of x.

In Step 2, given γ, Model (1) becomes a partially linear model. Then, β_0 can be estimated as:

$$\hat{\beta}(\gamma) = arg\min_{\beta\in\Theta_\beta} n^{-1}\sum_{i=1}^{n}[y_i - \hat{\alpha}(X_i;\beta,\gamma) - \beta I\{q_i > \gamma\}]^2 \hat{f}_h^2(X_i), \tag{3}$$

where $\hat{f}_h(X_i) = n^{-1}\sum_{i=1}^{n} K_h(X_i - x)$ works as the weighting function.

The work in Henderson et al. (2017) shows that $\hat{\beta}(\gamma)$ has the following mathematical expression:

$$\hat{\beta}(\gamma) = \left[n^{-1}\sum_{i=1}^{n}\left[\sum_{j=1}^{n} K_h(X_i - X_j)(I_i - I_j)\right]^2\right]^{-1} n^{-1}\sum_{i=1}^{n}\left[\sum_{j=1}^{n} K_h(X_i - X_j)(I_i - I_j)\sum_{j=1}^{n} K_h(X_i - X_j)(y_i - y_j)\right], \tag{4}$$

where we denote $I_i = I(q_i > \gamma)$.

In Step 3, we can estimate the threshold level γ_0 by solving the following optimization problem,

$$\hat{\gamma} = arg\min_{\gamma\in\Theta_\gamma}\left| n^{-1}\sum_{i=1}^{n}\left[y_i - \hat{\alpha}(X_i;\beta(\gamma),\gamma) - \hat{\beta}(\gamma)I\{q_i > \gamma\}\right] w(X_i)\right|, \tag{5}$$

where $w(\cdot)$ is a weighting function and is application dependent.

As mentioned in Section 1, the convergence rate of the threshold estimator of Henderson et al. (2017) is $\sqrt{n/h}$, which explodes faster than the usual parametric $\sqrt{n}$ rate. However, the unknown function $\alpha_0(\cdot)$ and the jump size β_0 converge at standard nonparametric rates of $\sqrt{nh^d}$ and $\sqrt{nh}$, respectively.

2.2. DKE and IDKE

Instead of using the absolute value of the weighted average of the sum of errors as the objective function, Delgado and Hidalgo (2000) considered using the difference between $\hat{E}[y|x_0, q = \gamma-]$ and $\hat{E}[y|x_0, q = \gamma+]$ as the objective function. Ideally, the closer γ approaches the true value, the larger the absolute value of the above difference should be. As a result, we are able to estimate the threshold level by choosing γ, which gives the most considerable gap between the two one-sided expectations. Therefore, the difference kernel estimator (DKE) can be obtained by:

$$\hat{\gamma}^{DKE} = arg\max_{\gamma\in\Theta_\gamma}\left(\frac{1}{n}\sum_{i=1}^{n} y_i K_{h,i}^{\gamma-} - \frac{1}{n}\sum_{i=1}^{n} y_i K_{h,i}^{\gamma+}\right)^2 \tag{6}$$

where we have:

$$K_{h,i}^{\gamma+} = K_h(X_i - x_0)\cdot k_h^{+}(q_i - \gamma),$$

$$K_{h,i}^{\gamma-} = K_h(X_i - x_0)\cdot k_h^{-}(q_i - \gamma),$$

if q_i is not part of X_i, and

$$K_{h,i}^{\gamma+} = K_h(X_{1i} - x_{10}) \cdot k_h^{+}(q_i - \gamma),$$

$$K_{h,i}^{\gamma-} = K_h(X_{1i} - x_{10}) \cdot k_h^{-}(q_i - \gamma),$$

if q_i is part of X_i, i.e., $X_i = [X_{1i}', q_i]'$, and $x_0 = [x_{10}', q_0]'$. Furthermore, $k_h^{+/-}(\cdot)$ is the one-sided kernel function with:

$$k_h^{+}(q_i - \gamma) = k(\frac{q_i - \gamma}{h})I(q_i > \gamma),$$

$$k_h^{-}(q_i - \gamma) = k(\frac{q_i - \gamma}{h})I(q_i \leq \gamma),$$

and $k(\cdot)$ is a second order kernel function.

Obviously, it is reasonable to expect that the DKE estimator is sensitive to the choice of x_0. Furthermore, the DKE suffers the curse of dimensionality problem as the convergence rate of the DKE, nh^{d-1}, depends on the dimension of the regressor. To fix these potential weaknesses, Yu et al. (2018) proposed an integrated difference kernel estimator, which allows $\hat{\gamma}$ not to rely on the single choice in x_0, but the expectation of all X. The $\hat{\gamma}^{IDKE}$ can be derived as follows:

$$\hat{\gamma}^{IDKE} = arg \max_{\gamma \in \Theta_\gamma} n^{-1} \sum_{i=1}^{n} \left(\frac{1}{n-1} \sum_{j=1, j\neq i}^{n} y_j K_{h,ij}^{\gamma-} - \frac{1}{n-1} \sum_{j=1, j\neq i}^{n} y_j K_{h,ij}^{\gamma+} \right)^2, \tag{7}$$

where:

$$K_{h,ij}^{\gamma+} = K_h(X_i - x_j) \cdot k_h^{+}(q_i - \gamma),$$

$$K_{h,i}^{\gamma-} = K_h(X_i - x_j) \cdot k_h^{-}(q_i - \gamma),$$

if q_i is not part of X_i, and

$$K_{h,i}^{\gamma+} = K_h(X_{1i} - x_{1j}) \cdot k_h^{+}(q_i - \gamma),$$

$$K_{h,i}^{\gamma-} = K_h(X_{1i} - x_{1j}) \cdot k_h^{-}(q_i - \gamma),$$

if q_i is part of X_i, i.e., $X_i = [X_{1i}', q_i]'$, and $x_j = [x_{1j}', q_j]'$. $k_h^{+/-}(\cdot)$ is defined the same as above.

The IDKE is super-consistent with convergence rate n. The work in Yu et al. (2018) showed that IDKE is consistent even if the threshold variable is endogenous. They explain that the role of the instruments of the endogenous regressors and the endogenous threshold variable is improving only the efficiency of the IDKE.

3. Estimation Difficulties in the Difference Kernel-Type Estimator with Near Boundary γ_0

In this section, we use a simple version of Model (1) to explain the estimation difficulties of the difference kernel-type estimators when γ_0 lies at the tails of the threshold variable distribution. This estimation difficulty motivates us to investigate the position effect of the true threshold level on the finite sample performance. Specifically, we consider the true model as:

$$y_i = I(X_i \geq \gamma_0), \tag{8}$$

where X_i is randomly drawn from a uniform distribution over the interval of $[-0.5, 0.5]$ for $i = 1, ..., n$.

The model above can be regarded as Model (1) with $\alpha_0(x) \equiv 0$, $\beta_0 = 1$, and $\varepsilon_i = 0$ for all $i = 1, ..., n$. Therefore, the DKE is based on the objective function:

$$\hat{Q}_n(\gamma)^{DKE} = [\frac{1}{n} \sum_{i=0}^{n} k\left(\frac{X_i - \gamma}{h}\right) I(X_i < \gamma) y_i - \frac{1}{n} \sum_{i=0}^{n} k\left(\frac{X_i - \gamma}{h}\right) I(X_i \geq \gamma) y_i]^2. \tag{9}$$

Letting $u_x = (X_i - \gamma)/h$ and applying the change of variables, we have the probability limit of $\hat{Q}_n(\gamma)$ equal to:

$$Q_n(\gamma)^{DKE} = h^2[\int_{\frac{-0.5-\gamma}{h}}^{\frac{0.5-\gamma}{h}} k(u_x)I(u_x < 0)I\left(u_x \geq \tfrac{\gamma_0-\gamma}{h}\right)du_x - \int_{\frac{-0.5-\gamma}{h}}^{\frac{0.5-\gamma}{h}} k(u)I(u_x \geq 0)I\left(u_x \geq \tfrac{\gamma_0-\gamma}{h}\right)du_x]^2, \quad (10)$$

where h is the bandwidth.

If $\gamma < \gamma_0$, we obtain:

$$Q_n(\gamma)^{DKE} = h^2[\int_{\frac{-0.5-\gamma}{h}}^{\frac{0.5-\gamma}{h}} k(u_x)du_x]^2, \quad (11)$$

and:

$$\frac{\partial Q_n(\gamma)^{DKE}}{\partial\gamma} = 2h\left(\int_{\frac{\gamma_0-\gamma}{h}}^{\frac{0.5-\gamma}{h}} k(u_x)du_x\right)\left[k\left(\frac{\gamma_0-\gamma}{h}\right) - k\left(\frac{0.5-\gamma}{h}\right)\right] > 0, \quad (12)$$

where the positive sign follows for all $\gamma_0 < 0.5$ for any second-order kernel function with a bell shape.

It is worth noting that as γ_0 approaches 0.5 from the left side, the difference between $k(\frac{\gamma_0-\gamma}{h}) - k(\frac{0.5-\gamma}{h})$ becomes smaller. As a result, for all γ, the above derivative goes to zero, which makes the objective function flat and leads to the estimation difficulty.

Similarly, if $\gamma > \gamma_0$, we have:

$$Q_n(\gamma)^{DKE} = h^2\left(\int_{\frac{\gamma_0-\gamma}{h}}^{0} k(u_x)du_x - \int_0^{\frac{0.5-\gamma}{h}} k(u_x)du_x\right)^2, \quad (13)$$

and:

$$\frac{\partial Q_n(\gamma)^{DKE}}{\partial\gamma} = 2h\left(\int_{\frac{\gamma_0-\gamma}{h}}^{0} k(u_x)du_x - \int_0^{\frac{0.5-\gamma}{h}} k(u_x)du_x\right)\left[k\left(\frac{\gamma_0-\gamma}{h}\right) + k\left(\frac{0.5-\gamma}{h}\right)\right] < 0, \quad (14)$$

where the negative sign follows for all $\gamma_0 > -0.5$ for any second-order kernel function with a bell shape.

Therefore, we observe that as γ_0 approaches -0.5 from the right side, for all γ, the difference between $\int_{\frac{\gamma_0-\gamma}{h}}^{0} k(u_x)du_x - \int_0^{\frac{0.5-\gamma}{h}} k(u_x)du_x$ becomes smaller, which makes the derivative go to zero, and this results in a flat objective function.

In summary, the DKE is asymptotically consistent with $\gamma_0 \in (-0.5, 0.5)$. However, it is reasonable to suspect that DKE may have poor finite performance with the true threshold level lying at the tails of the threshold variable distribution due to the estimation difficulty of the flat objective function.

Next, we assume that there are additional covariates, Z_i, which are randomly drawn from uniform distribution over the interval of $[-0.5, 0.5]$, for all $i = 1, ..., n$, and $\{X_i\}$ and $\{Z_i\}$ are independent. Therefore, the probability limit of the objective function of the IDKE is (with the same bandwidth):

$$\begin{aligned} &Q_n(\gamma)^{IDKE} \\ = \; & h^4\int_{-0.5}^{0.5}\Bigg[\int_{\frac{-0.5-\gamma}{h}}^{\frac{0.5-\gamma}{h}} k(u_z)k(u_x)I(u_x < 0)I(u_x \geq \frac{\gamma_0-\gamma}{h})du_x du_z \\ & - \int_{\frac{-0.5-z_0}{h}}^{\frac{0.5-z_0}{h}}\int_{\frac{-0.5-\gamma}{h}}^{\frac{0.5-\gamma}{h}} k(u_z)k(u_x)I(u_x \geq 0)I(u_x \geq \frac{\gamma_0-\gamma}{h})du_x du_z\Bigg]^2 dz_0 \end{aligned} \quad (15)$$

where $u_z = \frac{Z_i - z_0}{h}$.

Note that:

$$\frac{\partial Q_n(\gamma)^{IDKE}}{\partial\gamma} = h^2\int_{-0.5}^{0.5}\left(\int_{\frac{-0.5-z_0}{h}}^{\frac{0.5-z_0}{h}} k(u_z)du_z\right)^2 dz_0 \frac{\partial Q_n(\gamma)^{DKE}}{\partial\gamma}. \quad (16)$$

Consequently, in this typical example, $\frac{\partial Q_n(\gamma)^{IDKE}}{\partial \gamma}$ can be interpreted as a rescaled $\frac{\partial Q_n(\gamma)^{DKE}}{\partial \gamma}$, which implies the IDKE will suffer the same boundary problem as the DKE estimator.

4. Monte Carlo Designs

To assess the finite sample performance of the three nonparametric threshold estimators, we consider seven data-generating mechanisms, which are similar to those studied in Henderson et al. (2017); Yu et al. (2018).

- DGP 1:
$$y_i = 2I(x_i \geq \gamma_0) + \varepsilon_i \tag{17}$$
- DGP 2:
$$y_i = x_i + 2I(x_i \geq \gamma_0) + \varepsilon_i \tag{18}$$
- DGP 3:
$$y_i = sin(x_i) + 2I(x_i \geq \gamma_0) + \varepsilon_i \tag{19}$$
- DGP 4:
$$y_i = x_i^2 + 2I(x_i \geq \gamma_0) + \varepsilon_i \tag{20}$$
- DGP 5:
$$y_i = x_{1i} + x_{2i} + x_{3i} + 2I(x_{1i} \geq \gamma_0) + \varepsilon_i \tag{21}$$
- DGP 6:
$$y_i = x_{1i}^2 + x_{2i}x_{3i} + 2I(x_{1i} \geq \gamma_0) + \varepsilon_i \tag{22}$$
- DGP 7:
$$y_i = sin(x_{1i}) + cos(x_{2i}) + sin(x_{3i}) + 2I(x_{1i} \geq \gamma_0) + \varepsilon_i \tag{23}$$

where x_i is randomly drawn from a uniform distribution over the interval of $[-0.5, 0.5]$ for all $i = 1, ..., n$,[1] and ε_i is randomly drawn from the $N(0,1)$ distribution. All DGPs are based on the fixed threshold effect framework of Chan (1993) with both the exogenous threshold variable and exogenous regressors.

DGPs 1–4 are univariate threshold models. More specifically, DGPs 1–2 are typical linear threshold models. DGPs 3–4 are nonlinear threshold models modelling the periodicity and the quadraticity, respectively. DGPs 5–7 are multivariate threshold models. DGP 5 characterizes the multivariate linear threshold model. DGPs 6–7 are nonlinear threshold models extending DGPs 3–4 to multivariate specifications.

To examine the position effect of the true threshold level on the finite sample performance, we set γ_0 at different segments of the threshold variable distribution. Specifically, we set the true threshold, γ_0, as the pth quantile of the threshold variable with $p = 25$, 50 and 75 to place the true threshold level to the left tail, middle and the right tail of the threshold variable distribution, respectively.

We set $x_0 = x^{max}$ for the DKE estimate of Delgado and Hidalgo (2000), where x^{max} is the data with the greatest empirical density among all generated x_i''s for each simulation of each DGP.[2] We use the rule of thumb bandwidth, $h = C\hat{\sigma}_x n^{-1/(d+4)}$, where $C = \frac{4}{d+2}^{\frac{1}{d+4}}$, d is the dimension of x_i and $\hat{\sigma}_x$ is the sample standard deviation of $\{x_i\}$. We use the Gaussian kernel function. As suggested by

[1] With the uniform distribution, the intensity of the Poisson process would not change with the change in the true threshold location. Therefore, the limiting distribution of both the DKE and the IDKE is not affected given γ_0 is not on the boundary of Θ_γ.

[2] The theoretical density should be the same for all x due to the uniform distribution. The reason we use the data-driven choice of x_0 is because we do not know the true density in reality.

Yu et al. (2018), we use the one-sided rescaled Epanechnikov kernel with $k^{-}(q,0) = \frac{3}{4}(1-q^2)I(q<0)$ and $k^{+}(q,0) = k^{-}(-q,0)$ to estimate the DKE and the IDKE.

We repeat 2000 times for each simulation.[3] We set the sample size n = 100, 300 and 500. For each simulation, we report the average bias, mean squared error (or MSE) and the standard deviation (or stdev) of the threshold estimates. Tables 1–7 contain the details of the simulation results. Table 8 shows the realized convergence rate of the semi-parametric M-estimator of Henderson et al. (2017) and IDKE of Yu et al. (2018).

Table 1. Simulation results of nonparametric threshold estimators, Data-generating Mechanism 1 (DGP 1). IDKE, integrated difference kernel estimator.

γ_0 Is the 25th Quantile of the Threshold Variable									
		Bias			**MSE**			**Stdev**	
n	**Semi-M**	**DKE**	**IDKE**	**Semi-M**	**DKE**	**IDKE**	**Semi-M**	**DKE**	**IDKE**
100	0.0336	0.2705	0.0679	0.0144	0.0913	0.0225	0.1152	0.1345	0.1338
300	0.0015	0.2929	0.0870	0.0006	0.0986	0.0308	0.0241	0.1133	0.1525
500	0.0002	0.2632	0.1530	0.0001	0.0920	0.0544	0.0097	0.1509	0.1760
γ_0 Is the 50th Quantile of the Threshold Variable									
		Bias			**MSE**			**Stdev**	
n	**Semi-M**	**DKE**	**IDKE**	**Semi-M**	**DKE**	**IDKE**	**Semi-M**	**DKE**	**IDKE**
100	0.0056	−0.0346	−0.0183	0.0084	0.0154	0.0012	0.0916	0.1191	0.0288
300	0.0007	−0.0346	−0.0083	0.0009	0.0209	0.0002	0.0302	0.1406	0.0126
500	0.0008	−0.0347	−0.0055	0.0003	0.0233	0.0001	0.0166	0.1488	0.0080
γ_0 Is the 75th Quantile of the Threshold Variable									
		Bias			**MSE**			**Stdev**	
n	**Semi-M**	**DKE**	**IDKE**	**Semi-M**	**DKE**	**IDKE**	**Semi-M**	**DKE**	**IDKE**
100	−0.0397	−0.2485	−0.0666	0.0163	0.1082	0.0087	0.1215	0.2156	0.0650
300	−0.0028	−0.2590	−0.0377	0.0009	0.1143	0.0029	0.0299	0.2174	0.0391
500	−0.0004	−0.2841	−0.0287	0.0001	0.1288	0.0018	0.0118	0.2193	0.0308

This table reports the simulation results of three estimators, the semiparametric M-estimator of Henderson et al. (2017), the DKE of Delgado and Hidalgo (2000) and the IDKE of Yu et al. (2018) for the simple jump function defined as Equation (17). The first column gives the sample size that the simulation used. The third to fifth columns report the average bias. The sixth to eighth columns give the mean squared errors of the threshold estimates. The last three columns present the standard deviations.

Table 2. Simulation results of nonparametric threshold estimators, DGP 2.

γ_0 Is the 25th Quantile of the Threshold Variable									
		Bias			**MSE**			**Stdev**	
n	**Semi-M**	**DKE**	**IDKE**	**Semi-M**	**DKE**	**IDKE**	**Semi-M**	**DKE**	**IDKE**
100	0.0359	0.2272	0.0813	0.0154	0.0823	0.0250	0.1190	0.1752	0.1357
300	0.0053	0.2680	0.1019	0.0020	0.0954	0.0324	0.0442	0.1536	0.1485
500	0.0002	0.2632	0.1530	0.0001	0.0920	0.0544	0.0097	0.1509	0.1760

[3] All programming is finished in Matlab.

Table 2. *Cont.*

γ_0 Is the 50th Quantile of the Threshold Variable									
		Bias			MSE			Stdev	
n	Semi-M	DKE	IDKE	Semi-M	DKE	IDKE	Semi-M	DKE	IDKE
100	−0.0008	−0.0246	−0.0151	0.0082	0.0122	0.0009	0.0907	0.1077	0.0257
300	0.0002	−0.0147	−0.0067	0.0009	0.0130	0.0002	0.0306	0.1130	0.0107
500	0.0002	−0.0131	−0.0044	0.0000	0.0154	0.0001	0.0068	0.1233	0.0073
γ_0 Is the 75th Quantile of the Threshold Variable									
		Bias			MSE			Stdev	
n	Semi-M	DKE	IDKE	Semi-M	DKE	IDKE	Semi-M	DKE	IDKE
100	−0.0307	−0.2465	−0.1031	0.0119	0.1049	0.0159	0.1048	0.2101	0.0730
300	−0.0059	−0.2564	−0.0786	0.0023	0.1009	0.0086	0.0477	0.1876	0.0494
500	−0.0008	−0.2651	−0.0699	0.0003	0.1060	0.0065	0.0177	0.1891	0.0397

This table reports the simulation results of three estimators, the semiparametric M-estimator of Henderson et al. (2017), the DKE of Delgado and Hidalgo (2000) and the IDKE of Yu et al. (2018) for the univariate linear threshold model defined as Equation (18). The first column gives the sample size that the simulation used. The third to fifth columns report the average bias. The sixth to eighth columns give the mean squared errors of the threshold estimates. The last three columns present the standard deviations.

Table 3. Simulation results of nonparametric threshold estimators, DGP 3.

γ_0 Is the 25th Quantile of the Threshold Variable									
		Bias			MSE			Stdev	
n	Semi-M	DKE	IDKE	Semi-M	DKE	IDKE	Semi-M	DKE	IDKE
100	0.0303	0.2211	0.0785	0.0128	0.0791	0.0233	0.1092	0.1739	0.1310
300	0.0022	0.2725	0.1137	0.0014	0.0980	0.0373	0.0376	0.1541	0.1561
500	0.0005	0.2694	0.1570	0.0002	0.0961	0.0546	0.0131	0.1535	0.1730
γ_0 Is the 50th Quantile of the Threshold Variable									
		Bias			MSE			Stdev	
n	Semi-M	DKE	IDKE	Semi-M	DKE	IDKE	Semi-M	DKE	IDKE
100	0.0017	−0.0236	−0.0137	0.0073	0.0111	0.0008	0.0852	0.1027	0.0257
300	0.0002	−0.0220	−0.0061	0.0004	0.0132	0.0001	0.0196	0.1128	0.0101
500	−0.0003	−0.0114	−0.0041	0.0001	0.0149	0.0001	0.0112	0.1215	0.0067
γ_0 Is the 75th Quantile of the Threshold Variable									
		Bias			MSE			Stdev	
n	Semi-M	DKE	IDKE	Semi-M	DKE	IDKE	Semi-M	DKE	IDKE
100	−0.0358	−0.2471	−0.1036	0.0160	0.1031	0.0160	0.1212	0.2051	0.0725
300	−0.0027	−0.2592	−0.0822	0.0013	0.1041	0.0091	0.0360	0.1924	0.0482
500	−0.0007	−0.2637	−0.0686	0.0004	0.1031	0.0065	0.0203	0.1832	0.0422

This table reports the simulation results of three estimators, the semiparametric M-estimator of Henderson et al. (2017), the DKE of Delgado and Hidalgo (2000) and the IDKE of Yu et al. (2018) for the univariate threshold periodic model defined as Equation (19). The first column gives the sample size that the simulation used. The third to fifth report propose the average bias. The sixth to eighth columns give the mean squared errors of the threshold estimates. The last three columns present the standard deviations.

Table 4. Simulation results of nonparametric threshold estimators, DGP 4.

	γ_0 Is the 25th Quantile of the Threshold Variable								
		Bias			**MSE**			**Stdev**	
n	**Semi-M**	**DKE**	**IDKE**	**Semi-M**	**DKE**	**IDKE**	**Semi-M**	**DKE**	**IDKE**
100	0.0371	0.2754	0.1038	0.0168	0.0922	0.0348	0.1242	0.1278	0.1551
300	0.0065	0.2817	0.1479	0.0030	0.0921	0.0526	0.0545	0.1131	0.1754
500	0.0010	0.2884	0.2146	0.0005	0.0974	0.0794	0.0221	0.1196	0.1826
	γ_0 Is the 50th Quantile of the Threshold Variable								
		Bias			**MSE**			**Stdev**	
n	**Semi-M**	**DKE**	**IDKE**	**Semi-M**	**DKE**	**IDKE**	**Semi-M**	**DKE**	**IDKE**
100	0.0050	−0.0324	−0.0173	0.0086	0.0156	0.0016	0.0930	0.1205	0.0355
300	−0.0010	−0.0408	−0.0071	0.0012	0.0212	0.0002	0.0341	0.1400	0.0135
500	0.0000	−0.0340	−0.0051	0.0000	0.0222	0.0001	0.0038	0.1451	0.0086
	γ_0 Is the 75th Quantile of the Threshold Variable								
		Bias			**MSE**			**Stdev**	
n	**Semi-M**	**DKE**	**IDKE**	**Semi-M**	**DKE**	**IDKE**	**Semi-M**	**DKE**	**IDKE**
100	−0.0378	−0.2562	−0.0694	0.0157	0.1105	0.0089	0.1196	0.2120	0.0640
300	−0.0025	−0.2622	−0.0445	0.0007	0.1131	0.0037	0.0266	0.2107	0.0411
500	−0.0007	−0.2709	−0.0358	0.0004	0.1162	0.0024	0.0203	0.2070	0.0334

This table reports the simulation results of three estimators, the semiparametric M-estimator of Henderson et al. (2017), the DKE of Delgado and Hidalgo (2000) and the IDKE of Yu et al. (2018) for the univariate threshold quadratic model defined as Equation (20). The first column gives the sample size that the simulation used. The third to fifth report propose the average bias. The sixth to eighth columns give the mean squared errors of the threshold estimates. The last three columns present the standard deviations.

Table 5. Simulation results of nonparametric threshold estimators, DGP 5.

	γ_0 Is the 25th Quantile of the Threshold Variable								
		Bias			**MSE**			**Stdev**	
n	**Semi-M**	**DKE**	**IDKE**	**Semi-M**	**DKE**	**IDKE**	**Semi-M**	**DKE**	**IDKE**
100	0.0141	0.2560	0.0751	0.0060	0.1005	0.0213	0.0762	0.1871	0.1253
300	0.0005	0.2587	0.0421	0.0006	0.0970	0.0104	0.0253	0.1733	0.0931
500	0.0000	0.2696	0.0333	0.0000	0.0977	0.0085	0.0038	0.1583	0.0862
	γ_0 Is the 50th Quantile of the Threshold Variable								
		Bias			**MSE**			**Stdev**	
n	**Semi-M**	**DKE**	**IDKE**	**Semi-M**	**DKE**	**IDKE**	**Semi-M**	**DKE**	**IDKE**
100	−0.0035	−0.0232	−0.0167	0.0050	0.0248	0.0014	0.0710	0.1559	0.0335
300	0.0000	−0.0176	−0.0082	0.0001	0.0205	0.0003	0.0118	0.1420	0.0136
500	0.0001	−0.0330	−0.0057	0.0000	0.0222	0.0001	0.0041	0.1452	0.0106

Table 5. *Cont.*

γ_0 Is the 75th Quantile of the Threshold Variable									
		Bias			**MSE**			**Stdev**	
n	**Semi-M**	**DKE**	**IDKE**	**Semi-M**	**DKE**	**IDKE**	**Semi-M**	**DKE**	**IDKE**
100	−0.0203	−0.2778	−0.1173	0.0085	0.1239	0.0212	0.0900	0.2161	0.0864
300	−0.0007	−0.2878	−0.0958	0.0002	0.1256	0.0133	0.0154	0.2069	0.0639
500	0.0000	−0.2883	−0.0944	0.0000	0.1253	0.0119	0.0035	0.2056	0.0544

This table reports the simulation results of three estimators, the semiparametric M-estimator of Henderson et al. (2017), the DKE of Delgado and Hidalgo (2000) and the IDKE of Yu et al. (2018) for the multivariate linear threshold model defined as Equation (21). The first column gives the sample size that the simulation used. The third to fifth report propose the average bias. The sixth to eighth columns give the mean squared errors of the threshold estimates. The last three columns present the standard deviations.

Table 6. Simulation results of nonparametric threshold estimators, DGP 6.

γ_0 Is the 25th Quantile of the Threshold Variable									
		Bias			**MSE**			**Stdev**	
n	**Semi-M**	**DKE**	**IDKE**	**Semi-M**	**DKE**	**IDKE**	**Semi-M**	**DKE**	**IDKE**
100	0.0197	0.2495	0.0704	0.0082	0.0972	0.0188	0.0882	0.1871	0.1177
300	0.0002	0.2652	0.0364	0.0001	0.0997	0.0094	0.0114	0.1714	0.0898
500	0.0000	0.2738	0.0297	0.0000	0.1003	0.0074	0.0032	0.1594	0.0807
γ_0 **Is the 50th Quantile of the Threshold Variable**									
		Bias			**MSE**			**Stdev**	
n	**Semi-M**	**DKE**	**IDKE**	**Semi-M**	**DKE**	**IDKE**	**Semi-M**	**DKE**	**IDKE**
100	0.0019	−0.0107	−0.0158	0.0051	0.0242	0.0013	0.0711	0.1553	0.0323
300	−0.0004	−0.0251	−0.0074	0.0002	0.0216	0.0002	0.0138	0.1450	0.0125
500	0.0001	−0.0280	−0.0054	0.0000	0.0210	0.0001	0.0036	0.1422	0.0094
γ_0 **Is the 75th Quantile of the Threshold Variable**									
		Bias			**MSE**			**Stdev**	
n	**Semi-M**	**DKE**	**IDKE**	**Semi-M**	**DKE**	**IDKE**	**Semi-M**	**DKE**	**IDKE**
100	−0.0184	−0.2709	−0.1164	0.0082	0.1177	0.0207	0.0886	0.2105	0.0846
300	−0.0007	−0.2717	−0.0975	0.0004	0.1157	0.0131	0.0194	0.2048	0.0600
500	0.0002	−0.2647	−0.0889	0.0000	0.1080	0.0104	0.0042	0.1949	0.0497

This table reports the simulation results of three estimators, the semiparametric M-estimator of Henderson et al. (2017), the DKE of Delgado and Hidalgo (2000) and the IDKE of Yu et al. (2018) for the multivariate threshold quadratic model defined as Equation (22). The first column gives the sample size that the simulation used. The third to fifth columns report the average bias. The sixth to eighth columns give the mean squared errors of the threshold estimates. The last three columns present the standard deviations.

Table 7. Simulation results of nonparametric threshold estimators, DGP 7.

γ_0 Is the 25th Quantile of the Threshold Variable									
	Bias			**MSE**			**Stdev**		
n	**Semi-M**	**DKE**	**IDKE**	**Semi-M**	**DKE**	**IDKE**	**Semi-M**	**DKE**	**IDKE**
100	0.0207	0.2936	0.1292	0.0097	0.1086	0.0419	0.0964	0.1498	0.1588
300	0.0005	0.2915	0.1275	0.0003	0.1031	0.0393	0.0168	0.1347	0.1517
500	0.0003	0.2947	0.1378	0.0001	0.1048	0.0427	0.0105	0.1341	0.1542
γ_0 Is the 50th Quantile of the Threshold Variable									
	Bias			**MSE**			**Stdev**		
n	**Semi-M**	**DKE**	**IDKE**	**Semi-M**	**DKE**	**IDKE**	**Semi-M**	**DKE**	**IDKE**
100	−0.0034	0.0004	−0.0373	0.0051	0.0265	0.0074	0.0716	0.1630	0.0778
300	0.0013	0.0049	−0.0366	0.0003	0.0229	0.0029	0.0178	0.1514	0.0398
500	0.0003	0.0077	−0.0315	0.0001	0.0180	0.0019	0.0081	0.1339	0.0294
γ_0 Is the 75th Quantile of the Threshold Variable									
	Bias			**MSE**			**Stdev**		
n	**Semi-M**	**DKE**	**IDKE**	**Semi-M**	**DKE**	**IDKE**	**Semi-M**	**DKE**	**IDKE**
100	−0.0244	−0.2830	−0.2242	0.0106	0.1137	0.0575	0.0998	0.1834	0.0849
300	0.0000	−0.2798	−0.2068	0.0001	0.1074	0.0457	0.0084	0.1708	0.0539
500	0.0000	−0.2823	−0.1963	0.0000	0.1039	0.0403	0.0036	0.1558	0.0424

This table reports the simulation results of three estimators, the semiparametric M-estimator of Henderson et al. (2017), the DKE of Delgado and Hidalgo (2000) and the IDKE of Yu et al. (2018) for the multivariate threshold periodic model defined as Equation (23). The first column gives the sample size that the simulation used. The third to fifth columns report the average bias. The sixth to eighth columns give the mean squared errors of the threshold estimates. The last three columns present the standard deviations.

Table 8. Estimated convergence rate of the nonparametric threshold estimators.

Semiparametric M-Estimator of Henderson et al. (2017)							
	DGP 1	**DGP 2**	**DGP 3**	**DGP 4**	**DGP 5**	**DGP 6**	**DGP 7**
$p = 25$	−1.235	−1.202	−1.209	−1.280	−1.224	−1.347	−1.307
$p = 50$	−1.162	−1.195	−1.171	−1.234	−1.349	−1.335	−1.347
$p = 75$	−1.215	−1.251	−1.203	−1.205	−1.227	−1.234	−1.331
IDKE of Yu et al. (2018)							
	DGP 1	**DGP 2**	**DGP 3**	**DGP 4**	**DGP 5**	**DGP 6**	**DGP 7**
$p = 25$	−2.207	−2.126	−2.164	−2.541	−1.556	−1.436	−2.557
$p = 50$	−1.352	−1.287	−1.305	−1.335	−1.428	−1.348	−1.982
$p = 75$	−1.758	−1.949	−1.966	−1.757	−1.876	−2.115	−2.626

This table reports the realized convergence rates of the semiparametric M-estimator of Henderson et al. (2017) and the IDKE of Yu et al. (2018). The realized convergence rates are shown as the coefficient estimate by regressing the logarithm of $RMSE$ on the logarithm of the sample size for each DGP. Samples sizes used are $n = 100, 200, 300, 400, 500, 600$ and 700.

5. Monte Carlo Results

For the semi-parametric M-estimator introduced by Henderson et al. (2017), our results show that the performance was slightly affected by the position of the true threshold level. Meanwhile, as the sample size increased, this position effect gradually vanished.[4] In addition, we observed that the bias was smaller for multivariate models than univariate models. Using the bandwidth as defined in Section 4, which behaved roughly as $O(n^{-1/5})$ for univariate models and $O(n^{-1/7})$ for multivariate models, the theoretical convergence rates were $O(n^{-1.2})$ and $O(n^{-1.14})$ accordingly. From Table 8, the super-consistency was confirmed with the estimated convergence rate of $\hat{\gamma}$. Consistent with the theory, the realized convergence rate decreased as the dimension increased. It is quite interesting that, for almost all univariate models, the realized convergence rate of $\hat{\gamma}$ was faster when γ_0 was at the left- and right-tail position than when γ_0 was at the median position. However, for multivariate models, the realized rates seemed to be stable with the position of γ_0.

For the DKE, as we conjectured, it was severely affected by the position of the true threshold value for all DGPs, which may result from the estimation difficulties, as we argued in Section 3. Furthermore, even with the middle-positioned γ_0, the bias still showed a non-decreasing pattern with the increasing sample size under some multivariate specifications.[5] Intuitively, this may result from the choice of x_0, which distorts the result by providing useless information. According to the comment in the Supplementary Material of Yu et al. (2018), the choice of x_0 is crucial in identifying the DKE estimator. On the one hand, the optimal x_0 should make $[E(y|x_0, q = \gamma_0^-) - E(y|x_0, q = \gamma_0^+)]^2$ as large as possible. On the other hand, one needs the conditional density $f(x_0|q = \gamma_0)$ to be large enough to provide sufficient information. Therefore, theoretically, with a uniform distribution and univariate linear threshold model as in DGP2, the ideal x_0 should be at the middle of its distribution with the value of zero. However, in the simulation, we set x_0 equal to the value with the largest empirical density, which may appear at the two tails. This may lead to $[E(y|x_0, q = \gamma_0^-) - E(y|x_0, q = \gamma_0^+)]^2$ approaching zero. Moreover, with the multivariate and nonlinear specification, we can expect more distortion involved. As a result, the DKE performs the worst among all three competitors for all DGPs.

For the IDKE, our results reveal several features. Firstly, the IDKE was affected by the position of the actual threshold value. The influence was not as substantial as the DKE. Indeed, the integration allowed more local information to be used and alleviated the possible distortion due to the choice of x_0. Surprisingly, unlike the DKE, this position effect seemed to be asymmetric for the IDKE. For most of the DGPs, we observed that the absolute value of the average bias and MSE was larger with the left-tailed γ_0 than the right-tailed γ_0. The theoretical convergence rate of the IDKE estimator, n, is not related to either the bandwidth or the dimension, which is faster than the semi-parametric M-estimator of Henderson et al. (2017). This is consistent with our realized convergence rates, which are shown in Table 8. Moreover, for all DGPs, the realized convergence rates were faster with two-sided tailed γ_0 than the median γ_0.

In summary, the simulation results give some evidence that the finite sample performances were affected by the position of the true threshold level for all three nonparametric threshold estimators. However, this effect was heterogeneous. The position effect least influenced the semi-M estimator of Henderson et al. (2017). Meanwhile, the difference kernel-type estimators were severely distorted by the tailed γ_0, which confirms our conjecture made in Section 3. Furthermore, our results show that the position of the true threshold level also affects the realized convergence rate. We also found, for the semi-M estimator of Henderson et al. (2017) and the IDKE estimator, the tail distortion tended to be reduced in multivariate models.

As a robustness check of our findings, Figures 1–4 show the simulation results of DGP 2 and DGP 5 with γ_0 taking different positions along the threshold variable distribution. It is obvious that, for all figures, semi-M had lower average bias in absolute value than difference kernel-type estimators with tail γ_0. Furthermore, we found the gap between the average bias of the semi-M estimator and the

4 With n = 100, the bias, MSE and standard deviation were larger with γ_0 placed at two tails and γ_0 placed at the median point. However, with n = 500, there was no apparent difference between tail position γ_0 estimation and the median position γ_0 estimation.

5 For example, in Table 6, the bias monotonically increases with the in sample size.

average bias of the difference kernel-type estimators to drop greatly with γ_0 approaching the middle position of the threshold variable distribution.

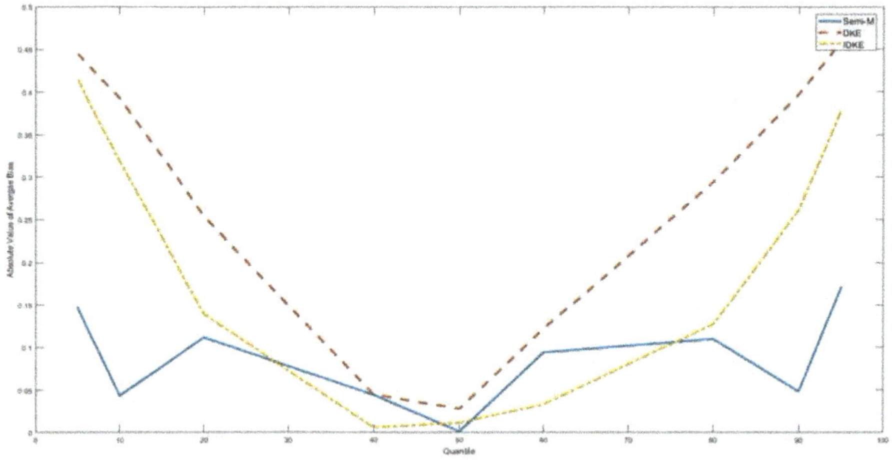

Figure 1. Average bias with γ_0 as various quantiles of the threshold variable, DGP 2, $n = 100$. This figure shows absolute values of the average bias with the true threshold level being several quantiles of the threshold variable (5th, 10th, 20th, 40th, 50th, 60th, 80th, 90th, 95th). The simulation is based on DGP 2. The sample size is 100.

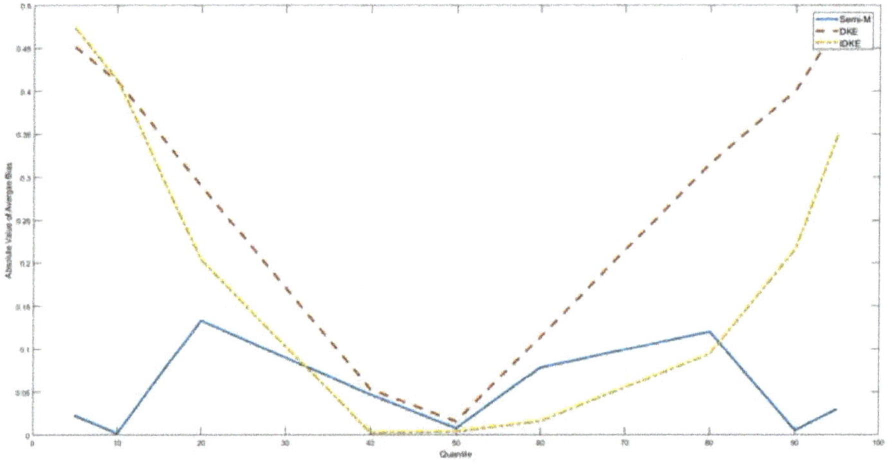

Figure 2. Average bias with γ_0 as various quantiles of the threshold variable, DGP 2, $n = 300$. This figure shows absolute values of the average bias with the true threshold level being several quantiles of the threshold variable (5th, 10th, 20th, 40th, 50th, 60th, 80th, 90th, 95th). The simulation is based on DGP 2. The sample size is 300.

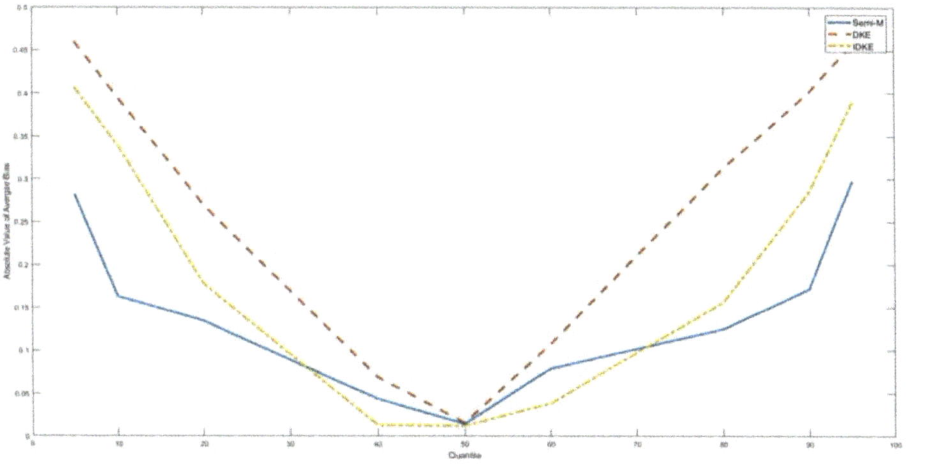

Figure 3. Average bias with γ_0 as various quantiles of the threshold variable, DGP 5, $n = 100$. This figure shows absolute values of the average bias with the true threshold level being several quantiles of the threshold variable (5th, 10th, 20th, 40th, 50th, 60th, 80th, 90th, 95th). The simulation is based on DGP 5. The sample size is 100.

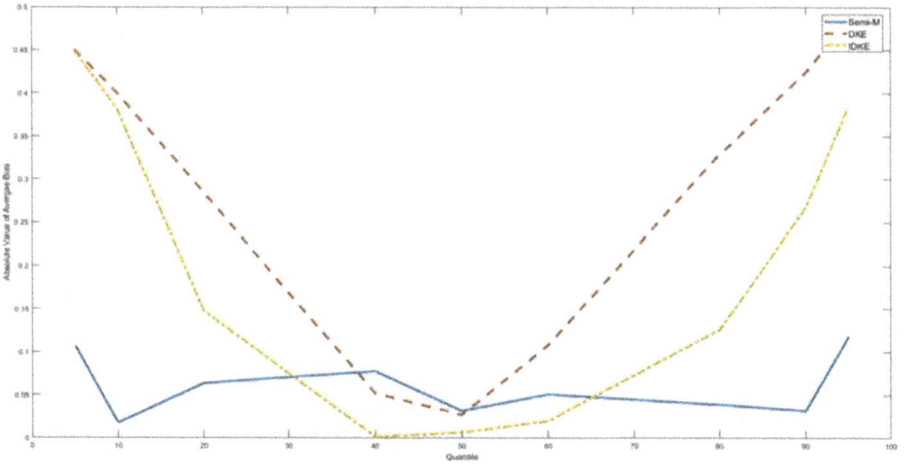

Figure 4. Average bias with γ_0 as various quantiles of the threshold variable, DGP 5, $n = 300$. This figure shows absolute values of the average bias with the true threshold level being several quantiles of the threshold variable (5th, 10th, 20th, 40th, 50th, 60th, 80th, 90th, 95th). The simulation is based on DGP 5. The sample size is 300.

6. Conclusions

In this paper, we evaluated the finite sample performance of three non-parametric threshold estimators and identified the relationship between the performances of different estimators and the position of the true threshold level with Monte Carlo methods.

The study shows, with all three estimators affected by the tail position of the true threshold value, that the semi-M estimator of Henderson et al. (2017) outperformed DKE and IDKE for roughly all DGPs considered in the paper. Interestingly, there appears to be some evidence that the distortion can be reduced if there are other covariates besides the threshold variable for the semi-M estimator and the IDKE. Consistent with the theory, we find that the realized convergence rates support the super-consistency in the threshold estimate for all three estimators. However, we find that the realized convergence rates are also affected by the position of the true threshold value. We therefore conclude that, in applied works, using the difference kernel-type estimation, researchers must be careful when the threshold estimate is at the left-tail or the right-tail of the threshold variable distribution.

Author Contributions: The two authors both contribute to the project formulation and paper preparation.

Funding: This research received no external funding.

Acknowledgments: We thank three anonymous referees for their helpful and constructive comments.

Conflicts of Interest: The authors declare no conflict of interest.

References

Afonso, Antonio, and Joao Tovar Jalles. 2013. Growth and productivity: The role of government debt. *International Review of Economics and Finance* 25: 384–407. [CrossRef]

Caner, Mehmet, and Bruce Hansen. 2004. Instrumental variable estimation of a threshold model. *Econometric Theory* 20: 813–43. [CrossRef]

Caner, Mehmet, Thomas J. Grennes, and Friederike N. Koehler-Geib. 2010. *Finding the Tipping Point—When Sovereign Debt Turns Bad*. Policy Research WP, No. 5391. New Delhi: Policy Research, pp. 1–13.

Cecchetti, Stephen G., Madhusudan Mohanty, and Fabrizio Zampolli. 2011. The Real Effects of Debt. Working paper, Bank for International Settlements, Basel, Switzerland.

Chan, Kung-Sik. 1993. Consistency and Limiting Distribution of the Least Squares Estimator of a Threshold Autoregressive Model. *Annals of Statistics* 21: 520–33. [CrossRef]

Delgado, Miguel A., and Javier Hidalgo. 2000. Nonparametric inference on structural breaks. *Journal of Econometrics* 96: 113–44. [CrossRef]

Hansen, Bruce E. 2000. Sample splitting and threshold estimation. *Econometrica* 68: 575–603. [CrossRef]

Hansen, Bruce E. 2011. Threshold Autoregression in Economics. *Statistics and Its Interface* 4: 123–27. [CrossRef]

Heckman, James J. 1979. Sample Selection Bias as a Specification Error. *Econometrica* 47: 153–61. [CrossRef]

Henderson, Daniel J., Christopher F. Parmeter, and Liangjun Su. 2017. Nonparametric Threshold Regression: Estimation and Inference. Working paper, Research Collection School of Economics, Singapore.

Kourtellos, Andros, Thanasis Stengos, and Chih Ming Tan. 2016. Structural Threshold Regression. *Econometric Theory* 32: 827–60. [CrossRef]

Kourtellos, Andros, Thanasis Stengos, and Yiguo Sun. 2017. Endogeneity in Semiparametric Threshold Regression. Working paper, University of Cyprus and University of Guelph, Guelph, ON, Canada.

Potter, Simon M. 1995. A Nonlinear Approach to US GNP. *Journal of Applied Econometrics* 10: 109–25. [CrossRef]

Seo, Myung Hwan, and Oliver Linton. 2007. A smoothed least squares estimator for threshold regression models. *Journal of Econometrics* 141: 704–35. [CrossRef]

Seo, Myung Hwan, and Yongcheol Shin. 2016. Dynamic Panels with Threshold Effect and Endogeneity. *Journal of Econometrics* 195: 169–86. [CrossRef]

Yu, Ping, and Peter C. B. Phillips. 2018. Threshold Regression with Endogeneity. *Journal of Econometrics* 203: 50–68. [CrossRef]

Journal of
Risk and Financial Management

MDPI

Article

Risk, Return and Volatility Feedback: A Bayesian Nonparametric Analysis

Mark J. Jensen [1] **and John M. Maheu** [2,*]

1 Federal Reserve Bank of Atlanta, 1000 Peachtree St NE, Atlanta, GA 30309, USA; Mark.Jensen@atl.frb.org
2 DeGroote School of Business, McMaster University, 1280 Main Street W., Hamilton, ON L8S4M4, Canada
* Correspondence: maheujm@mcmaster.ca

Received: 27 July 2018; Accepted: 1 September 2018; Published: 5 September 2018

Abstract: In this paper, we let the data speak for itself about the existence of volatility feedback and the often debated risk–return relationship. We do this by modeling the contemporaneous relationship between market excess returns and log-realized variances with a nonparametric, infinitely-ordered, mixture representation of the observables' joint distribution. Our nonparametric estimator allows for deviation from conditional Gaussianity through non-zero, higher ordered, moments, like asymmetric, fat-tailed behavior, along with smooth, nonlinear, risk–return relationships. We use the parsimonious and relatively uninformative Bayesian Dirichlet process prior to overcoming the problem of having too many unknowns and not enough observations. Applying our Bayesian nonparametric model to more than a century's worth of monthly US stock market returns and realized variances, we find strong, robust evidence of volatility feedback. Once volatility feedback is accounted for, we find an unambiguous positive, nonlinear, relationship between expected excess returns and expected log-realized variance. In addition to the conditional mean, volatility feedback impacts the entire joint distribution.

Keywords: dependent Bayesian nonparametrics; Dirichlet process prior; slice sampling

JEL Classification: C11; C14; C32; G12

1. Introduction

In this paper, we investigate the risk–return relationship, along with the impact of volatility feedback, by estimating a Bayesian nonparametric model of the joint distribution of market excess returns and realized variance. In contrast to the existing risk–return literature where the conditional mean of excess stock market returns is modeled as a linear relationship with the conditional volatility, we allow the observed monthly returns and realized variances calculated from daily returns to determine the relationship between the conditional mean of excess returns and the contemporaneous log-realized variance.[1] Distinguishing between lagged and contemporaneous relationships has implications for the risk–return relationship which can be indirectly derived from the contemporaneous model.

Past risk–return research finds conflicting evidence on the direction and level of significance a change in a GARCH model's conditional variance can have on the conditional mean return.[2] Recent results on risk and return has helped to resolve some of these conflicts. Scruggs (1998) and

---

1 Ludvigson and Ng (2007) also utilize realized variance as a measure of conditional volatility. As we will show using realized variance provides additional flexibility in modeling the joint distribution and provides a better signal on volatility by using daily data to estimate monthly ex post variance.
2 A good summary of this research is found in Lettau and Ludvigson (2010).

Guo and Whitelaw (2006) show that additional predetermined conditional variables can affect the sign and significance of risk. Lundblad (2007) argues that longer samples are necessary in order to find a significant relationship between the market risk premium and expected volatility with GARCH specifications. Bandi and Perron (2008) document a long-run relationship between expected excess market returns and past market variance, while Maheu and McCurdy (2007) find the long-run component of realized variance is priced in annual data. Recently, Ghysels et al. (2013) established a positive risk and return relationship over sample periods that excluded financial crises.[3]

Most of the research on risk–return assumes excess returns are conditionally normally distributed. Harvey (2001) argues one should dispense with the parametric assumptions around the conditional expectations given the contemporaneous log realized variance that normality assumes. Gaussianity also ignores the potential role higher order moments like skewness and leptokurtosis play in the predictability of returns (see Campbell and Hentschel 1992). Using daily data, Maheu et al. (2013) find the conditional variance and conditional skewness, due to jumps in returns, is significantly priced. Hence, ignoring the higher ordered moments for excess returns may confound the evidence of a positive risk and return relation.

In this paper, we relax the normality assumption and let the data determine the joint distribution between excess returns and volatility.[4] This borrows from the parametric approach of Brandt and Kang (2004) by jointly modeling the distribution of returns and log-volatility but now nonparametrically. A nonparametric estimate of the joint distribution also allows us to study the risk–return relationship from a flexible uninformed standpoint and to avoid having to address those issues pointed out by Scruggs (1998) and Guo and Whitelaw (2006) over which predetermined conditioning variables to include.

Our nonparametric estimator is an extension of the Bayesian Dirichlet process mixture (DPM) model (see Lo (1984)). Most DPM models consist of an infinite mixture of normal distributions whose means, covariances, and mixture probabilities are estimated by applying the relatively uninformative Dirichlet process (DP) prior to the infinite number of unknowns (see Ferguson (1973)). Being almost surely a discrete distribution, the DP prior essentially shrinks the number of unknowns down to just a few important mixture clusters, thus enabling us to overcome the common nonparametric problem of having more unknowns than observations. For conditional distributions, which govern the risk–return relationship, the DPM is an infinite mixture of conditional normals but whose mixture probabilities, means and variances all depend on the value of the conditioning variables (see Muller et al. (1996) and Taddy and Kottas (2010)). The DPM representation and estimation of the conditional distribution allows for a more flexible relationship between the conditional mean of excess returns and contemporaneous realized variance than is possible under Gaussianity.

Because of its straightforward nature and good empirical performance, the DPM approach has become the gold standard for Bayesian nonparametric estimation of unknown distributions.[5] For investigating the risk–return relationship, we extend the DPM by assuming the means of the infinite mixture of normals depend on intertemporal variables. Rather than modelling the joint distribution of excess returns and log realized variances as a mixture over the unconditional bivariate mean vectors, we include contemporaneous and lagged excess returns and log realized variances in the means and mix over each covariates coefficient. By including contemporaneous and lagged variables in the mixture, our bivariate DPM model is a semi-nonparametric estimator since it accounts for structural economic relationships like volatility feedback and known empirical regularities like persistence in volatility, while not imposing any fixed parametric relationship over the risk premium or volatility

---

3 Ghysels et al. (2013) updates the results in Ghysels et al. (2005) which had a coding error.

4 Harrison and Zhang (1999) also relaxes the normality assumption by applying Gallant and Tauchen (1989) semi-nonparametric estimator but only to the conditional distribution of excess returns.

5 For example, see Chib and Hamilton (2002); Burda et al. (2008); Conley et al. (2008); Delatola and Griffin (2013); Griffin and Steel (2004); and Chib and Greenberg (2010); Jensen and Maheu (2010, 2013, 2014) for recent applications of the DPM model.

feedback. We design a Markov chain Monte Carlo (MCMC) algorithm that uses the slice sampler methodology of Walker (2007) to deliver posterior draws of the unknowns from which estimates are obtained that account for uncertainty in the risk–return trade-off and volatility effect through the unknown joint distribution.

Volatility feedback is the causal relationship between the variance and price changes and can be an important source of asymmetry in returns. Campbell and Hentschel (1992) show that volatility feedback plays an important role in finding a positive risk and return relationship. They find a positive relationship with a model derived from economic restrictions that linearly relate log-returns to log-prices and log-dividends.[6]

Our nonparametric approach differs in several important ways from the existing volatility feedback literature. First, while almost all the literature has studied volatility feedback from a tightly parameterized model, we use a flexible approach with no economic restrictions. Second, we use realized variance which is an accurate ex post measure of the variance of returns and permits the joint modelling of returns and variance. Third, we nonparametrically model the relationship between contemporaneous excess returns and log-realized variance. Volatility feedback implies an instantaneous causal relationship between volatility innovations and price levels or returns and our contemporaneous model is designed to investigate this relationship directly. Fourth, our nonparametric approach allows for conditioning on predetermined conditioning variables.

Using a long calender span of monthly US stock market data, we find strong robust evidence of volatility feedback. Expected excess returns are always positive when volatility shocks are small; however, they become negative once the volatility shock becomes larger. This risk–return relationship is very nonlinear and depends on the current level of expected volatility. Ignoring these dynamics will result in confounding evidence for risk and return. Once volatility feedback is accounted for, there is an unambiguous positive relationship between expected excess returns and expected log-realized variance. Conditional quantile and contour plots support these findings and display significant deviations from the monotonic changes in the conditional distribution of the parametric model. We find strong evidence of the volatility feedback affecting the whole distribution of excess returns and not just its conditional mean.

This paper is organized as follows. The data and construction of realized variance are discussed in the next section followed by Section 3, which motivates our model and the link to risk and return and volatility feedback. The nonparametric model for excess market returns and log-realized variance is introduced in Section 4. Section 5 discusses estimation of the conditional distribution and conditional mean of excess returns given log-realized variance. Empirical results are found in Section 6 followed by the conclusions.

2. Return and Realized Variance Data

Using high frequency daily returns permits the construction of monthly realized variance—an ex post, observable variance that is the focus of our study. Although the realized variance has been used in empirical finance for some time French et al. (1987), there exists a strong theoretical foundation for using it as an essentially nonparametric measure of ex post volatility (for recent reviews, see Andersen and Benzoni (2008) and McAleer and Medeiros (2008)). For example, in the factor analysis investigation of the risk–return trade-off by Ludvigson and Ng (2007), the nonparametric realized variance affords them the luxury of not having to specify a potentially restrictive parametric form for volatility. For our purpose, the strength of realized variance is it being a consistent estimate of

---

[6] The approximation is based on Campbell and Shiller (1988). Additional papers that build on this approach and find empirical support for volatility feedback include Turner et al. (1989); Kim et al. (2004); Kim et al. (2005); Bollerslev et al. (2006); and Calvet and Fisher (2007).

return volatility. This property means that we can directly model the distribution of return volatility by treating the realized variances as a time series of observed volatilities.

To compute the monthly realized variances, we obtain daily price data from Bill Schwert[7] for February 1885–December 1925, and from CRSP for January 1926–December 2011 on the value-weighted portfolio with distributions for the S&P500. The price data is converted to continuously compounded daily returns. If $r_{t,\iota}$ denotes the continuously compounded return for day ι in month t, then we compute month t's realized variance according to

$$RV_t^q = \hat{\gamma}_0 + 2\sum_{j=1}^{q}(1 - j/(q+1))\hat{\gamma}_j, \quad \hat{\gamma}_j = \sum_{\iota=1}^{N_t - j} r_{t,\iota} r_{t,\iota+j}, \ j = 0, \ldots, q, \tag{1}$$

where N_t denotes the number of daily returns in month t. This estimate of return volatility contains a bias adjustment of order q to account for market microstructure dynamics and stale prices and follows Hansen and Lunde (2006). The Bartlett weights in Equation (1) ensure that RV_t^q is always positive. In this paper, we set $q = 1$ and let $RV_t \equiv RV_t^q$.

Monthly returns are taken from the associated monthly files from Schwert and CRSP S&P500. The risk-free rate is obtained from Amit Goyal's website for February 1885–December 1925, and, after this time period, the risk-free rate equals the one-month rate from the CRSP Treasury bill file.

Our risk–return analysis dataset thus consists of monthly excess returns r_t and monthly realized variance RV_t from January 1885–December 2011 for a total of 1519 monthly observations. Returns are scaled by 12 and RV_t by 144 in order for our findings to be interpreted in terms of annual returns. When estimating the model, we reserve the first 22 observations as conditioning variables. The information set is denoted by $I_t = \{r_1, RV_1, \ldots, r_t, RV_t\}$, for $t = 1, \ldots, T$.

Table 1 reports various summary statistics for monthly excess returns and realized variance. Compared to squared returns, realized variance is less noisy. Returns standardized by realized variance are approximately normal with sample skewness of 0.003 and sample kurtosis of 2.6856. Log-realized variance is closer to being bell-shaped than the levels of RV_t. Figure 1 displays a scatter plot of market excess returns and $\log(RV_t)$ which is the basis of our time-series models.

Table 1. Summary statistics.

	Mean	Variance	Skewness	Kurtosis	Min	Max
r_t	0.0514	0.3884	−0.4047	10.0461	−4.0710	4.1630
r_t^2	0.3907	1.3474	9.7037	119.5948	0.0000	17.3300
RV_t	0.3790	0.5611	7.0305	69.4529	0.0116	11.3000
$\log(RV_t)$	−1.5602	0.8846	0.8051	4.2910	−4.4595	2.4245
$z = r_t/\sqrt{RV_t}$	0.2296	1.0789	0.0030	2.6856	−2.4080	2.8580

This table reports summary statistics for the monthly data on excess returns r_t and monthly realized volatility RV_t. Data is from January 1885–December 2011 giving 1519 observations.

[7] For details on the construction of these data, see Schwert (1990).

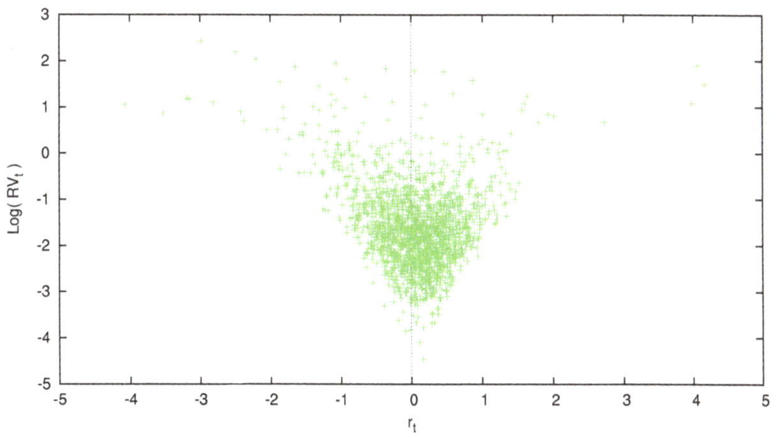

Figure 1. Excess return versus $\log(RV_t)$.

3. Risk Return and Volatility Feedback

This section will provide some motivation for the econometric model studied in this paper. Consider the following specification based on Equation (7) from French et al. (1987) for excess returns

$$r_t = E[r_t|I_{t-1}] + \alpha_1(RV_t - E[RV_t|I_{t-1}]) + \text{error}_t. \tag{2}$$

The first term on the RHS is the expected excess return conditional on the information set I_{t-1}. Hence, it can be a function of $E[RV_t|I_{t-1}]$. In French et al. (1987), the first term comes from an ARMA model on realized variance or standard deviation. This component is ex ante and captures the traditional positive risk–return relationship that the literature has focused on.

The second term of Equation (2) is the volatility innovation and is the ex post adjustment that volatility feedback operates through. If variance risk is priced, an unexpected increase in stock market volatility raises future required stock returns, and thus lowers stock prices (see Campbell and Hentschel (1992)). In this case, $\alpha_1 < 0$ would hold. Therefore, if volatility is priced, a positive shock to volatility will have a positive impact on the first term and a negative effect on the second term. Thus, volatility feedback obscures any risk–return relationship. Note that, in this specification, only when the variance shock is zero ($RV_t = E[RV_t|I_{t-1}]$) does the conditional mean of excess returns contain a pure risk–return effect.

Our goal is to nonparametrically model these two components of excess returns. To fully capture the two opposing effects on excess returns, it is critical to jointly model excess returns and the contemporaneous variance. In addition, the conditional mean of excess returns should be a function of the ex post variance. The other conditional expectations we will model nonparametrically. These considerations lead to a nonparametric joint model of excess returns and log-realized variance.

4. Nonparametric Model of Market Excess Returns and Realized Variance

In this section, we provide the intuition behind the nonparametric model that we will use to flexibly estimate the joint relationship between excess returns and contemporaneous realized variance. As pointed out by Brandt and Kang (2004), there are no theoretical reasons that a particular parametric relationship should hold between the conditional mean and variance of excess returns. Without a theoretical relationship to guide us, we choose to let the data inform us about the risk–return trade-off by modeling the joint probability distribution of excess returns and realized variance as an unknown distribution and fitting it nonparametrically.

Our nonparametric approach consists of approximating the unknown joint distribution's density with the infinite mixture of bivariate densities

$$p(r_t, \log(RV_t)|I_{t-1}, \Omega, \Theta) = \sum_{j=1}^{\infty} \omega_j f(r_t, \log(RV_t)|\theta_j, I_{t-1}), \tag{3}$$

where $\Omega = (\omega_1, \omega_2, \ldots,)$ are the mixture probabilities such that $\omega_j \geq 0$, $j = 1, \ldots, \infty$, and $\sum_{j=1}^{\infty} \omega_j = 1$, and $\Theta = (\theta_1, \theta_2, \ldots)$ are the mixture parameters. The function $f(\cdot, \cdot|\theta_j, I_{t-1})$ is the jth mixture components smooth, bivariate, probability density function given the mixture parameter θ_j and information set I_{t-1}.

It it well understood that any continuous bivariate distribution can be approximated to arbitrary accuracy by selecting an appropriate density function for $f(\cdot, \cdot|\theta_j, I_{t-1})$ and by estimating the unknown mixture weights ω_j and mixture parameters θ_j, for $j = 1, \ldots, \infty$ (Ghosal et al. 1999). In the next section, we discuss how the infinite number of unknowns can be estimated with a finite number of observation. For now, we only consider how we can obtain a nonparametric representation of the risk–return relationship from Equation (3) through the conditional distribution of excess returns given log-realized variance. To reduce the clutter from carrying around excessive notation on the conditional mixture arguments, we drop Θ and Ω from $p(r_t, \log(RV_t)|I_{t-1}, \Omega, \Theta)$ when it is clear to do so.

By the law of total probability, the joint distribution in Equation (3) can be written as the product of the marginal and conditional distributions

$$f(r_t, \log(RV_t)|\theta_j, I_{t-1}) \equiv f(r_t|\log(RV_t), \theta_j, I_{t-1}) f(\log(RV_t)|\theta_j, I_{t-1}). \tag{4}$$

Drawing on the theoretical considerations of Andersen et al. (2003), the known empirical bell-shaped distribution of $\log(RV_t)$, and the approximately normally distributed standardized excess returns, we choose to let the conditional and marginal probability density functions be

$$f(r_t|\log(RV_t), \theta_j, I_{t-1}) = f_N\left(r_t|\alpha_{0,j} + \alpha_{1,j} RV_t, \eta_{1,j}^2 RV_t\right), \tag{5}$$

$$\begin{aligned} f(\log(RV_t)|\theta_j, I_{t-1}) &= f_N\Bigg(\log(RV_t)\,\Bigg|\,\gamma_{0,j} + \gamma_{1,j}\log(RV_{t-1}) + \frac{\gamma_{2,j}}{6}\sum_{i=1}^{6}\log(RV_{t-i}) \\ &\quad + \gamma_{3,j}\frac{r_{t-1}}{\sqrt{RV_{t-1}}} + \gamma_{4,j}\left|\frac{r_{t-1}}{\sqrt{RV_{t-1}}}\right|, \eta_{2,j}^2\Bigg), \end{aligned} \tag{6}$$

where $f_N(\cdot|\mu, \sigma^2)$ is the normal density function with mean μ and variance σ^2. The jth-cluster's mixture parameter vector is $\theta_j = (\alpha_{0,j}, \alpha_{1,j}, \eta_{1,j}, \gamma_{0,j}, \ldots, \gamma_{4,j}, \eta_{2,j})'$ and the conditioning set is $I_{t-1} = (RV_{t-1}, RV_{t-2}, \ldots, RV_{t-5}, r_{t-1})$. Although the jth mixture component in Equations (5) and (6) are normally distributed, mixing them over the infinite set of different valued θ_js produces joint distributions of excess returns and log-realized variances with non-zero higher ordered moments, multiple modes, and a wide variety of curvatures.

What is novel about Equations (5) and (6) is that their mixture locations and scales are functions of contemporaneous and lagged realized variances and lagged returns. Previous infinite mixture models directly mix over the conditional means and variances and do not allow for covariates in the mixture moments. By including contemporaneous and intertemporal variables, our mixture model's means and covariances explicitly depend on intertemporal values of returns and volatility and contemporaneous values of volatility. For example, the values of RV_t can impact the mixture means and variances of excess returns. Note that, under certain conditions, RV_t will be an unbiased estimate of the variance of returns, but we allow for deviations that are captured by the $\eta_{1,j}$s in the mixture model.

Although not the focus of this study, the model allows for a leverage effect or asymmetric response of past return shocks to future $\log(RV_t)$. This occurs in Equation (6) through the terms $\frac{r_{t-1}}{\sqrt{RV_{t-1}}}$ and $|\frac{r_{t-1}}{\sqrt{RV_{t-1}}}|$ and, since this enters the mixture, allows for a general nonlinear leverage effect.

The intertemporal form of Equations (5) and (6) is not based on theory, but on empirical regularities known to exist in stock market returns and their volatility. For instance, the conditional mean of $\log(RV_t)$ in Equation (6) is along the lines of the models found in Andersen et al. (2007), Corsi (2009) and the joint models of Maheu and McCurdy (2007, 2011), as adapted to monthly data. It features an expected volatility comprised of an intertemporal six month component that captures the significant persistence known to exist in realized variances.[8] The last two terms of the conditional mean in Equation (5) also accounts for an asymmetric volatility relationship by including an asymmetric response in the mixture means of log-realized variances to lagged returns.

In the conditional density of Equation (5), any potentially nonlinear function of $\log(RV_t)$ can be conditioned on; eg., $\log(RV_t)$ or $RV_t = \exp(\log(RV_t))$. This conditional density function of excess returns captures the empirical regularity of excess returns being normally distributed when standardized by $\sqrt{RV_t}$. The conditional mixture mean implicitly includes a risk–return relationship (positive) as well as a volatility feedback effect (positive or negative).[9] As a result, the signs of the mixture parameters $\alpha_{1,j}$s are left ambiguous. Essentially, we are nonparametrically modeling through Equation (3), Campbell and Hentschel (1992) reduced form equation of excess returns without imposing any theoretical restrictions. For this reason, we place no restrictions on the $\alpha_{0,j}$ and $\alpha_{1,j}$, $j = 1, \ldots, \infty$. The implications for the risk–return trade-off can be indirectly derived from the contemporaneous model and are discussed later.

4.1. Conditional Distribution of Returns Given Realized Variance

From the mixture representation of the joint distribution of excess returns and realized variances in Equation (3), it directly holds that the probability density function of excess returns conditional on contemporaneous log-realized variance equals

$$p(r_t|\log(RV_t), I_{t-1}) = \frac{p(r_t, \log(RV_t)|I_{t-1})}{p(\log(RV_t)|I_{t-1})} = \frac{\sum_{j=1}^{\infty} \omega_j f(r_t, \log(RV_t)|\theta_j, I_{t-1})}{\sum_{j=1}^{\infty} \omega_j f(\log(RV_t)|\theta_j, I_{t-1})} \tag{7}$$

$$= \sum_{j=1}^{\infty} q_j(\log(RV_t)|\Theta, I_{t-1}) f(r_t|\log(RV_t), \theta_j, I_{t-1}), \tag{8}$$

where $f(r_t|\log(RV_t), \theta_j, I_{t-1}) \equiv f(r_t, \log(RV_t)|\theta_j, I_{t-1}) / f(\log(RV_t)|\theta_j, I_{t-1})$ is the conditional probability density function of the jth cluster and $f(\log(RV_t)|\theta_j, I_{t-1})$ is the associated marginal density function for $\log(RV_t)$.

The mixture weights in Equation (8) have the particular form

$$\begin{aligned} q_j(\log(RV_t)|\Theta, I_{t-1}) &= \frac{\omega_j f(\log(RV_t)|\theta_j, I_{t-1})}{\sum_{i=1}^{\infty} \omega_i f(\log(RV_t)|\theta_i, I_{t-1})}, \\ &\propto \omega_j f_N\left(\log(RV_t) \middle| \gamma_{0,j} + \gamma_{1,j}\log(RV_{t-1}) + \frac{\gamma_{2,j}}{6}\sum_{i=1}^{6}\log(RV_{t-i}) \right. \\ &\quad \left. + \gamma_{3,j}\frac{r_{t-1}}{\sqrt{RV_{t-1}}} + \gamma_{4,j}\left|\frac{r_{t-1}}{\sqrt{RV_{t-1}}}\right|, \eta_{2,j}^2\right), \end{aligned} \tag{9}$$

so that they sum to one. From Equation (10), we see that those clusters providing a better *fit* of $\log(RV_t)$ receive more weight in the mixture representation. Components whose $\gamma_{\cdot,j}$ and $\eta_{2,j}^2$ result in larger likelihoods play a bigger role in accounting for the risk–return trade-off and the volatility feedback

---

[8] A preliminary analysis showed the importance of a six-month component.

[9] Several different functional forms for the conditional mean of r_t given $\log(RV_t)$ result in similar findings and are discussed in Section 6.4. The current specification provides flexibility in modeling.

effect. Note that different values of $\log(RV_t)$ produce smooth changes in the conditional distribution of excess returns and, hence, in its mean.

Our interest rests in the risk–return and volatility feedback relationship; in other words, the conditional expectation of market excess returns given log-realized volatility. Since the expectation of a mixture distribution is equivalent to the mixture of the expectations, from the conditional mixture means of excess returns in Equation (5), the expectation of Equation (8) is the conditional expectation

$$E[r_t|\log(RV_t), I_{t-1}] = \sum_{j=1}^{\infty} q_j(\log(RV_t)|\Theta, I_{t-1})E[r_t|\log(RV_t), \theta_j, I_{t-1}] \tag{10}$$

$$= \sum_{j=1}^{\infty} q_j(\log(RV_t)|\Theta, I_{t-1})\left[\alpha_{0,j} + \alpha_{1,j}RV_t\right]. \tag{11}$$

A linear parametric risk–return relationship is nested in Equation (11) by simply letting there be only one mixture component. As more mixture components are added and a greater mixture of differently valued $\alpha_{0,j}$s and $\alpha_{1,j}$s are included, the conditional mean of excess returns as a function of RV_t, moves away from linearity. This mixing allows Equation (11) to become more flexible and capable of modeling a wider array of different types of risk–return and volatility feedback relationships.

Being a function of realized variance, the mixture representation in Equation (11) differs from previous work by nonparametrically modelling excess returns and ex post variance. The conditional mean of excess returns given realized variance will contain an ex ante risk–return component and an ex post volatility feedback component.

A plot of the conditional expectation of excess returns as a function of $\log(RV_t)$ will be a smoothly changing function that weights each of the cluster specific conditional expectations according to how the weight function $q_j(\log(RV_t)|\Theta, I_{t-1})$ changes as $\log(RV_t)$ changes. This is true even if each cluster's expectation, $E[r_t|\log(RV_t), \theta_j, I_{t-1}]$, is constant. In this way, we can see the contemporaneous relationship of log-volatility on the conditional mean of excess returns. As mentioned above, volatility feedback occurs simultaneously and this specification is designed to shed light on it.

4.2. Dirichlet Process Prior for the Infinite Number Of Unknowns

Because our nonparametric model of excess returns and log-realized variance joint probability distribution consists of an infinite number of unknown mixture weights, ω_j, and parameter vectors, θ_j, we resort to a Bayesian prior to shrink the number of unknowns to a feasible number while not forsaking the flexibility that comes from an infinite mixture model. The prior we choose is the Dirichlet process prior (DP). The Dirichlet process prior has a long history, beginning with Ferguson (1973), of use in Bayesian nonparametric problems. It was used as a prior in countable infinite mixtures for density estimation in Ferguson (1983) and Lo (1984), but applications were limited until modern computational techniques. The seminal paper by Escobar and West (1995) shows how to perform Bayesian nonparametric density estimation with Gibbs sampling.

The DP prior essentially partitions the parameter space into a finite number of sets such that parameter vectors drawn from a particular set all have the same unique value. Such a prior promotes clustering among the mixture components resulting in only having to estimate a few unknown mixture parameter vectors. The probability of a particular mixture parameter vector occurring is equal to the probability over a member set of the partition as defined by the DP prior.

To be explicit, we assume the Dirichlet process prior, $DP(G_0, \kappa)$, for the unknown ω_j and θ_j, $j = 1, \ldots, \infty$ of Equation (3). Sethuraman (1994) shows that a $DP(G_0, \kappa)$ prior for the mixture unknowns has the representation of being almost surely draws from

$$\omega_1 = v_1, \;\; \omega_j = v_j \prod_{i=1}^{j-1}(1 - v_i), \;\; v_j \overset{iid}{\sim} Beta(1, \kappa), \tag{12}$$

$$\theta_j \overset{iid}{\sim} G_0, \tag{13}$$

for $j = 1, \ldots, \infty$. In Equation (13), each mixture cluster parameter vector θ_j is a unique vector independently drawn from the base distribution G_0. This base distribution is our best guess at how the θ_js are distributed. In Equation (12), the mixture weights are drawn from what is referred to as a stick breaking process since the unit interval is successively broken into the mixture weights, ω_j, $j = 1, \ldots, \infty$, by breaking off random $Beta(1, \kappa)$ portions of the remaining part of the unit length stick. This stick breaking process ensures the mixture weights sum to one while also promoting clustering in the θs.

The positive scalar κ, known as the Dirichlet processes' concentration parameter, controls the degree of clustering in the mixture components. A κ close to zero results in only a few mixture weights being nonzero, putting most of the weight on only a few unique draws from G_0. As κ gets larger more ω_js become nonzero, and, hence, there is less clustering and more unique θ_js. In the limit as κ approaches infinity, the partition of the mixture parameter space is no longer finite and discrete. Instead, the parameter sets within the partition becomes so fine and large in number that the θ_js no longer cluster to a finite set of unique value but instead will be continuously distributed as G_0. In other words, when $\kappa \to \infty$, the mixture weights are uniformly distributed, no clustering occurs and the prior for the θs is essentially G_0.

4.3. Hierarchical Representation

The Dirichlet process mixture model defined in Equations (3)–(6), (12) and (13) also has the hierarchical representation where $r_t, \log(RV_t)|\theta_t^*, I_{t-1}$ is distributed

$$r_t, \log(RV_t)|\theta_t^*, I_{t-1} \sim f(r_t, \log(RV_t)|\theta_t^*, I_{t-1}), \qquad t = 1, \ldots, T, \tag{14}$$

$$\theta_t^*|G \overset{iid}{\sim} G, \qquad t = 1, \ldots, T, \tag{15}$$

$$G|G_0, \kappa \sim DP(G_0, \kappa). \tag{16}$$

In Equation (15), the distribution of the parameter vector $\theta_t^* = (\alpha_{0,t}^*, \alpha_{1,t}^*, \eta_{1,t}^*, \gamma_{0,t}^*, \ldots, \gamma_{4,t}^*, \eta_{2,t}^*)'$ is the unknown distribution, G, whose prior is modeled in Equation (16) by the Dirichlet process prior $DP(G_0, \kappa)$. Given the stick breaking definition of the Dirichlet process in Equations (12) and (13), the prior distribution for G is almost surely equal to the discrete distribution

$$G(\theta_t^*) = \sum_{j=1}^{\infty} \omega_j \delta_{\theta_j}(\theta_t^*), \tag{17}$$

where $\delta_{\theta_j}(\cdot)$ denotes a point mass at θ_j, and ω_j and θ_j are the random realizations defined in Equations (12) and (13).

Equation (17) helps us better appreciate the clustering behavior of the DP prior. Since G is almost surely a discrete distribution, there will be duplicates among the θ_t^*, $t = 1, \ldots, T$. As a result, several of the observations will share the same mixture parameter vector, θ_j.

If volatility risk is priced, a positive volatility shock requires an increase in returns which discounts all future cash flows at a higher rate. This discounting results in a drop in the current price. As a result, if any unexpected news arrives be it good or bad, uncertainty increases causing the innovation to volatility, v_t, to be positive. If a volatility feedback effect exists the effect good news has on returns will be dampened, whereas the effect of the bad news will be amplified. Therefore, a price increase from good news will be less than what would occur without volatility feedback while a price decrease from bad news will be steeper. Dynamics of this sort occur when $\alpha^*_{1,t}$ is negative. On the other hand, if volatility shocks are small, the net impact on the conditional mean of excess returns will be a reward for risk which can be captured by a positive $(\alpha^*_{0,t} + \alpha^*_{1,t}RV_t)$.

By connecting the clustering property of the DP with the volatility feedback parameter, $\alpha^*_{1,t}$, our nonparametric model will have a unique $\alpha_{1,j}$ during similar market environments. Two months with similar market behavior will have the same volatility feedback, $\alpha_{1,j}$. However, the volatility feedback for months where the market dynamics are different will not equal $\alpha_{1,j}$.

4.4. Posterior Simulation

To sample the posterior density of our nonparametric joint distribution model, we will exploit the mixture representation in Equation (3) and a slice sampler based on Walker (2007); Kalli et al. (2011); and Papaspiliopoulos (2008).[10] This Markov chain Monte Carlo (MCMC) algorithm introduces a random auxiliary, latent, variable, $u_t \in (0,1)$, which slices away any mixtures clusters with a weight ω_j less than u_t. In this way, the infinite mixture model is reduced to a finite mixture.

Introducing the latent variable u_t, we define the joint conditional density of the observed variables $(r_t, \log(RV_t))$ and u_t as,

$$p(r_t, \log(RV_t), u_t|\Omega, \Theta, I_{t-1}) = \sum_{j=1}^{\infty} \mathbf{1}(u_t < \omega_j) f(r_t, \log(RV_t)|\theta_j, I_{t-1}). \tag{18}$$

This infinite mixture is truncated to only include *alive* clusters with $u_t < \omega_j$ while *dead* clusters have a weight of 0 and can be ignored. If u_t has a uniform distribution, then integration of $p(r_t, \log(RV_t), u_t|\Omega, \Theta, I_{t-1})$ with respect to u_t gives back the original model $p(r_t, \log(RV_t)|\Omega, \Theta, I_{t-1})$. On the other hand, the marginal density of u_t is $\sum_{j=1}^{\infty} \mathbf{1}(u_t < \omega_j)$.

We augment the parameter space to include estimation of $S = (s_1, \ldots, s_T)$. Let $U = (u_1, \ldots, u_T)$, $\Omega_K = (\omega_1, \ldots, \omega_K)$ and $\Theta_K = (\theta_1, \ldots, \theta_K)$, then the full likelihood is

$$\prod_{t=1}^{T} p(r_t, \log(RV_t), u_t, s_t|\Omega_K, \Theta_K, I_{t-1}) = \prod_{t=1}^{T} \mathbf{1}(u_t < \omega_{s_t}) f(r_t, \log(RV_t)|\theta_{s_t}, I_{t-1}) \tag{19}$$

and the joint posterior is

$$p(\Omega_K) \left[\prod_{i=1}^{K} p(\theta_i)\right] \prod_{t=1}^{T} \mathbf{1}(u_t < \omega_{s_t}) f(r_t, \log(RV_t)|\theta_{s_t}, I_{t-1}), \tag{20}$$

where the number of mixture clusters, K, is the smallest natural number that satisfies the condition $\sum_{j=1}^{K} \omega_j > 1 - \min\{U\}$. This value of K ensures that there are no $\omega_k > u_t$ for $k > K$. In other words, we have the set of all clusters that are alive, $\{j : u_t < \omega_j\}$.

Posterior simulation consists of sampling from the following densities:

1. $\pi(\theta_j|\mathbf{r}, \mathbf{RV}, S) \propto g_0(\theta_j) \prod_{\{t:s_t=j\}} f(r_t, \log(RV_t)|\theta_j, I_{t-1}), j = 1, \ldots, K$.
2. $\pi(v_j|S) \propto \text{Beta}(v_j|a_j, b_j), j = 1, \ldots, K$, with $a_j = 1 + \sum_{t=1}^{T} \mathbf{1}(s_t = j)$, $b_j = \kappa + \sum_{t=1}^{T} \mathbf{1}(s_t > j)$.
3. $\pi(u_t|\Omega_K, S) \propto \mathbf{1}(0 < u_t < \omega_{s_t}), t = 1, \ldots, T$.
4. Find the smallest K such that $\sum_{j=1}^{K} \omega_j > 1 - \min\{U\}$.
5. $P(s_t = j|r, \mathbf{RV}, \Theta_K, U, \Omega_K) \propto \sum_{j=1}^{K} \mathbf{1}(u_t < \omega_j) f(r_t, \log(RV_t)|\theta_{s_t}, I_{t-1})$.

[10] Alternative methods Escobar and West (1995) based on the hierarchical form of the model in Equation (14) are more difficult as our model and prior are non-conjugate.

where $\boldsymbol{r} = (r_1, \ldots, r_T)'$ and $\boldsymbol{RV} = (RV_1, \ldots, RV_T)'$.

The first step depends on the model and the base density $g_0(\cdot)$ to the DP priors' base measure, G_0. For the kernel densities in Equations (5) and (6), specifying a normal prior for the regression coefficients and an independent inverse gamma prior for the variance, in other words, defining $G_0 \equiv N(\underline{b}, \underline{V}) \times G(\underline{v}/2, \underline{s}/2)$, we can employ standard Gibbs sampling techniques in Step 1 (see Greenberg (2013) for details on the exact form of these conditional distributions). Step 2 results from the conjugacy of the generalized Dirichlet distribution and multinomial sampling Ishwaran and James (2001). Given Ω_K and S, each u_t is uniformly distributed on $(0, \omega_{s_t})$. The next step updates the truncation parameter K. If K is incremented, Step 4 will also involve drawing additional ω_j and θ_j from the DP prior. The final step is a multinomial draw of the cluster assignment variable s_t based on a mixture with equal weights.

Repeating all these steps forms one iteration of the sampler. The MCMC sampler yields the following set of variables at each iteration i,

$$\{(\theta_{i,j}, v_{i,j}), j = 1, 2, \ldots, K_i; (s_{i,t}, u_{i,t}), t = 1, \ldots, T\}. \tag{21}$$

Note that $v_{i,j}, j = 1, 2, \ldots, K_i$, implies $\omega_{i,j}, j = 1, 2, \ldots, K_i$, through Equation (12). After dropping the burn-in phase from the above sampler, we collect $i = 1, \ldots, N$ samples.

Each ith iteration of the algorithm produces a draw of the unknown mixing distribution G from its posterior $[G|\boldsymbol{r}, \boldsymbol{RV}]$ as

$$G_i = \sum_{j=1}^{K_i} \omega_{i,j} \delta_{\theta_{i,j}} + \left(1 - \sum_{j=1}^{K_i} \omega_{i,j}\right) G_0(\theta). \tag{22}$$

We will make use of these posterior realizations of G to form the predictive density and conditional expectations.

5. Nonparametric Conditional Density Estimation

To flexibly estimate the conditional density $p(r_t | \log(RV_t), I_{t-1})$ found in Equation (8), or the conditional mean in Equation (11), we use the method of Muller et al. (1996). This is an elegant approach to nonparametric estimation that allows the conditional density and expectation of excess returns to depend on covariates, in this case $\log(RV_t)$. The method requires the joint modeling of the predictor variable and its covariates and uses well know estimation methods for Dirichlet process mixture models. We extend Muller et al. (1996) to the slice sampler to accommodate the non-Gaussian data densities and nonconjugate priors found in our nonparametric model of market excess returns and realized variances.[11]

Based on the previous section, and given G_i, the ith realization from the posterior of the joint conditional predictive density for the generic return, log-realized variance combination, $(r, \log(RV))$, is

$$p(r, \log(RV)|G_i, I_{t-1}) = \int f(r, \log(RV)|\theta, I_{t-1}) G_i(d\theta), \tag{23}$$

where the predictive is conditional on the information set $I_{t-1} = \{r_{t-1}, RV_{t-1}, \ldots, r_1, RV_1\}$.

[11] Additional papers that also build on Muller et al. (1996) are Rodriguez et al. (2009); Shahbaba and Neal (2009); and Taddy and Kottas (2010).

Substituting in the stick breaking representation for G_i found in Equation (22), the posterior draw of the predictive density has the equivalent representation

$$\begin{aligned} p(r, \log(RV)|G_i, I_{t-1}) &= \sum_{j=1}^{K_i} w_{i,j} f(r, \log(RV)|\theta_{i,j}, I_{t-1}) \\ &\quad + \left(1 - \sum_{j=1}^{K_i} w_{i,j}\right) p(r, \log(RV)|G_0, I_{t-1}), \end{aligned} \tag{24}$$

where $p(r, \log(RV)|G_0, I_{t-1}) = \int f(r, \log(RV)|\theta, I_{t-1}) G_0(d\theta)$ is the expectation of Equation (14) over G_0. To integrate out the uncertainty associated with G, one averages Equation (24) over the posterior realizations, $G_i \sim [G|\boldsymbol{r}, \boldsymbol{RV}]$, $i = 1, \ldots, N$, to obtain the posterior predictive density

$$p(r, \log(RV)|\boldsymbol{r}, \boldsymbol{RV}) \approx \frac{1}{N} \sum_{i=1}^{N} p(r, \log(RV)|G_i, I_{t-1}). \tag{25}$$

Now, the predictive density of r given $\log(RV)$ can be estimated as well. For each draw of G_i, we have

$$\begin{aligned} p(r|\log(RV), G_i, I_{t-1}) &= \frac{p(r, \log(RV)|G_i, I_{t-1})}{p(\log(RV)|G_i, I_{t-1})}, \\ &= \frac{p(r, \log(RV)|G_i, I_{t-1})}{\sum_{j=1}^{K_i} w_{i,j} f(\log(RV)|\theta_{i,j}, I_{t-1}) + (1 - \sum_{j=1}^{K_i} w_{i,j}) f(\log(RV)|G_0, I_{t-1})}, \\ &= \sum_{j=1}^{K_i} q_{i,j}(\log(RV)) f(r|\log(RV), \theta_{i,j}) \\ &\quad + \left(1 - \sum_{j=1}^{K_i} q_{i,j}(\log(RV))\right) f(r|\log(RV), G_0, I_{t-1}), \end{aligned} \tag{26}$$

where $f(r|\log(RV), \theta_{i,j}, I_{t-1})$ is the conditional density of Equation (5), $f(\log(RV)|\theta_{i,j}, I_{t-1})$ is the marginal density of Equation (6) and

$$\begin{aligned} q_{i,j}(\log(RV)) = w_{i,j} f\left(\log(RV)\,|\theta_{i,j}, I_{t-1}\right) \Bigg/ \Bigg[&\sum_{l=1}^{K_i} w_{i,l} f\left(\log(RV)|\theta_{i,l}, I_{t-1}\right) \\ &+ \left(1 - \sum_{l=1}^{K_i} w_{i,l}\right) f(\log(RV)|G_0, I_{t-1}) \Bigg]. \end{aligned} \tag{27}$$

The denominator of $q_{i,j}(\log(RV))$ is the marginal of Equation (24) obtained by integrating out r. $f(\log(RV)|\theta_{i,j}, I_{t-1})$ is the marginal data density of $\log(RV)$ for the jth cluster with the marginal cluster parameter θ_j and $f(\log(RV)|G_0, I_{t-1})$ is the marginal data density with mixing over the base measure. The terms in Equations (26) and (27) involving G_0 are defined as follows:

$$f(r|\log(RV), G_0, I_{t-1}) = \frac{\int f(r, \log(RV)|\theta, I_{t-1}) G_0(d\theta)}{\int f(\log(RV)|\theta, I_{t-1}) G_0(d\theta)}, \tag{28}$$

$$f(\log(RV)|G_0, I_{t-1}) = \int f(\log(RV)|\theta, I_{t-1}) G_0(d\theta). \tag{29}$$

Assuming that the marginal data density $f(\log(RV)|\theta, I_{t-1})$ is available in analytic form, both of these expressions can be approximated by the usual MCMC methods. For instance, $f(\log(RV)|G_0, I_{t-1}) \approx N^{-1} \sum_{i=1}^{N} f(\log(RV)|\theta^{(i)}, I_{t-1})$, where $\theta^{(i)} \sim G_0$, with a similar expression for the numerator of Equation (28).

The posterior predictive conditional density is estimated by averaging Equation (26) over the posterior simulations of G_i as

$$p(r|\log(RV), I_{t-1}, \boldsymbol{r}, \boldsymbol{RV}) \approx \frac{1}{N}\sum_{i=1}^{N} p(r|\log(RV), G_i, I_{t-1}). \tag{30}$$

Using this approximation, features of the conditional distribution such as conditional quantiles can be derived.

5.1. Nonparametric Conditional Mean Estimation

Our focus will be on the conditional expectation that can be estimated from these results. First, the conditional expectation of r given $\log(RV)$, G_i and the information set I_{t-1} is

$$\begin{aligned} E[r|\log(RV), G_i, I_{t-1}] &= \sum_{j=1}^{K_i} q_{i,j}(\log(RV))E[r|\log(RV), \theta_{i,j}, I_{t-1}] \\ &+ \left(1 - \sum_{j=1}^{K_i} q_{i,j}(\log(RV))\right) E[r|\log(RV), G_0, I_{t-1}], \end{aligned} \tag{31}$$

where $E[r|\log(RV), G_0, I_{t-1}]$ is taken with respect to Equation (28). Note that this final term is only a function of G_0 and can be computed once, at the start of estimation, for a grid of values of $\log(RV_t)$. It is estimated as[12]

$$E[r|\log(RV), G_0, I_{t-1}] = \frac{\int E[r|\log(RV), \theta, I_{t-1}]f(\log(RV)|\theta, I_{t-1})G_0(d\theta)}{\int f(\log(RV)|\theta, I_{t-1})G_0(d\theta)}, \tag{32}$$

$$\approx \frac{N^{-1}\sum_{i=1}^{N} E[r|\log(RV), \theta^{(i)}, I_{t-1}]f(\log(RV)|\theta^{(i)}, I_{t-1})}{N^{-1}\sum_{i=1}^{N} f(\log(RV)|\theta^{(i)}, I_{t-1})} \tag{33}$$

for $\theta^{(i)} \sim G_0, i = 1, \ldots, N$.

Given G_i, Equation (31) shows the conditional expectation of r is a convex combination of cluster specific conditional expectations $E[r|\log(RV), \theta_j, I_{t-1}], j = 1, \ldots, K_i$, along with the expectation taken with respect to the base measure G_0. The weighting function changes with the conditioning variable $\log(RV)$, which in turn changes for each I_{t-1}.

Finally, with this, we can obtain the posterior predictive conditional mean estimate by averaging over Equation (31) as follows:

$$E[r|\log(RV), I_{t-1}, \boldsymbol{r}, \boldsymbol{RV}] \approx \frac{1}{N}\sum_{i=1}^{N} E[r|\log(RV), G_i, I_{t-1}], \tag{34}$$

in order to integrate out uncertainty concerning G.[13] Point-wise density intervals of the conditional mean can be estimated from the quantiles of $E[r|\log(RV), G_i, I_{t-1}]$.

We evaluate the predictive conditional mean for a grid of values over $\log(RV)$. This will produce a smooth curve and we will have a unique curve for each information set I_{t-1} in our sample $t = 1, \ldots, T$.

---

12 This result makes use of expressing the numerator as $\int xp(x,y|\theta)p(\theta)d\theta dx = \int xp(x|y,\theta)p(y|\theta)p(\theta)d\theta dx = \int E[x|y,\theta]p(y|\theta)p(\theta)d\theta$.

13 Note that the quantity $E[r_t|\log(RV_t), I_{t-1}]$ in (11) assumes parameters are known. In our case, they need to be estimated by the posterior density using the full sample of data $\boldsymbol{r}$, $\boldsymbol{RV}$. Therefore, our estimate implicitly conditions on the observed $\boldsymbol{r}$ and $\boldsymbol{RV}$ in $E[r|\log(RV), I_{t-1}]$.

6. Empirical Findings

For our empirical analysis, we specify the following priors. The base measure G_0 contains priors for each regression parameter in Equations (5) and (6) as independent $N(0,1)$ while $\eta_{1,j}^{-2} \overset{iid}{\sim} G(5/2, 5/2)$ and $\eta_{2,j}^{-2} \overset{iid}{\sim} G(6/2, 3/2)$, $j = 1, \ldots, \infty$, where $G(a,b)$ denotes a gamma distribution with mean a/b. Note that we expect the $\eta_{1,j}^2$s to be close to 1 and the prior reflects this with $E[\eta_{1,j}^{-2}] = 1$ but allows for deviations from this. These prior beliefs cover a wide range of empirically realistic values and robustness to other choices is discussed below. The concentration parameter of the Dirichlet process, κ, is estimated and has a prior $G(2, 10)$. Each cluster contains the nine parameters found in θ_j.

We use 5000 initial iterations of the posterior sampler for burn-in and then collect the following 20,000 for posterior inference. The Markov chain mixes well and the posterior mean (0.95 density interval) for κ is 0.2046, $(0.0439, 0.4831)$ and the posterior mean (0.95 density interval) for the number of alive clusters is 2.6, $(2, 4)$. In other words, about 2.6 components are used to fit the joint model of r_t and $\log(RV_t)$.

Before we turn to the estimates from our nonparametric DPM model, a parametric version of the model is reported in Table 2. This is a one state model. The coefficient α_1 on RV_t in the excess return equation is significantly negative and hence evidence of the volatility feedback mechanism at work. η_1^2 is close to 1 and indicates no systematic bias in RV_t. The estimates of γ_1 and γ_2 indicate persistence in $\log(RV_t)$. The lagged standardized excess return terms entering the log-volatility equation show asymmetry. A negative return shock results in a larger conditional mean for log-volatility next period compared to a positive shock.

Table 2. Parametric model estimates.

	Mean	0.95 Density Interval
α_0	0.1922	(0.1672, 0.2171)
α_1	−0.2801	(−0.3895, −0.1748)
η_1^2	1.0177	(0.9460, 1.0962)
γ_0	−0.3319	(−0.4151, −0.2470)
γ_1	0.3766	(0.3179, 0.4329)
γ_2	0.4505	(0.3817, 0.5180)
γ_3	−0.1518	(−0.1842, −0.1170)
γ_4	0.1258	(0.0680, 0.1861)
η_2^2	0.3981	(0.3702, 0.4278)

This table reports posterior summary statistics for the parametric model: $r_t = \alpha_0 + \alpha_1 RV_t + \eta_1 \sqrt{RV_t} z_t,\ z_t \sim NID(0,1)$; $\log(RV_t) = \gamma_0 + \gamma_1 \log(RV_{t-1}) + \gamma_2 \frac{1}{6} \sum_{i=1}^{6} \log(RV_{t+1-i}) + \gamma_3 \frac{r_{t-1}}{\sqrt{RV_{t-1}}} + \gamma_4 \left| \frac{r_{t-1}}{\sqrt{RV_{t-1}}} \right| + \eta_2 v_t,\ v_t \sim NID(0,1)$.

Figure 2 displays the contemporaneous relationship between expected excess returns and $\log(RV)$ for the estimated parametric model.[14] The conditional expectation of excess returns given log-realized variance is computed over a grid of 100 log-variance values between −4.0 to 2.0. Using a straight line, we interpolate between the values of $E[r|\log(RV), I_{t-1}, \boldsymbol{r}, \boldsymbol{RV}]$ at the different values of log variance in order to approximate the smooth relationship between $E[r|\log(RV), I_{t-1}, \boldsymbol{r}, \boldsymbol{RV}]$ and $\log(RV)$. Although the estimated model is a fixed linear relationship between excess returns and RV, this parametric model yields the nonlinear relations between the conditional mean of excess returns and log-realized variance found in Figure 2.

[14] For convenience, our figures drop the conditioning set $\boldsymbol{r}, \boldsymbol{RV}$.

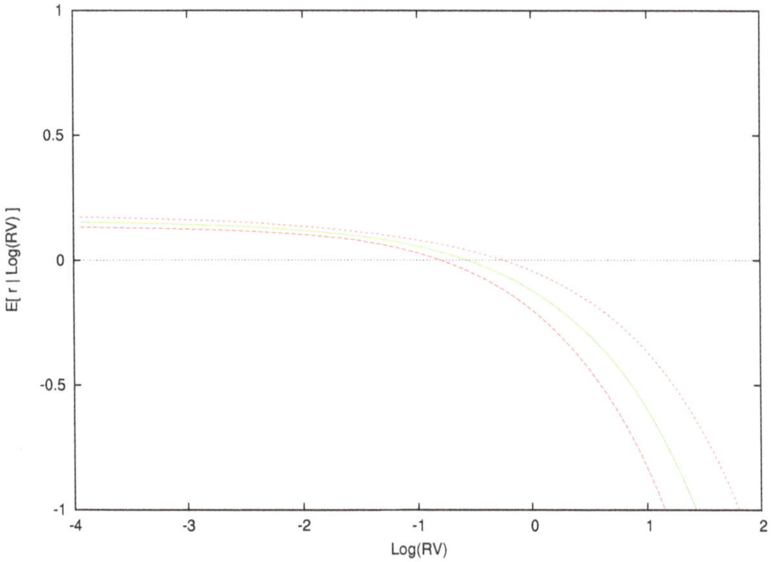

Figure 2. Expected excess return given log realized variance for the parametric model. This figure displays the expected excess return and 0.90 density intervals as a function of log realized variance for the parametric model.

In Figure 3, the conditional expectation of excess returns as a function of log-realized variance for our nonparametric model is plotted for every information set, I_{t-1}, $t = 1, \ldots, T$, in our dataset. Note that the parametric relationship in Figure 2 is the same for every information set and is not affected by low or high volatility periods. Overall, there is a general increase in the conditional mean of excess returns in Figure 3 as log-realized variance increases from low levels of volatility to a point where expected returns become negative. This is a general pattern found in all of the plots of Figure 3. However, the log-variance argument that causes the conditional mean of excess returns to begin to decline does differ for the different information sets I_{t-1}. It is clear that, if one averaged over these expectations, you could obtain a positive value for expected excess returns or a negative value.[15] To really understand the relationship between the conditional mean of excess returns and log-realized variance, we need to consider the conditional expectation and the innovation of log-volatility as well.

To do this, we isolate three months in our sample where market volatility is low (October, 1964), average (February, 1996) and high (December, 2008) and plot in Figures 4–6 the conditional expectations of excess returns against different values of log-realized variance during these three months. In addition to plotting the conditional expectation of market excess returns, the three figures also include the conditional expectation of log-realized variance, $E[\log(RV_t)|I_{t-1}, \boldsymbol{r}, \boldsymbol{RV}]$, as a vertical blue line, and the observed realized value of log-realized variance for that month, $\log(RV_t)$, as a vertical dashed line. Point-wise 90% probability density intervals are included for the expected excess return.

[15] In fact, averaging the curves from the nonparametric model would give something close to the parametric model in Figure 2.

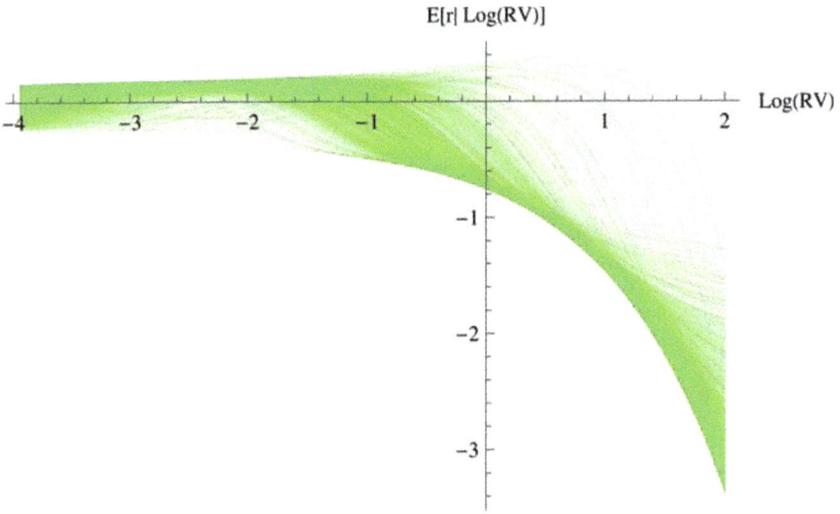

Figure 3. Expected return given log realized variance for each of the information sets I_{t-1}, $t = 2, \ldots, T$.

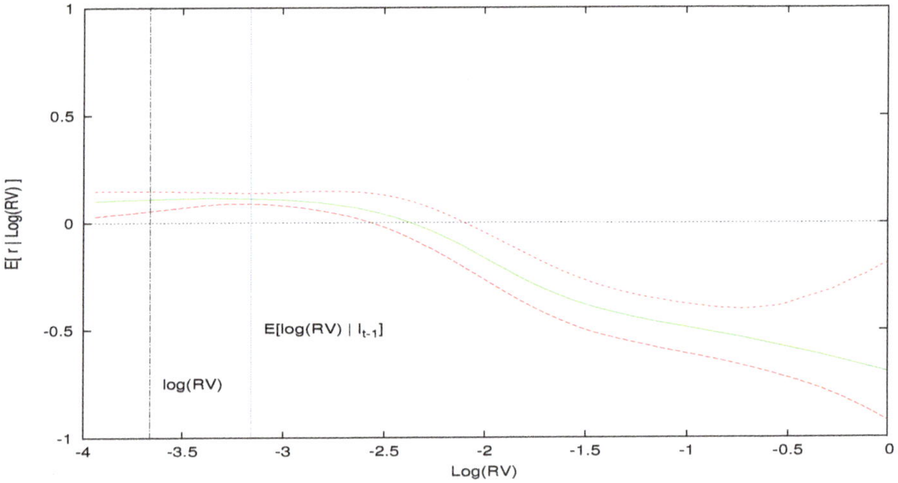

Figure 4. Expected excess return given log realized variance for the information set I_{t-1} where volatility is low. This figure displays the expected excess return and 0.90 density intervals as a function of $\log(RV)$ conditional on the information set I_{t-1}, $t = 1964 : 10$, which is a low volatility period. The expected log-realized volatility based on the model is blue, while the actual log-realized volatility for $t = 1964 : 10$ is the black vertical line.

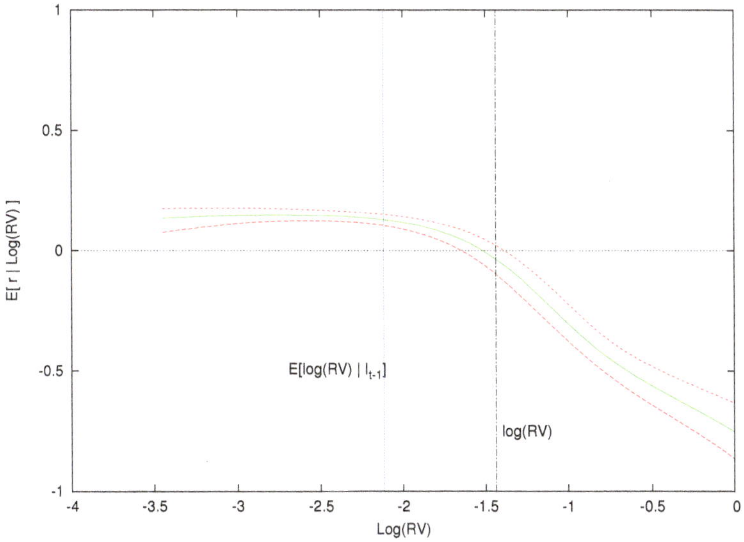

Figure 5. Expected excess return given log realized variance for the information set I_{t-1} where volatility is near its average level. This figure displays the expected excess return and 0.90 density intervals as a function of $\log(RV)$ conditional on regressors in the information set from I_{t-1}, $t = 1996:2$, which is an average volatility period. The expected log-realized volatility based on the model is blue while the actual log-realized volatility for $t = 1996:2$ is the black vertical line.

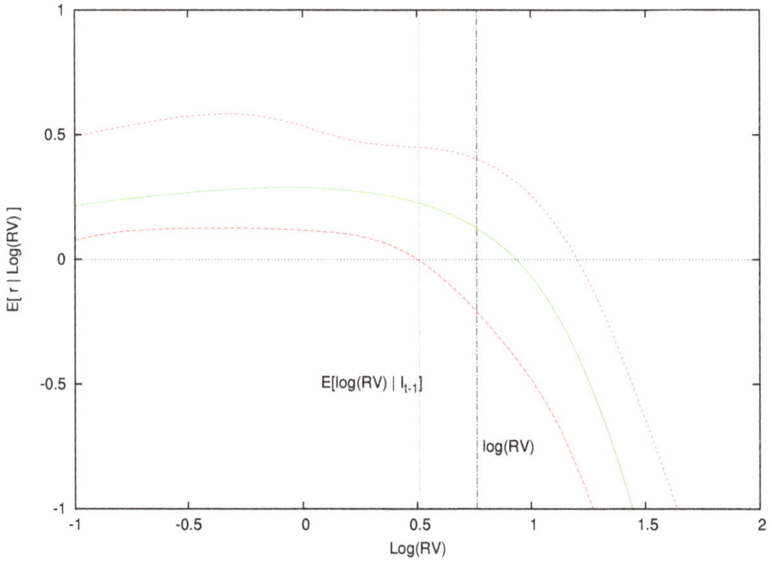

Figure 6. Expected excess return given log realized variance for the information set I_{t-1} where volatility is high. This figure displays the expected excess return and 0.90 density intervals as a function of $\log(RV)$ conditional on regressors in the information set from I_{t-1}, $t = 2008:12$, which is a high volatility period. The expected log-realized volatility based on the model is blue while the actual log-realized volatility for $t = 2008:12$ is the black vertical line.

6.1. Volatility Effect

Recalling our discussion on volatility feedback, if volatility is priced and a positive volatility shock arrives, then, all things being equal, the required rate of return increases which discounts all future cash flows at a higher rate and results in a simultaneous drop in the current price so as to deliver a higher future return consistent with the increase in risk. Only when the observed log-variance is equal to its expected value will the volatility feedback effect be zero. Hence, if volatility risk is priced, values of log-variance greater (less) than its expected value will cause current prices to fall (rise).

This is exactly what we find in Figures 4–6 for an unexpected positive volatility shock where log-variance is greater than the expected value of log-realized variance. For instance, consider Figure 4, which conditions on the low volatility information set, $I_{1964:10}$.[16] In this month of low market volatility, the model's expected log-realized variance is -3.158. The expected excess return is positive for values of log-variance below and slightly above this expected value, but eventually the expected excess return becomes negative as $\log(RV)$ increases above -2.25. In other words, when market volatility is low, if the volatility shock is sufficiently larger than zero, we expect a contemporaneous decrease in prices from the volatility feedback effect.

Figure 5 displays a similar pattern for the month where volatility is not unusual but typical for the equity market. The period is for the information set $I_{1996:2}$ and our model finds the expected value of $\log(RV)$ to be -2.117. As before, expected excess returns are positive for values of log-variance less than and slightly greater than -2.117, but eventually becomes negative when log-realized variance is larger than -1.5. If the log-volatility shock is sufficiently large (about +0.68), then the expected excess return is negative and continues to decrease as the size of the volatility shock grows. In addition, notice that the whole posterior curve of $E[r|\log(RV), I_{1996:2}, \boldsymbol{r}, \boldsymbol{RV}]$ has shifted rightward as the expected $\log(RV)$ has increased from Figures 4 to 5 (low to average $\log(RV)$). This suggests an increase in compensation for the higher perceived volatility risk when the market moves from an unusually calm market to one that is typical.

A highly volatility market corresponding to the information set $I_{2008:12}$ is found in Figure 6. Just as before, $E[r|\log(RV), I_{2008:12}, \boldsymbol{r}, \boldsymbol{RV}]$ is essentially linear and flat for values of $\log(RV)$ smaller than $E[\log(RV)|I_{2008:12}, \boldsymbol{r}, \boldsymbol{RV}]$. In other words, the expected excess returns do not respond to negative volatility shocks. However, for values of $\log(RV)$ greater than 0.5, expected excess returns start to decline and become negative when log-realized variance is almost one.[17] This is consistent with the volatility feedback effect. Note that, in each of these three figures, the effect of volatility feedback on returns gets stronger where the impact of a positive volatility shock on expected returns increases as the the market moves from a low volatility state to a market with average volatility and then to a market where volatility is exceptionally high.

Figure 7 plots $E[r|\log(RV), I_{t-1}, \boldsymbol{r}, \boldsymbol{RV}]$ for each of the three information sets, $I_{1964:10}$, $I_{1996:2}$ and $I_{2008:12}$. As $E[\log(RV)|I_{t-1}, \boldsymbol{r}, \boldsymbol{RV}]$ increases, the conditional expectation of excess returns shifts rightward and up. This is consistent with a positive and increasing reward for bearing higher levels of risk.

In summary, we find a robust volatility feedback effect that is most notable for positive shocks to volatility. Expected excess returns are positive below $E[\log(RV)|I_{t-1}, \boldsymbol{r}, \boldsymbol{RV}]$ but after this value eventually become negative. Thus, small news events have little effect on expected returns, whereas large news events cause expected excess returns to decline. This suggests that risk is priced and the previous figure is consistent with this.

---

16 From Table 1, average $\log(RV)$ is -1.5602 with a minimum of -4.4595 and maximum of 2.4245.

17 $E[\log(RV)|I_{t-1}, \boldsymbol{r}, \boldsymbol{RV}]$ denotes the in-sample Bayesian estimate of the expectation of $\log(RV)$ given I_{t-1}. This conditions on regressors in the information set $t-1$ but uses the full posterior density based on $\boldsymbol{r}$,$\boldsymbol{RV}$ for the model parameters to integrate out parameter uncertainty.

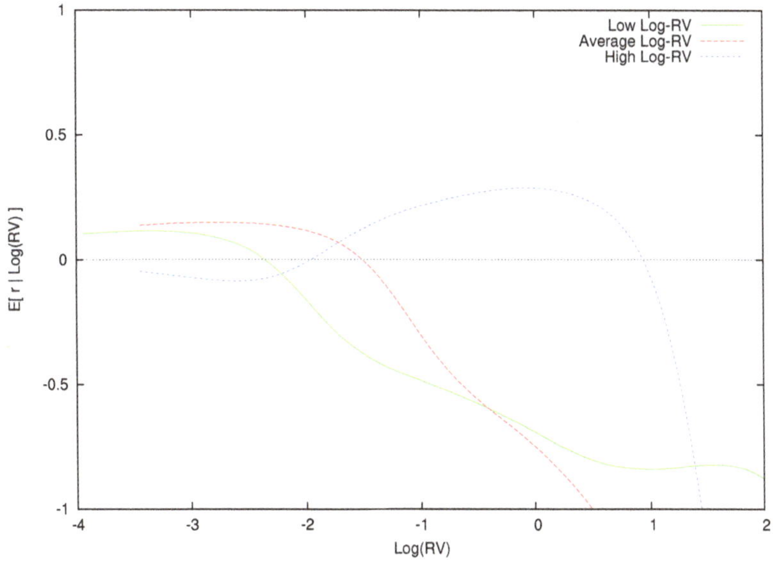

Figure 7. Expected excess return given $\log(RV)$ for various periods. This figure displays the expected excess return as a function of $\log(RV)$ conditional on regressors I_{t-1} taken from $t = 1964:10$ "Low Log-RV", $t = 1996:2$, "Average Log-RV" and $t = 2008:12$ "High Log-RV".

6.2. Risk and Return Trade-Off

To focus on risk and return, we need to account for the volatility feedback effect. In each of our figures, the point on the $E[r|\log(RV), I_{t-1}, \boldsymbol{r}, \boldsymbol{RV}]$ line that corresponds to $\log(RV) = E[\log(RV)|I_{t-1}, \boldsymbol{r}, \boldsymbol{RV}]$ is exactly the point with no volatility feedback. This point is where the investor receives exactly the reward for risk with no adjustment for volatility feedback because the volatility shock is zero. This will be at a different place in each of our curves of $E[r|\log(RV), I_{t-1}, \boldsymbol{r}, \boldsymbol{RV}]$. Using interpolation between each of the grid values, we can estimate the value of $E[r|\log(RV), I_{t-1}, \boldsymbol{r}, \boldsymbol{RV}]$ at $\log(RV) = E[\log(RV)|I_{t-1}, \boldsymbol{r}, \boldsymbol{RV}]$ for each time period t. This represents a *pure* risk and return relationship which nets out volatility feedback.

Figure 8 displays the equity risk premium over time from the nonparametric model when volatility feedback has been removed. The premium is everywhere positive. Figure 9 displays the pure risk and return relationship. It shows the expected excess return as a function of expected log-realized variance according to our model estimates when volatility feedback is removed. Each dot represents the point of $E[r|\log(RV), I_{t-1}, \boldsymbol{r}, \boldsymbol{RV}]$ in which volatility feedback is zero given the information set I_{t-1}. The relationship is unambiguously positive and increasing in $\log(RV)$, which accords with theory. The relationship is nonlinear. It is approximately linear for a small value of log-volatility but increases sharply as expected log-volatility surpasses zero.

In contrast to Campbell and Hentschel (1992) and the subsequent literature on volatility feedback, we find evidence of a positive risk and return relationship and a volatility feedback effect without imposing any economic restrictions. The key is flexibly modeling the contemporaneous distribution of market excess returns and log-realized variance and accounting for the volatility shock.

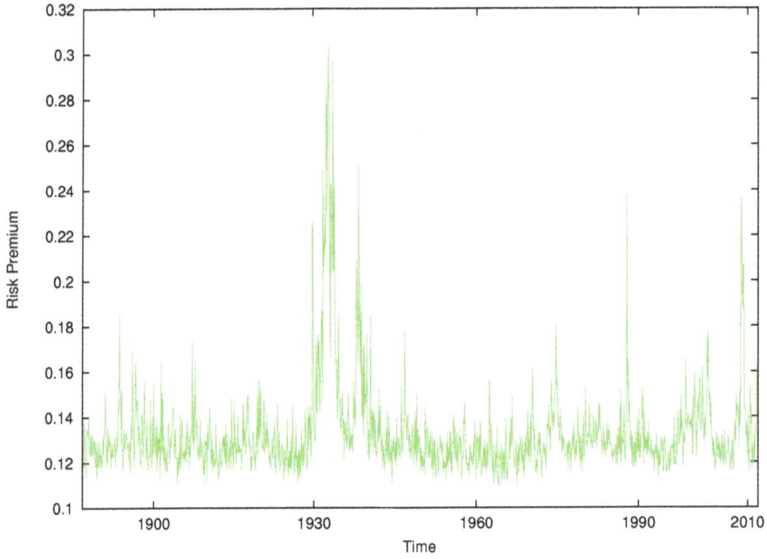

Figure 8. Time series of equity risk premium.

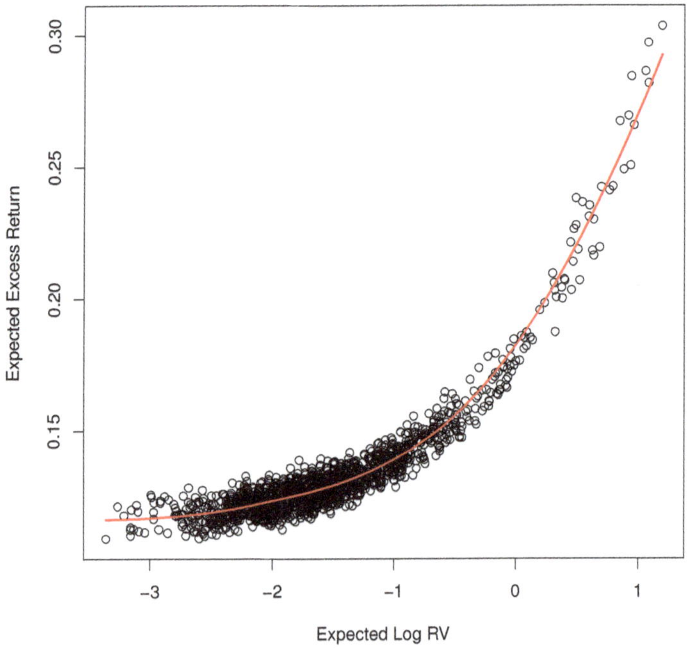

Figure 9. Expected excess return when volatility feedback is zero.

6.3. Conditional Quantiles and Contour Plots

Figures 10–13 display conditional quantile plots of the distribution of excess returns given different values of $\log(RV)$ for the parametric model and several cases of the nonparametric model. In each figure, the green line is the conditional mean that was discussed above.

For the parametric model, as before, the conditional quantiles do not change for different information sets. The estimated weights and component densities in the mixture model of Equation (8), however, are sensitive to the information set and result in very different conditional distributions. Each of the conditional quantile plots show a highly nonlinear distribution that is at odds with the parametric model.

Recall from the previous discussion that the conditional expectations of the low, average and high levels of $\log(RV_t)$ were -3.158, -2.117 and 0.509, respectively. In Figures 11–13, the bulk of the distribution is above zero at each of these points. Investors are most likely to receive a positive excess return from the market at the value of the expected value of log-realized variance. As $\log(RV)$ increases and the volatility shock becomes larger, most of the mass in each conditional density is over a negative range of excess returns. Here, investors are likely to have a loss from investing in the market.

The upper quantiles show the most nonlinear behavior given low (Figure 11) and average (Figure 12) levels of volatility. Volatility feedback has an impact on the whole distribution and not just the conditional mean. The changes in the density, as $\log(RV)$ increases, are non-monotonic. In Figures 11 and 12, there is an increase in the spread of the density followed by a decrease and final increase. The point of these changes in the conditional density is to the right of the conditional mean of $\log(RV_t)$. The parametric quantile plot is inconsistent with these features.

Although volatility feedback is the most likely explanation of our results, Veronesi (1999) shows that, in the presence of uncertainty about the economic regime, prices overreact to bad news in good times and underreact to good news in bad times. This results in negative returns coupled with high volatility such as seen in the conditional quantile plots.

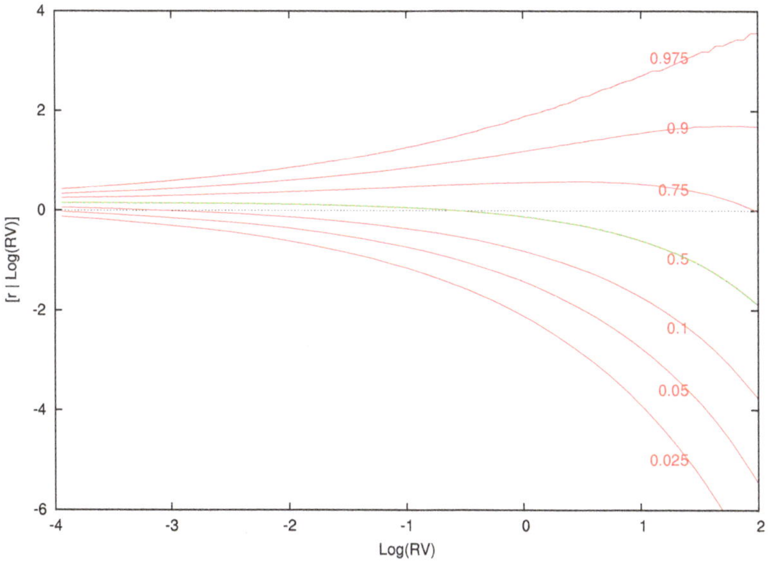

Figure 10. Quantiles of excess returns given $\log(RV)$ for the parametric model. This figure displays the quantiles of the distribution of excess returns conditional on $\log(RV)$ for the parametric model. The green dotted line is the expected excess return given $\log(RV)$.

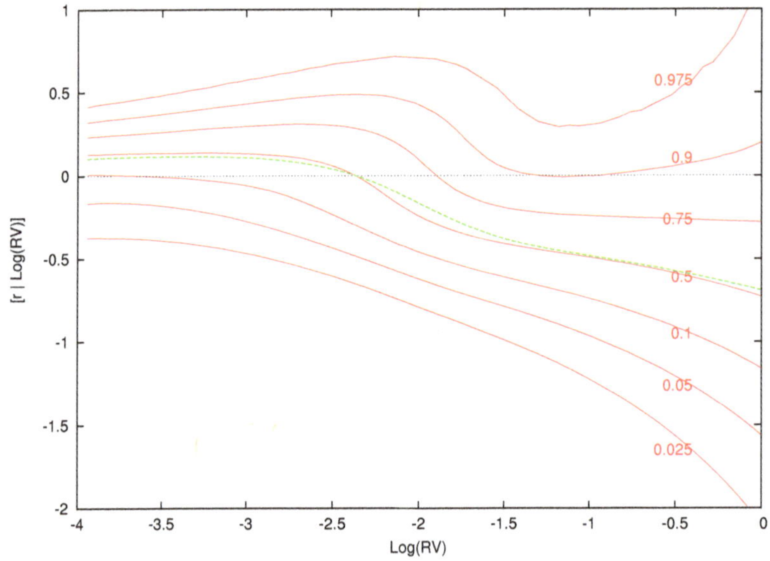

Figure 11. Quantiles of excess returns given $\log(RV)$ for low volatility. This figure displays the quantiles of the distribution of excess returns conditional on $\log(RV)$ for $I_{t-1}, t = 1964:10$. The green dotted line is the expected excess return given $\log(RV)$.

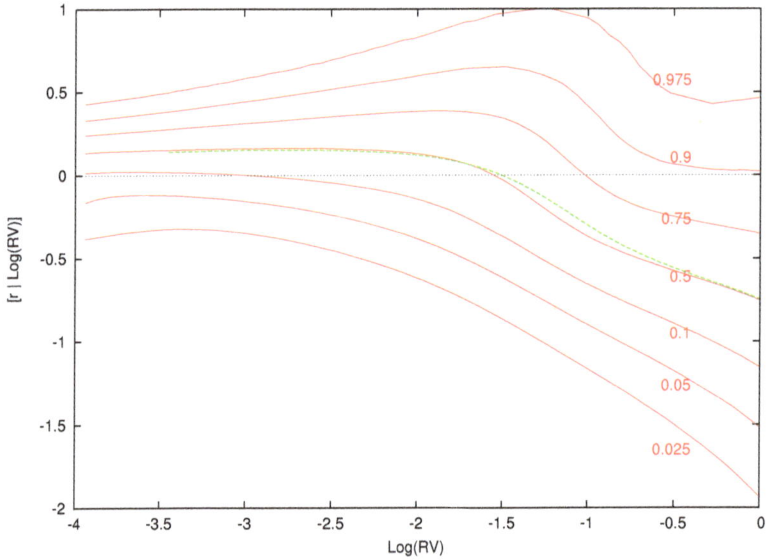

Figure 12. Quantiles of excess returns given $\log(RV)$ for average volatility. This figure displays the quantiles of the distribution of excess returns conditional on $\log(RV)$ for $I_{t-1}, t = 1996:2$. The green dotted line is the expected excess return given $\log(RV)$.

Contour plots of the conditional joint predictive density for excess returns and log-realized variances, for the three different months of market volatility, are found in Figures 14–16. Each of the figures are consistent with deviations from Gaussian behavior in the conditional bivariate distribution. It is clear that the conditional distribution changes a great deal over time and is not a result of changes in location and/or scale. There is a thick tail for small values of r and larger values of $\log(RV)$ in each figure, but the shape of the distributions tail is very different depending on I_t. These important changes in the conditional density are the features that our nonparametric model are designed to capture. Conventional parametric approaches cannot accommodate these features.

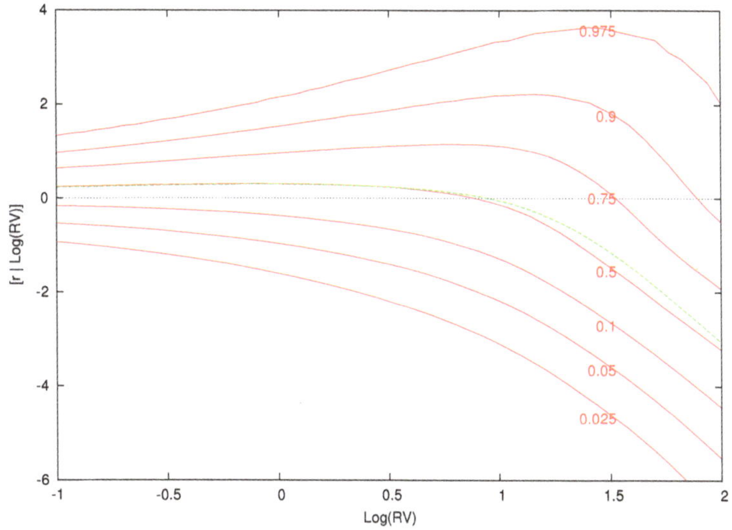

Figure 13. Quantiles of excess returns given $\log(RV_t)$ for high volatility. This figure displays the quantiles of the distribution of excess returns conditional on $\log(RV)$ for I_{t-1}, $t = 2008:12$. The green dotted line is the expected excess return given $\log(RV)$.

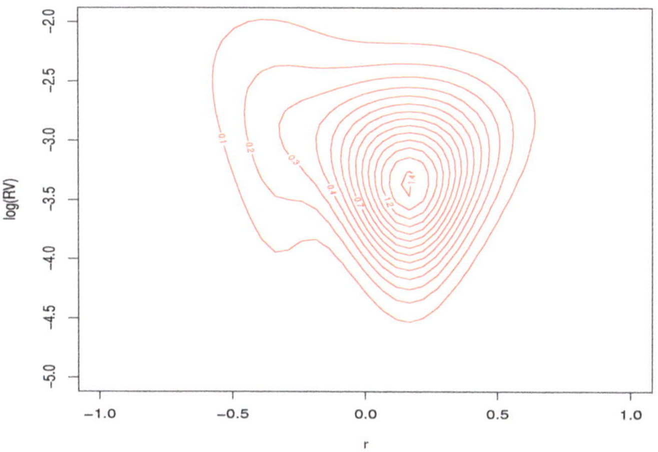

Figure 14. Predictive density for $r, \log(RV)$ for low volatility I_{t-1}, $t = 1964:10$.

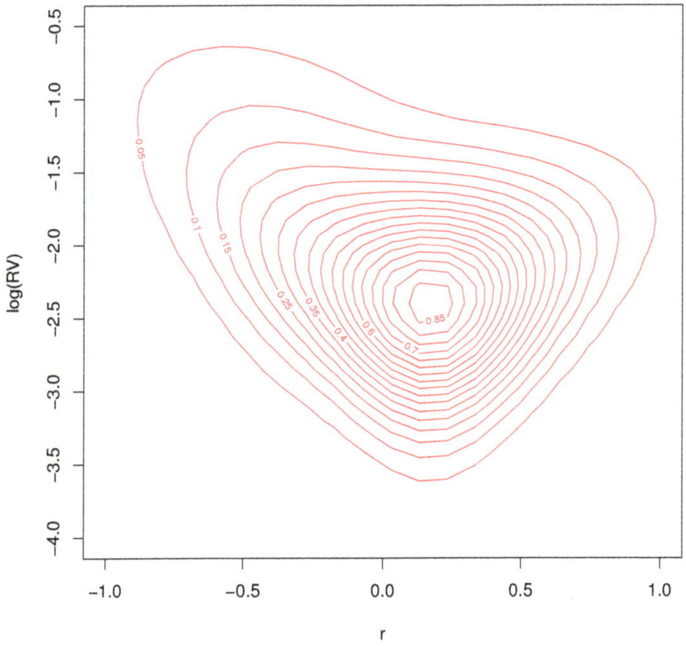

Figure 15. Predictive density for $r, \log(RV)$ for average volatility I_{t-1}, $t = 1996:2$.

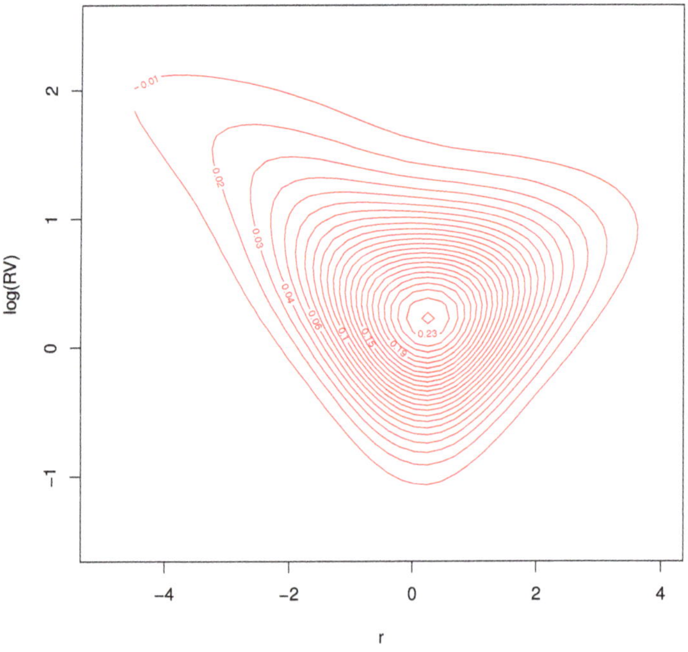

Figure 16. Predictive density for $r, \log(RV)$ for high volatility I_{t-1}, $t = 2008:12$.

6.4. Parameter Estimates and Robustness

Figures 17 and 18 display the posterior mean of each of the model parameters contained in the vector θ_t^* for $t = 1, \ldots, T$. A parametric model would be a straight line. We see considerable switching between clusters in all the plots and the size of the change between the cluster's parameter values is often large. This shows that multiple mixture components in our nonparametric model is a significant feature of the data. Compared to the parametric model results found in Table 2, $\alpha_{1,t}^*$, the coefficient on RV_t is negative and positive over different time periods. The variability of the parameters in the figures is well beyond the 95% density intervals for the parametric model reported in Table 2. Although the parametric model estimate of η_1^2 is close to one, the nonparametric parameter estimates, $\eta_{1,t}^*$, $t = 1, \ldots, T$, varies between 0.4 to 0.85. This is due to the significantly improved fit that the nonparametric model offers in the conditional mean, which contributes to a lower innovation variance.

Our results are robust to changes in the priors and the model for the data density. For instance, we obtain the same qualitative results for $E[r|\log(RV), I_{t-1}, \boldsymbol{r}, \boldsymbol{RV}]$ if we omit from Equation (5) RV_t by setting $\alpha_{1,j} = 0$, $j = 1, \ldots, \infty$, or drop the lagged return terms from Equation (6) by making $\gamma_{3,j} = \gamma_{4,j} = 0$ for $j = 1, \ldots, \infty$. Although our priors are quite diffuse and provide a wide range of empirically realistic parameter values, making them more diffuse produces similar results, but the density intervals for $E[r|\log(RV), I_{t-1}, \boldsymbol{r}, \boldsymbol{RV}]$ are generally larger. If RV_t is replaced by $\log(RV_t)$ in the conditional mean of excess returns (5), we obtain the same results for $E[r|\log(RV), I_{t-1}, \boldsymbol{r}, \boldsymbol{RV}]$.

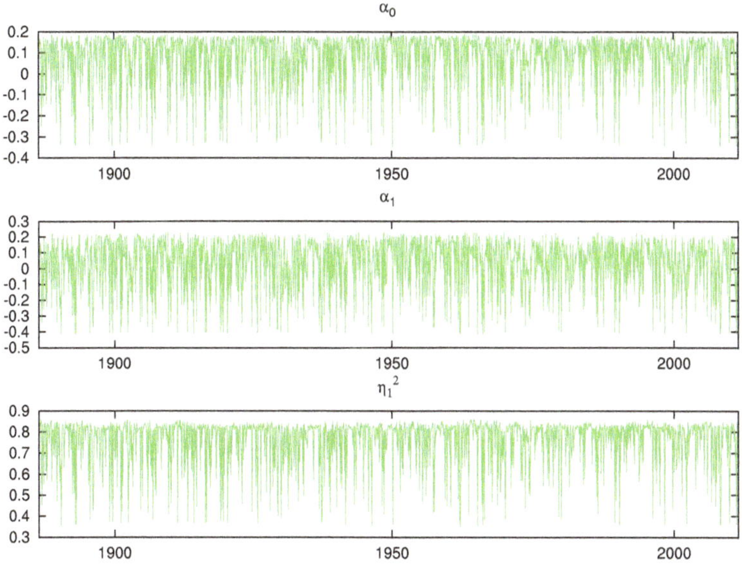

Figure 17. Posterior means of α_{0,s_t}, α_{1,s_t} and η_{1,s_t}^2.

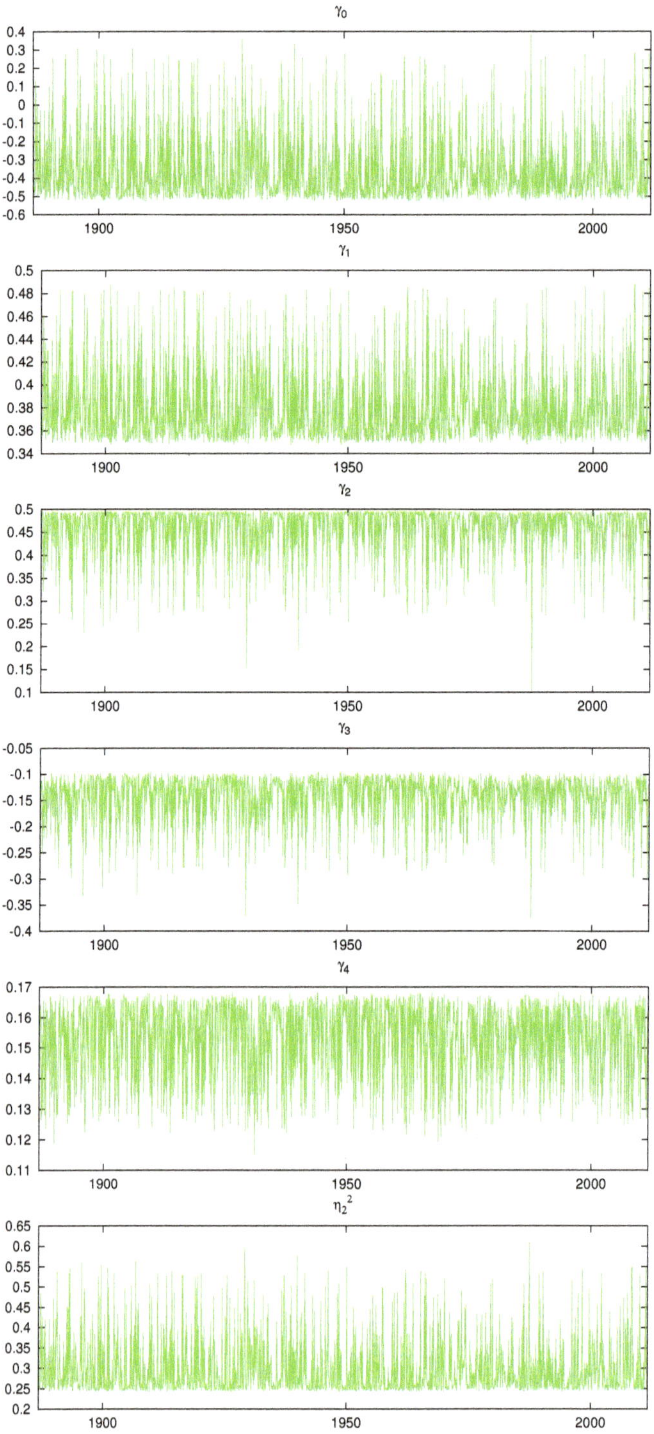

Figure 18. Posterior means of $\gamma_{0,s_t}, \ldots, \gamma_{4,s_t}$ and η^2_{2,s_t}.

7. Conclusions

This paper nonparametrically models the contemporaneous relationship between market excess returns and realized variances. An infinite mixture of distributions is given a flexible Dirichlet process prior. From this, the nonparametric conditional distribution of returns given realized variance consists of an infinite mixture representation whose probabilities and arguments depend on the value of realized variance. This allows for a smooth nonlinear relationship between the conditional mean of market excess returns and realized variance. The model is estimated with MCMC techniques based on slice sampling methods that extends the posterior sampling methods in the literature.

Applied to a long span of monthly data, we find strong robust evidence of volatility feedback. Once volatility feedback is accounted for, there is an unambiguous positive relationship between expected excess returns and expected log-realized variance. In contrast to the existing literature, we find evidence of a positive risk and return relationship and a volatility feedback effect without imposing any economic restrictions. We show that the volatility feedback impacts the whole distribution and not just the conditional mean.

Due to the nonlinear risk and return relationship and the presence of volatility feedback, simple regression techniques or models that ignore these facts are likely to give misleading estimates of risk.

Several questions remain from our work. Would higher frequency data also display a positive risk and return relationship once volatility feedback is modeled? Would more accurate ex post variance measures computed from intraday data improve estimation accuracy? We leave these questions for future work.

Author Contributions: Both authors are equal contributors.

Funding: Maheu's research is supported by the Social Sciences and Humanities Research Council of Canada.

Acknowledgments: We are grateful for helpful comments from the Editor, four anonymous referees, Tolga Cenesizoglu, Christian Dorion and Georgios Skoulakis and conference participants at CFE'12, NBER-NSF SBIES 2013, the Bayesian RCEA workshop 2013 and the Applied Financial Time-series workshop HEC 2014 and seminar participants at McMaster University and University of Toronto. A previous version of this work was titled "A Bayesian Nonparametric Analysis of the Relationship between Returns and Realized Variance." We are grateful to Tom McCurdy who supplied the data. The views expressed here are ours and not necessarily those of the Federal Reserve Bank of Atlanta or the Federal Reserve System. J.M.M. is grateful to the SSHRC for financial support.

Conflicts of Interest: The authors declare no conflict of interest.

References

Andersen, Torben G., Tim Bollerslev, Francis X. Diebold, and Paul Labys. 2003. Modeling and forecasting realized volatility. *Econometrica* 71: 529–626. [CrossRef]

Andersen, Torben G., and Luca Benzoni. 2008. Realized Volatility. FRB of Chicago Working Paper No. 2008-14. Available online: http://ssrn.com/abstract=1092203 (accessed on 1 September 2018).

Andersen, Torben G., Tim Bollerslev, and Francis X. Diebold. 2007. Roughing it up: Including jump components in the measurement, modeling, and forecasting of return volatility. *The Review of Economics and Statistics* 89: 701–20. [CrossRef]

Bandi, Federico M., and Benoit Perron. 2008. Long-run risk–return trade-offs. *Journal of Econometrics* 143: 349–74. [CrossRef]

Bollerslev, Tim, Julia Litvinova, and George Tauchen. 2006. Leverage and volatility feedback effects in high-frequency data. *Journal of Financial Econometrics* 4: 353–84. [CrossRef]

Brandt, Michael W., and Qiang Kang. 2004. On the relationship between the conditional mean and volatility of stock returns: A latent var approach. *Journal of Financial Economics* 72: 217–57. [CrossRef]

Burda, Martin, Matthew Harding, and Jerry Hausman. 2008. A Bayesian mixed logit–probit model for multinomial choice. *Journal of Econometrics* 147: 232–46. [CrossRef]

Calvet, Laurent E., and Adlai J. Fisher. 2007. Multifrequency news and stock returns. *Journal of Financial Economics* 86: 178–212. [CrossRef]

Campbell, John Y., and Ludger Hentschel. 1992. No news is good news: An asymmetric model of changing volatility in stock returns. *Journal of Financial Economics* 31: 281–318. [CrossRef]

Campbell, John Y., and Robert J. Shiller. 1988. The dividend-price ratio and expectations of future dividends and discount factors. *Review of Financial Studies* 1: 195–228. [CrossRef]

Chib, Siddhartha, and Edward Greenberg. 2010. Additive cubic spline regression with dirichlet process mixture errors. *Journal of Econometrics* 156: 322–36. [CrossRef]

Chib, Siddhartha, and Barton Hamilton. 2002. Semiparametric Bayes analysis of longitudinal data treatment models. *Journal of Econometrics* 110: 67–89. [CrossRef]

Conley, Timothy G., Christian B. Hansen, Robert E. McCulloch, and Peter E. Rossi. 2008. A semi-parametric Bayesian approach to the instrumental variable problem. *Journal of Econometrics* 144: 276–305. [CrossRef]

Corsi, Fulvio. 2009. A simple approximate long-memory model of realized volatility. *Journal of Financial Econometrics* 7: 174–96. [CrossRef]

Delatola, Eleni-Ioanna, and Jim E. Griffin. 2013. A Bayesian semiparametric model for volatility with a leverage effect. *Computational Statistics & Data Analysis* 60: 97–110.

Escobar, Michael D. and Mike West. 1995. Bayesian density estimation and inference using mixtures. *Journal of the American Statistical Association* 90: 577–88. [CrossRef]

Ferguson, Thomas S. 1973. A Bayesian analysis of some nonparametric problems. *The Annals of Statistics* 1: 209–30. [CrossRef]

Ferguson, Thomas S. 1983. Bayesian Density Estimation by Mixtures of Normal Distribution. In *Recent Advances in Statistics*. Edited by M. Haseeb Rizvi, Jagdish S. Rustagi and David Siegmund. New York: Academic Press Inc., pp. 287–302.

French, Kenneth R., G. William Schwert, and Robert F. Stambaugh. 1987. Expected stock returns and volatility. *Journal of Financial Economics* 19: 3–29. [CrossRef]

Gallant, Ronald A., and George Tauchen. 1989. Seminonparametric estimation of conditionally constrained heterogeneous processes: Asset pricing applications. *Econometrica* 57: 1091–120. [CrossRef]

Ghosal, S., J. K. Ghosh, and R. V. Ramamoorthi. 1999. Posterior consistency of Dirchlet mixtures in density estimation. *Annals of Statistics* 27: 143–58.

Ghysels, Eric, Alberto Plazzi, and Rossen Valkanov. 2013. The Risk–Return Relationship and Financial Crises. Working paper, University of North Carolina at Chapel Hill, Department of Economics, Chapel Hill, NC, USA.

Ghysels, Eric, Pedro Santa-Clara, and Rossen Valkanov. 2005. There is a risk–return trade-off after all. *Journal of Financial Economics* 76: 509–48. [CrossRef]

Greenberg, Edward. 2013. *Introduction to Bayesian Econometrics*, 2nd ed. New York: Cambridge University Press.

Griffin, Jim E., and Mark F. J. Steel. 2004. Semiparametric Bayesian inference for stochastic frontier models. *Journal of Econometrics* 123: 121–52. [CrossRef]

Guo, Hui, and Robert F. Whitelaw. 2006. Uncovering the risk–return relation in the stock market. *The Journal of Finance* 61: 1433–63. [CrossRef]

Hansen, Peter R., and Asger Lunde. 2006. Realized variance and market microstructure noise. *Journal of Business & Economic Statistics* 24: 127–61.

Harrison, Paul, and Harold H. Zhang. 1999. An investigation of the risk and return relation at long horizons. *The Review of Economics and Statistics* 81: 399–408. [CrossRef]

Harvey, Campbell R. 2001. The specification of conditional expectations. *Journal of Empirical Finance* 8: 573–637. [CrossRef]

Ishwaran, Hemant, and Lancelot F. James. 2001. Gibbs sampling methods for the stick breaking priors. *Journal of the American Statistical Association* 96: 161–73. [CrossRef]

Jensen, Mark J., and John M. Maheu. 2010. Bayesian semiparametric stochastic volatility modeling. *Journal of Econometrics* 157: 306–16. [CrossRef]

Jensen, Mark J., and John M. Maheu. 2013. Bayesian semiparametric multivariate GARCH modeling. *Journal of Econometrics* 176: 3–17. [CrossRef]

Jensen, Mark J., and John M. Maheu. 2014. Estimating a semiparametric asymmetric stochastic volatility model with a dirichlet process mixture. *Journal of Econometrics* 178: 523–38. [CrossRef]

Kalli, Maria, Jim Griffin, and Stephen Walker. 2011. Slice sampling mixture models. *Statistics and Computing* 21: 93–105. [CrossRef]

Kim, Chang-Jin, James C. Morley, and Charles R. Nelson. 2004. Is there a positive relationship between stock market volatility and the equity premium? *Journal of Money, Credit, and Banking* 36: 339–60. [CrossRef]

Kim, Chang-Jin, James C. Morley, and Charles R. Nelson. 2005. The structural break in the equity premium. *Journal of Business & Economic Statistics* 23: 181–91.

Lettau, Martin, and Sydney Ludvigson. 2010. Measuring and Modeling Variation in the Risk-Return Trade-Off. In *Handbook of Financial Econometrics*. Edited by Yacine Ait-Shalia and Lars-Peter Hansen. New York: Elsevier.

Lo, Albert Y. 1984. On a class of Bayesian nonparametric estimates. I. density estimates. *The Annals of Statistics* 12: 351–57. [CrossRef]

Ludvigson, Sydney C., and Serena Ng. 2007. The empirical risk–return relation: A factor analysis approach. *Journal of Financial Economics* 83: 171–222. [CrossRef]

Lundblad, Christian. 2007. The risk return trade-off in the long run: 1836–2003. *Journal of Financial Economics* 85: 123–50. [CrossRef]

Maheu, John M., and Thomas H. McCurdy. 2007. Components of market risk and return. *Journal of Financial Econometrics* 5: 560–90. [CrossRef]

Maheu, John M., and Thomas H. McCurdy. 2011. Do high-frequency measures of volatility improve forecasts of return distributions? *Journal of Econometrics* 160: 69–76. [CrossRef]

Maheu, John M., Thomas H. McCurdy, and Xiaofei Zhao. 2013. Do jumps contribute to the dynamics of the equity premium? *Journal of Financial Economics* 110: 457–77. [CrossRef]

McAleer, Michael, and Marcelo C. Medeiros. 2008. Realized volatility: A review. *Econometric Reviews* 27: 10–45. [CrossRef]

Muller, Peter, Alaattin Erkanli, and Mike West. 1996. Bayesian curve fitting using multivariate normal mixtures. *Biometrika* 83: 67–79. [CrossRef]

Papaspiliopoulos, Omiros. 2008. A note on posterior sampling from Dirichlet mixture models. Department of Economics, Universitat Pompeu Fabra, Barcelona, Spain. Unpublished manuscript.

Rodriguez, Abel, David B. Dunson, and Alan E. Gelfand. 2009. Bayesian nonparametric functional data analysis through density estimation. *Biometrika* 96: 149–62. [CrossRef] [PubMed]

Schwert, G. William. 1990. Indexes of U.S. stock prices from 1802 to 1987. *Journal of Business* 63: 399–426. [CrossRef]

Scruggs, John T. 1998. Resolving the puzzling intertemporal relation between the market risk premium and conditional market variance: A two-factor approach. *Journal of Finance* 53: 575–603. [CrossRef]

Sethuraman, Jayaram. 1994. A constructive definition of Dirichlet priors. *Statistica Sinica* 4: 639–50.

Shahbaba, Babak, and Radford Neal. 2009. Nonlinear models using dirichlet process mixtures. *Journal of Machine Learning Research* 10: 1829–50.

Taddy, Matthew A., and Athanasios Kottas. 2010. A Bayesian nonparametric approach to inference for quantile regression. *Journal of Business & Economic Statistics* 28: 357–69.

Turner, Christopher M., Richard Startz, and Charles R. Nelson. 1989. A Markov model of heteroskedasticity, risk, and learning in the stock market. *Journal of Financial Economics* 25: 3–22. [CrossRef]

Veronesi, Pietro. 1999. Stock market overreaction to bad news in good times: A rational expectations equilibrium model. *The Review of Financial Studies* 12: 975–1007. [CrossRef]

Walker, Stephen G. 2007. Sampling the dirichlet mixture model with slices. *Communications in Statistics—Simulation and Computation* 36: 45–54. [CrossRef]

Journal of
Risk and Financial Management

MDPI

Article

Forecasting of Realised Volatility with the Random Forests Algorithm

Chuong Luong and Nikolai Dokuchaev *

School of Electrical Engineering, Computing and Mathematical Sciences, Curtin University, GPO Box U1987, Perth 6845, Western Australia, Australia; p.luong@postgrad.curtin.edu.au
* Correpondence: N.Dokuchaev@curtin.edu.au

Received: 8 September 2018; Accepted: 9 October 2018; Published: 11 October 2018

Abstract: The paper addresses the forecasting of realised volatility for financial time series using the heterogeneous autoregressive model (HAR) and machine learning techniques. We consider an extended version of the existing HAR model with included purified implied volatility. For this extended model, we apply the random forests algorithm for the forecasting of the direction and the magnitude of the realised volatility. In experiments with historical high frequency data, we demonstrate improvements of forecast accuracy for the proposed model.

Keywords: realised volatility; heterogeneous autoregressive model; purified implied volatility; classification; random forests; machine learning

1. Introduction

In this paper, the estimation of historical volatility is considered for financial time series generated by stock prices and indexes. This estimation is a necessary step for the volatility forecast which is crucial for the pricing of financial derivatives and for optimal portfolio selection. The methods of estimation and forecast of volatility have been intensively studied (see, e.g., the references in Andersen and Bollerslev (1997) and in De Stefani et al. (2017); Dokuchaev (2014)).

In pricing of derivatives, option traders use volatility as the input for determining the value of an option using underlying models such as the Black–Scholes' (Black and Scholes 1973) and Heston's (1993) option pricing models. Hence, being able to forecast the direction and magnitude of the future volatility on different time horizons will provide advantages in terms of pricing risks and the development of trading strategies.

There is an enormous body of research on modelling and forecasting volatility. Engle (1982) and Bollerslev (1986) first proposed the ARCH model and the GARCH model for forecasting volatility. These models have been extended in a number of directions based on the empirical evidences that the volatility process is non-linear, asymmetry, and has a long memory. Such extensions can be referred to EGARCH—Nelson (1991), GJR-GARCH—Glosten et al. (1993), AGARCH—Engle (1990), and TGARCH—Zakoian (1994). However, studies have found that those models cannot describe the whole-day volatility information well enough because they were developed within low-frequency time sequences.

With the appearance of high-frequency data, Andersen et al. (2003) introduced a new volatility measure. This proxy was known as realized volatility (RV). In comparison with the GARCH-type measures, realised volatility is preferred as it is a model-free measure. Hence, it provides convenience for calculation. In addition, the realised volatility takes high-frequency data into consideration and exhibits the long memory property. There have been many forecasting models that have been developed to predict the realised volatility. Among those models, the heterogeneous autogressive model for realised volatility (HAR) by Corsi (2003) is one to name. The HAR-RV model was developed in accordance with the heterogeneous market hypothesis proposed by Muller et al. (1997) and the long memory character of realised volatility by Andersen et al. (2003). Empirical studies have shown that the HAR model has high forecasting performance for future volatility, especially for out-of-sample data with different time horizons (Corsi 2003; Khan 2011).

Another commonly used volatility measure is the implied volatility. The implied volatility is often derived from the observed market option prices and is regarded as the fear gauge Whaley (2000). The implied volatility fluctuates with stock movement, strike price, interest rate, time-to-maturity, and option price. To reduce the impact of stock price movement, a so-called "purified" implied volatility was introduced in Luong and Dokuchaev (2014). In the present paper, we show that that this volatility measure contains some information about the future volatility.

To produce rules for prediction for the classes and the regression of the outcome variables, classification and regression tree models and other machine learning techniques have been developed in the literature (see the references in De Stefani et al. (2017)). This paper explores the related random forests algorithm to improve the forecasting of realised volatility in the machine learning setting.

This algorithm is constructed to predict both the direction and the magnitude of realised volatility, based on the HAR model framework with the inclusion of the purified implied volatility.

The paper is structured as follows. In Section 2, we provide the background of the volatility measures, the classical HAR model, and the random forests algorithm. We then discuss our proposed model and methodology and their results in Section 3. Section 4 provides discussion of the study, and we conclude the results of this study in Section 5.

2. Materials and Methods

2.1. Random Forests Algorithm

Breiman (2001) introduced the random forests (RF) algorithm as an ensemble approach that can also be thought of as a form of nearest neighbour predictor. The random forest starts with a standard machine learning technique called "decision trees". We provide a brief summary of this algorithm in this section.

2.1.1. Decision Trees

The decision trees algorithm is an approach that uses a set of binary rules to calculate a target class or value. Different from predictors like linear or polynomial regression where a single predictive formula is supposed to hold over the entire data space, decision trees aim to sub-divide the data into multiple partitions using a recursive method, and then fit simple models to each cell of the partition. Each decision tree has three levels:

- Root nodes: entry points to a collection of data;
- Inner nodes: a set of binary questions where each child node is available for every possible answer;
- Leaf nodes: respond to the decision to take if reached.

For example, in order to predict a response or class Y from inputs $X_1, X_2, ..., X_n$, a binary tree is constructed based on the information from each input. At the internal nodes in the tree, a test to one of the inputs is run for a given criterion with logical outcomes: **TRUE** or **FALSE**. Depending on the outcome, a decision is drawn to the next sub-branches corresponding to the **TRUE** or **FALSE** response. Eventually, a final prediction outcome is obtained at the leaf node. This prediction aggregates or averages all of the training data points which reach that leaf. Figure 1 illustrates the binary tree concept.

Algorithm 1 describes how a decision tree can be constructed using CART from (Breiman et al. 1984). This algorithm is computationally simple and quick to fit the data. In addition, as it requires no parametric, no formal distributional assumptions are required. However, one of the main disadvantages of tree-based models is that they exhibit instability and high variance, i.e., a small change in the data can result in a very different series of split, or over-fitting. To overcome such a major issue, we used an alternative ensemble approach known as the random forests algorithm.

Algorithm 1: Classification And Regression Trees - CART algorithm for building decision trees.

1: Let N be the root node with all available data.
2: Find the feature F and threshold value T that split the samples assigned to N into subsets I_{TRUE} and I_{FALSE}, to maximise the label purity within these subsets.
3: Assign the pair (F, T) to N.
4: If $I(s)$ is too small to be split, attach a 'child' leaf node to L_{TRUE} and L_{FALSE} to N and assign the leaves with the most present label in I_{TRUE} and I_{FALSE}, respectively.
If subset $I(s)$ is large enough to be split, attach child nodes N_{TRUE} and N_{FALSE} to N, and then assign $I(s)$ to them, respectively.
5: Repeat steps 2–4 for the new nodes $N = N_{TRUE}$ and $N = N_{FALSE}$ until the new subsets can no longer be split.

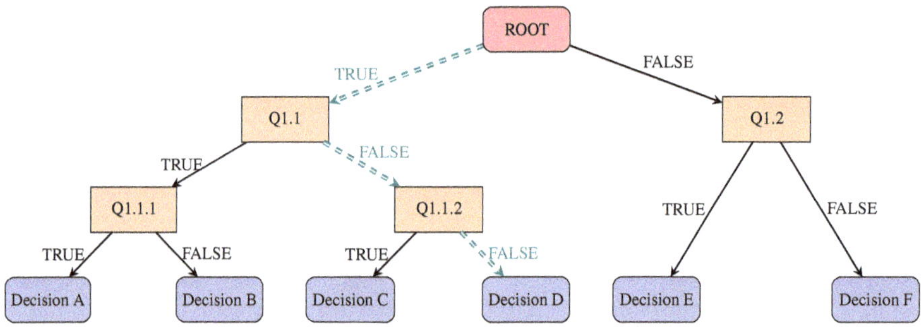

Figure 1. A binary tree—starting from the root node, multiple criteria are selected based on the information from each input. A decision is drawn at a particular leaf, i.e., Decision D, if all criteria along its path "==" are satisfied.

2.1.2. Random Forests

A random forest can be considered to be a collection or ensemble of simple decision trees that are selected randomly. It belongs to the class of so-called bootstrap aggregation or bagging technique which aims to reduce the variance in an estimated prediction function. Particularly, a number of decision trees are constructed and random forests will either "vote" for the best decision (classification problems) or "average" the predicted values (regression problems). Here, each tree in the collection is formed by firstly selecting, at random, at each node, a small group of input coordinates (also called features or variables hereafter) to split on and secondly, by calculating the best split based on these features in the training set. The tree is grown using the CART algorithm to maximum size, without pruning. The use of random forests can lead to significant improvements in prediction accuracy (i.e., better ability to predict new data cases) in comparison with a single decision tree, as discussed in the previous section. Algorithm 2 from Breiman (2001) details how the random forests can be constructed.

For $m = 1$, the algorithm uses random splitter selection. m can also be set to the total number of predictor variables which is known as Breiman's bagger parameter (Breiman 2001). In this paper, we set m as equal to the maximum number of variables of interest used in the proposed model.

Applications of the random forests algorithm can be found in machine learning, pattern recognitions, bio-infomatics, and big data modelling. Recently, a number of financial literatures have applied the random forests algorithm to the forecasting of stock prices as well as in developing the investment strategies found in Theofilatos et al. (2012) and Qin et al. (2013). Here, we introduce an application of the random forests algorithm involving the forecasting of the realised volatility.

Algorithm 2: Random forests

1: Draw a number of bootstrap samples from the original data (n_{tree}) to be grown.
2: Sample N cases at random with replacement to create a subset of the data. The subset is then split into in-bag and out-of-bag samples at a selected ratio (i.e., 7:3).
3: At each node, for a preselected number m, m predictor variables (m_{try}) are chosen at random from all the predictor variables.
4: The predictor variable that provides the best split, according to some objective function, is used to build a binary split on that node.
5: At the next node, choose another m variables at random from all predictor variables.
6: Repeat 3–5 until all nodes are grown.

2.2. *Volatility Measures*

Volatility, often measured by the standard deviation or variance of returns from a financial security or market index, is an important component of asset allocation, risk management, and pricing derivatives. In this section, we discuss the two measures of volatility known as the realised volatility and the purified implied volatility.

2.2.1. Realised Volatility

The realised volatility measure was proposed by Andersen et al. (2003) in 2003 based on the use of high frequency data.

Let $S(t)$ represent the asset price which is observed at equally-spaced discrete points within a given time interval $[t-\delta, t]$, where $0 \leqslant t-\delta \leqslant t \leqslant T$, $s(t) = \log S(t)$ and $r(t,\delta) = s(t) - s(t-\delta)$. We assume that $S(t)$ is represented by the following Ito equation

$$ds(t) = \mu(t)dt + \sigma(t)dW(t), \quad 0 \leqslant t \leqslant T, \tag{1}$$

where $W(t)$ is a standard Brownian process, $\mu(t)$ and $\sigma(t)$ are predictable processes with $\sigma(t)$ being the standard deviation of $ds(t)$ and independent of $dW(t)$. Therefore, the processes $\mu(t)$ and $\sigma(t)$ represent the instantaneous conditional mean and volatility of the return. Hence,

$$r(t,\delta) = s(t) - s(t-\delta) = \int_{t-\delta}^{t} \mu(\tau)d\tau + \int_{t-\delta}^{t} \sigma(\tau)W(t). \tag{2}$$

Following this result, let us assume that the time interval $[t-\delta, t]$ is observed evenly at $\triangle$ steps in discrete time. The realised volatility (RV) of $S(t)$ can be estimated by

$$RV_{t-\delta,t} = \sqrt{\sum_{j=0}^{M-1} r^2_{t-j\triangle}}, \tag{3}$$

where $r_{t-j\triangle} = s(t-j\triangle) - s(t-(j+1)\triangle)$, $\triangle = \frac{1}{M}$, and M is the number of observations within that time interval.

2.2.2. The Purified Implied Volatility

The implied volatility is often known as the ex-ante measure of volatility, and is derived from either the Black–Scholes' options pricing model from Black and Scholes (1973) (model-based estimation) or from theoptions market price formula by Carr and Wu (2006) (model-free estimation). Such measures depend on several inputs, such as time-to-expiration, stock price, exercise price, risk-free-rate-of-interest, and observed call/put price. Hence, the implied volatility will vary in accordance with the fluctuations of these inputs. In order to reduce the impact of the stock price movements, the purified implied volatility (PV) was introduced in Luong and Dokuchaev (2014). The purified implied volatility is derived from the Black–Scholes options pricing model, where the market option prices are replaced by artificial option prices that reduce the impact of the market price from the observed option prices. The paper also shows that the purified implied volatility does contain information about the traditional volatility measure (i.e., the standard deviation of the low-frequency daily returns). In this paper, we include the purified implied volatility as an extended variable of the HAR model.

2.3. Models for Volatility

2.3.1. Heterogeneous Autoregressive Model for Realised Volatility

Corsi (2003) (see also Corsi and Reno (2009)) proposed the heterogeneous autoregressive model for realised volatility as an extension of the Heterogenous ARCH (HARCH) class of models analysed by Muller et al. (1997), which recognizes the presence of heterogeneity in the traders. The idea stems from the "Fractal Market Hypothesis" (Peters 1994), "Interacting Agent View" (Lux and Marchesi 1999) and "Mixture of Distribution" hypotheses (Andersen and Bollerslev 1997) in the realised volatility process.

It is noted that the definition of realised volatility involves two time parameters: (1) the intraday return interval $\triangle$ and (2) the aggregation period one day. For the heterogeneous autoregressive model of realised volatility from Corsi (2003), it is considered that the latent realised volatility is viewed over time horizons longer than one day. The n days historical realised volatility at time t (i.e., $RV_{t-n,t}$) is estimated as an average of the daily realised volatility between $(t-n)$ and t. The daily HAR is expressed by

$$RV_{t,t+1} = \beta_0 + \beta_D RV_{t-1,t} + \beta_W RV_{t-5,t} + \beta_M RV_{t-22,t} + \varepsilon_{t,t+1}, \tag{4}$$

where $W = 5$ days, $M = 22$ days, and $RV_{t-5,t}, RV_{t-22,t}$ present the average realised volatility of the last 5 days and 22 days, respectively. The HAR model can be extended by including the jump component proposed by Barndorff-Nielsen and Shephard (2001) such that

$$\sum_{t-\delta \leqslant \tau \leqslant t} J^2(\tau) \equiv max\{RV(t-\delta,t) - BV(t-\delta,t), 0\}, \tag{5}$$

where BV is the realised bi-power variation Barndorff-Nielsen and Shephard (2004). Hence, the general form of the model is

$$RV_{t,t+k} = \beta_0 + \beta_D RV_{t-1,t} + \beta_W RV_{t-5,t} + \beta_M RV_{t-22,t} + \beta_J J_{t-k,t} + \varepsilon_{t,t+k}. \tag{6}$$

Most recently, the heterogeneous structure was extended with the inclusion of the leverage effect observed by Black (1976)—the asymmetry in the relationship between returns and volatility noticed by Corsi and Reno (2009). For a given period of time, the leverage level at time t is measured as the average aggregated negative and positive returns during that period where

$$r^+_{t-k,t} = \frac{1}{M}\sum_{j=0}^{M-1} r_{t-j\triangle,t} I_{\{r_{t-k,t},\ldots,r_{t,t} \geqslant 0\}};\, r^-_{t-k,t} = \frac{1}{M}\sum_{j=0}^{M-1} r_{t-j\triangle,t} I_{\{r_{t-k,t},\ldots,r_{t,t} \leqslant 0\}},$$

with M being the number of observations between $t-k$, t, and $\triangle$ is the time step. Therefore, one would include the leverage effect as a predictor for the realised volatility in the next k days as follows:

$$\begin{aligned} RV_{t,t+k} = {} & \beta_0 + \beta_D RV_{t-1,t} + \beta_W RV_{t-5,t} + \beta_M RV_{t-22,t} \\ & + \beta_J J_{t-k,t} + \alpha_P r^+_{t-k,t} + \alpha_N r^-_{t-k,t} + \varepsilon_{t,t+k}. \end{aligned} \tag{7}$$

Often, the coefficients $\beta_0, \beta_D, \beta_W, \beta_M, \beta_J, \alpha_P, \alpha_N$ are obtained by using the Ordinary-Least-Squares (OLS) estimation for linear regression models.

2.4. The Modified HAR Model for Realised Volatility and Forecasting the Direction

We define two states of the world outcome on the volatility direction as "UP" and "DOWN". Let D_δ be the direction of the realised volatility observed at the time δ, such that

$$D_\delta = \begin{cases} UP & \text{if } \dfrac{RV_\delta}{RV_{\delta-1}} > 1, \\ DOWN & \text{if } \dfrac{RV_\delta}{RV_{\delta-1}} < 1. \end{cases} \tag{8}$$

In order to forecast the direction of realised volatility, a set of predictors (or technical indicators) is used which are derived from the historical price movement of the underlying asset and its realised volatility. Since all available historical information is used, D_δ does not follow a Markov chain. We investigated a number of indicators and through the feature selection process (using variable importance ranking from the random forest algorithm), we found that the following indicators were best for forecasting the realised volatility's direction.

1. The Average True Range (ATR): The ATR is an indicator that measures volatility by using the high–low range of the daily prices. ATR is based on n-periods and can be calculated on an intraday, daily, weekly, or monthly basis. It is noted that ATR is often used as a proxy for volatility. To estimate ATR_t, we are required to compute the "true range" (TR) such that

$$TR_\delta = max\{H_\delta - L_\delta, |H_\delta - C_{\delta-1}|, |L - C_{\delta-1}|\}, \tag{9}$$

   where H_δ, L_δ, $C_{\delta-1}$ are the current highest return, the current lowest return, and the previous last return of a selected period, respectively, with absolute values to ensure TR_δ is always positive. Hence, the average true range within n-days is

$$ATR_{\delta-n,\delta} = \frac{(n-1)ATR_{\delta-n-1,\delta} + TR_\delta}{n}. \tag{10}$$

2. Close Relative To Daily Range (CRTDR): The location of the last return within the day's range is a powerful predictor of next-returns. Here, CRTDR is estimated by

$$CRTDR_\delta = \frac{C_\delta - L_\delta}{H_\delta - L_\delta}, \tag{11}$$

   where, H_δ, L_δ and C_δ are the high, low, and close returns at time δ for a selected time period using high frequency returns.
3. Exponential Moving Average of realised volatility (EMARV): Exponential moving averages reduce the lag effect in time-series by applying more weight to recent prices. The weighting applied to the most recent price depends on the number of periods (n) in the moving average and the weighting multiplier (κ). The formula for EMARV of n-periods is as follows:

$$EMARV_{\delta-n,\delta} = RV_\delta - \kappa \times EMARV_{\delta-n-1,\delta} + EMARV_{\delta-n-1,\delta}. \tag{12}$$

4. Moving average convergence/divergence oscillator (MACD) measure of realised volatility: The MACD is one of the simplest and most effective momentum indicators. It turns two moving averages into a momentum oscillator by subtracting the longer moving average (m-days) from the shorter moving average (n-days). The MACD fluctuates above and below the zero line as the moving averages converge, cross, and diverge. We estimate the MACD for realised volatility as

$$MACDRV_{\delta,m,n} = EMARV_{\delta,m} - EMARV_{\delta,n}. \tag{13}$$

5. Relative Strength Index for realised volatility (RSIRV): This is also a momentum oscillator that measures the speed and change of volatility movements. We define RSIRV as

$$RSIRV_{\delta-n,\delta} = 1 - \frac{1}{1 + \dfrac{\overline{RV}^{+}_{\delta-n,\delta}}{\overline{RV}^{-}_{\delta-n,\delta}}}, \tag{14}$$

where $\overline{RV}^{+}_{\delta-n,\delta}$ is the average increase in volatility and $\overline{RV}^{-}_{\delta-n,\delta}$ is the average decrease in volatility within n-days.

The steps that we take to forecast the volatility direction are listed in Algorithm 3.

Algorithm 3: Forecasting the direction of realised volatility

---

1: Obtain the direction of the realised volatility.
2: Compute the above technical indicators for each observation.
3: Split the data into a training set and a testing set.
4: Apply the random forests algorithm to the training set to develop the pattern solution of the realised volatility using the above indicators.
5: Use the solution from Step 4 to predict the direction of the testing set.

Figure 2 demonstrates a possible decision tree that was built for forecasting the direction of realised volatility D_δ using the above steps. In this example, node #4 can be reached when RSI-RV(5) $\geqslant 0.5$ and TR(10) < 0.0084, with 19% of the in-sample data falling into this category and 91% of these observations being classified as "DOWN". Likewise, node #27 is reached when RSI-RV(5) $\leqslant 0.5$, $r^{+} \geqslant 0.014$, and $0.0049 \leqslant TR(10) < 0.0072$. In random forests, we can construct similar trees but with different structures to classify the direction of the realised volatility based on the information from other predictors.

Let $\widehat{D}_{t,t+k}$ denote the predicted direction of the realised volatility at time $t+k$ using Algorithm 3.

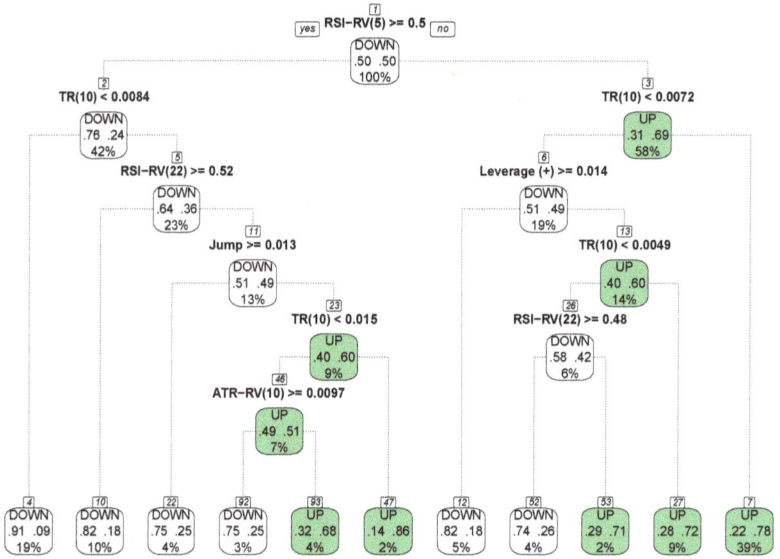

Figure 2. A possible decision tree for classifying the daily realised volatility direction using the technical indicators from the previous day.

2.5. Forecasting the Realised Volatility—The Proposed Model

To forecast the realised volatility, we consider the heterogeneous autoregression model as discussed in Section 2.3.1. We further include the purified implied volatility and the predicted direction of the future volatility as new predictive variables. Particularly, the model (7) is extended to

$$\begin{aligned} RV_{t,t+k} = & \beta_0 + \beta_D RV_{t-1,t} + \beta_W RV_{t-5,t} + \beta_M RV_{t-22,t} + \beta_J J_{t-k,t} + \alpha_1 r^+_{t-k,t} \\ & + \alpha_2 r^-_{t-k,t} + \gamma PV_{t-k,t+22} + \kappa \widehat{D}_{t,t+k} + \varepsilon_{t,t+k}. \end{aligned} \quad (15)$$

We also consider the logarithmic form of this model, as the logarithmic of the realised volatility is often believed to be a smoother process. Thus, we model $\log RV$ as

$$\begin{aligned} \log RV_{t,t+k} = & \beta_0 + \beta_D \log RV_{t-1,t} + \beta_W \log RV_{t-5,t} + \beta_M \log RV_{t-22,t} + \beta_J \log(1 + J_{t-k,t}) \\ & + \alpha_1 \log |r^+_{t-1,t}| + \alpha_2 \log |r^-_{t-1,t}| + \gamma log(PV_{t-k,t+22}) + \kappa \widehat{D}_{t,t+k} + \varepsilon_{t,t+k}, \end{aligned} \quad (16)$$

where $k = \{1, 5, 22\}$ for 1-day, 5-day, and 22-day time horizons. We use $\log(1 + J_{t-k,t})$ instead of $\log(J_{t-k,t})$ to allow for the cases where $J_{t-k,t} = 0$, and the leverage effect is measured by $\log |r^*_{t-1,t}|$ to allow for the average aggregated negative returns.

The parameters in models (15) and (16) (HAR-JL-PV-D) are fitted using the random forests regression algorithm. It is important to note that for the in-sample data, we replace $\widehat{D}_{t,t+k}$ with the actual direction $D_{t,t+k}$ to measure the impact of the direction variable on the forecasting of the realised volatility.

3. The results

3.1. Measuring Errors

Since the paper focuses on forecasting both the realised volatility's direction and its magnitude, we used the following measures to compare each model.

3.1.1. Classification Problem

In forecasting the direction of the realised volatility, the classification problem consists of only two stages. We measured the accuracy of the forecast as follows.

Let us define the following terms

- True positive (TP): The number of days that are observed with "DOWN" signals that were correctly predicted.
- False positive (FP): The number of days that are observed with "DOWN" signals that were predicted to have "UP" signals.
- False negative (FN): The number of days that are observed with "UP" signals that were predicted to have "DOWN" signals.
- True negative (TN): The number of days that are observed with "UP" signals that were correctly predicted.
- Accuracy: the proportion of the total number of correct predictions

$$\text{Accuracy} = \frac{TP + TN}{TP + FP + TN + FN}. \quad (17)$$

3.1.2. Regression Problem

We split our data into two subsets: the training (in-sample) data and the test (out-of-sample) data. Since we used the random forests algorithm, we measured the accuracy of the model proposed method for training data and test data separately.

Measuring Error for Training Data

For the random forests algorithm, an estimate of the error rate can be obtained based on the training as follows:

1. For each bootstrap, predict the out-of-bag values using the tree grown within the bootstrap sample.
2. Aggregate the Out-of-bag (OOB) predictions and calculate the mean square error rate by

$$MSE_{OOB} = \frac{1}{m}\sum_{t=1}^{n}\left\{RV_t - \overline{RV_t}^{OOB}\right\}^2 \quad (18)$$

   where m is the number of observations in the OOB data (i.e., $m < N$) and $\overline{RV_t}^{OOB}$ is the average of the OOB predictions for the tth observation.
3. Estimate the percentage variance explained as a measure of goodness of fit by

$$1 - \frac{MSE_{OOB}}{\sigma^2_{RV}} \quad (19)$$

   where σ^2_{RV} is the variance in the OOB sample.

Measuring Error for Test Data

Let RV_t denote the tth observation, $\widehat{RV_t}$ denote its forecast, and k be the number of data points observed in the selected period. The error measures include:

- The mean absolute error

$$MAE = \frac{1}{k}\sum_{t=1}^{k}|RV_t - \widehat{RV_t}|. \quad (20)$$

- The mean absolute percentage error

$$MAPE = \frac{1}{k}\sum_{t=1}^{k}\frac{|RV_t - \widehat{RV_t}|}{RV_t}. \quad (21)$$

- The root mean square error

$$RMSE = \sqrt{\frac{1}{k}\sum_{t=1}^{k}(RV_t - \widehat{RV_t})^2}. \quad (22)$$

- The root mean square percentage error

$$RMSPE = \sqrt{\frac{1}{k}\sum_{t=1}^{k}\left(\frac{RV_t - \widehat{RV_t}}{RV_t}\right)^2}. \quad (23)$$

3.2. *Empirical Results*

3.2.1. Data Description

We demonstrate the proposed model by analysing the S&P ASX 200 Index high frequency returns data and their realised volatility. Our dataset was collected from Reuters (2015) for the period 1 January 2008 to 31 December 2014. The Australian Stock Exchange is open between 10:00 a.m. to 4:00 p.m. We collected the tick-by-tick S&P 200 levels; hence, the prices were not recorded at equispaced time points. We used the previous tick aggregation method to force the observed prices into an equispaced grid, i.e., by taking the last price realized before each grid point and obtaining the 15-s frequency data. The daily realised volatility (with 1762 observations) was then estimated using these 15-s prices. The data from 2008 to 2013 were used for training purposes and 2014 data were used for validation purposes. This was to account for over-fitting and bias effects of the time-series data with the random forests algorithm.

The experiment was performed in a cloud-based Linux environment that stored seven years worth of high frequency data. The data aggregation was processed on a 2.5 GHz Intel Xeon Platinum 8175 instance with 32 GB of RAM. The function *rxDForest* from RevoScaleR package in R was used for the random forests algorithm. This allowed us to effectively handle the large dataset and to execute the computation in parallel. A fixed value of random seed was also set to ensure that the results between each run were comparable and reproducible.

3.2.2. The Results

Below we report the results of our experiment which were the best results obtained via cross-validation and hyper parameter tuning of the *rxDForest* function.

Table 1 provides a summary of the 15-s realised volatility measured using different time-windows. It was observed that both non-logarithmic and logarithmic series are skewed and non-normal. This suggests that the Ordinary Least Squares estimation approach is not applicable for our dataset. As a result, we compared the maximum likelihood estimation (MLE) with the random forests algorithm instead. In terms of correlation coefficients between the series, we observed that the computed realised volatility exhibits the long memory effect. Further, the purified implied volatility was shown to be strongly correlated with the realised volatility measures, which indicates that PV can be a useful predictor of realised volatility.

Table 2 compares the in-sample forecast results of the proposed model. For the selected time horizons, the inclusion of purified implied volatility improved the forecast accuracy against the original HAR-JL model (based on the RMSE measure and % OOB variance explained), where the logarithmic RV series performed better than the non-logarithmic RV series. It is also observed that the direction indicator further improved the forecast results; this was most significant for the 1-day forecast (with 79.28% and 80.55% variance explained for RV and log RV in comparison with 57.81% and 61.66% from the HAR-JL model respectively). For the 5-day and 22-day in-sample forecasts, we observed slight improvements in RMSE with a better goodness of fit.

In forecasting the direction of the out-sample realised volatility, we obtained the accuracy of the hit-rate at 80.05%, 72.85%, and 65.22% for 1-day, 5-day and 22-day forecasts respectively. This suggests our classification model can perform better for short-term forecasts than long-term forecasts. This can be explained by the fact that long-term forecasts require not only technical indicators but also fundamental indicators and long-term expectations from the market.

Table 3 provides a summary of the forecast errors for the out-sample data. In general, the out-of-sample performances of the proposed model are in line with the in-sample performances. The MAPE and RMSPE for the 1-day forecast of the RV from the HAR-JL-PV-D reduced by 8% and 11%, respectively, while the MAPE and RMSPE for the 5-day and 22-day forecasts reduced by 3% and 5%. When comparing the HAR-JL-PV model against the HAR-JL-D model, it can be seen that the forecast errors were smaller for the HAR-JL-PV model for these time horizons. This was anticipated as we found that the forecast in the long-term direction was less accurate for the 5-day and 22-day forecasts. However, the HAR-JL-D model still performed better than the HAR-JL alone, and the HAR-JL-PV-D model provided the best fit.

We present in Figure 3 the actual S&P200's realised volatility measured under different time horizons from 1 January 2014 to 31 December 2014, with the predicted realised volatility using the maximum likelihood estimation for the HAR-JL model (left panel) and using the random forests estimation for the HAR-JL-PV-D model (right panel). Such separation in the time frame was implemented to measure the realised values of our metrics, in order to avoid the over-fitting effect that can possibly be caused by the random forests algorithm.

Table 1. Statistical summary of S&P/ASX 200's 15-second realised volatility at different time horizons from 1 January 2008 to 31 December 2014 and their correlations matrix.

Series	Mean	Std. Dev.	Skew.	Kurt.	Min.	Max.	$RV_{t-1,t}$	$RV_{t-5,t}$	$RV_{t-22,t}$	PV
$RV_{t-1,t}$	0.1335	0.0848	2.4957	8.9530	0.0328	0.7811	1	0.8441	0.7523	0.7757
$RV_{t-5,t}$	0.1335	0.0721	2.0481	5.4748	0.0484	0.5453	0.8441	1	0.9042	0.8919
$RV_{t-22,t}$	0.1331	0.0664	1.8304	3.9311	0.0593	0.4228	0.7523	0.9042	1	0.9180
PV	0.1614	0.0705	1.5181	2.8461	0.0698	0.5004	0.7757	0.8919	0.9180	1
Series	**Mean**	**Std. Dev**	**Skew.**	**Kurt.**	**Min.**	**Max.**	$\log RV_{t-1,t}$	$\log RV_{t-5,t}$	$\log RV_{t-22,t}$	$\log PV$
$\log RV_{t-1,t}$	−2.1588	0.5139	0.5678	0.2336	−3.4184	−0.2471	1	0.8548	0.7739	0.7936
$\log RV_{t-5,t}$	−2.1244	0.4499	0.6619	0.0960	−3.0274	−0.6064	0.8548	1	0.9124	0.8972
$\log RV_{t-22,t}$	−2.113	0.4213	0.7156	−0.0407	−2.8248	−0.8608	0.7739	0.9124	1	0.9017
$\log PV$	−1.9044	0.3893	0.5190	−0.3229	−2.6618	−0.6923	0.7936	0.8972	0.9017	1

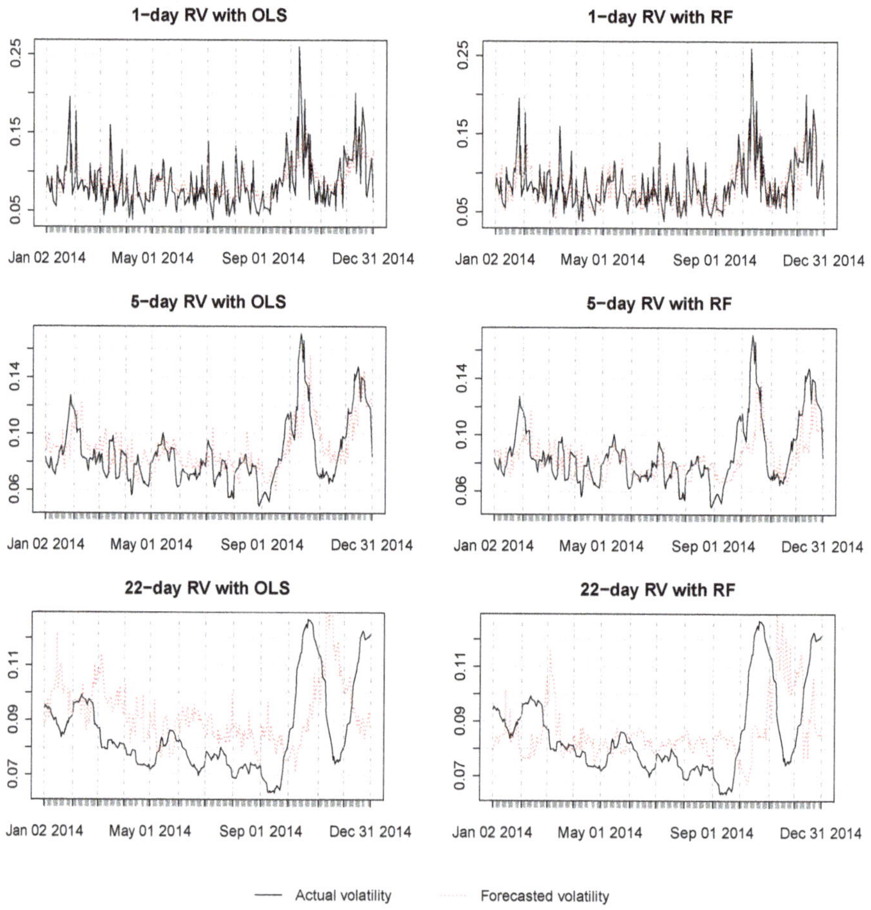

Figure 3. Predicted vs. actual realised volatility using the HAR-JL-PV-D model with the maximum likelihood estimation and random forests estimation.

Table 2. Forecasting error of the realised volatility for the in-sample data from 1 January 2008 to 31 December 2013.

		1-Day				5-Day				22-Day			
		HAR-JL	**HAR-JL-PV**	**HAR-JL-D**	**HAR-JL-PV-D**	**HAR-JL**	**HAR-JL-PV**	**HAR-JL-D**	**HAR-JL-PV-D**	**HAR-JL**	**HAR-JL-PV**	**HAR-JL-D**	**HAR-JL-PV-D**
RV	RMSE	0.0031	0.0029	0.0018	0.0018	0.002	0.0011	0.0010	0.0010	0.0011	0.0010	0.0009	0.0001
	% OOB Var	57.81	59.61	74.68	75.58	79.28	80.28	81.13	81.81	74.47	76.44	78.09	79.44
log RV	RMSE	0.0996	0.0957	0.0509	0.0502	0.0378	0.0336	0.0326	0.0295	0.0383	0.0323	0.0339	0.0287
	% OOB Var	61.66	63.12	80.39	80.65	80.55	82.70	83.25	84.83	77.48	81.97	80.05	83.12

Table 3. Forecasing error of the realised volatility for the out-sample data from 1 January 2014 to 31 December 2014.

		1-Day				5-Day				22-Day			
		HAR-JL	**HAR-JL-PV**	**HAR-JL-D**	**HAR-JL-PV-D**	**HAR-JL**	**HAR-JL-PV**	**HAR-JL-D**	**HAR-JL-PV-D**	**HAR-JL**	**HAR-JL-PV**	**HAR-JL-D**	**HAR-JL-PV-D**
RV	MAE	0.0212	0.0205	0.0176	0.0171	0.0147	0.0135	0.0137	0.0127	0.0184	0.0142	0.017	0.0137
	MAPE	0.2715	0.2516	0.2042	0.1974	0.1814	0.1573	0.1670	0.1500	0.2245	0.1630	0.2094	0.1576
	RMSE	0.0285	0.0277	0.0247	0.0235	0.0192	0.0182	0.0180	0.0168	0.0223	0.0182	0.0209	0.0176
	RMSPE	0.3610	0.3245	0.2709	0.2568	0.2352	0.2025	0.2181	0.1926	0.2745	0.2046	0.2602	0.1973
log RV	MAE	0.0206	0.0201	0.0170	0.0165	0.0143	0.0135	0.0130	0.0129	0.0170	0.0138	0.0156	0.0135
	MAPE	0.2525	0.2331	0.1947	0.1878	0.1740	0.1553	0.1574	0.1481	0.2058	0.1576	0.1881	0.1532
	RMSE	0.0279	0.0280	0.0239	0.0233	0.0185	0.0185	0.0175	0.0175	0.0206	0.0177	0.0191	0.0174
	RMSPE	0.3250	0.2929	0.2573	0.2454	0.2230	0.1980	0.2116	0.1913	0.2499	0.1958	0.2310	0.1912

Note: as the random forests algorithm requires a random selection process, for consistent comparison across models, we reset the random seed to a specific value before applying the algorithm to each of the above models.

4. Discussion

Forecasting problems for financial time series are challenging since these series have a significant noise component. Currently, there is no consensus on the possibility of forecasting for asset prices using a technical analysis or a mathematical algorithm. The forecasting of parameters of stochastic models for financial time series, including volatility, is also challenging. Moreover, even statistical inference for parameters of financial time series is usually difficult. An additional difficulty is that these parameters are not directly observable; they are defined by the underlying model and by many other factors. For example, it appears that the volatility depends on the sampling frequency and on the delay parameter in the model equation see, e.g., Luong and Dokuchaev (2016). In addition, there is no a unique comprehensive model for stock price evolution; for example, there are many models with stochastic equations for volatility, with jumps, with fractional noise, etc. Respectively, even a modest improvement in forecasting for the parameters of financial time series would be beneficial for the practitioners.

Our paper explored the HAR (Corsi and Reno 2009) model with the main focus being to extend this model family via two new features, the purified volatility and the forecast volatility movement, and the implementation of this machine learning algorithm to improve the forecast of realised volatility.

By utilising the availability of high frequency data, we showed that the direction of the realised volatility can be forecast with the random forests algorithm by using the proposed technical indicators, with an accuracy of above 80% for the selected time series. However, this accuracy could be further improved if we could integrate fundamental indicators such as financial news.

The errors in forecasting the realised volatility with our proposed features also showed further improvement on top of the existing HAR-JL model. Particularly, this was done through the addition of information derived from the purified volatility and the predicted direction of the volatility. We believe that the predictions of realised volatility would further be improved by using other tree-based algorithms such as Extreme Gradient Boosting (XGBoost) or Bayesian additive regression trees (BART). However, we leave this for future study.

5. Conclusions

This paper introduces an application of the random forests algorithm for forecasting the realised volatility. For the classification problem, our study showed that by using the selected feature choices, it was able to forecast the direction of the realised volatility. For the regression problem with its non-linear structure, the technique was able to reduce the forecasting error rate from volatility clustering systematically under different time horizons. The empirical results of S&P 200 show that the existing HAR model framework was improved by including the purified implied volatility and applying this machine learning technique. We suggest that further investigation of the roles of the purified implied volatility and random forests algorithm in other high frequency models of volatility should be done.

Author Contributions: C.L. conceived, planned, and carried out the experiment. N.D. helped supervise the project. C.L. and N.D. provided critical feedback and helped shape the research, analysis and the manuscript.

Funding: This work was supported by ARC grant of Australia DP120100928.

Conflicts of Interest: The authors declare no conflicts of interest.

References

Andersen, Torben G., and Tim Bollerslev. 1997. Heterogeneous information arrivals and return volatility dynamics: Uncovering the long run in high frequency data. *Journal of Finance* 52: 975–1005. [CrossRef]

Andersen, Torben G., Tim Bollerslev, Francis X. Diebold, and Paul Labys. 2003. Modeling and forecasting realized volatility. *Econometrica* 71: 529–626. [CrossRef]

Barndorff-Nielsen, Ole E., and Neil Shephard. 2001. Econometric Analysis of Realised Volatility and its Use in Estimating Stochastic Volatility Models. *Journal of the Royal Statistical Society* 64: 253–80. [CrossRef]

Barndorff-Nielsen, Ole E., and Neil Shephard. 2004. Power and bipower variation with stochastic volatility and jumps. *Journal of Financial Econometrics* 2: 1–37. [CrossRef]

Black, Fischer, and Myron Scholes. 1973. The Pricing of Options and Corporate Liabilities. *Journal of Political Economy* 81: 637–54. [CrossRef]

Black, Fischer. 1976. The pricing of commodity contracts. *Journal of Financial Economics* 3: 167–79. [CrossRef]

Bollerslev, Tim. 1986. Generalized Auto Regressive Conditional Heteroskedasticity. *Journal of Econometrics* 31: 307–27. [CrossRef]

Breiman, Leo, J. H. Friedman, R. A. Olshen, and C. J. Stone. 1984. *Classification and Regression Trees*. Monterey: Wadsworth and Brooks.

Breiman, Leo. 2001. Random Forests. *Machine Learning* 45: 5–32. [CrossRef]

Carr, Peter, and Liuren Wu. 2006. A tale of two indices. *Journal of Derivatives* 3: 13–29. [CrossRef]

Corsi, Fulvio, and Roberto Reno. 2009. HAR Volatility Modelling With Heterogeneous Leverage and Jumps. Available online: https://web.stanford.edu/group/SITE/archive/SITE_2009/segment_1/s1_papers/corsi.pdf (accessed on 10 October 2018).

Corsi, Fulvio. 2003. A Simple Approximate Long-Memory Model of Realized Volatility. *Journal of Financial Econometrics* 7: 174–96. [CrossRef]

De Stefani, Jacopo, Olivier Caelen, Dalila Hattab, and Gianluca Bontempi. 2017. Machine Learning for Multi-step Ahead Forecasting of Volatility Proxies. Available online: https://pdfs.semanticscholar.org/39cf/3536e780ff195d400902076e1b3e7b2e638d.pdf (accessed on 20 September 2015).

Dokuchaev, Nikolai. 2014. Volatility estimation from short time series of stock prices. *Journal of Nonparametric Statistics* 26: 373–84. [CrossRef]

Engle, Robert F. 1982. Autoregressive conditional heteroskedasticity with estimates of variance of UK inflation. *Econometrica* 50: 987–1008. [CrossRef]

Engle, Robert F. 1990. Discussion: Stock market volatility and the crash of 87. *Review of Financial Studies* 3: 103–6. [CrossRef]

Glosten, Lawrence R., Ravi Jagannathan, David E. Runkle. 1993. On the relationship between the expected value and the volatility of the nominal excess return on stocks. *Journal of Finance* 46: 1779–801. [CrossRef]

Heston, Steven L. 1993. A closed-form solution for options with stochastic volatility with applications to bond and currency options. *The Review of Financial Studies* 6: 327–43. [CrossRef]

Khan, Md Ashraful Islam. 2011. Financial Volatility Forecasting by Nonlinear Support Vector Machine Heterogeneous Autoregressive Model: Evidence from Nikkei 225 Stock Index. *International Journal of Economics and Finance* 3: 138–50. [CrossRef]

Luong, Chuong, and Nikolai Dokuchaev. 2014. Analysis of market volatility via a dynamically purified option price process. *Annals of Financial Economics* 9: 1450006. [CrossRef]

Luong, Chuong, and Nikolai Dokuchaev. 2016. Modelling dependency of volatility on sampling frequency via delay equations. *Annals of Financial Economics* 11: 1650007. [CrossRef]

Lux, Thomas, and Michele Marchesi. 1999. Scaling and criticality in a stochastic multi-agent model of financial market. *Nature* 397: 498–500. [CrossRef]

Müller, Ulrich A., Michel M. Dacorogna, Rakhal D. Davé, Richard B. Olsen, Olivier V. Pictet, and Jacob E. Von Weizsäcker. 1997. Volatilities of different time resolutions: Analyzing the dynamics of market components. *Journal of Empirical Finance* 4: 213–39. [CrossRef]

Nelson, Daniel B. 1991. Conditional Heteroskedasticity in Asset Returns: A New Approach. *Econometrica* 59: 347–70. [CrossRef]

Peters, Edgar. 1994. Fractal Market Analysis. In *A Wiley Finance Edition*. New York: John Wiley & Sons.

Qin, Qin, Qing-Guo Wang, Jin Li, and Shuzhi Sam Ge. 2013. Linear and Nonlinear Trading Models with Gradient Boosted Random Forests and Application to Singapore Stock Market. *Journal of Intelligent Learning Systems and Applications* 5: 1–10. [CrossRef]

Reuters, Thomson. 2015. Thomson Reuters Tick History. Available online: http://www.sirca.org.au/ (accessed on 20 September 2015).

Theofilatos, Konstantinos, Spiros Likothanassis, and Andreas Karathanasopoulos. 2012. Modeling and Trading the EUR/USD Exchange Rate Using Machine Learning Techniques. *ETASR—Engineering, Technology & Applied Science Research* 2: 269–72.

Whaley, Robert E. 2000. The investor fear gauge. *The Journal of Portfolio Management* 6: 12–17. [CrossRef]

Zakoian, Jean-Michel. 1994. Threshold Heteroscedastic Models. *Journal of Economic Dynamics and Control* 18: 931–55. [CrossRef]

Journal of
Risk and Financial Management

MDPI

Article

Growth and Debt: An Endogenous Smooth Coefficient Approach

Mustafa Koroglu

Independent Researcher, Guelph, ON N1G 0G1, Canada; koroglu4943@yahoo.com

Received: 21 January 2019; Accepted: 25 January 2019; Published: 1 February 2019

Abstract: The new growth theories with an emphasis on fundamental determinants such as institutions suggest a non-linear cross-country growth process. In this paper, we investigate the public debt and economic growth relationship using the semi-parametric smooth coefficient approach that allows democracy to influence this relationship and parameter heterogeneity in the unknown functional form and addresses the endogeneity of variables. We find results consistent with the previous literature that identified a significant adverse effect of public debt on growth for the countries below a particular democracy level. However, we also find conclusive evidence that countries with high institutional quality have an adverse effect of public debt on growth for the period 1980–2009, as well as for the extended period including the years 2010–2014. A 10-percentage point increase in the debt-to-GDP ratio is associated with a 0.12% and 0.07% decrease in the subsequent 10-year period real GDP growth rate for the zero democracy countries and for the countries with a democracy score of 10, respectively.

Keywords: functional coefficients; local linear regression; nonparametric 2SLS estimator; series estimator; Solow economic growth convergence model

1. Introduction

In the aftermath of the recent global financial crisis, government debt has increased substantially across the world. For advanced economies, the public debt-to-GDP ratio rose on average from about 66% in 2007 to 105% by the end of 2015. Particularly, Greece, Ireland, Japan, Portugal, Spain, and the United Kingdom, when compared to other countries, experienced a rapid and higher increase in public debt-to-GDP ratio between 2008 and 2012. A growing concern behind these facts is that countries may not achieve debt sustainability, implying higher vulnerability to an economic and financial crisis (Cecchetti et al. (2010); Bohn (1995)). In fact, over the last two centuries, there were twenty financial crises followed by debt build-up periods, which lasted more than a decade and are associated with lower growth than during other periods (Reinhart et al. (2012)). Therefore, a relevant policy question centers on the long-term growth effects of high public debt.

The relationship between public debt and economic growth is still unresolved in both the theoretical and empirical literature. Theoretically, the conventional view of public debt is that fiscal deficits in the short-run can have a positive effect on economic growth by stimulating aggregate demand and output, whereas it also may have a potential crowding out effect on private investment in the long run (Elmendorf and Mankiw (1999)). On the other hand, much of the economic growth literature reveals some evidence of nonlinearity in the effect of public debt on growth, mainly focusing on threshold levels. The idea is to detect a debt level beyond which economic growth is adversely affected, implying a concave (inverted-U shape) relationship between debt and growth. Using a basic nonparametric technique (i.e., a histogram, to investigate a correlation between public debt and growth), Reinhart and Rogoff (2010) found a threshold level of 90% for 20 advanced countries between 1945 and 2009. Their findings are striking in that an average of real GDP growth decreases substantially (at about 4%) when public debt-to-GDP ratio is beyond the 90% threshold as compared to other public debt-to-GDP ratios. Moreover, the debt-growth link disappears for the public debt ratios below the 90% threshold.

In the empirical growth literature, an extensive number of studies have tried to examine the sensitivity of Reinhart and Rogoff's 90% threshold level to model specifications, alternative sets of included and excluded variables, and different data series. Table A1 in the Appendix A provides a summary of recent studies aimed at unveiling the nonlinear relationship between government debt and economic growth. An important observation gleaned from this table is that there is no common finding for the threshold level, except for a small number of studies that found a turning point for a public debt-to-GDP ratio at around 90%. In one study in the latter group of papers, Cecchetti et al. (2011) examined a panel of 18 OECD countries (all from advanced economies) for the period 1980–2006. Using least squares dummy variables threshold estimation within the context of the dynamic fixed-effects panel data model, they found a negative relationship between government debt and growth beyond the 85% threshold level after controlling for other determinants of growth including trade openness, inflation rate, and total dependency ratio (related to aging). Their approach avoided a possible feedback effect from economic growth to public debt by using five-year averages of growth, so that regressors were predetermined. Their results suggest that, on average, a ten-percentage points increase in the debt-to-GDP ratio is predicted to reduce economic growth by 0.13 percentage points per year. In Checherita-Westphal and Rother (2012), a study of 12-Euro area economies from 1970–2008, they aimed to investigate nonlinearity in the debt-growth link by using a quadratic equation in debt. To control for endogeneity of the public debt variable, the authors used a lagged value of debt and average debt of the other countries in the sample. They found a public debt threshold level between 90% and 100%, beyond which economic growth was negatively affected. Baum et al. (2013) dealt with the endogeneity problem arising from the dynamic model specification in their study of 12-Euro area countries from 1990–2007 and 2010. They found a threshold level of the public debt-to-GDP ratio at 95% for the extended period. In another study, Woo and Kumar (2015) surveyed 38 advanced and emerging economies from 1970–2008. Using several estimation strategies and subsamples, the authors examined non-linearity in the debt-growth relationship by fitting the data to the dynamic panel regression model. They also found a 90% threshold level beyond which public debt had a negative and significant effect on economic growth. Panizza and Presbitero (2014) accounted for the potential endogeneity of public debt using the share of foreign currency debt in total public debt as an instrument. Using the same dataset and empirical approach of Cecchetti et al. (2011), as well as performing various robustness checks, they found little evidence of the adverse effect of high public debt on future growth in advanced economies.

Other studies provide evidence of a threshold level of public debt different from 90% of GDP. For example, Caner et al. (2010) studied a cross-section of 101 developed and emerging market economies from 1980–2008. Using threshold estimation, they found a turning point of the public debt-to-GDP ratio at 77% for the full sample controlling for initial GDP per capita, trade openness, and inflation rate; this value was lower at 64% of GDP for the subsample of developing countries. In the Wright and Grenade (2014) study of 13 Caribbean countries from 1990–2012, the authors found a threshold level of 61% of GDP beyond which debt had a negative effect on economic growth and investment. Some research studies closely replicated the research of Reinhart and Rogoff (2010) using different econometric techniques. For example, Minea and Parent (2012) employed the panel smooth transition regression model of Gonzáles et al. (2005) and found an adverse and gradually decreasing effect of public debt on growth below the threshold level of 115%. Their finding supported the presence of nonlinearity in the effect of debt on growth for the debt-to-GDP ratio above 90%. On the other hand, they found a positive growth effect of debt for the debt level above 115%. In a related study, using nonlinear threshold models for the same dataset used in Reinhart and Rogoff (2010), Égert (2015) found limited evidence for a negative nonlinear correlation between public debt and growth. The author's findings suggest that a debt threshold level can be lower than 90% of GDP depending on data coverage (regarding country coverage and time dimension), model specification, and different measures of the public debt. Eberhardt and Presbitero (2015) provided strong evidence of different non-linearities in the debt-growth relationship across 118 countries from 1961–2012 by doing a comprehensive analysis of dynamic panel time series estimation (see Eberhardt and Presbitero (2013) for the earlier version of the authors' work). They employed a common factor framework to uncover possible heterogeneity in the effect of public debt stock on economic growth by considering latent factors of growth and public debt, which include a country's debt composition, macroeconomic policies related to past crises, and institutional framework. They found no evidence for the common threshold effect for all countries in their sample.

A primary purpose of the above-discussed research studies was to reveal a nonlinear relationship between public debt and economic growth depending on the public debt level. In other words, these researchers tried to expose the nonlinear growth effect of high public debt levels. However, this point of view ignores potential variables, either omitted from the model or included as a regressor, that may govern the debt-growth relationship. This concern raises an important question: Is the high public debt a primary source of the negative relationship between debt and growth? Kourtellos et al. (2013) studied 82 countries in a 10-year panel from 1980–2009 to test formally for several threshold variables including democracy, trade openness, fertility, life expectancy, and inflation rate, among others. They employed the structural threshold regression model of Kourtellos et al. (2016) to account for the endogeneity of both the threshold variable and the regressors. The authors found strong evidence in favor of heterogeneity in the debt-growth relationship in the sense that the effect of public debt on economic growth depends on the institutional quality of a country. Notably, they found that, holding other factors fixed, countries with low institutional quality experienced a negative and significant effect of public debt on economic growth, while public debt had a positive, but insignificant effect on growth for countries with high institutional quality. Jalles (2011) investigated the impact of democracy and corruption on the external debt-growth relationship in a panel of 72 developing countries from 1970–2005. Using fixed effects and GMM estimation strategies under various model specifications (linear and quadratic terms in debt-to-GDP ratio), the author found a negative growth effect of external debt in countries with higher levels of corruption. These findings are consistent with the such new growth theories as the suggestion of Azariadis and Drazen (1990) of a highly nonlinear cross-country growth process (see also Temple (1999) for further reading).

Institutional differences across countries are perceived as one of the primary factors in the cross-country income gap. In a seminal paper by Acemoglu et al. (2001), the authors documented a positive relationship between democracy and per capita GDP after controlling for the endogeneity of institutions from an exogenous source of variation (see also Acemoglu et al. (2015) for recent work on the same subject). Another argument is that the democracy variable is not correctly measured as many institutional measures reflect the outcome of dictatorial choices and, therefore, should be seen as institutional outcome variables, not predictors of it (see, for example, Glaeser et al. (2004) and Acemoglu et al. (2005)). On the other hand, Minier (2007) examined democracy as a source of heterogeneity in the relationship between economic growth and its determinants, and the author provided some evidence of an indirect effect of institutions regarding the link between trade openness and economic growth.

Given that the relationship between public debt and growth appears to be heterogeneous and complex and there may be other factors that contribute to the marginal impacts of variables on economic growth, our aim in this paper is to examine whether democracy may influence the relationship between public debt and economic growth in our sample of countries. The limitations of the existing debt-growth literature coupled with the lack of explicit theoretical argument on the debt-growth link in advanced economies suggests that a flexible approach may be more appropriate for estimating the effect of debt on growth and seeking other factors to characterize this relationship. We, therefore, present an augmented conventional Solow economic growth model with public debt-to-GDP ratio and country-specific parameters, which relax the homogeneity assumption of a standard growth regression. Specifically, as a first assumption, we model parameters to be a function of one or more covariates including democracy, fertility, and life expectancy, among others. Our approach is also related to the empirical growth studies that use nonparametric and semiparametric models to model parameter heterogeneity in the cross-country growth process. Examples include Liu and Stengos (1999) and Ketteni et al. (2007) for an additive semiparametric partially linear model; Vaona and Schiavo (2007) for a semiparametric partial linear model; Durlauf et al. (2001), Mamuneas et al. (2006), Kourtellos (2011), and Kumbhakar and Sun (2012) for a varying coefficient model; and Henderson et al. (2011) for a nonparametric model.

To ensure that our regression model captures the heterogeneous effects of variables, we further assume the parameters to be unknown measurable smooth functions. This assumption enables us to use nonparametric techniques, which essentially allows the data to decide the functional form of each parameter. Moreover, the coefficient estimates avoid bias by the misspecification of parameter heterogeneity, which occurs in a parametric form in the existing debt-growth studies. Furthermore, economic theory does not suggest a functional form for the regression model of debt-growth relationship or even for the parameter heterogeneity in the debt-growth link. Therefore, nonparametric techniques permit unknown functions to be governed by country-specific characteristics such as the country's initial conditions, state of development variables, institutional quality, and macroeconomic policies playing an indirect role in explaining a nonlinear relationship between growth and its determinants across countries and the time domain. For this study, we used a recently-developed smooth coefficient instrumental variable estimator of Delgado et al. (2015) that assumes linearity in the regressors, but allows the intercept and slope coefficients to be an unknown function of a covariate (e.g., democracy). Moreover, with this estimator, we can control for endogeneity of a covariate in the unknown functional coefficients.

We fit the semiparametric smooth coefficient model to a dataset including 82 countries for the three 10-year averages spanning from 1980–2009. We also extend this dataset by adding recent years from 2010–2014 for 78 countries. We find strong evidence of heterogeneity in the effect of public debt with respect to institutional quality of countries. Additionally, we find conclusive evidence in support of the recently shifted focus in the debt-growth relationship that institutions may be one of the factors that influence this relationship. Specifically, our results are consistent with the literature that identified an average negative and statistically-significant effect of public debt on growth. However, our empirical results also show that for high democracy countries, a higher debt-to-GDP ratio leads to lower economic growth where everything else is equal. Our core results suggest that a ten percentage point increase in the debt-to-GDP ratio is associated with a 0.12% (and 0.071%) decrease in the subsequent ten-year period real GDP growth rate for zero democracy countries (and for the countries with a democracy score of 10).

Our findings are robust to different measures of democracy, different country groupings, and to the inclusion of additional control variables. Our results from prediction exercises also suggest that our semiparametric model can better describe the underlying process that generated the data than the parametric models. We, therefore, are contributing to the empirical debt-growth literature by explaining parameter heterogeneity in the cross-country growth process through fundamental determinants of economic growth proposed by new growth theories.

The remainder of this paper is organized as follows. Section 2 describes our empirical methodology. Section 3 describes our data. Section 4 presents the empirical results of the study. Section 5 presents our robustness checks. Section 6 presents the conclusion.

2. Empirical Methodology

2.1. The Augmented Solow Growth Model

In this section, we provide a brief description of a linear Solow growth model augmented with the debt-to-GDP ratio to investigate the impact of country's debt level on its economic growth rate.

This model assumes a common regression across countries, as well as constant coefficient estimates for all economic variables, which intuitively explains the average effect of the variables.

$$g_i = X_i^T\beta + u_i = \beta_0 + S_i^T\beta_s + \beta_d debt_i + u_i, i = 1, .., n, \quad (1)$$

where $X_i = [1, S_i^T, debt_i]^T$ is a $(d_s + 2) \times 1$ vector of regressors consisting of a constant term, a d_s-dimensional vector of standard Solow growth determinants, including $ln(yin_i)$, the logarithm of the ith country's real GDP per worker in the initial year of each 10-year period; $ln(s_i)$, the logarithm of the ith country's average saving rate; $ln(n_i + 0.05)$, the logarithm of the ith country's population growth plus 0.05; $ln(sch_i)$, the logarithm of the ith country's average years of secondary and tertiary schooling for the male population over 25 years of age; and $debt_i$, which is defined as the ith country's public debt-to-GDP ratio. Moreover, S_i includes a time trend. u_i is an identically and independently distributed error term.

2.2. An Endogenous Smooth Coefficient Model

We consider the following semiparametric varying coefficient model of Delgado et al. (2015) for the augmented Solow growth model:

$$\begin{cases} g_i = \theta_0(Z_i) + \sum_{j=1}^{d_s}\theta_{sj}(Z_i)S_{ji} + \theta_d(Z_i)debt_i + \epsilon_i \\ Z_i = \mu_Z + a_1(E_{i,1}) + a_2(E_{i,2}) + ... + a_p(E_{i,p}) + u_i, i = 1, ..., n, \end{cases} \quad (2)$$

$$(i) E[u_i|\mathbf{E}_i] = 0$$
$$(ii) E[\epsilon_i|\mathbf{E}_i, u_i] = E[\epsilon_i|u_i], i = 1, ..., n,$$

where Z_i is an endogenous variable defined as an additive nonparametric function of E_{ij}, $j = 1, ..., p$, where $\mathbf{E}_i = [E_{i,1}, E_{i,2}, ..., E_{i,p}] = [S_i^T, debt_i, W_i^T]^T$ is a $p \times 1$ vector of continuous variables including a d_w-dimensional vector of instrumental variables, W_i^T. $a_t(\cdot)$, $t = 1, ..., p$, $\theta_0(\cdot), \theta_s(\cdot)$, $\theta_d(\cdot)$ are all unknown smooth measurable functions, and u_i is a zero-mean error term.

In Equation (2), the object of estimation is the structural model that necessitates different identification strategies than standard nonparametric regression, which is used to estimate conditional expectations. The additive separability of Z and the conditional mean of ϵ and u given in (i) and (ii) in Equation (2) are nonparametric restrictions for identification in this model.[1]

After setting $E[\epsilon_i|u_i] \equiv b(u_i)$ and denoting $v_i \equiv \epsilon_i - b(u_i)$, which satisfies $E[v_i|\mathbf{E}_i, u_i] = 0$, we can rewrite Model (2) as:

$$g_i = \theta_0(Z_i) + \sum_{j=1}^{d_s}\theta_{sj}(Z_i)S_{ji} + \theta_d(Z_i)debt_i + b(u_i) + v_i, i = 1, .., n, \quad (3)$$

provided that $b(\cdot)$ is an unknown smooth function. Equation (3) consists of two additive components, $\theta_0(Z_i)$ and $b(u_i)$, together with the functional coefficient terms, $\sum_{j=1}^{d_s}\theta_{sj}(Z_i)S_{ji}$ and $\theta_d(Z_i)debt_i$. According to Newey et al. (1999), identification of unknown functions in Equation (3) is the same as identification in Equation (2), as the additive structure of Equation (3) is equivalent to conditional mean restriction (Assumption (ii)) in Equation (2). The sufficient condition for identification of unknown functions in Equation (3) is, therefore, assuming no additive functional relationship between Z_i and u_i (see Newey et al. (1999), Theorems 2.1 and 2.2 on pp. 567–68).

1 In another paper Newey and Powell (2003), the conditional mean of disturbances given instruments was assumed to be zero without imposing an additive structure for the endogenous variables.

If we assume that Z and all conditioning variables are exogenous, then the first equation in (2) is a pure varying coefficient model that can be consistently estimated using the nonparametric kernel estimator of Li et al. (2002); otherwise, this estimator yields a bias in estimation of unknown functional coefficients. Assuming the exogeneity of covariates seems to be strong in the present growth application; we, therefore, allow variables representing Z to be endogenous. This endogeneity assumption is that growth regression is formulated as in the structural form of Model (2), called a triangular nonparametric simultaneous equations model.

Nonparametric estimators for regression models that include endogeneity problem have been proposed in the context of varying coefficient models, for example Das (2005), Cai et al. (2006), and Cai and Li (2008). However, these papers allow for endogenous variables in the parametric part of a regression. The estimator proposed by Delgado et al. (2015), on the other hand, deals with endogenous variables that appear in the nonparametric part of a smooth coefficient model. This estimator is applicable to the economic studies, where the endogenous variable has a potential interaction effect with the other regressors on the response variable. For example, child care use may have a potential indirect effect on students' test scores that can be modeled as in the functional coefficient form that varies with respect to mother's education, age, and experience, among other regressors (see Bernal and Keane (2011) for a parametric estimation and full description of the regressors and Ozabaci et al. (2014) for an additive nonparametric regression estimation).

To circumvent the endogeneity problem, Delgado et al. (2015) used the control function approach in the estimation of the structural function of interest. Since u enters Equation (3) as a conditioning variable and it is generally unobserved, Delgado et al. (2015), first, calculated $\hat{u}$ from the regression of Z on $\boldsymbol{E_i}$ using the second equation of Model (2). Then, they estimated $\theta(Z_i)$ and $b(\hat{u})$ via the sieve approximation approach by an ordinary least squares method. In the third step, they used a local linear regression method to estimate $\theta(Z_i)$ and $\theta'(Z_i)$. They showed that their estimator was oracle efficient in the sense that large sample distribution of the estimator was the same regardless of whether the function $b(\cdot)$ was known. It is also noted that the third-step estimator is not affected by the errors in the first two steps of estimation. The estimation procedure is given in detail as follows.

In the first step, Delgado et al. (2015) approximated unknown functions $a_1(\cdot),...,a_p(\cdot)$ by series expansions[2]:

$$a_m^*(e) = \sum_{l=1}^{L_n} \alpha_{ml}\phi_l(e), \tag{4}$$

for $m = 1,...,p$, where $\alpha_m = (\alpha_{m1}, \alpha_{m2}, ..., \alpha_{mL_n})^T$ is an $L_n \times 1$ vector of unknown coefficients, $\{\phi_j(\cdot)\}_{j=1}^{L_n}$ is a sequence of square integrable orthonormal basis functions over the interval $[0,\infty)$, and L_n denotes the number of basis functions. It is noteworthy that the Laguerre polynomial series is used to approximate the unknown functions, as it is one of the common choices for series expansions when a function has a domain over $[0,\infty)$ (see, e.g., Assumption 1(ii) in Delgado et al. (2015) and Chen (2007) for further details).

The coefficients α_m, $m = 1,...,p$ in (4) can be consistently estimated from the ordinary least squares (or OLS) regression of Z_i on $a_1^*(E_{i,1}), a_2^*(E_{i,2}), ..., a_p^*(E_{i,p})$. Then, the OLS estimator of the unknown function is given by $\hat{a}_m(e) = \sum_{l=1}^{L_n} \hat{\alpha}_{ml}\phi_l(e)$, $m = 1,...,p$. Fitted values and the residuals from the OLS regression can be calculated as $\hat{Z}_i = \hat{\mu} + \hat{a}_1(E_{i,1}) + \hat{a}_2(E_{i,2}) + ... + \hat{a}_p(E_{i,p})$ and $\hat{e}_i = Z_i - \hat{Z}_i$ for all $i = 1,...,n$, respectively.

[2] The authors used B-spline smoothing in the first two steps assuming the domain of the basis functions over the closed interval.

In the second step, using series expansions, they approximate unknown functions $\theta(z)$ and $b(\hat{\epsilon}_i)$, respectively, by:

$$\theta_k^*(z) = \sum_{l=1}^{L_n} \beta_{kl}\phi_l(z), \qquad \text{and} \qquad b^*(\hat{\epsilon}) = \sum_{l=1}^{L_n} \gamma_l\phi_l(\hat{\epsilon}), \tag{5}$$

where $\beta_k = (\beta_{k1}, \beta_{k2}, ..., \beta_{kL_n})^T$ for $k = 0, ..., d_s + 1$, and $\gamma = (\gamma_1, \gamma_2, ..., \gamma_{L_n})^T$ are all $L_n \times 1$ vectors of unknown coefficients. Model (3) can be, now, approximated by substituting equalities in (5) for $\theta_k(z)$, $k = 0, ..., d_s + 1$, and $b(\hat{\epsilon})$ in Model (3).

$$g_i \approx \sum_{k=0}^{d_s+1} \sum_{l=1}^{L_n} \beta_{kl}\phi_l(z)X_{ki} + \sum_{l=1}^{L_n} \gamma_l\phi_l(\hat{\epsilon}_i) + v_i, i = 1, .., n, \tag{6}$$

where residual $\hat{\epsilon}_i$ is calculated from the first step. The least squares problem is, then, defined as follows:

$$[\hat{\beta}^T, \hat{\gamma}^T]^T = \arg\min_{(\beta,\gamma)} \sum_{i=1}^{n} \left\{ g_i - \sum_{k=0}^{d_s+1} \sum_{l=1}^{L_n} \beta_{kl}\phi_l(z)X_{ki} + \sum_{l=1}^{L_n} \gamma_l\phi_l(\hat{\epsilon}_i) \right\}^2. \tag{7}$$

In the third step, Delgado et al. (2015) used the local linear regression approach to estimate the functional coefficients, $\theta(\cdot)$, and its first-order derivatives, $\theta'(\cdot)$. Following Delgado et al. (2015), we assume that the unknown function, $\theta(Z)$, is continuously differentiable up to second order, so that we can apply a first order Taylor series approximation of $\theta(Z)$ around a given point z, technically by $\theta(Z) \approx \theta(z) + \theta'(z)(Z - z)$. We, further, assume $K(\cdot)$ to be a kernel weight function assigning more weights to the observations closer to point z, satisfying: (i) $\int K(a)da = 1$, (ii) $K(a) = K(-a)$, and (iii) $\int a^2K(a)da > 0$. In the case of the higher dimensional covariate vector, Z, which includes continuous and discrete covariates, the kernel function is the product kernel, $K = WL(Z^d, z^d, \lambda)$, where $W = W((Z^c - z^c)/h)$, Z^c is the continuous covariate, L_λ is the kernel function for the discrete variable, Z^d, and λ is the smoothing parameter for the discrete covariate; see Racine and Li (2004) for further details about kernel functions for the categorical variables. We use a single continuous covariate in the kernel function given in (8).

Replacing $b(\epsilon_i)$ in Equation (3) by $\hat{b}(\hat{\epsilon}_i)$ calculated from the second-step estimation and treating $\hat{g}_i = g_i - \hat{b}(\hat{\epsilon}_i)$ as a dependent variable, Delgado et al. (2015) showed that a consistent estimate of $(\theta(\cdot), \theta'(\cdot))$ can be obtained from a minimization of a kernel-weighted objective function:

$$\min_{\theta(z),\theta'(z)} \sum_{i=1}^{n} [\hat{g}_i - X_i^T\theta(z) - X_i^T\theta'(z)(Z_i - z)]^2 K((Z_i - z)/h), \tag{8}$$

where $\theta'(z)$ reflects the partial effects $\partial\theta(z)/\partial z$ and h is the bandwidth controlling the size of the local neighborhood around an interior point z.

Letting $\delta(z) = [\theta(z), \theta'(z)]$, the solution of Problem (8) is given by:

$$\hat{\delta}(z) = (\mathbf{X}^T\mathbf{K}\mathbf{X})^{-1}\mathbf{X}^T\mathbf{K}\hat{g}, \tag{9}$$

where $\mathbf{X}$ is an $n \times 2(d_s + 2)$ matrix having $(X_i^T, X_i^T(Z_i - z))$ as its ith row and $\mathbf{K}$ is a $n \times n$ diagonal matrix with the ith diagonal element being $K((Z_i - z)/h)$.

The bandwidth parameter has a particular importance in the estimation of non-/semiparametric models as it determines the degree of smoothing. We use a cross-validation method, a data-driven approach, to choose the bandwidth parameter so that the bias-variance trade-off in the estimation is optimized by using the data themselves. We also provide wild-bootstrap standard errors, which are robust to heteroscedasticity, using 399 bootstrap replications Härdle and Marron (1991).

We use three goodness-of-fit measures including in-sample R^2, out-of-sample R^2, and average squared predicted error (ASPE). The out-of-sample measures are robust to over-fitting of the model, which, therefore, implies that the model of interest may better describe the underlying process that generated the data. The predictive exercises are based on 1000 bootstrap replications. We use 80 percent of the data to estimate the model parameters and evaluate on the hold-out data; see Henderson and Parmeter (2015).

3. Data

We employ the same dataset as used in Kourtellos et al. (2013) to investigate the long-run growth effect of public debt. We provide the source and definition of each variable in Table A3 in the Appendix A. We have a balanced 10-year period panel dataset covering 82 countries from 1980–1989, 1990–1999, and 2000–2009. Working with 10-year averages allows us to avoid any short-run fluctuations in macroeconomic variables. We also obtain an extended dataset and construct 10-year and five-year averages for a sample of 78 countries using the latest version of Penn World Table (PWT 9.0).[3]

We use the per capita real GDP growth rate as a measure of economic growth. We include traditional Solow regressors as control variables in our model. These variables are the initial level of income at the beginning of each ten-year period, which is expected to be negatively related to economic growth rates, the population growth rate, and the rate of physical capital investment; these are used as proxies for the growth rate of input factors in the aggregate production function. Additional regressors are the public debt and the logarithm of the percent of public debt to GDP, which is the primary variable that we are interested in in this study, coming from the International Monetary Fund historical public debt database. The inflation rate is included as a finance-related variable that is expected to be positively related to public debt, which may help to explain the causal effect of debt on growth partly.

The main covariate, or auxiliary variable, in this study is democracy, for which we use a democracy index as a proxy for institutions constructed by the Center for Systemic Peace as in the Polity IV project. The democracy index ranges from 0–10, and higher scores indicate a greater extent of institutionalized democracy that incorporates "the presence of institutions and procedures through which citizens can express effective preferences about alternative policies and leaders," "the existence of institutionalized constraints on the exercise of power by the executive," and "the guarantee of civil liberties to all citizens in their daily lives and in acts of political participation" (Marshall et al. (2016)).

It is believed that there are many determinants of economic growth that may be correlated with institutions, but are omitted from the regression model. Moreover, the democracy indicators are viewed as noisy measures of "true" institutional quality and subject to considerable measurement error, which potentially result in attenuation bias in the estimate. For example, Acemoglu et al. (2001) used the mortality rates of European settlers in the colonial countries as an instrument for the institutions and eliminated these two potential bias sources simultaneously. In a more recent study, Acemoglu et al. (2015) used regional waves of democratization after 2011 as an instrument for the democracy variable. They also constructed a new measure of democracy variables to circumvent measurement error problems in the standard dynamic panel regression estimation. In our paper, we rely on lagged values of democracy, which may still lead to underestimation of its impact, but may eliminate omitted variable bias.

We also use another set of variables as the threshold variables that resulted in a rejection of the null hypothesis of global linearity in the model of Kourtellos et al. (2013). These covariates include fertility, the logarithm of the average total fertility rate; life expectancy, the logarithm of the average life expectancy at birth; government consumption, the logarithm of average ratios of government consumption to real GDP per capita; and trade openness, the average ratio for each period of exports plus imports to GDP.

---

[3] Excluded countries are Guyana, Nicaragua, Papua New Guinea, and Syria. Guyana and Papua New Guinea are excluded since they were not reported in PWT 9.0. Data for Syria were not available in the IMF public debt database beyond 2010.

4. Estimation Results

4.1. Homogeneous Models and Mean Parameter Estimates

We present estimates from various model specifications for the augmented Solow growth model and an endogenous semiparametric smooth coefficient model in Table 1. We first compared mean parameter estimates from the semiparametric specifications with those from parametric model regression estimation. Columns 1–7 show estimates for four homogeneous model specifications from ordinary least squares (or OLS) and three model specifications from two-stage least squares (or 2SLS) estimation method. Since semiparametric models take democracy into account through the functional coefficients, we included democracy as an additional conditioning variable in the standard growth model specifications. The year indicator is another factor that was controlled for in the parametric regression models in Columns 1–7. Columns 1–4 show that the OLS estimates for the coefficient of public debt were negative and significant at the 5% and 10% levels with their values ranging from −0.0058–−0.0080. The OLS regression in Column 3 suggests that a 10 percentage point increase in the debt-to-GDP ratio was, on average, associated with a 0.060% decrease in the subsequent 10-year period real per capita GDP growth rate.

The 2SLS estimates for public debt variable in Columns 5–7 were also significant at the 10% level within the same magnitude level as the OLS estimates. The 2SLS estimate of the impact of democracy on economic growth, 0.0022, was highly significant with a standard error of 0.0007. This estimate was larger than the OLS estimates in Column 3, which suggests that there was a downward bias in the OLS estimates of democracy variable, possibly due to measurement error in the democracy index that created attenuation bias (an estimate biased toward zero) or endogeneity.[4]

Table 1. Summary of the results. ASPE, average squared predicted error.

Variable	OLS				2SLS			SPSCM-IV		
	(1)	(2)	(3)	(4)	(5)	(6)	(7)	(8)	(9)	(10)
Intercept	0.0355 ^{b}	0.0258 ^{c}	−0.0203	−0.0126	0.0236 ^{c}	−0.0068	−0.0068	0.0409	0.0196	−0.0171
	0.0143	0.0143	0.0437	0.0450	0.0144	0.0444	0.0457	0.005	0.0391	0.0346
Public Debt	−0.0080 ^{b}	−0.0067 ^{b}	−0.0060 ^{c}	−0.0058 ^{c}	−0.0064 ^{c}	−0.0058 ^{c}	−0.0055 ^{c}	−0.0071 ^{a}	−0.0073 ^{a}	−0.0053 ^{b}
	0.0034	0.0033	0.0033	0.0033	0.0033	0.0033	0.0033	0.0011	0.0025	0.0023
Democracy		0.0012 ^{a}	0.0014 ^{b}	0.0014 ^{b}	0.0015 ^{b}	0.0022 ^{a}	0.0021 ^{a}	—	—	—
		0.0004	0.0006	0.0006	0.0004	0.0007	0.0007			
Initial Income			−0.0049	−0.0051		−0.0060 ^{a}	−0.0061 ^{c}		−0.0097 ^{a}	−0.0081 ^{a}
			0.0035	0.0035		0.0021	0.0034		0.0024	0.0024
Investment Rate			0.0178 ^{a}	0.0176 ^{a}		0.0183 ^{a}	0.0181 ^{a}		0.0077 ^{c}	0.0077 ^{b}
			0.0053	0.0053		0.0053	0.0053		0.004	0.0039
Population Growth Rate			−0.0111	−0.0102		−0.0073	−0.0069		−0.0283 ^{b}	−0.028 ^{b}
			0.0248	0.0248		0.0247	0.0248		0.0142	0.014
Schooling			0.0050	0.0051		0.0047	0.0048		0.0090 ^{a}	0.0090 ^{a}
			0.0039	0.0040		0.0039	0.0040		0.0029	0.003
Inflation Rate				−0.0015			−0.0017			−0.0028 ^{b}
				0.0012			0.0012			0.0011
Trend	0.0054 ^{a}	0.0041 ^{b}	0.0023	0.0017	0.0038 ^{c}	0.0019	0.0013			
	0.0018	0.0019	0.0023	0.0018	0.0020	0.0017	0.0018			
In-Sample R^2	0.0832	0.1211	0.2093	0.2154	0.1191	0.2025	0.2094	0.1744	0.3799	0.4257
Out-of-Sample R^2	0.0982	0.1399	0.2684	0.2767	0.1379	0.2600	0.2698	0.1187	0.3099	0.3411
ASPE	0.00048	0.00046	0.00044	0.00044	0.00047	0.00073	0.00074	0.00049	0.00041	0.00040

1. Semiparametric model specifications allow coefficients to vary with respect to democracy. 2. We use Gaussian kernel function for all semiparametric estimation. The cross-validated bandwidth in column 9 is 1.62. Moreover, L_n is equal to 1. 3. Statistically significant parameter estimates: ^{a}, significance at 1%; ^{b}, significance at 5%; ^{c}, significance at 10%. 4. Column 8–10 reports the mean coefficient estimates and their respective standard errors. 5. Out-of-sample R^2 and ASPE report mean of 1000 bootstrap replications.

Columns 8–10 report the average of semiparametric smooth coefficient instrumental variable (or SPSCM-IV) regression estimates and their standard errors. Columns 8 and 9 show that the coefficient

4 Acemoglu et al. (2001) evaluated the difference between OLS and 2SLS estimates of the democracy variable using executive constraints as an instrument. They expected that using this variable as an instrument would not solve the endogeneity problem, but that it would correctly address the measurement error if it was properly measured. The estimated effect of the institutions variable from the 2SLS method was 0.87 and highly significant. They concluded that measurement error in the institutions variable could be the primary difference between the OLS and 2SLS estimates.

estimates of public debt were negative and statistically significant at the 5% and 1% levels with values around −0.0071 and −0.0073, respectively. The estimated effect suggests that a 10 percentage point increase in the debt-to-GDP ratio may be associated with a 0.073% decrease in the subsequent 10-year period real GDP growth rates, on average. Comparing Columns 9 and 3, we observe that the mean value of public debt coefficient estimates from the semiparametric model estimation is almost in agreement with that of the ordinary least squares estimation.

Nevertheless, the in-sample goodness of fit of the semiparametric model (38%) is higher than that of the parametric model (20%). This comparison holds for all specifications between semiparametric and parametric regression models. We further investigate the model's out-of-sample performance to decide whether this improvement reflects over-fitting. In each semiparametric model in Columns 8–10, the out-of-sample R^2 (ASPE) was in general higher (lower) than in the corresponding parametric models. These results indicate that the semiparametric smooth coefficient model in Column 9 was 7.3% more efficient than the parametric linear model in Column 3 regarding out-of-sample predictive ability, which, therefore, implies that the semiparametric model may better describe the underlying process that generated the data than does the parametric model. One may be concerned that higher-order polynomial terms in the homogeneous model may be sufficient to capture the parameter heterogeneity. We examined this concern with the bias-variance trade-off in both the parametric and nonparametric model estimation. Adding polynomial terms in a parametric regression model reduced the bias of the estimates (since more information was used in the estimation), but the parameters were less accurately estimated (i.e., standard errors were larger). Therefore, nonlinearity in the parametric model may be captured at the cost of efficiency. The nonparametric regression model, on the other hand, allowed controlling the bias-variance trade-off through the selection of a bandwidth parameter, which essentially determines the local sample size for the estimation of each point of interest. Furthermore, one can choose the bandwidth using the data via the cross-validation method. In other words, the nonparametric modeling approach allows a researcher to use the data to optimize the bias-variance trade-off. One also might ask whether a linear interaction term in a parametric model might explain the idea that public debt may have a different effect for countries that have different institutional quality. Since the estimate for public debt reflects the average effect on growth rate for all countries and since adding an interaction term for each variable in the model can result in loss of efficiency, a parametric model with an interaction term may not fully explain the parameter heterogeneity. However, the smooth coefficient approach models the interaction effect among regressors and some covariates in a flexible way as opposed to a predetermined structure considered in the parametric specifications. It should be emphasized that both the parametric and semiparametric models approximate the unknown true relationships in their capacity; however, the non-semiparametric model imposes fewer restrictions than the parametric model and thus is believed to enable a better fit to the data and a more reliable inference.

The coefficients on other explanatory variables (i.e., initial per capita income, investment rate, population growth rate, and average years of schooling) in Columns 9 and 10 were of the predicted sign and significant at conventional levels. Column 10 reports the mean estimates for the semiparametric regression model, which controls for inflation rate additionally. All variables had statistically-significant coefficient estimates at conventional levels, but the magnitude of the coefficient estimate of public debt decreased by more than half as the inflation rate accounts for part of its negative effect on economic growth. This result is consistent with the theoretical literature on inflation and economic growth (Barro and Salai-Martin (1995)). Homogeneous model specifications in Columns 4 and 7, on the other hand, did not estimate an economically-significant drop in the growth effect of public debt when the inflation rate was included as an additional conditioning variable.

4.2. Parameter Heterogeneity

Figure 1 displays country-specific coefficient estimates for the public debt variable from the semi-parametric regression model in Table 1's Column 10 along with 95% bootstrap percentile confidence intervals.[5] We first observe that more public debt leads to lower economic growth for countries with democracy scores less than one and higher than 7.6, holding other factors fixed. This result is partially consistent with the existing literature that found an adverse effect of more public debt on growth for countries with weak institutional quality. However, we also found that countries with a high democracy score had a statistically-significant negative relationship between public debt and economic growth in the long run. We found that public debt had no significant effect on growth for the countries with a democracy score between one and 7.6. Notably, the impact of public debt on growth for countries with a median level of democracy score reduced to values around zero, which is therefore economically insignificant as well.

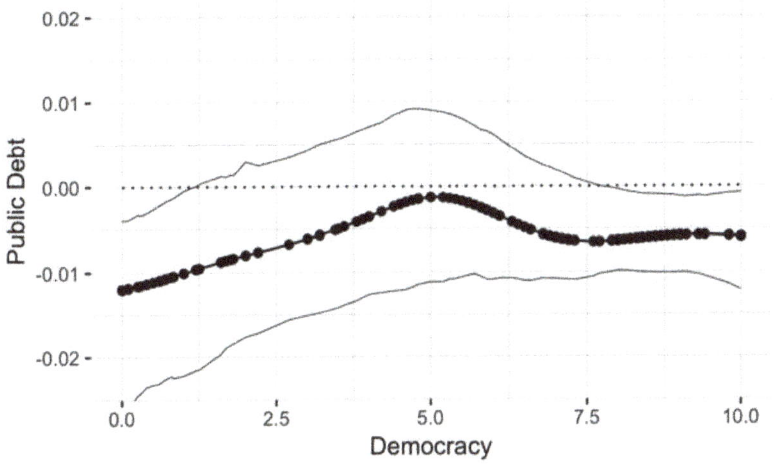

Figure 1. Estimated coefficient curve for the public debt variable from the model in Column 9 of Table 1. The figure corresponds to the functional coefficient $\theta_d(\cdot)$, graphing the semiparametric smooth coefficient instrumental variable estimate (solid line with small circles) with 95% bootstrap percentile confidence intervals (solid lines).

We find that the quartile values for the public debt coefficient estimates were −0.0093, −0.0071, and −0.0064, respectively, for the 25th, 50th, and 75th percentiles. Moreover, countries with zero democracy had the maximum value of estimates −0.012, whereas advanced countries with a democracy score of 10 had the median coefficient estimate. This result implies heterogeneity in the effect of debt on growth with different magnitudes for the two country groups. From another perspective, we found evidence of heterogeneity observing geographical differences within these two groups of countries. These results are particularly relevant to policy decisions suggesting fiscal policy sustainability for the low-income countries, as well as emerging and developed countries. However, we should note that debt sustainability is important for highly indebted Euro area countries such as Greece, Portugal, and Spain, but not the case for Japan.

5 Henderson et al. (2012) suggest to plot gradient estimates in a 45o plot to expose parameter heterogeneity that exists in the estimates. Their suggestion is useful especially when covariate vector is more than one dimension. Since in our model estimation the coefficients vary with respect to only one variable, from the graphical point of view it is better to plot coefficient estimates on a Cartesian coordinate system.

We should emphasize that our results did not indicate any tipping point or threshold level for the debt-to-GDP ratio beyond which economic growth is adversely affected. For the two country groups separately, we observed debt-to-GDP ratios at different levels ranging from 16%–560% for the low democracy group and from 9%–196% for the high democracy group.

We did not find conclusive evidence in support of the direct effect of democracy on the coefficient of public debt as their effect appeared to be insignificant for all countries and economically insignificant for the advanced countries. In other words, if the democracy score of countries were to increase in the 10-year averages, it may not be indicative that these countries have an increasing or decreasing effect of public debt on growth in the long run.

4.2.1. Including the Period 2010–2014

We further investigated the relationship between public debt and economic growth including the years from 2010–2014. Guyana, Nicaragua, Papua New Guinea, and Syria were not included in the extended dataset. Figure 2 displays functional coefficient estimates for the public debt variable using this dataset. In contrast to Figure 1, we found a statistically-significant negative effect of public debt on the growth for the countries with a democracy score higher than three. On average, public debt had a stronger effect on growth with an estimate of −0.0106 (1.5-fold increase) compared to the estimate from Column 9 in Table 1. We observed that countries with the highest democracy had a larger negative effect of public debt on growth at −0.013 than the effect obtained from the initial dataset. Moreover, the largest effect in magnitude was −0.018 for the countries having a democracy score of 3.5.[6]

Our results strongly suggest heterogeneity in the relationship between debt and growth as the countries in different geographical regions had statistically-significant estimates of different magnitudes. We also did not find any evidence on the direct effect of democracy on the public debt coefficient, which indicates the neutral effect of democracy on the public debt coefficient for all countries.

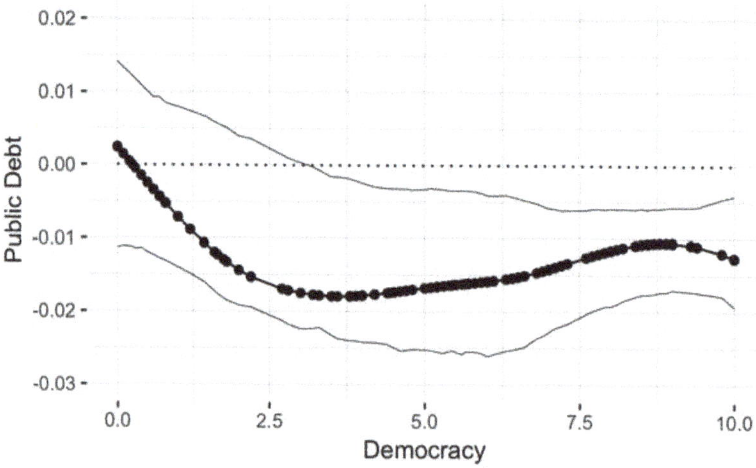

Figure 2. Functional coefficient estimates for the public debt variable for the period 1980–2014. The figure corresponds to the functional coefficient $\theta_d(\cdot)$, graphing the semiparametric smooth coefficient instrumental variable estimate (solid line with small circles) with 95% bootstrap percentile confidence intervals (solid lines).

---

6 These countries are the Central African Republic and Malawi for the year 1990.

4.2.2. Policy Implications

We now turn to the contradictory result that we found in both Figures 1 and 2 for the advanced countries. One may believe that good institutions, which we proxy by democracy in this paper, may help to alleviate the adverse effect of high public debt to ensure fiscal policy sustainability, to use government spending in productive sectors such as education and health, and to promote sustainable growth, among others. Japan is an example of this case having the largest debt-to-GDP ratio among advanced countries with strong economic indicators. The question may be then highly related to the quality of institutions of advanced countries. Relatedly, it has been widely discussed for the Euro area countries that the root of the public debt crisis in Europe is an excessive risk-taking behavior of economies due to over-borrowing (see Allen et al. (2015) and Yener et al. (2015)). In other words, countries within a widespread financial system rely heavily on external funds to finance their excess consumption, which eventually results in unsustainable public debt levels. To overcome this problem, governments adopt austerity fiscal policies with the risk of recession. Greece has been one of the examples of this situation.

The main reason behind our findings is that our democracy variables used in this paper captured only the political institutions of countries as explained in Section 3. However, it is widely argued that economic institutions, which are determined by the political process of a country, are one of the determinants of the prosperity of countries in the economic history (see Acemoglu and Robinson (2012) for further details). Therefore, our analysis requires additional variable such as the financial risk index, which can be a proxy for economic institutions and may have a variability within the advanced country group. We defer this analysis for future research.

In Section 5.1, we show the results from robustness checks conducted by excluding the most indebted advanced countries (i.e., Japan, Greece, Belgium, Ireland, Portugal, Italy, and Jamaica) to examine whether these countries may drive the main results for advanced countries. We found that the statistically-significant negative relationship between debt and growth for the advanced countries remained the same, which suggests that our core results for the highest democracy countries may be driven by country- and time-specific factors and spillover effects. Moreover, debt trajectory may have more explanatory power in the debt-growth nexus than the level of public debt (see Chudik et al. (2017) and Yener et al. (2017)). In fact, in our available dataset, we find all above-listed countries to have rising public debt levels regardless of their initial debt-to-GDP ratios. Lastly, we included Germany in the dataset to investigate whether our main results can be altered or not. With the inclusion of Germany in the analysis, our main results remained exactly the same.

4.2.3. Parameter Heterogeneity in the Relationship between Growth and Other Regressors

The curves in Figure 3 show how democracy affects the coefficients of other conditioning variables. Figure 3a shows that countries with an institutionalized democracy, a score higher than 4.7, had an increasing significant negative effect of initial income on economic growth, which confirms the conditional β-convergence hypothesis. The curve in Figure 3b exhibits a significant positive and an inverse U-shaped relationship between the real investment rate and the real GDP per capita growth rate for the countries with a democracy score between 1.2 and 7. Figure 3c indicates that a higher population growth rate was associated with a slowdown in economic growth for the countries with a democracy score greater than 6.6. Figure 3d shows that schooling had a significant positive effect on the growth rate for the countries with a democracy score greater than 6.3. For each regressor, except for the investment rate, there was a heterogeneous relationship in the effect of the variable on the economic growth rate for the mid- and high-level democracy score countries.

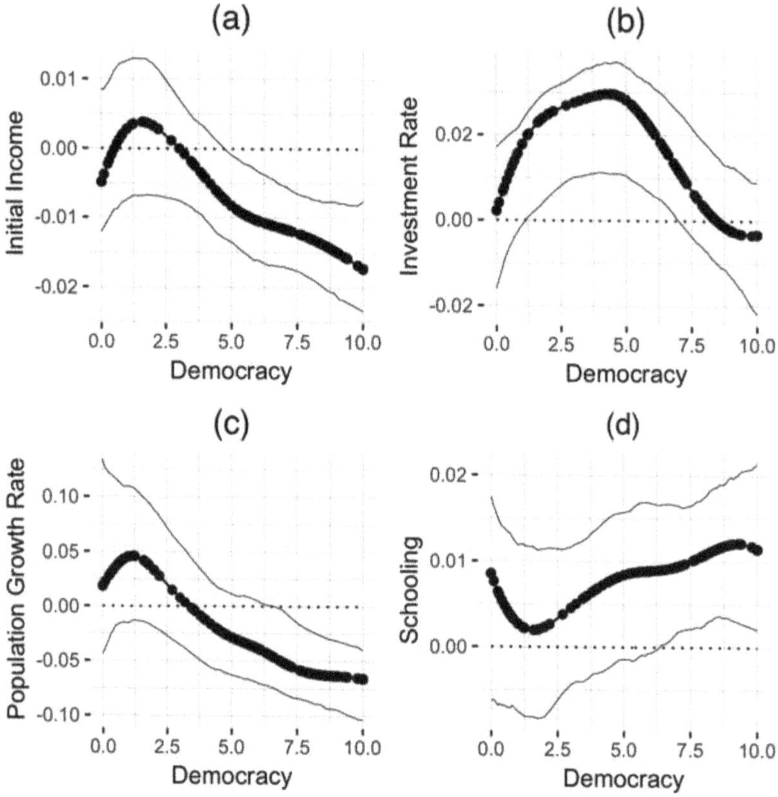

Figure 3. Functional coefficient estimates for other regressors. Plot (**a**) corresponds to the functional coefficient of initial income. Plot (**b**) corresponds to the functional coefficient of investment rate. Plot (**c**) corresponds to the functional coefficient of population growth rate. Plot (**d**) corresponds to the functional coefficient of schooling. Each plot graphs the semiparametric smooth coefficient instrumental variable estimate (solid line with small circles) with 95% bootstrap percentile confidence intervals (solid lines).

5. Robustness Checks

In this section, we describe how various robustness exercises used to examine whether our core results remain the same using additional model specifications.[7]

5.1. Influential Countries

Our primary investigation was undertaken to understand how sensitive the results are for advanced countries notated in Figure 1 and using respective datasets. In the dataset for the period 1980–2009, Japan, Jamaica, and Belgium are the countries with a democracy score of 10 having the highest public debt-to-GDP ratio. When we only exclude Japan, our core results in Figure 1 remain the same. When we exclude the three countries listed above, we lose the statistical significance of the estimates for countries with high democracy scores. In part, the insignificant coefficient estimates for advanced countries occurs because we lose nine data points in the neighborhood of each point

[7] The figures and detailed results obtained in this section are available upon request from the author.

estimation. We also ran our semi-parametric regression model with the initial dataset excluding Guyana, Nicaragua, Papua New Guinea, and Syria, as these countries are not available in the extended dataset. We find the same functional coefficient curve as in Figure 2 with fewer countries having statistically-significant coefficient estimates (i.e., countries with democracy scores higher than 6.8). For further investigation, we performed two additional econometric exercises by excluding Guyana only and testing Nicaragua, Papua New Guinea, and Syria together from the initial dataset. We found that the Guyana dataset might have driven our main finding for low democracy countries in Figure 1.

We performed the same econometric exercise for the extended dataset (i.e., for the years 1980–2014), excluding Japan, Greece, Belgium, Ireland, Portugal, Italy, and Jamaica. When we excluded Japan and Greece from the dataset, our core results in Figure 2 remained the same. When we excluded all seven countries listed above, our core results in Figure 2 remained the same with the same magnitude and functional coefficient curve. Thus, these results indicate that a high debt-to-GDP ratio may not be the main factor for the statistically-significant negative relationship between public debt and growth for the highest democracy countries. Specifically, in our study, being consistent with Kourtellos et al.'s (2013) findings, we find that low and high democracy countries have a negative effect of debt on growth regardless of their public debt-to-GDP ratio.

5.2. Alternative Measure for Democracy

We examined whether our main results were sensitive to different measures of institutional quality such as executive constraints obtained from the same data source, Polity IV. We found that countries with an executive constraint score less than 2.2 and higher than 5.8 had a statistically-significant negative relationship between public debt and growth for the period 1980–2009. This result does not alter the conclusions drawn from our main results; that is, institutional quality is an essential factor that governs the effect of public debt on growth.

We further tested our main results using Freedom House's historical data on political rights and civil liberties. For the period 1980–2009, our findings indicated that countries with an index of political rights above 2.7 and below 4.5 (and with an index of civil liberties between 3.1 and 5.0) had a statistically-significant negative estimate of public debt on economic growth. For the period 1980–2014, we found a statistically-significant negative effect of public debt on growth for the countries whose political rights index was between 5.1 and 6.7 and whose civil liberty index was between 3.9 and 6.4. Overall, our core results were robust to different measures of democracy. However, we lost the statistical significance of a public debt coefficient estimate for the advanced countries.

5.3. Additional Control Variables

We estimated the semiparametric smooth coefficient model that includes such additional country characteristics as government spending, trade openness, fertility, and life expectancy. In separate econometric exercises for each additional control variable, we revealed similar results as shown in Figures 1 and 2. Thus, the qualitative implications of our core results remained unchanged in the model.

6. Conclusions

In this study, we employed a semi-parametric smooth coefficient model with an endogenous variable in the nonparametric part to analyze the heterogeneous relationship between debt and growth with two different time frames. Our paper contributes to the literature by taking the institutional differences across countries into account in a flexible modelling approach and provides conclusive evidence of heterogeneity in the debt-growth relationship in the given sample.

Our results are consistent with the previous literature that identified an average negative and statistically-significant effect of public debt on growth. However, our semi-parametric model also identifies heterogeneity in the growth effect of public debt. Mainly, we find strong evidence that countries we studied with a democracy score less than one and higher than 7.6 have an adverse effect of debt on growth for the period 1980–2009. The magnitude of the effect of public debt on growth varies across countries with different institutional quality. Our findings for the period 1980–2014 also provide conclusive evidence in support of the negative and significant relationship between debt and growth for the countries with a democracy score higher than three. Our core results from Figure 1 suggest that a 10-percentage point increase in the debt-to-GDP ratio is associated with a 0.12% and 0.071% decrease in the subsequent 10-year period real GDP growth rate for the zero democracy countries and for the countries with a democracy score of 10, respectively. The public debt appears to have a more profound effect on growth for the advanced countries after the most recent years are considered. Specifically, the 10-year average real GDP growth rate decreased by 0.13% when the debt-to-GDP ratio surged by ten percentage points.

In future research, we will certainly incorporate more variables that are among the determinants of economic institutions of countries to better understand the effect of public debt on economic growth.

Acknowledgments: We would like to thank two anonymous referees for their insightful and instructive comments. We also thank Thanasis Stengos, Yiguo Sun, Alex Maynard, Miana Plesca, and the participants at the June 2017, 51st Annual Conference of the Canadian Economics Association hosted by Saint Francis Xavier University in Antigonish.

Conflicts of Interest: The author declares no conflict of interest.

Appendix A

Table A1. Summary statistics.

	Mean	Std. Dev.	Min	Max
Panel A. Penn World Table 7.0 (1980–2009)				
Growth	0.014	0.023	−0.099	0.083
Initial income	8.42	1.27	5.87	10.71
Lag of initial income	8.34	1.23	5.78	10.55
Investment rate	3.05	0.35	1.87	3.89
Lag of investment rate	3.05	0.39	1.74	4.31
Population growth rate	−2.71	0.16	−3.23	−2.38
Lag of population growth rate	−2.69	0.16	−3.08	−2.28
Government consumption	2.19	0.44	1.06	3.56
Lag of government consumption	2.19	0.48	1.01	3.69
Trade openness	66.51	36.49	9.77	199.86
Lag of trade openness	61.01	35.80	9.70	180.09
Panel B. Penn World Table 9.0 (1980–2014)				
Growth	0.025	0.029	−0.061	0.114
Initial income	8.77	1.17	6.42	11.20
Investment rate	2.96	0.45	0.65	3.92
Population growth rate	−2.71	0.15	−3.07	−2.38
Schooling	0.77	0.32	0.036	1.31
Panel C. World Bank				
Inflation rate	2.30	1.17	−1.95	7.57
Lag of inflation rate	2.34	1.19	−1.46	8.26
Life expectancy	4.17	0.17	3.63	4.41
Lag of life expectancy	4.14	0.18	3.63	4.38
Fertility	3.62	1.73	1.21	7.78
Lag of fertility	4.06	1.89	1.17	7.82
Panel D. IMF				
Public debt	4.08	0.61	2.17	6.33
Lag of public debt	3.92	0.73	1.12	6.46
Panel E. Barro and Lee (2000)				
Schooling	0.60	0.77	−2.18	1.97
Lag of schooling	0.32	0.90	−2.66	1.90
Panel F. Polity IV				
Democracy	5.74	3.83	0.00	10.00
Lag of democracy	5.02	4.17	0.00	10.00
Executive constraints	4.96	2.05	1.00	7.00
Lag of executive constraints	4.51	2.33	1.00	7.00
Panel G. Freedom House				
Political rights	4.82	1.93	1.00	7.00
Lag of political rights	4.53	2.08	1.00	7.00
Civil liberties	4.67	1.68	1.00	7.00
Lag of civil liberties	4.45	1.77	1.00	7.00

Table A2. Data description. PWT, Penn World Table.

Variable	Source	Definition
Growth	PWT 7.0 & 9.0	Growth rate of real per capita GDP in chain series for the periods 1980–1989, 1990–1999, 2000–2009, and 2010–2014 (for extended data).
Initial income	PWT 7.0 & 9.0	Logarithm of real per capita GDP in chain series at 1980, 1990, 2000, and 2010 (for extended data). Lagged values correspond to 1975, 1985, 1995, and 2005 (for extended data).
Investment rate	PWT 7.0 & 9.0	Logarithm of average ratios over each period of investment to real GDP per capita for the periods 1980–1989, 1990–1999, 2000–2009, and 2010–2014 (for extended data). Lagged values correspond to 1975–1979, 1985–1989, 1995–1999, 2005–2009 (for extended data).
Population growth rate	PWT 7.0 & 9.0	Logarithm of average population growth rates plus 0.05 for the periods 1980–1989, 1990–1999, 2000–2009, and 2010–2014 (for extended data). Lagged values correspond to 1975–1979, 1985–1989, 1995–1999, 2005–2009 (for extended data).
Schooling	Barro and Lee (2000)	Logarithm of average years of male secondary and tertiary school attainment for ages above 25 in 1980, 1990, 1999, and 2010 (for extended data). Lagged values correspond to 1975, 1985, 1995, and 2005 (for extended data).
Public debt	IMF, Debt Database Fall 2011 Vintage	Logarithm of average percentages over each period of public debt to GDP for the periods 1980–1989, 1990–1999, 2000–2009, and 2010–2014 (for extended data). Lagged values correspond to 1975–1979, 1985–1989, 1995–1999, and 2005–2009 (for extended data).
Fertility	World Bank	Logarithm of average total fertility rate in 1980–1989, 1990–1999, 2000–2009, and 2010–2014 (for extended data). Lagged values correspond to 1975–1979, 1985–1989, 1995–1999, 2005–2009 (for extended data).
Life expectancy	World Bank	Logarithm of average average life expectancy at birth for the periods 1980–1989, 1990–1999, 2000–2009, and 2010–2014 (for extended data). Lagged values correspond to 1975–1979, 1985–1989, 1995–1999, and 2005–2009 (for extended data).
Trade openness	PWT 7.0 & 9.0	Average ratios for each period of exports plus imports to real GDP per capita for the periods 1980–1989, 1990–1999, 2000–2009, and 2010–2014 (for extended data). Lagged values correspond to 1975–1979, 1985–1989, 1995–1999, 2005–2009 (for extended data).
Government consumption	PWT 7.0 & 9.0	Logarithm of average ratios for each period of government consumption to real GDP per capita for the periods 1980–1989, 1990–1999, 2000–2009, and 2010–2014 (for extended data). Lagged values correspond to 1975–1979, 1985–1989, 1995–1999, 2005–2009 (for extended data).
Inflation rate	World Bank	Logarithm of average inflation plus 1 for the periods 1980–1989, 1990–1999, 2000–2009, and (for extended data). Lagged values correspond to 1975–1979, 1985–1989, 1995–1999, and 2005–2009 (for extended data).
Democracy	Polity IV	An index ranges from 0 to 10 where higher values equals a greater extent of institutionalized democracy. Average for the periods 1980–1989, 1990–1999, 2000–2009, and 2010–2014 (for extended data). Lagged values correspond to 1975–1979, 1985–1989, 1995–1999, and 2005–2009 (for extended data).
Executive constraints	Polity IV	An index ranges from 1 to 7 where higher values equals a greater extent of institutionalized constraints on the power of chief executives. Average for the periods 1980–1989, 1990–1999, 2000–2009, and 2010–2014 (for extended data). Lagged values correspond to 1975–1979, 1985–1989, 1995–1999, 2005–2009 (for extended data).
Political rights	Freedom House	An index ranges from 1 to 7 where higher values equals a greater extent of institutionalized constraints on the power of chief executives. Average for the periods 1980–1989, 1990–1999, 2000–2009, and 2010–2014 (for extended data). Lagged values correspond to 1975–1979, 1985–1989, 1995–1999, and 2005–2009 (for extended data).
Civil liberties	Freedom House	An index ranges from 1 to 7 where higher values equals a greater extent of institutionalized constraints on the power of chief executives. Average for the periods 1980–1989, 1990–1999, 2000–2009, and 2010–2014 (for extended data). Lagged values correspond to 1975–1979, 1985–1989, 1995–1999, and 2005–2009 (for extended data).

Table A3. List of countries grouped into coefficient estimates from SPSCM-IVand democracy score from the Polity IV dataset.

Negative and Significant			Insignificant
≤1	≥7.6 & ≤9	≥9	
Algeria (1980, 1990)	Argentina (2000)	Australia (1980, 1990, 2000)	Argentina (1980, 1990)
Bangladesh (1980)	Bolivia (1990, 2000)	Austria (1980, 1990, 2000)	Benin (1990, 2000)
Benin (1980)	Botswana (2000)	Belgium (1980, 1990, 2000)	Bangladesh (1990, 2000)
Burundi (1980, 1990)	Brazil (1990, 2000)	Canada (1980, 1990, 2000)	Bolivia (1980)
Cameroon (1980, 1990, 2000)	Chile (1990, 2000)	Costa Rica (1980, 1990, 2000)	Botswana (1980, 1990)
Central African Republic (1980)	Colombia (1980, 1990)	Cyprus (1980, 1990, 2000)	Brazil (1980)
Chile (1980)	Dominican Republic (2000)	Denmark (1980, 1990, 2000)	Burundi (2000)
Cote'd Ivoire (1980, 1990)	Ecuador (1980, 1990)	Finland (1980, 1990, 2000)	Central African Republic (1990, 2000)
Egypt (1980, 1990, 2000)	France (1980)	France (1990, 2000)	Congo Republic (1990)
Gabon (1980, 1990, 2000)	Greece (1980)	Greece (1990, 2000)	Cote'd Ivoire (2000)
Gambia (2000)	Guatemala (2000)	Ireland (1980, 1990, 2000)	Colombia (2000)
Ghana (1980)	India (1980, 1990, 2000)	Italy (1980, 1990, 2000)	Dominican Republic (2000)
Guyana (1980)	Republic of Korea (2000)	Israel (1980, 1990, 2000)	Ecuador (2000)
Indonesia (1980, 1990)	Lesotho (2000)	Jamaica (1980, 1990, 2000)	Gambia (1980, 1990)
Iran (1980)	Mexico (2000)	Japan (1980, 1990, 2000)	Ghana (1980, 1990)
Kenya (1980, 1900)	Panama (1990, 2000)	Netherlands (1980, 1990, 2000)	Guatemala (1990)
Lesotho (1980)	Paraguay (2000)	New Zealand (1980, 1990, 2000)	Guyana (1990, 2000)
Malawi (1980)	Peru (2000)	Norway (1980, 1990, 2000)	Honduras (1980, 1990, 2000)
Mali (1980)	Philippines (2000)	Portugal (1980, 1990, 2000)	Kenya (2000)
Mauritania (1980, 2000)	Senegal (2000)	Spain (1980, 1990, 2000)	Lesotho (1990)
Morocco (1980, 1990, 2000)	South Africa (1990, 2000)	Sweden (1980, 1990, 2000)	Malaysia (1980, 2000)
Nicaragua (1980, 1990)	Thailand (1990)	United Kingdom (1980, 1990, 2000)	Malawi (1990, 2000)
Niger (1980)	Trinidad & Tobago (1990, 2000)	United States (1980, 1990, 2000)	Mali (1990, 2000)
Panama (1980)	Turkey (1990, 2000)	Uruguay (1990, 2000)	Mexico (1980, 1990)
Paraguay (1980)	Venezuela (1980, 1990)		Nepal (1980, 1990, 2000)
Sierra Leone (1980)			Nicaragua (1990)
Swaziland (1980, 1990, 2000)			Niger (1990, 2000)
Syria (1980, 1990, 2000)			Pakistan (1980, 1990, 2000)
Togo (1980, 1990, 2000)			Papua New Guinea (1980, 1990, 2000)
Tunisia (1980, 1990, 2000)			Paraguay (1990)
Zambia (1980)			Republic of Korea (1980, 1990)
Zimbabwe (1990)			Peru (1980, 1990)
			Sierra Leone (1980, 2000)
			South Africa (1980)
			Sri Lanka (1980, 1990, 2000)
			Thailand (2000)
			Turkey (1980)
			Venezuela (2000)
			Zambia (1990, 2000)
			Zimbabwe (1980, 2000)

Table A4. List of literature on the relationship between public debt and economic growth.

Paper	Sample	Empirical Methodology	Debt Measure	Instrumental Variable	Findings
Caner et al. (2010)	101 developing and developed countries (1980–2008)	Cross-section; Threshold Least Squares	General government gross debt (% GDP) from IMF	No instruments	Significant negative effect; debt threshold is 77% for all countries; 64% for the sample of developing countries only
Cecchetti et al. (2011)	18 OECD countries (1980–2010)	Panel data; FE; panel threshold; LSDV	General government debt from IMF	No instruments	Significant negative effect; threshold level is 85%
Checherita-Westphal and Rother (2012)	12 Euro area countries (1970–2008)	Panel data; FE; 2SLS; GMM	Gross government debt (% GDP) from AMECO	Lagged debt-to-GDP ratio up to the 5th lag; average of the debt levels of the other countries in the sample	Significant negative effect; debt turning point is in between 90% and 100%
Minea and Parent (2012)	20 advanced countries as in Reinhart and Rogoff (2010) (1945–2009)	Panel data; panel smooth threshold regression	Public debt from IMF	No instruments	Negative effect below the threshold level of 115%; positive effect beyond this level of debt
Baum et al. (2013)	12 Euro area countries (EMU) (1990–2007/2010)	Panel data (yearly); non-/dynamic panel threshold model; OLS; GMM	Public debt from AMECO	No instrument for debt variable	Significant positive effect below the threshold level of 67% for the period 1990–2007; insignificant effect beyond that threshold; significant negative effect beyond the threshold level of 95% for the period 1990–2010
Kourtellos et al. (2013)	82 countries (1980–2009)	Panel data (10-year averages); structural threshold regression; 2SLS; GMM	Public debt (% of GDP) from IMF	Lag of public debt	Threshold variable is democracy; significant negative effect for low-democracy regime countries; insignificant effect for countries in high-democracy regime

Table A5. List of literature on the relationship between public debt and economic growth (Cont'd.).

Paper	Sample	Empirical Methodology	Debt Measure	Instrumental Variable	Findings
Wright and Grenade (2014)	13 Caribbean countries (1990–2012)	Panel data; PDOLS	Debt/GDP from IMF	No instruments	61% is the threshold level
Eberhardt and Presbitero (2015)	118 countries (1961–2012)	Unbalanced panel data; panel time series approach; ECM	Gross general government debt from WDI and IMF	No instruments	No common threshold level of public debt for all countries; evidence for differences in debt-growth relationship across countries
Égert (2015)	20 advanced and 21 emerging economies (1946–2009)	Panel data; threshold regression	Central government debt from the same source in Reinhart and Rogoff (2011)	No instruments	Little evidence on 90% threshold level; some evidence for lower threshold level
Woo and Kumar (2015)	38 advanced and emerging economies (1970–2008)	Panel data; BE; pooled OLS; FE; SGMM	Gross government debt (% of GDP) from IMF	5t lag of debt variable	Significant negative effect; threshold level of 90%, beyond which debt has a negative effect

1. European Commission AMECO (AMECO is the annual macro-economic database of the European Commission's Directorate General for Economic and Financial Affairs.) database. 2. LSDV stands for the Least Squares Dummy Variables. 3. ECM stands for the Error Correction Model. 4. PDOLS refers to the panel dynamic ordinary least squares. 5. WDI stands for the World Development Indicators. 6. BE refers to the Between Estimator. 7. Woo and Kumar (2015) found the threshold level by adding interaction terms into the model. 8. Égert's (2015) dataset for advanced countries excludes Ireland and includes Switzerland.

References

Acemoglu, Daron, Simon Johnson, and James A. Robinson. 2001. The colonial origins of comparative development: An empirical investigation. *American Economic Review* 91: 1369–401. [CrossRef]

Acemoglu, Daron, Simon Johnson, James A. Robinson, and Pierre Yared. 2005. From education to democracy? *American Economic Review* 95: 44–49. [CrossRef]

Acemoglu, Daron, Suresh Naidu, Pascual Restrepo, and James A. Robinson. 2015. Democracy does cause growth. *Journal of Political Economy*. [CrossRef]

Acemoglu, Daron and James A. Robinson. 2012. *Why Nations Fail: The Origins of Power, Prosperity, and Poverty*. New York: Currency.

Allen, Franklin, Elena Carletti, Itay Goldstein, and Agnese Leonello. 2015. Moral hazard and government guarantees in the banking industry. *Journal of Financial Regulation* 1: 1–21. [CrossRef]

Azariadis, Costas, and Allan Drazen. 1990. Threshold externalities in economic development. *The Quarterly Journal of Economics* 105: 501–26. [CrossRef]

Barro, Robert J., and Xavier I. Salai-Martin. 1995. *Economic Growth*. New York: McGraw-Hill.

Baum, Anja, Cristina Checherita-Westphal, and Philipp Rother. 2013. Debt and growth: New evidence for the euro area. *Journal of International Money and Finance* 32: 809–21. [CrossRef]

Bernal, Raquel, and Michael P. Keane. 2011. Child care choices and children's cognitive achievement: the case of single mothers. *Journal of Labor Economics* 29: 459–12. [CrossRef]

Bohn, Henning. 1995. The sustainability of budget deficits in a stochastic economy. *Journal of Money, Credit and Banking* 27: 257–71. [CrossRef]

Cai, Zongwu, Mitali Das, Huaiyu Xiong, and Xizhi Wu. 2006. Functional coefficient instrumental variables models. *Journal of Econometrics* 133: 207–41. [CrossRef]

Cai, Zongwu, and Qi Li. 2008. Nonparametric estimation of varying coefficient dynamic panel data models. *Econometric Theory* 24: 1321–42. [CrossRef]

Caner, Mehmet, Thomas Grennes, and Fritzi Koehler-Geib. 2010. *Finding the Tipping Point-When Sovereign Debt Turns Bad*. Technical Report. Washington, DC: The World Bank.

Cecchetti, Stephen G., Madhusudan S. Mohanty, and Fabrizio Zampolli. 2010. *The Future of Public Debt: Prospects and Implications*. Technical Report. Basel: Bank for International Settlements.

Cecchetti, Stephen G., Madhusudan S. Mohanty, and Fabrizio Zampolli. 2011. *The Real Effects of Debts*. Technical Report. Basel: Bank for International Settlements.

Checherita-Westphal, Cristina, and Philipp Rother. 2012. The impact of high government debt on economic growth and its channels: An empirical investigation for the euro area. *European Economic Review* 56: 1392–405. [CrossRef]

Chen, Xiaohong. 2007. Large sample sieve estimation of semi-nonparametric models. In *Handbook of Econometrics*. Edited by James J. Heckman and Edward E. Leamer. New York: Springer, vol. 6B, pp. 5549–32.

Chudik, Alexander, Kamiar Mohaddes, Hashem M. Pesaran, and Mehdi Raissi. 2017. Is there a debt-threshold effect on output growth? *The Review of Economics and Statistics* 99: 135–50. [CrossRef]

Das, Mitali. 2005. Instrumental variables estimators for nonparametric models with discrete endogenous variables. *Journal of Econometrics* 124: 335–61. [CrossRef]

Delgado, Michael S., Deniz Ozabaci, Yiguo Sun, and Subal C. Kumbhakar. 2015. *Smooth Coefficient Models With Endogenous Environmental Variables*. Technical Report. West Lafayette: Purdue University.

Durlauf, Steven N., Andros Kourtellos, and Artur Minkin. 2001. The local solow growth model. *European Economic Review* 45: 928–40. [CrossRef]

Eberhardt, Markus, and Andrea F. Presbitero. 2013. *This Time They Are Different: Heterogeneity and Nonlinearity in The Relationship Between Debt and Growth*. Technical Report. Washington, DC: IMF.

Eberhardt, Markus, and Andrea F. Presbitero. 2015. Public debt and growth: heterogeneity and non-linearity. *Journal of International Economics* 97: 45–58. [CrossRef]

Égert, Balázs. 2015. Public debt, economic growth and nonlinear effects: Myth or reality? *Journal of Macroeconomics* 43: 226–38. [CrossRef]

Elmendorf, Douglas W., and N. Gregory Mankiw. 1999. Government debt. In *Handbook of Macroeconomics*. Edited by John B. Taylor. Oxford: Taylor and Michael Woodford.

Glaeser, Edward L., Rafael La Porta, Florencio Lopez-De-Silanes, and Andrei Shleifer. 2004. Do institutions cause growth? *Journal of Economic Growth* 9: 271–303. [CrossRef]

Gonzáles, Andrés, Timo Teräsvirta, and Dick VanDijk. 2005. *Panel Smooth Transition Regression Models*. Technical Report. Stockholm: Stockholm School of Economics.

Härdle, Wolfgang, and Steve J. Marron. 1991. Bootstrap simultaneous error bars for nonparametric regression. *The Annals of Statistics* 19: 778–96. [CrossRef]

Henderson, Daniel J., Subal C. Kumbhakar, and Christopher F. Parmeter. 2012. A simple method to visualize results in nonlinear regression models. *Economics Letters* 117: 578–81. [CrossRef]

Henderson, Daniel J., Chris Papageorgiou, and Christopher F. Parmeter. 2011. Growth empirics without parameters. *The Economic Journal* 122: 125–54. [CrossRef]

Henderson, Daniel J., and Christopher F. Parmeter. 2015. *Applied Nonparametric Econometrics*. New York: Cambridge University Press.

Jalles, Joao T. 2011. The impact of democracy and corruption on the debt-growth relationship in developing countries. *Journal of Economic Development* 36: 41–72.

Ketteni, Elena, Theofanis P. Mamuneas, and Thanasis Stengos. 2007. Nonlinearities in economic growth: A semiparametric approach applied to information technology data. *Journal of Macroeconomics* 29: 555–68. [CrossRef]

Kourtellos, Andros. 2011. Modeling parameter heterogeneity in cross-country regression models. In *Economic Growth and Development (Frontiers of Economics and Globalization)*. Edited by O. de La Grandville. Bingley: Emerald Group Publishing Limited, pp. 579–604.

Kourtellos, Andros, Thanasis Stengos, and Chih Ming Tan. 2013. The effect of public debt on growth in multiple regimes. *Journal of Macroeconomics* 38: 35–43. [CrossRef]

Kourtellos, Andros, Thanasis Stengos, and Chih Ming Tan. 2016. Structural thresold regression. *Econometric Theory* 32: 827–60. [CrossRef]

Kumbhakar, Subal C., and Kai Sun. 2012. Estimation of tfp growth: A semiparametric smooth coefficient approach. *Empirical Economics* 43: 1–24. [CrossRef]

Li, Qi, Cliff J. Huang, Dong Li, and Tsu-Tan Fu. 2002. Semiparametric smooth coefficient models. *Journal of Business and Economic Statistics* 20: 412–22. [CrossRef]

Liu, Zhenjuan, and Thanasis Stengos. 1999. Non-linearities in cross-country growth regressions: A semiparametric approach. *Journal of Applied Econometrics* 14: 527–38. [CrossRef]

Mamuneas, Theofanis P., Andreas Savvides, and Thanasis Stengos. 2006. Economic development and the return to human capital: A smooth coefficient semiparametric approach. *Journal of Applied Econometrics* 21: 111–32. [CrossRef]

Marshall, Monty G., Ted R. Gurr, and Keith Jaggers. 2016. *Polity Iv Project: Dataset Users' Manual*. Technical Report. Vienna: Center for Systemic Peace.

Minea, Alexandru, and Antoine Parent. 2012. *Is High Public Debt Always Harmful to Economic Growth? Reinhart And Rogoff and Some Complex Nonlinearities*. Technical Report. Clermont-Ferrand: Centre d'Études et de Recherches sur le Développement International.

Minier, Jenny A. 2007. Institutions and parameter heterogeneity. *Journal of Macroeconomics* 29: 595–611. [CrossRef]

Newey, Whitney K., and James L. Powell. 2003. Instrumental variable estimation of nonparametric models. *Econometrica* 71: 1565–78. [CrossRef]

Newey, Whitney K., James L. Powell, and Francis Vella. 1999. Nonparametric estimation of triangular simultaneous equations models. *Econometrica* 67: 565–603. [CrossRef]

Ozabaci, Deniz, Daniel J. Henderson, and Liangjun Su. 2014. Additive nonparametric regression in the presence of endogenous regressors. *Journal of Business & Economic Statistics* 32: 555–75.

Panizza, Ugo, and Andrea F. Presbitero. 2014. Public debt and economic growth: is there a causal effect. *Journal of Macroeconomics* 41: 21–41. [CrossRef]

Racine, Jeffrey S., and Qi Li. 2004. Nonparametric estimation of regression functions with both categorical and continuous data. *Journal of Econometrics* 119: 99–130. [CrossRef]

Reinhart, Carmen M., Vincent R. Reinhart, and Kenneth S. Rogoff. 2012. Public debt overhangs: advanced-economy episodes since 1800. *Journal of Economic Perspectives* 26: 69–86. [CrossRef]

Reinhart, Carmen M., and Kenneth S. Rogoff. 2010. *Growth in a Time of Debt*. NBER Working Paper No. 15639, NBER, Cambridge, MA, USA.

Temple, Jonathan. 1999. The new growth evidence. *Journal of Economic Literature* 37: 112–56. [CrossRef]

Vaona, Andrea, and Stefano Schiavo. 2007. Nonparametric and semiparametric evidence on the long-run effects of inflation on growth. *Economics Letters* 94: 452–58. [CrossRef]

Woo, Jaejoon, and Manmohan S. Kumar. 2015. Public debt and growth. *Economica* 82: 705–39. [CrossRef]

Wright, Alan, and Kari Grenade. 2014. Determining optimal public debt and debt-growth dynamics in the caribbean. *Research in Applied Economics* 6: 87–115. [CrossRef]

Yener, Haluk, Thanasis Stengos, and Ege M. Yazgan. 2015. *Survival Maximizing Leverage of an Economy: The Case of Greece*. Technical Report, Discussion Paper. Guelph: University of Guelph.

Yener, Haluk, Thanasis Stengos, and Ege M. Yazgan. 2017. Analysis of the seeds of the debt crisis in europe. *The European Journal of Finance* 23: 1589–610. [CrossRef]

Journal of
Risk and Financial Management

MDPI

Article

Smoothed Maximum Score Estimation of Discrete Duration Models

Sadat Reza [1] **and Paul Rilstone** [2,*]

1 Nanyang Business School, Nanyang Technological University, Singapore 639798, Singapore; SReza@ntu.edu.sg
2 Department of Economics, York University, Toronto, ON M3J 1P3, Canada
* Correspondence: pril@yorku.ca

Received: 7 March 2019; Accepted: 9 April 2019; Published: 15 April 2019

Abstract: This paper extends Horowitz's smoothed maximum score estimator to discrete-time duration models. The estimator's consistency and asymptotic distribution are derived. Monte Carlo simulations using various data generating processes with varying error distributions and shapes of the hazard rate are conducted to examine the finite sample properties of the estimator. The bias-corrected estimator performs reasonably well for the models considered with moderately-sized samples.

Keywords: maximum score estimator; discrete duration models; efficient semiparamteric estimation

---

1. Introduction

Parametric discrete-time duration models are used extensively within econometrics and the other statistical sciences. Since misspecification of these models can lead to invalid inferences, a variety of semiparametric alternatives have been proposed. However, even these alternative semiparametric estimators exploit certain smoothness and moment conditions, which may be untenable in some circumstances. To address these shortcomings, we propose a new estimator, based on Horowitz (1992)'s smoothed maximum score estimator of single-period binary choice models, which relaxes these assumptions. To motivate and contextualize this estimator, we use this Introduction to review the relevant literature on discrete duration and binary choice models and indicate how our proposed estimator fills a gap in the literature.

In econometrics, discrete-time duration models are typically framed as a sequence of binary choices. The probability of remaining in a state at time s (the continuation probability) is denoted $F_s(\beta_0)$, and the hazard rate is simply $h_s(\beta_0) = 1 - F_s(\beta_0)$. Many parametric forms have been employed for the hazard rate in these models including extreme value, logistic, normal and other parsimonious specifications. Examples using a logistic specification include: Huff-Stevens (1999), Finnie and Gray (2002), Bover et al. (2002) and D'Addio and Rosholm (2005); normal distribution: Meghir and Whitehouse (1997) and Chan and Huff-Stevens (2001); extreme value (also known as the complementary log-log model): Baker and Rea (1998), Cooper et al. (1999), Holmas (2002), Fennema et al. (2006) and Gullstrand and Tezic (2008). These and others were reviewed in Allison (1982) and Sueyoshi (1995). Hess (2009) has suggested using the generalized Pareto distribution, which nests the extreme value and logistic distributions. These specifications lead naturally to maximum likelihood estimation of β_0, although it is useful to note that there are alternative ways to estimate β_0 including nonlinear regression, treating $F_s(\beta_0)$ as a conditional mean. As with any parametric approach, misspecification of the hazard rate can lead to invalid inferences. In this regard, we consider various relevant semiparametric alternatives, which relax the parametric assumptions.

We note first that semiparametric estimation of continuous-time models has been the focus of substantial research in the discipline. Numerous authors have developed distribution theory for semiparametric estimation of various continuous-time duration models including Horowitz (1999),

Nielsen et al. (1998), Van der Vaart (1996) and Bearse et al. (2007). While these and other semiparametric estimators allow for the relaxation of some parametric assumptions associated with continuous-time duration models, they are not generally appropriate when the duration random variable has a discrete distribution.

We adopt the standard approach in econometrics of constructing the continuation probability from an underlying latent regression structure. In a standard single-period basic binary choice model, we would observe $Y = 1[Y^* \geq 0]$ with $Y^* = Z + U$ where $1[\cdot]$ is the usual indicator function, Z is an index function of observable random variables and unknown parameters and U has a distribution function F. With discrete-time duration models, the observed duration is the sum of a sequence of indicators so that $T = \sum_{s=1}^{S} Y_s$, where $Y_s = Y_{s-1}1[Z_s + U_s > 0]$ with $Y_0 = 1$, and the distribution function of U_s is denoted by F_s.

There is a large literature on semiparametric estimation of single-period binary choice models. We briefly review this, highlighting how it has been adapted for certain multivariate discrete choice and/or discrete-duration models and finally how our proposed estimator fills a gap in this research. Since in some cases, the conditional mean of Y in the single-period case can be written as $F(\beta_0)$, the parameter of interest, β_0, can be estimated from a semi-parametric regression. This was suggested by Ichimura (1993) to obtain a $\sqrt{N}$-consistent estimator of β_0. With respect to duration models and exploiting the fact that F_s can also be written as the conditional mean of the choice variable, Reza and Rilstone (2014) minimized a sum of squared semiparametric residuals to estimate the parameters of interest. In a similar vein, Klein and Spady (1993) developed a semi-parametric maximum likelihood estimator of β_0 with the single observation likelihood function written as $l(\beta) = F(\beta)^Y(1 - F(\beta))^{1-Y}$. Klein and Spady's (1993) estimator essentially consists of replacing F with a nonparametric conditional mean function. Reza and Rilstone (2016) adapted Klein and Spady's (1993) estimator to the discrete duration case. They also derived the efficiency bounds and showed that their estimator obtained these bounds. We note that the approaches in Ichimura (1993) and Klein and Spady (1993) require continuity of F in the underlying covariates and are limited with respect to the forms of allowable heteroskedasticity (for example, heteroskedasticity from time-varying parameters is precluded). Another problem is simply that identification may not be possible under the mean-independence restriction that $\mathbb{E}[U|Z] = 0$.[1] By extension, the estimators of Reza and Rilstone (2014, 2016) suffer the same shortcomings as applied to duration models.

With respect to single-period binary choice models, Manski's (1975, 1985) Maximum Score (MS) estimator circumvents these limitations using simply the median-independence restriction that $\text{Median}[U|Z] = 0$. The MS estimator can be written as the maximizer of:

$$\Psi^*_N(\beta) = \frac{1}{N}\sum_{i=1}^{N}(2Y_i - 1)1[Z_i(\beta) > 0] \tag{1}$$

where $Z_i(\beta)$ is an index function of the observable covariates. As is usually the case, a normalization of β is necessary. For the estimator to be consistent, a few restrictions need to be imposed, in particular with respect to the distribution of U. The shortcomings of the estimator are that it is only $N^{1/3}$-consistent, and its asymptotic distribution, a form of Brownian motion, is not amenable for use in the applied work.

From one perspective, the shortcomings of the MS estimator derive from its use of the non-differentiable indicator function. Horowitz (1992) largely circumvented its limitations in this regard by replacing the indicator function with a smoothed indicator function, $K^+(Z_i(\beta)/\gamma)$. The objective function for the Smoothed Maximum Score (SMS) estimator is:

---

1 Horowitz (1998) gave a discussion of these issues.

$$\Psi_N(\beta) = \frac{1}{N}\sum_{i=1}^{N}(2Y_i - 1)K^{\dagger}(Z_i(\beta)/\gamma). \tag{2}$$

The SMS is typically better than $N^{1/3}$-consistent, but slower than $\sqrt{N}$, the speed of convergence depending on the smoothness of $K^{\dagger}$ and the distribution of the random components of the model. Note that the $\sqrt{N}$-convergence of the estimators such as Klein and Spady's (1993) is linked to the manner in which they use kernels. These estimators are a form of double averages. However, the objective functions for MS and SMS are nonparametric point estimators, which are single averages. With some caveats, the SMS estimator reflects the fact that the only exploitable information is at or close to the median of the U's. The $\sqrt{N}$ estimators effectively use all the data points.

The main objective of this paper is to show how to extend SMS to estimate discrete duration models. The MS and SMS estimators have been used in other situations such as Lee (1992) and Melenberg and Van Soest (1996), who extended the MS and SMS, respectively, to ordered-response models. De Jong and Woutersen (2011) have extended the SMS estimator to binary choices with dynamic time series data. Fox (2007) adapted the MS estimator to multinomial choices. Charlier et al. (1995) extended the SMS to panel data. Other researchers have modified the MS and SMS estimators to improve their sampling properties. Kotlyarova and Zinde-Walsh (2010) suggested using a weighted average of different SMS estimators to reduce mean squared error. Iglesias (2010) derived the second-order bias, which can be used to reduce the bias of the SMS estimator. Jun et al. (2015) proposed a Laplace estimator alternative to improve on the $N^{1/3}$-consistency of the MS estimator. To our knowledge, neither the MS nor SMS estimators have been extended to duration models.

Sections 2 and 3 discuss the class of models considered and present the basic estimator along with its main asymptotic properties. Section 4 provides some simulation results concerning the sampling distribution of the estimator, and Section 5 concludes.

2. Modelling

As mentioned, a standard approach for modelling a discrete duration process is to construct it as a sequence of binary choice models, with observed and unobserved heterogeneity. The standard binary choice model is adapted such that in each time period, s, a choice is made by individual i to continue in a state if the latent variable:

$$Y_{is}^{*} = Z_{is}(\beta_0) + U_{is}, \qquad s = 1, 2, \ldots, S \tag{3}$$

is greater than zero. Here, $Z_{is}(\beta) = X_{is}^{*} + X_{is}^{\top}\beta$[2] is an index where X_{is}^{*} is a scalar random variable and X_{is} is a $k \times 1$ vector, which may include a function of s, while β is a $k \times 1$ vector of constants.

We assume the U_{is}'s and X_{is}^{*}, X_{is}'s are jointly i.i.d. We observe $Y_{is} = 1[Y_{is}^{*} > 0]Y_{is-1}$ and X_{is}^{*}, X_{is}, $s = 1, \ldots, S$. A natural adaptation of Manski's setup is the additional assumption that $\text{Median}[U_s|X_s, Y_{s-1}] = 0$, $s = 1, \ldots, S$. We estimate the parameters by effectively estimating the density of $Z_{is}(\beta_0)$ at zero by nonparametric methods. For notational convenience, we often suppress the i subscripts. Another way to view the modelling is that in any given period s with $Y_{s-1} = 1$, this is a standard binary choice variable with the key difference being that the index Z is a function of some covariates and the number of completed periods, s. The duration variable for period s is simply $T_s = \sum_{j=0}^{s-1} Y_j$ with $Y_0 = 1$, $Y_{S+1} = 0$.[3] The evolution of the Y_s's, conditional on the covariates and duration, is given by:

$$Y_s = 1[Z_s(\beta_0) + U_s \geq 0]Y_{s-1}, \qquad s = 1, \ldots, S. \tag{4}$$

2 Some normalization of the parameter space is necessary. We find it most convenient to impose a unit coefficient on X_{is}^{*} immediately.
3 The model is easily reformulated to incorporate functions of the Y_j's, $j \leq s$ as conditioning variables.

Note that this representation is such that Y_s is zero if the subject left the state prior to period s and becomes a standard binary choice model in period s if the subject elected to continue in the state in period $s-1$.

We put an upper limit, S, on the length of spells. This is common in empirical work.[4] Allowing for unbounded S introduces technical difficulties that are not readily resolved. Put $\mathcal{Z}_s = \{X_{ij}^*, X_{ij}, Y_{i,j-1}\}_{j=1}^{s}$. It is useful to note that by iterated expectations:

$$\mathbb{E}[Y_s|\mathcal{Z}_s] = \mathbb{E}[Y_s|Z_s(\beta_0), Y_{s-1}] = F_s Y_{s-1} \tag{5}$$

so that, tautologically, F_s, the continuation probability function, is:

$$F_s = \mathbb{E}[Y_s|Z_s(\beta_0), Y_{s-1}=1] = \Pr[Y_s=1|Z_s(\beta_0), Y_{s-1}=1]. \tag{6}$$

3. The Estimator

Adapting the SMS estimator to the discrete duration model as outlined in Section 2, the objective function is:

$$\Psi_N(\beta) = \frac{1}{N}\sum_{i=1}^{N}\sum_{s=1}^{S} Y_{is-1}(2Y_{is}-1)K^{\dagger}(Z_{is}(\beta)/\gamma). \tag{7}$$

$K^{\dagger}(w)$, a smoothed indicator function, is the anti-derivative of $K(w) = dK^{\dagger}(w)/dw$ and has the properties: $|K^{\dagger}(w)| \leq M < \infty$, $\lim_{w\to-\infty} K^{\dagger}(w) = 0$, $\lim_{w\to\infty} K^{\dagger}(w) = 1$. In most kernel density estimation, K is a density function and $K^{\dagger}$ is its associated cumulative distribution function. The technical requirements here sometimes require use of a higher order kernel.

Note that the objective function is of the same form as the usual SMS estimator with the modifications that there is a double summand over individuals and time periods and each of the summands at period s is multiplied by Y_{s-1}, so that after exit, there is no further contribution to the objective function by that individual.

Implicitly, we impose the identification condition that the coefficient on X_{is}^* is unity[5] (e.g., Li and Racine 2007). Horowitz (1992) discussed the identification issue. X_{is}^* is assumed to have a continuous distribution, conditional on X_{is} and Y_{is-1}. Let:

$$Y_i = \begin{pmatrix} Y_{i1} \\ \vdots \\ Y_{iS} \end{pmatrix}, \quad X_i = \begin{pmatrix} X_{i1} \\ \vdots \\ X_{iS} \end{pmatrix}, \quad X_i^* = \begin{pmatrix} X_{i1}^* \\ \vdots \\ X_{iS}^* \end{pmatrix}, \quad Z_i = \begin{pmatrix} Z_{i1} \\ \vdots \\ Z_{iS} \end{pmatrix}. \tag{8}$$

The estimator solves the first-order conditions $\psi_N(\widehat{\beta}) = 0$, which are given by:

$$\begin{aligned} \psi_N(\beta) &= \frac{1}{N}\sum_{i=1}^{N} q_i(\beta), \quad q_i(\beta) = \sum_{s=1}^{S} q_{is}(\beta), \\ q_{is}(\beta) &= Y_{is-1}(2Y_{is}-1)\frac{1}{\gamma}K\left(\frac{Z_{is}(\beta)}{\gamma}\right)X_{is}. \end{aligned} \tag{9}$$

Concerning notation, when a function's argument β is suppressed, it is evaluated at β_0, e.g., $q_i = q_i(\beta_0)$. $q_i^{(1)}(\beta) = \partial q_i(\beta)/\partial\beta^{\top}$, a $k \times k$ matrix. Thus,

---

4 For example, Cameron and Heckman (1998) defined S as the upper limit to years of education. In practice, for programming purposes, it suffices to set S equal to the longest duration in the dataset being used. In the simulations reported in Section 4, the maximum duration was 37.

5 This has two aspects: one is that it implies that estimates of the other β's are all to scale and that we know the sign of the first coefficient.

$$\psi_N^{(1)}(\beta) = \frac{1}{N}\sum_{i=1}^{N} q_i^{(1)}(\beta), \quad q_i^{(1)}(\beta) = \sum_{s=1}^{S} q_{is}^{(1)}(\beta),$$
$$q_{is}^{(1)}(\beta) = Y_{is-1}(2Y_{is}-1)\frac{1}{\gamma^2}K^{(1)}\left(\frac{Z_{is}(\beta)}{\gamma}\right)X_{is}X_{is}^{\top}.$$

$G(u_s|z_s, x_s, y_{s-1})$ and $g(u_s|z_s, x_s, y_{s-1})$ denote the cumulative distribution and density functions of U_s conditional on $Z_s, X_s, Y_{s-1} = 1$, and $f(z_s|x_s, y_{s-1})$ denotes the density functions of Z_s conditional on X_s, Y_{s-1}. The superscript $[j]$ indicates the jth derivative of a function with respect to z_s, and in particular, we have $G^{[j]}(-z_s|z_s, x_s, y_{s-1}) = d^j G(-z_s|z_s, x_s, y_{s-1})/dz_s^j$. $0 \le M < \infty$ is a generic constant. Put:

$$\begin{aligned} B &= -2\frac{\mu_m}{m!}\mathbb{E}\left[\sum_{s=1}^{S}\sum_{j=1}^{m}\binom{m}{j}G^{[j]}(0|0, X_s, Y_{s-1})f^{[m-j]}(0|X_s, Y_{s-1})X_s Y_{s-1}\right], \\ C &= \mathbb{E}\left[\sum_{s=1}^{S} f(0|X_s, Y_{s-1})X_s X_s^{\top} Y_{s-1}\right]\int K(w)^2 dw, \\ Q &= 2\mathbb{E}\left[\sum_{s=1}^{S} G^{[1]}(0|0, X_s, Y_{s-1})f(0|X_s Y_{s-1})X_s X_s^{\top} Y_{s-1}\right]. \end{aligned} \tag{10}$$

Let $\Pr[u_s, x_s, x_s^*|\mathcal{Z}_{s-1}]$ denote the probability distribution of U_{is}, X_{is}, X_{is}^* given $\mathcal{Z}_{i,s-1}$. The distributional assumptions we make are as follows.

Assumption 1. *$\{Y_i, X_i, X_i^*\}_{i=1}^N$ is a random sample where $Y_{is} = 1[Z_{is}(\beta_0) + U_{is} \ge 0]Y_{is-1}$. $\Pr[u_s, x_s, x_s^*|\mathcal{Z}_{s-1}] = \Pr[u_s, x_s, x_s^*|Y_{s-1}]$. $Z_{is}(\beta) = X_{is}^* + X_{is}^{\top}\beta$. $Y_{i0} = 1$ for all i.*

Assumption 2. *For $s = 1, \ldots, S$, (a) the support of the distribution of x_s^*, x_s is not contained in any proper linear subspace of $\mathbb{R}^{k+1}$, (b) $0 < \Pr(y_s = 1|x_s^*, x_s, y_{s-1} = 1) < 1$ for almost every x_s^*, x_s and (c) for almost every x_s, y_{s-1}, the distribution of x_s^* conditional on x_s, y_{s-1} has everywhere positive density with respect to the Lebesgue measure.*

Assumption 3. *$Median(u_s|x_s^*, x_s, Y_{s-1}) = 0$ for almost every x_s, Y_{s-1}, $s = 1, \ldots, S$.*

Assumption 4. *$\beta_0 \in \mathcal{B}$, a compact subset of $\mathbb{R}^k$.*

Assumption 5. *The elements of X_s have finite fourth moments, $s = 1, \ldots, S$.*

Assumption 6. *$(\log N)/(N\gamma^4) \to 0$ as $N \to \infty$*

Assumption 7. *(a) $K^{\dagger}$ is twice differentiable everywhere; K and $K^{[1]}$ are uniformly bounded; and each of the following integrals over $(-\infty, \infty)$ is finite: $\int K(w)^4 dw$, $\int [K^{[1]}(w)]^2 dw$, $\int l w^2 K^{[1]}(w)|dw$. (b) For some integer $m > 2$ and each integer j, $j = 2, \ldots, m-1$ $\int w^j K(w)dw = 0$, $\int w^m K(w)dw = \mu_m$, $|\mu_m| < \infty$. (c) For $j = 2, \ldots, m-1$, $\gamma \to 0$, any $\eta > 0$, $\gamma^{j-m}\int_{|\gamma w|>\eta}|w^j K(w)|dw \to 0$, $\gamma^{-1}\int_{|\gamma w|>\eta}|K^{[1]}(w)|dw \to 0$*

Assumption 8. *$f(z_s|x_s, y_{s-1})$ is m-times continuously differentiable with respect to z in a neighbourhood of zero, almost every x_s, y_{s-1}, and $|f^{[j]}(-z_s|z_s, x_s, y_{s-1})| \le M$, $s = 1, \ldots, S$.*

Assumption 9. *$G(-z_s|z_s, x_s, y_{s-1})$ is m-times continuously differentiable with respect to z_s in a neighbourhood of zero, almost every x_s, y_{s-1} and $|G^{[j]}(-z_s|z_s, x_s, y_{s-1})| < M$, $j = 1, \ldots, m$, $s = 1, \ldots, S$.*

Assumption 10. *β_0 is an interior point of $\mathcal{B}$.*

Assumption 11. *Q is negative definite.*

These assumptions adapt those in Horowitz (1992) to allow for the dependency structure. They also embed Manski's (1985) assumptions with $S = 1$. Notice that the random sampling assumption refers to N random draws within each being the potentially S observations.

Identification (see Proof of Proposition 1 in Appendix A) follows by adapting Manski's (1985) proof for the MS estimator. Of interest here is that we wish to allow for time dependence. Note that for the MS/SMS case, nothing precludes the inclusion of a constant in the index so long as, say, x_s is not co-linear[6] (in fact, simulation and empirical results such as in Horowitz (1998) indicate good results for intercept estimates). For the m-multinomial choice model, Lee (1992) included m non-stochastic threshold parameters (including a constant). In our case, the same applies for including certain non-stochastic functions of s in x_s, such as including indicators for each s or a polynomial in s. For parsimony in our numerical/empirical work, we have included quadratics to allow for increasing, decreasing and non-monotonic time dependency. This allows for straight-forward testing. In this regard, we note that the semiparametric information matrix derived in Reza and Rilstone (2016) was singular for this class of models. There is no contradiction here, since the singularity indicates that those parameters are not estimable at the $\sqrt{N}$-rate; it does not imply that they cannot be identified or estimated at a less than $\sqrt{N}$-rate, which we do here.

We have the following lemma, which permits simple derivation of the asymptotic properties of the estimator.

Lemma 1. *Let Assumptions 1–11 hold. Then, (a)* $\mathbb{E}[q_i^{(1)}(\beta_0)] = Q + o(1)$*, (b)* $\gamma^m \mathbb{E}[q_i(\beta_0)] = B + o(1)$ *and (c)* $\gamma \mathbb{E}[q_i(\beta_0) q_i(\beta_0)^\top] = C + o(1)$.

The asymptotic distribution of the estimator can be summarized easily using the following result.

Proposition 1. *Let Assumptions 1–11 hold. Then, (a)* $\widehat{\beta}$ *is consistent and (b)* $\sqrt{N\gamma}(\widehat{\beta} - \beta_0 - \gamma^m Q^{-1} B) \xrightarrow{d} N(0, Q^{-1} C Q^{-1})$.

The proofs are in Appendix A. In the statement of the proposition, note the presence of the first-order bias, $\gamma^m Q^{-1} B$, for which it may be advisable to adjust the raw estimator. One of the benefits of this estimator is that one can effectively ignore the dependence of the observations, pool all the observations across individuals for whose $Y_{i,s-1} = 1$ and use standard SMS optimization procedures. This is what we have done in the simulations. Reza and Rilstone's (2016) setup (extension of Klein and Spady 1993) allows for estimation of the hazard rate, $1 - F_s$, with a natural estimate of time dependence from the semiparametric estimates of $\Delta h_s = F_{s-1} - F_s$. Note that Reza and Rilstone's (2016) estimator of Δh_s only has a $\sqrt{N\gamma}$-rate of convergence.

As for the SMS estimator, we can consider the optimal choice of window width. As with Horowitz (1992), we consider choices that minimize an MSE criterion. Therefore, if we consider that the asymptotic results correspond to the distribution of a random variable, say W, with mean $\gamma^m Q^{-1} B$ and variance $Q^{-1} C Q^{-1}/(N\gamma)$, we can consider minimizing, say, the inner product MSE of $\Omega^{1/2} W$, where Ω is a positive definite weighting matrix, i.e., minimize $\mathbb{E}[W^\top \Omega W]$ with respect to γ. This results in:

$$\gamma^* = \arg\min MSE(\gamma), \quad MSE(\gamma) = \gamma^{2m} B^\top Q^{-1\top} \Omega Q^{-1} B + \frac{1}{N\gamma} \text{Trace}\left[\Omega Q^{-1} C Q^{-1}\right] \tag{11}$$

$$\gamma^* = N^{-1/(2m+1)} \left(\frac{\text{Trace}[\Omega Q^{-1} C Q^{-1}]}{2m B^\top Q^{-1\top} \Omega Q^{-1} B} \right)^{1/(2m+1)}. \tag{12}$$

[6] In this case, the random sampling assumption should be interpreted as referring to the stochastic elements of x_s.

For inferences it is necessary to obtain consistent estimates of the components of the first-order bias and variance. These cannot be directly estimated as they depend on the distribution of the unobservable U's. However, by extension of the arguments in Horowitz (1992), they may be obtained through various derivatives of the objective function. Specifically, put:

$$\begin{aligned} \widehat{B}(\widehat{\beta}) &= \frac{1}{\gamma^m}\psi_N(\widehat{\beta}), \quad \widehat{Q}(\widehat{\beta}) = \psi_N^{(1)}(\widehat{\beta}) \\ \widehat{C}(\widehat{\beta}) &= \frac{1}{N\gamma}\sum_{i=1}^{N}\sum_{s=1}^{S} q_{is}(\widehat{\beta})X_{is}^{\top}K(Z_{is}(\widehat{\beta})/\gamma). \end{aligned} \tag{13}$$

By the uniform law of large numbers, $\widehat{B}(\widehat{\beta}) \xrightarrow{p} B$, $\widehat{Q}(\widehat{\beta}) \xrightarrow{p} Q$ and $\widehat{C}(\widehat{\beta}) \xrightarrow{p} C$.

It is well known that the first-order asymptotic results may provide a poor approximation to the sampling distribution of the SMS estimator. Thus, it may be preferable to use some higher order method to approximate the distribution. Apart from Iglesias (2010) who applied the results in Rilstone et al. (1996) to derive the second-order bias of $\widehat{\beta}$, little is known (explicitly) about the second-order properties of the SMS estimator. Estimates can be bootstrapped. In this regard, we note that one should resample individuals. That is, bootstrap estimates should be based on resamples: $\{\mathcal{Z}_{iS}^*\}_{i=1}^N$, where the $*$'s indicate random draws from the original data. Horowitz (2002) documents some of the issues associated with bootstrapping the distribution of $\widehat{\beta}$. In particular, the corresponding re-estimates: $\widehat{\beta}_j^*$, say, and corresponding standard errors should be calculated using an under-smoothing window-width such as $\gamma \in [.5\gamma^*, \gamma^*]$.

4. Simulation Exercise

To examine the estimator's performance in finite samples, we conducted Monte Carlo simulations with several Data Generating Processes (DGPs). We adapted simulations in Horowitz (1992) by augmenting the models with duration dependence, and a variety of error distributions. The latent processes we considered included those with homoskedastic errors:

$$\begin{aligned} Y_{is}^* &= 1.5 + 2(s/100) - (s/100)^2 + X_{1is} + X_{2is} - u_{is}, \\ u_{is} &\sim N(0,1) \end{aligned} \tag{14}$$

and those with heteroskedastic errors:

$$\begin{aligned} Y_{is}^* &= 1.5 + 2(s/100) - (s/100)^2 + X_{1is} + X_{2is} - v_{is}, \\ v_{is} &= 0.25(1 + (X_{1is} + X_{2is})^2) \cdot u_{is}, \\ u_{is} &\sim N(0,1). \end{aligned} \tag{15}$$

We conducted the simulations for two sample sizes, $N = 500$ and $N = 1000$. The X's were drawn as i.i.d. $N(0,1)$. For the DGP with homoskedastic normal errors, this resulted in duration times with averages of 5.7 ($N = 500, 1000$) and standard deviations also 5.7 ($N = 500, 1000$). With heteroskedastic errors, the average duration times were 8.7 ($N = 500, 1000$) with standard deviations of 9.6 ($N = 500$) and 9.5 ($N = 1000$). For identification purposes, the coefficient on X_1 was normalized to one, and our key parameter of interest was the coefficient on X_2, with a true value of one. We conducted 500 replications for each specification. We followed Horowitz (1992) to estimate the parameters in two steps: first using simulated annealing to find the approximate maximizer of $\Psi_N(\beta)$ followed by gradient methods for greater precision. We then used the bias correction described in the previous section to bias-adjust the parameter estimates. We used a Gaussian kernel with a window-width

$\gamma = N^{-1/6}$.[7] Standard errors and the bias correction were based on the consistent estimators $\widehat{B}(\widehat{\beta})$, $\widehat{Q}(\widehat{\beta})$ and $\widehat{C}(\widehat{\beta})$ from Equation (13).

Tables 1–3 report the summary statistics of the simulations for the estimates of the coefficients on X_2, $(s/100)$ and $(s/100)^2$, respectively. We also conducted corresponding probit estimates as benchmarks. Note that, with normal errors, the probit estimates were fully efficient. The summary statistics indicated that the semiparametrically-estimated coefficients on X_2 were very close to the true parameter. The bias and standard deviation both decreased with sample size. This is particularly true compared to the (misspecified) probit estimator when the errors were heteroskedastic. As for the coefficient on the linear duration dependence term $(s/100)$, there appeared to be some bias, particularly in the presence of heteroskedasticity. However, the bias and RMSE of the SMS estimators diminished with sample size. This was not the case with the probit estimators. As indicated earlier, estimating duration dependence term at the $\sqrt{N}$-rate was not possible. The estimates of the coefficient on the quadratic term of the duration dependence were somewhat biased, although the bias decreased with the sample as did the RMSE. Larger sample sizes than used here may be required to estimate, with precision, more nuanced forms of duration dependence using the proposed SMS in these contexts.

Table 1. Simulation summary statistics—parameter: coefficient on X_2.

No. of Observations	**Spec (1) Normal Error**		**Spec (2) Normal, Heteroscedastic Error**	
	500	**1000**	**500**	**1000**
Using second order kernel				
True value	1.000	1.000	1.000	1.000
Estimates				
Mean	1.013	0.982	1.034	1.001
Standard dev.	0.114	0.081	0.094	0.063
RMSE	0.115	0.083	0.100	0.063
Skewness	0.452	0.481	0.491	0.308
Kurtosis	3.167	3.305	4.226	3.652
Using normal cdf as continution probability				
True value	1.000	1.000	1.000	1.000
Estimates				
Mean	1.017	1.003	0.937	0.939
Standard dev.	0.093	0.032	0.063	0.045
RMSE	0.094	0.032	0.090	0.076
Skewness	0.260	0.114	0.163	−0.082
Kurtosis	2.712	2.924	2.900	2.970

[7] Estimates using a fourth-order kernel as in Horowitz (1992) yielded very similar results. The non-stochastic window-width was used, rather than, say, a plug-in window-width, to keep the simulations manageable.

Table 2. Simulation summary statistics—parameter: coefficient on $(s/100)$.

No. of Observations	Spec (1) Normal Error		Spec (2) Normal, Heteroscedastic Error	
	500	1000	500	1000
Using second order kernel				
True value	2.000	2.000	2.000	2.000
Estimates				
Mean	2.359	2.112	1.737	1.790
Standard dev.	3.426	2.356	1.854	1.340
RMSE	3.441	2.356	1.871	1.355
Skewness	0.126	0.181	−0.280	−0.065
Kurtosis	4.233	3.986	8.149	4.617
Using normal cdf as continution probability				
True value	2.000	2.000	2.000	2.000
Estimates				
Mean	2.577	2.343	1.813	1.633
Standard dev.	1.544	1.010	0.830	0.623
RMSE	1.647	1.066	0.850	0.722
Skewness	0.126	−0.042	0.304	0.433
Kurtosis	3.150	3.092	2.894	3.344

Table 3. Simulation summary statistics—parameter: coefficient on $(s/100)^2$.

No. of Observations	Spec (1) Normal Error		Spec (2) Normal, Heteroscedastic Error	
	500	1000	500	1000
Using second order kernel				
True value	−1.000	−1.000	−1.000	−1.000
Estimates				
Mean	−2.147	−1.554	0.685	0.042
Standard dev.	14.302	9.805	6.804	3.911
RMSE	14.334	9.810	7.003	4.043
Skewness	0.182	−3.846	2.400	1.283
Kurtosis	7.844	43.237	21.338	8.266
Using normal cdf as continution probability				
True value	−1.000	−1.000	−1.000	−1.000
Estimates				
Mean	−4.032	−2.678	−1.435	−0.922
Standard dev.	6.113	3.609	1.798	1.273
RMSE	6.819	3.977	1.848	1.274
Skewness	−0.929	−0.655	−1.135	−1.576
Kurtosis	4.467	4.051	5.005	9.012

We also examined the distribution of the estimates. Figures 1–3 graph the QQ-plots of the standardized SMS estimates of the coefficients on X_2, $s/100$ and $(s/100)^2$, respectively. Most of the standardized estimates appeared to be close to the standard normal quantiles, except for a few extreme values. The extreme values are potentially due to difficulties with numerical optimization. This would seem to indicate that the sampling distributions of the estimators in our simulation exercise were reasonably well approximated by a normal distribution.

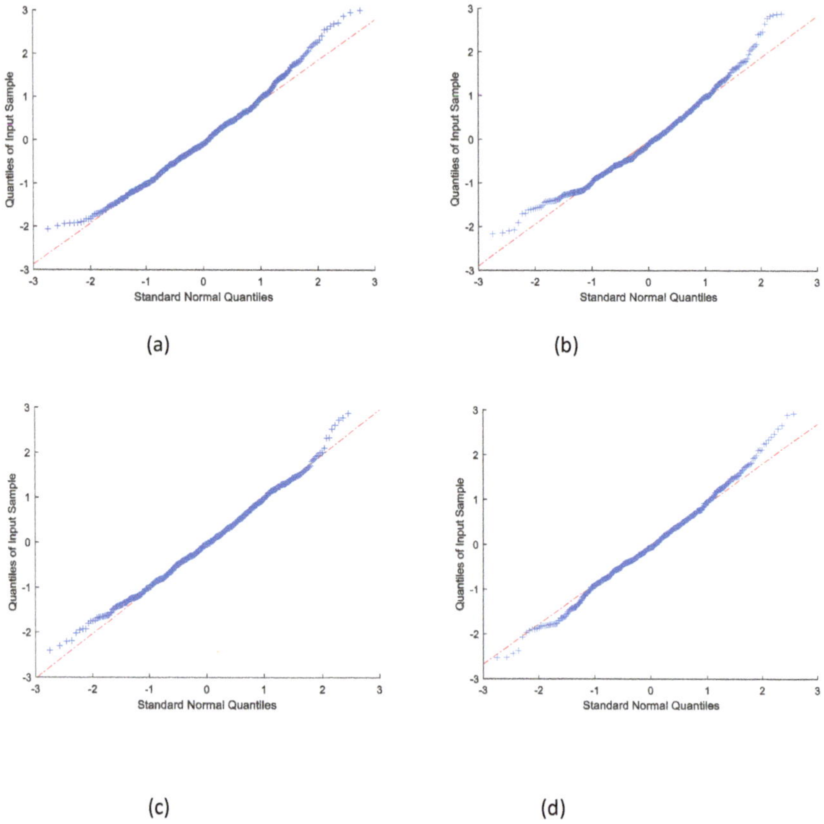

Notes: (a) Normal error, 500 observations per replication; (b) Normal error, 1000 observations per replication; (c) Heteroscedastic error, 500 observations per replication; (d) Heteroscedastic error, 1000 observations per replication.

Figure 1. QQ plot of estimated coefficient on X_2.

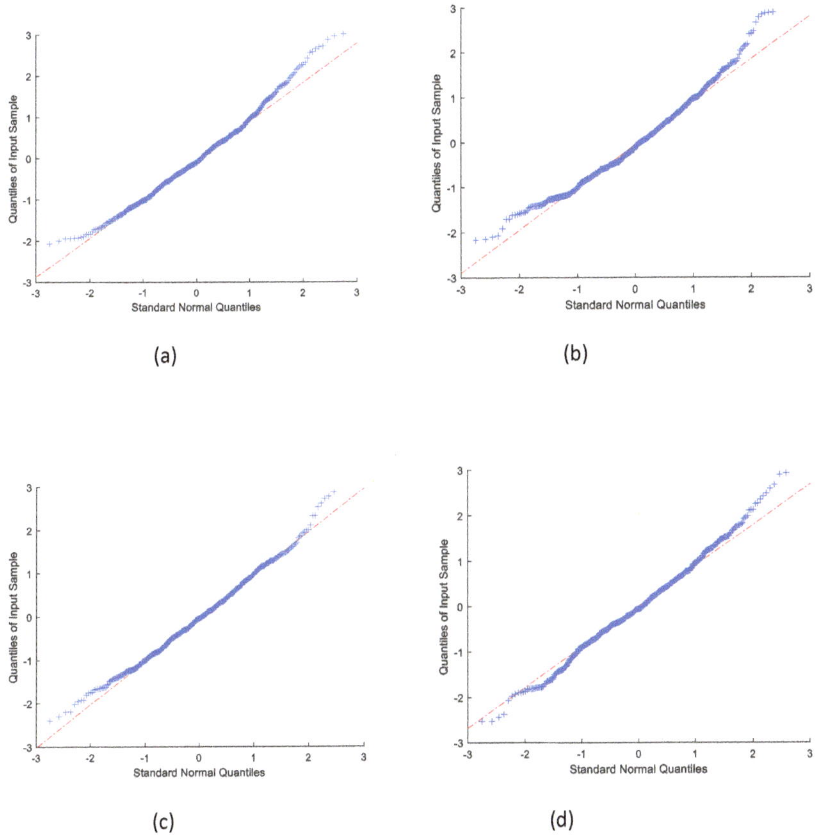

Notes: (a) Normal error, 500 observations per replication; (b) Normal error, 1000 observations per replication; (c) Heteroscedastic error, 500 observations per replication; (d) Heteroscedastic error, 1000 observations per replication.

Figure 2. QQ plot of estimated coefficient on $s/100$.

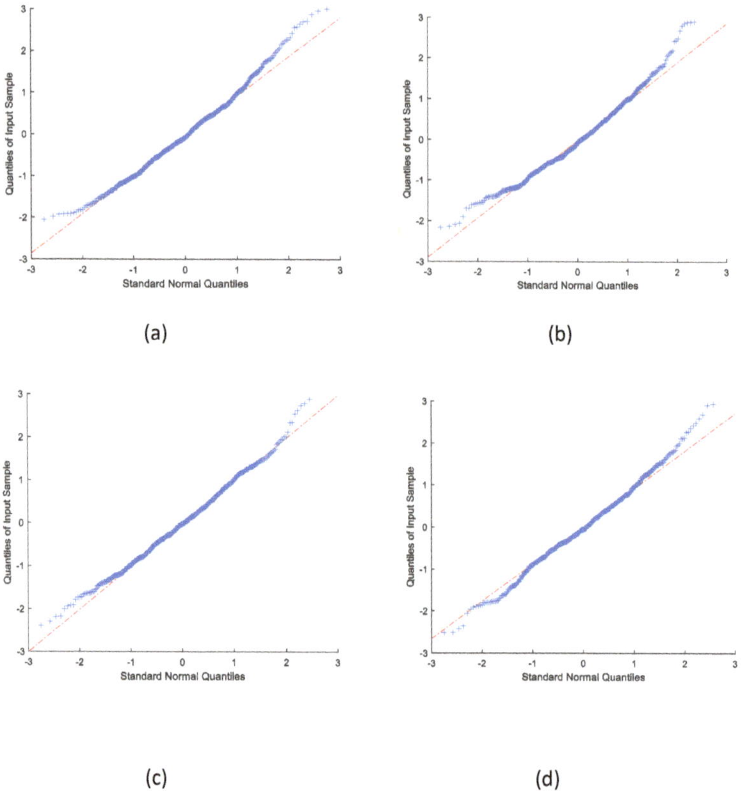

Notes: (a) Normal error, 500 observations per replication; (b) Normal error, 1000 observations per replication; (c) Heteroscedastic error, 500 observations per replication; (d) Heteroscedastic error, 1000 observations per replication.

Figure 3. QQ plot of estimated coefficient on $(\frac{s}{100})^2$.

5. Conclusions

This paper has shown that the SMS estimator can be readily adapted to consistently estimate the parameters of a popular class of discrete duration models, while relaxing the distributional assumptions of parametric models and certain semiparametric models. The asymptotic distribution of the estimators was derived and can be readily approximated using standard software. Simulations illustrated the viability of the approach. We are currently working on an empirical application of the estimator.

Author Contributions: Coceptualization, formal analysis, writing, P.R.; software, validation, S.R.

Funding: This research received no external funding.

Acknowledgments: The authors appreciate comments from Richard Blundell, Christian Bontemps, Juan Rodríguez-Poo and seminar participants at the 2016 African Meetings of the Econometric Society in South Africa and the 2017 International Conference on Panel Data in Thessaloníki. The authors are responsible for any errors.

Conflicts of Interest: The authors declare no conflict of interest.

Appendix A

Proof of Lemma 1 (a). To derive the expected value of $q_{is}^{(1)}(\beta_0)$, suppress the i subscripts, and write:

$$\begin{aligned}\mathbb{E}[q_s^{(1)}|X_s, Y_{s-1}] &= \mathbb{E}[Y_{s-1}(2Y_s - 1)K^{(1)}(Z_s/\gamma)X_sX_s^\top]/\gamma^2 \\ &= \mathbb{E}[A_s|X_s, Y_{s-1}]X_sX_s^\top Y_{s-1}\end{aligned} \tag{A1}$$

where $A_s = (21[Z_s + U_s \geq 0] - 1)\frac{1}{\gamma^2}K^{(1)}(Z_s/\gamma)$, suppressing the X_s and Y_{s-1} arguments in $g(u_s|z_s, x_s, y_{s-1})$ and $h(z_s|x_s, y_{s-1})$.

$$\begin{aligned}\mathbb{E}[A_s|Z_s] &= \int (21[Z_s + u_s \geq 0] - 1)K^{(1)}(Z/\gamma)g(u_s|Z_s)du_s/\gamma^2 \\ &= \left(\int_{-Z_s}^{\infty} + \int_{-\infty}^{-Z_s}\right)(21[Z_s + u_s \geq 0] - 1)K^{(1)}(Z_s/\gamma)g(u_s|Z_s)du_s/\gamma^2 \\ &= K^{(1)}(Z_s/\gamma)\left(\int_{-Z_s}^{\infty} - \int_{-\infty}^{-Z_s}\right)g(u_s|Z_s)du_s.\end{aligned} \tag{A2}$$

$$\begin{aligned}\mathbb{E}[A_s] &= \int K^{(1)}(z_s/\gamma)\left(\int_{-z_s}^{\infty} - \int_{-\infty}^{-z_s}\right)g(u_s|z_s)du_s/\gamma^2 f(z_s)dz_s \\ &= \int K^{(1)}(w)\left(\int_{-w\gamma}^{\infty} - \int_{-\infty}^{-w\gamma}\right)g(u_s|w\gamma)f(w\gamma)du_s dw/\gamma \\ &= \int K^{(1)}(w)\left((1 - G(-w\gamma|w\gamma) - G(-w\gamma|w\gamma)\right)f(w\gamma)dw/\gamma \\ &= \int K^{(1)}(w)\left((1 - 2G(-w\gamma|w\gamma)\right)f(w\gamma)dw/\gamma \\ &= -\int K(w)(((1 - 2G(-w\gamma|w\gamma))f(w\gamma))^{[1]}dw \\ &\to -(((1 - 2G(-z_s|z_s))f(z_s))_{z_s=0}^{[1]} \\ &= 2G^{[1]}(0|0)f(0)\end{aligned} \tag{A3}$$

To prove Part (b), make substitutions as in (a), with:

$$\mathbb{E}[q_s|X_s, Y_{s-1}] = \mathbb{E}[A_s|X_s, Y_{s-1}]X_sY_{s-1} \tag{A4}$$

where $A_s = (21[Z_s + U_s \geq 0] - 1)K(Z_s/\gamma)/\gamma$.

$$\begin{aligned}\mathbb{E}[A_s|Z_s] &= \int (21[Z_s + u_s \geq 0] - 1)K(Z_s/\gamma)g(u_s|Z_s)du_s/\gamma \\ &= K(Z_s/\gamma)\left(\int_{-Z_s}^{\infty} + \int_{-\infty}^{-Z_s}\right)(21[Z_s + u_s \geq 0] - 1)g(u_s|Z_s)du_s/\gamma \\ &= K(Z_s/\gamma)\left(\int_{-Z_s}^{\infty} - \int_{-\infty}^{-Z_s}\right)g(u_s|Z_s)du_s/\gamma \\ &= K(Z_s/\gamma)\left(1 - 2G(-Z_s|Z_s)\right)/\gamma\end{aligned} \tag{A5}$$

so that:

$$\begin{aligned}\mathbb{E}[A_s] &= \int K(z_s/\gamma)\left(1 - 2G(-z_s|z_s)\right)f(z_s)dz_s/\gamma \\ &= \int K(w)\bar{A}(w\gamma)dw\end{aligned}$$

where $\bar{A}(\gamma) = (1 - 2G(-w\gamma|w\gamma))f(w\gamma)$ and:

$$\int K(w)\bar{A}(w\gamma)dw = \int K(w)\left(\bar{A}(0) + \sum_{j=1}^{s-1}\frac{\bar{A}^{[j]}(0)(w\gamma)^j}{j!} + \frac{\bar{A}^{[m]}(\bar{\gamma})(w\gamma)^m}{m!}\right)dw. \tag{A6}$$

Note that $\bar{A}(0) = 0$ and all the middle terms in Equation (A6) are zero from $\int w^j K(w)dw = 0$, $j = 1, \ldots, m-1$. As for the third term, first note that:

$$\int K(w)\left(\bar{A}^{[m]}(\bar{\gamma}) - \bar{A}^{[m]}(0)\right)w^m dw \bar{A}^{[m]}(\gamma) = o(1) \tag{A7}$$

by dominated convergence, uniformly on x_s, Y_{s-1}. There are a few ways to write $\bar{A}^{[m]}(0)$. It is simplest to note first that:

$$\int K(w)A^{[m]}(0)w^j dw = \mu_m A^{[m]}(0) \tag{A8}$$

and by the binomial theorem:

$$\begin{aligned} A^{[m]}(0) &= \sum_{j=1}^{m}\binom{m}{j}(1 - 2G(-u|u))^{[m-j]}f^{[j]}(z)\Big|_{u=0} \\ &= -2\sum_{j=1}^{m-1}\binom{m}{j}G^{[m-j]}(-z|z)f^{[j]}(u)\Big|_{z=0}. \end{aligned} \tag{A9}$$

To prove Part (c):

$$\gamma\mathbb{E}[q_s q_\tau^\top|X_s, Y_{s-1}, X_\tau, Y_{\tau-1}] = \mathbb{E}[A_{s\tau}|X_s, Y_{s-1}, X_\tau, Y_{\tau-1}]X_s Y_{s-1} X_\tau^\top Y_{\tau-1} \tag{A10}$$

where $A_{s\tau} = (21[Z_s + U_s \geq 0] - 1)K(Z_s/\gamma)(21[Z_\tau + U_\tau \geq 0] - 1)K(Z_\tau/\gamma)/\gamma^2$. From Assumption 1, we have:

$$\mathbb{E}[A_{s\tau}|X_s, Y_{s-1}, X_\tau, Y_{\tau-1}] = \begin{cases} \mathbb{E}[(21[Z_s + U_s \geq 0] - 1)^2 K(Z_s/\gamma)^2)/\gamma^2|X_s, Y_{s-1}], & s = \tau \\ (\mathbb{E}[(21[Z_s + U_s \geq 0] - 1)^2 K(Z_s/\gamma)/\gamma|X_s, Y_{s-1}])^2 = O(1), & s \neq \tau. \end{cases} \tag{A11}$$

It suffices to only consider when $s = \tau$, as it converges at a slower rate than when $s \neq \tau$.

$$\begin{aligned} \mathbb{E}[A_{s\tau}|Z_s] &= K(Z_s/\gamma)^2\int(21[Z_s + u_s \geq 0] - 1)^2 g(u_s|Z_s)du_s/\gamma^2 \\ &= K(Z_s/\gamma)^2\left(\int_{-\infty}^{-Z_s} + \int_{-Z_s}^{\infty}\right)(21[Z_s + u_s \geq 0] - 1)^2 g(u_s|Z_s)du_s/\gamma^2 \\ &= K(Z_s/\gamma)^2\left(\int_{-\infty}^{-Z_s} + \int_{-Z_s}^{\infty}\right)g(u_s|Z_s)du_s/\gamma^2 \end{aligned} \tag{A12}$$

so that:

$$\begin{aligned} \mathbb{E}[A_{s\tau}] &= \int K(z_s/\gamma)^2\left(\int_{-\infty}^{-z_s} + \int_{-z_s}^{\infty}\right)g(u_s|z_s)du_s/\gamma^2 f(z_s)dz_s/\gamma^2 \\ &= \int K(z_s/\gamma)^2((1 - G(u_s|s_s) + G(u_s|z_s)))f(z_s)dz_s/\gamma^2 \\ &= \int K(w)^2 f(w\gamma)dw/\gamma \end{aligned}$$

and $\gamma\mathbb{E}[A_{s\tau}] \to f(0)\int K(w)^2 dw$. □

Lemma A1. *Assume* $\bar{\beta} \xrightarrow{p} \beta_0$. *Then, under Assumptions* 1–11, $\psi_N^{(1)}(\bar{\beta}) = Q + o_p(1)$.

Proof of Lemma A1. For $\psi_N^{(1)}(\bar{\beta})$, note that by the uniform law of large numbers and Slutsky's theorem, $\psi_N^{(1)}(\bar{\beta}) \to \lim_{N\to\infty} \mathbb{E}[q_i^{(1)}(\beta_0)] = Q$. □

Proof of Proposition 1. (a) Consistency is shown by combining and extending the results of Manski (1985) and Horowitz (1992). Following Manski, define a population objective function $\Psi^*(\beta) = \sum_{s-1}^{S}(2\Pr(Y_s = 1, Z_s(\beta) \geq 0|Y_{s-1}) - \Pr(Z_s(\beta) \geq 0|Y_{s-1}))\Pr(Y_{s-1} = 1)$. [8] As per Manski, $\Psi^*(\beta)$ is maximized uniquely at $\beta = \beta_0$, is continuous and $\Psi_N^*(\beta)$ converges uniformly to $\Psi^*(\beta)$. Extending Horowitz, we have $|\Psi_N^*(\beta) - \Psi_N(\beta)| \xrightarrow{p} 0$ uniformly in β, and hence, $\widehat{\beta}$ is consistent. (b) To derive the asymptotic distribution, use a Taylor series expansion of the first-order conditions, rearranging them so that:

$$\sqrt{N\gamma}(\widehat{\beta} - \beta_0) = (\psi_N^{(1)}(\bar{\beta}))^{-1}\sqrt{N\gamma}(\psi_N(\beta_0) - \mathbb{E}\psi_N(\beta_0)) \tag{A13}$$

and from Lemmas 1 and A1:

$$\sqrt{N\gamma}(\widehat{\beta} - \beta_0 - \gamma^m Q^{-1}B) = (Q^{-1} + o_P(1))\sqrt{N\gamma}\frac{1}{N}\sum \tilde{q}_i + o_P(\sqrt{N\gamma}\gamma^m). \tag{A14}$$

Application of the central limit theorem completes the result. □

References

Allison, Paul D. 1982. Discrete-Time Methods for the Analysis of Event Histories. In *Sociological Methodology 1982*. Edited by S. Leinhardt. San Francisco: Jossey-Bass Publishers, pp. 61–98.

Baker, Michael, and Samuel A. Rea. 1998. Employment Spells and Unemployment Insurance Eligibility Requirements. *Review of Economics and Statistics* 80: 80–94. [CrossRef]

Bearse, Peter, José Canals-Cerda, and Paul Rilstone. 2007. Efficient Semiparametric Estimation of Duration Models with Unobserved Heterogeneity. *Econometric Theory* 23: 281–308. [CrossRef]

Bover, Olympia, Manuel Arellano, and Samuel Bentolila. 2002. Unemployment Duration, Benefit Duration and the Business Cycle. *Economic Journal* 112: 223–65.

Cameron, Stephen V., and James J. Heckman. 1998. Life cycle schooling and dynamic selection bias: Models and evidence for five cohorts of American males. *Journal of Political Economy* 106: 262–333. [CrossRef]

Chan, Sewin, and Ann Huff-Stevens. 2001. Job Loss and Employment Patters of Older Workers. *Journal of Labor Economics* 19: 484–521. [CrossRef]

Charlier, Erwin, Bertrand Melenberg, and Arthur H. O. van Soest. 1995. A Smoothed Maximum Score estimator for the Binary Choice Data Model with an Application to Labour Force Participation. *Statistica Neerlandica* 49: 324–42. [CrossRef]

Cooper, Russell, John Haltiwanger, and Laura Power. 1999. Machine Replacement and the Business Cycle: Lumps and Bumps. *American Economic Review* 89: 921–46. [CrossRef]

D'Addio, Anna C., and Michael Rosholm. 2005. Exits from Temporary Jobs in Europe: A competing Risks Analysis. *Labour Economics* 12: 449–68. [CrossRef]

De Jong, Robert M., and Tiemen Woutersen. 2011. Dynamic Time Series Binary Choice. *Econometric Theory* 27: 673–702.

Fennema, Julian, Wilko Letterie, and Gerard Pfann. 2006. The Timing of Investment Episodes in the Netherlands. *De Economist* 154: 373–88. [CrossRef]

Finnie, Ross, and David Gray. 2002. Earnings Dynamics in Canada: An Econometric Analysis. *Labour Economics* 9: 763–800. [CrossRef]

[8] This corresponds to Manski for $S = 1$.

Fox, Jeremy T. 2007. Semiparametric estimation of multinomial discrete–choice models using a subset of choices. *Rand Journal of Economics* 38: 1002–19. [CrossRef]

Gullstrand, Joakim, and Kerem Tezic. 2008. Who Leaves After Entering the Primary Sector? Evidence from Swedish Micro-level Data. *European Review of Agricultural Economics* 35: 1–28. [CrossRef]

Hess, Wolfgang. 2009. *A Flexible Hazard Rate Model for Grouped Duration Data*. Mimeo. Lund: Lund University.

Holmas, Tor H. 2002. Keeping Nurses at Work: A Duration Analysis. *Health Economics* 11: 493–503. [CrossRef]

Horowitz, Joel L. 1992. A Smoothed Maximum Score Estimator for the Binary Response Model. *Econometrica* 60: 505–31. [CrossRef]

Horowitz, Joel L. 1998. *Semiparametric Methods in Econometrics*. New York: Springer.

Horowitz, Joel L. 1999. Semiparametric Estimation of a Proportional Hazard Model with Unobserved Heterogeneity. *Econometrica* 67: 1001–28. [CrossRef]

Horowitz, Joel L. 2002. Bootstrap Critical Values for Tests Based on the Smoothed Maximum Score Estimator. *Journal of Econometrics* 111: 141–67. [CrossRef]

Huff-Stevens, Ann. 1999. Climbing out of Poverty, Falling Back in - Measuring the Persistence of Poverty over Multiple Spells. *The Journal of Human Resources* 34: 534–56.

Ichimura, Hidehiko. 1993. Semiparametric least squares (SLS) and weighted SLS estimation of single-index models. *Journal of Econometrics* 58: 71–120. [CrossRef]

Iglesias, Emma M. 2010. First and Second Order Asymptotic Bias Correction of Nonlinear Estimators in a Non-Parametric Setting and an Application to the Smoothed Maximum Score Estimator. *Studies in Nonlinear Dynamics and Econometrics* 14: 1–30. [CrossRef]

Jun, Sung Jae, Joris Pinkse, and Yuanyuan Wang. 2015. Classical Laplace estimation for $N^{1/3}$-consistent estimators: Improved convergence rates and rate-adaptive inference. *Journal of Econometrics* 187: 201–16. [CrossRef]

Klein, Roger W., and Richard H. Spady. 1993. An Efficient Semiparametric Estimator for Binary Response Models. *Econometrica* 61: 387–421. [CrossRef]

Kotlyarova, Yulia, and Victoria Zinde-Walsh. 2010. Robust estimation in binary choice models. *Communications in Statistics–Theory and Methods* 39: 266–79. [CrossRef]

Lee, Myoung-Jae. 1992. Median regression for ordered discrete response. *Journal of Econometrics* 51: 59–77. [CrossRef]

Li, Qi, and Jeffrey S. Racine. 2007. *Nonparametric Econometrics*. Princeton: Princeton University Press.

Manski, Charles F. 1975. Maximum Score Estimation of the Stochastic Utility Model of Choice. *Journal of Econometrics* 3: 205–28. [CrossRef]

Manski, Charles F. 1985. Semiparametric Analysis of Discrete Response: Asymptotic Properties of the Maximum Score Estimator. *Journal of Econometrics* 32: 65–108 .

Meghir, Costas, and Edward Whitehouse. 1997. Labour Market Transitions and Retirement of men in the UK. *Journal of Econometrics* 79: 327–54. [CrossRef]

Melenberg, Bertrand, and Arthur H. O. Van Soest. 1996. Parametric and semi-parametric modelling of vacation expenditures. *Journal of Applied Econometrics* 11: 59–76. [CrossRef]

Nielsen, Jens P., Oliver Linton, and Peter J. Bickel. 1998. On a semiparametric survival model with flexible covariate effect. *The Annals of Statistics* 26: 215–41. [CrossRef]

Reza, Sadat, and Paul Rilstone. 2014. A simple root-N-consistent semiparametric estimator for discrete duration models. *Statistics and Probability Letters* 95: 150–54. [CrossRef]

Reza, Sadat, and Paul Rilstone. 2016. Semiparametric efficiency bounds and efficient estimation of discrete duration models with unspecified hazard rate. *Econometric Reviews* 35: 693–726. [CrossRef]

Rilstone, Paul, Virendra K. Srivastava, and Aman Ullah. 1996. The Second-Order Bias, and Mean Squared Error of Nonlinear Estimators. *Journal of Econometrics* 75: 369–95. [CrossRef]

Sueyoshi, Glenn T. 1995. A Class of Binary Response Models for Grouped Duration Data. *Journal of Applied Econometrics* 10: 411–31. [CrossRef]

Van der Vaart, Aad. 1996. Efficient Maximum Likelihood Estimation in Semiparametric Mixture Models. *The Annals of Statistics* 24: 862–78. [CrossRef]

Journal of
Risk and Financial Management

MDPI

Article

Nonparametric Approach to Evaluation of Economic and Social Development in the EU28 Member States by DEA Efficiency

Lukáš Melecký [1], Michaela Staníčková [1,*] and Jana Hančlová [2]

[1] Department of European Integration, Faculty of Economics, VŠB—Technical University of Ostrava, Sokolská třída 33, 702 00 Ostrava 1, Czech Republic; lukas.melecky@vsb.cz

[2] Department of System Engeneering, Faculty of Economics, VŠB—Technical University of Ostrava, Sokolská třída 33, 702 00 Ostrava 1, Czech Republic; jana.hanclova@vsb.cz

* Correspondence: michaela.stanickova@vsb.cz; Tel.: +420-597-322-237

Received: 27 March 2019; Accepted: 22 April 2019; Published: 24 April 2019

Abstract: Data envelopment analysis (DEA) methodology is used in this study for a comparison of the dynamic efficiency of European countries over the last decade. Moreover, efficiency analysis is used to determine where resources are distributed efficiently and/or were used efficiently/inefficiently under factors of competitiveness extracted from factor analysis. DEA measures numerical grades of the efficiency of economic processes within evaluated countries and, therefore, it becomes a suitable tool for setting an efficient/inefficient position of each country. Most importantly, the DEA technique is applied to all (28) European Union (EU) countries to evaluate their technical and technological efficiency within the selected factors of competitiveness based on country competitiveness index in the 2000–2017 reference period. The main aim of the paper is to measure efficiency changes over the reference period and to analyze the level of productivity in individual countries based on the Malmquist productivity index (MPI). Empirical results confirm significant disparities among European countries and selected periods 2000–2007, 2008–2011, and 2012–2017. Finally, the study offers a comprehensive comparison and discussion of results obtained by MPI that indicate the EU countries in which policy-making authorities should aim to stimulate national development and provide more quality of life to the EU citizens.

Keywords: competitiveness; country competitiveness index; DEA; efficiency; European Union; factors; indicators; Malmquist productivity index

1. Introduction

It is generally accepted that the level of economic development is not uniform across territories. On the contrary, it substantially differs. This plays an essential role in many research studies that sought to assign an appropriate evaluation of economic and social development in the European area (e.g., Balcerowicz et al. 2013; Easterly and Levine 2012; Watt and Botsch 2010; Ghosh et al. 2009). As human activities are related to economic development and affected by territorial development, the way of measurement of the conditions of national development is essential in the determination of a country's socio-economic policies (Halkos and Tzeremes 2005). The issue of socio-economic advancement, as well as disparities of territories, is closely linked to the setting and evaluation of competitiveness (Gardiner et al. 2004; Lukovics 2009; Ocubo 2012).

The pursuit and the promotion of competitiveness increasingly shape the dynamics of economic, social, political, and cultural change in the contemporary world. The economy's entry into the globalization phase radically altered the nature of competition. Numerous new actors from every market in the world are simultaneously in competition on every market. This new competition accentuated the interdependence of the different levels of globalization. Globalization obliged all countries to raise their standards of economic efficiency, resulting in a growing interest in and concern about competitiveness; nations, regions, and cities have no option but to strive to be competitive in order to survive in the new global marketplace and the "new competition" being forged by the further information or knowledge-driven economy (Gardiner et al. 2004).

Policy-makers at all levels are being swept up in this competitiveness fever. This growing interest may perhaps be partly attributable to their awareness of the fact that all countries have to contend with raised standards of economic efficiency as a result of the globalization of goods and factor markets. The economy may be competitive, but if the society and the environment suffer too much, the country will face significant difficulties and vice versa. Therefore, governments, in the long run, cannot focus alone on the economic competitiveness of their country; instead, they need an integrated approach to govern the country. The complexity of competitiveness, decomposed by Esser et al. (1995), in the view of efficiency analysis is used in this paper—every country has standard features which affect and drive the competitiveness of all the entities located there, even if the variability of competitiveness level of the entities within the country may be very high.

In the European Union (EU), the process of achieving an increasing trend and a higher level of competitiveness is significantly complicated by the heterogeneity of countries and regions in many areas. Although the EU is one of the most developed parts of the world with high living standards, there exist significant and substantial economic, social, and territorial disparities influencing a level of worldwide production and efficiency; so far, the EU competitiveness stands as a global player in the world economy. Considering the increasing importance of economic growth in the society and competitive world, evaluation of territorial performance is remarkably considered, and various measures are brought up as criteria in the assessment of territorial performance. The EU competitiveness depends on a multiplicity of actions that can optimize the potentials within its countries. All EU member states possess development opportunities; however, enough use of these options will increase the competitiveness of the EU countries and, thus, they must be efficient enough.

From this point of view, the purpose of the paper is to achieve a more detailed productivity analysis and assessment of EU28 countries based on the concept of country competitiveness index (Annoni and Kozovska 2010; Annoni and Dijkstra 2013; Annoni et al. 2017) using a multivariate method of factor analysis (FA), identifying the main factors of socioeconomic development determining the competitiveness level of European countries. These factors of competitiveness are used for further productivity score evaluation performed using an advanced data envelopment analysis (DEA) approach—Malmquist productivity index (MPI) (Färe et al. 1994a, 1994b) in the reference period 2000–2017. The application of MPI allows providing an efficiency analysis of EU member states in three selected periods, 2000–2007 (pre-crisis period), 2008–2011 (crisis period), and 2012–2017 (post-crisis period), concerning the internal and external assumption for their economic growth and competitive position.

2. Theoretical Background

At a time when the EU member states have to deal with increased pressure on public balances, stemming from demographic trends and globalization, the improvement of the efficiency and effectiveness of public spending features high on the political agenda. The current economic situation determined by persisting effects of the crisis is causing the governments of countries worldwide to streamline their processes in terms of collecting revenue from the state budget and then redistributing it on the principle of performance and economic efficiency. Therefore, this resulted in the fact that markets provided by developed countries will be more critical for developing countries and their trade practices, as well as commercial practices of national or/and private companies (MacGregor Pelikánová 2017). Comparative analysis of efficiency in the public sector is, thus, a starting point for studying the role of efficiency, effectiveness, and total performance regarding economic governance of resource utilization by general management for achieving medium/long-term objectives of economic recovery and sustainable development of national economies (Mihaiu et al. 2010).

The analysis of efficiency and effectiveness is about the relationships between inputs (entries), outputs (results), and outcomes (effects). Farrell (1957) already investigated the question of how to measure efficiency and highlighted its relevance for economic policy-makers. Since that time, techniques to measure efficiency improved, and investigations of efficiency are more frequent. Nevertheless, the measurement of efficiency and effectiveness of countries remains a conceptual challenge. Problems arise because public spending has multiple objectives and because public sector outputs are often not sold on the market, which implies that price data are not available and that the output cannot be quantified (Mandl et al. 2008). Efficiency is, thus, a central issue in analyses of economic growth, the effects of fiscal policies, the pricing of capital assets, the level of investments, the technology changes and production technology, and other economic topics and indicators. Efficiency can be achieved under the conditions of maximizing the results of action about the resources used, and it is calculated by comparing the effects obtained by their efforts. In a competitive economy, therefore, the issue of efficiency, particularly dynamic efficiency, can be resolved by comparing these economic issues.

The ratio of inputs to outputs gives the efficiency, but there is a difference between the technical efficiency and the allocative efficiency. The technical efficiency implies a relationship between inputs and outputs on the frontier production curve; however, not any form of technical efficiency makes sense in economic terms, and this efficiency is captured through the allocative efficiency that requires a cost/benefit ratio. The effectiveness, in terms of this meaning, implies a relationship between outputs and outcomes. In this sense, the distinction between the output and the outcome must be made. The outcome is often linked to welfare or growth objectives and, therefore, may be influenced by multiple factors (including outputs, as well as exogenous "environment" factors). The effectiveness is, thus, more challenging to assess than efficiency, since the outcome is influenced by political choice. There are thus three key topics for the article concept: competitiveness–productivity–stage of development, and their interdependence is as follows, resp. for the logical interconnection of theoretical and empirical part see Figure 1.

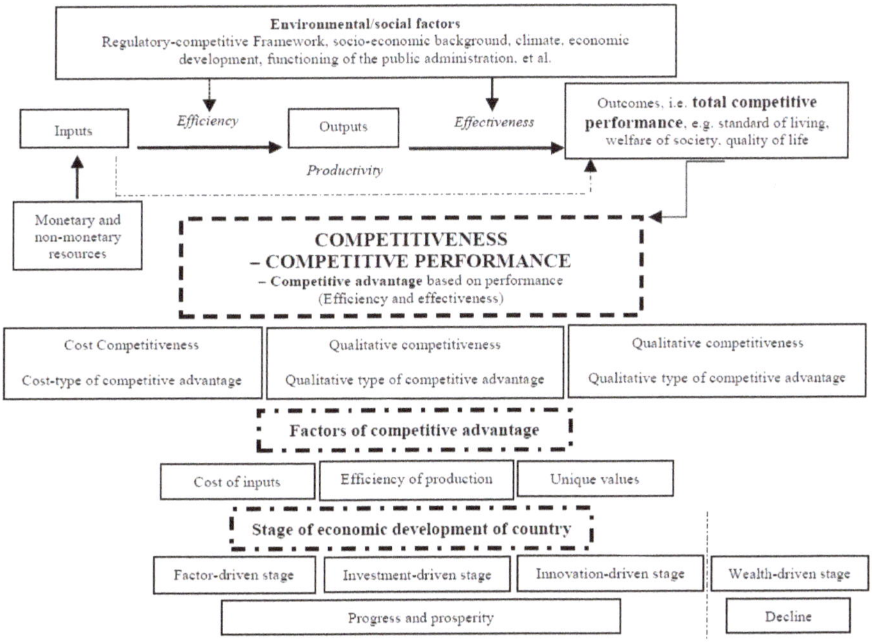

Figure 1. The relationship between the efficiency and the effectiveness impacting competitiveness (source: Mandl et al. 2008; own extension and elaboration).

Drucker (2001) believes that there is no efficiency without effectiveness because it is more important to do well what you proposed (the effectiveness) than do well something else that was not necessarily concerned. The relationship between efficiency and effectiveness is that of a part to the whole; the effectiveness is a necessary condition for achieving efficiency. This implies that efficiency and effectiveness are not always easy to isolate.

3. Materials and Methods

The most common quantitative methods convenient for a high number of multivariate measured variables can be identified as multivariate statistical methods. Multivariate analysis is an ever-expanding set of techniques for data analysis, encompassing a wide range of possible research situations (Hair et al. 2009). Between collections of multivariate statistical methods, we can include, e.g., principal component analysis, factor analysis, cluster analysis, or data envelopment analysis.

3.1. Factor Analysis

Many scientific studies feature the fact that "numerous variables are used to characterize objects". Because of these big numbers of variables that are in play, the study can become rather complicated. Moreover, it could well be that some of the variables measure different aspects of the same underlying variable. For situations such as these, factor analysis (FA) was invented. FA is the statistical approach that can be used to analyze interrelationships among a large number of variables and to explain these variables in terms of their standard underlying dimensions, i.e., factors. The main applications of FA techniques are, thus, to reduce the number of variables and to detect structure in the relationships among variables, so as to classify variables. The objective of FA is to reduce the number of variables by grouping them into a smaller set of factors; for this purpose, FA is applied in the paper.

FA is a collection of methods for investigating whether some variables of interest ($Y_1, Y_2, \ldots, Y_n$) are linearly related to a smaller number of unobservable factors ($F_1, F_2, \ldots, F_k$). If we suggest that one measured variable, Y_1, is a function of two underlying factors, F_1 and F_2, then it is assumed that Y variable is linearly related to the two factors F, as follows (Hair et al. 2009):

$$Y_1 = \beta_{10} + \beta_{11}F_1 + \beta_{12}F_2 + e_1. \quad (1)$$

The error terms e_1 serves to indicate that the hypothesized relationships are not exact. In the specialized vocabulary of FA, the parameters $\beta_{i,j}$ are referred to as loadings, e.g., β_{12} is called the loading of variable Y_1 on factor F_2.

Why carry out factor analyses? If we can summarize a multitude of measurements with a smaller number of factors without losing too much information, we achieve some economy of description, which is one of the goals of scientific investigation. It is also possible that FA will allow us to test theories involving variables, which are hard to measure directly. Finally, at a more prosaic level, FA can help us establish that sets of questionnaire items (observed variables) are in fact all measuring the same underlying factor (perhaps with varying reliability) and, hence, can be combined to form a more reliable measure of that factor. There are some different varieties of FA (Stevens 1986).

For an elaboration of FA, the software IBM SPSS Statistics 25 is used in the paper.

3.2. DEA-Based Malmquist Productivity Index

Charnes et al. (1978) first proposed data envelopment analysis (DEA). Since DEA was first introduced, researchers in some fields quickly recognized that it is an excellent and easily used methodology for modeling operational processes for efficiency evaluations, accompanied by other developments. There are several researchers which also employed the DEA method in the context of studies about a country's macroeconomy and Knowledge-based economies (KBE) (see Appendix A); Melecký (2018) and Staníčková (2017) also consider DEA as a convenient tool for measuring efficiency as a mirror of national and regional competitiveness. Several studies using the DEA approach also focused its attention on efficiency analysis in the context of EU member states in research and development (Conte et al. 2009).

DEA is based on the simple Farrell model (Farrell 1957) for measuring the efficiency of decision-making units (DMUs) with one input and one output. This method was initially expanded in 1978 by Charnes, Cooper, and Rhodes (CCR model) assuming constant returns to scale (CRS), and it was later modified in 1984 by Banker, Charnes, and Cooper (BCC model) assuming variable returns to scale (VRS). DEA methods also include advanced additive models, such as the slack-based model (SBM) performed by Tone in 2002 or free disposal hull (FDH) and free replicability hull (FRH) models that were firstly formulated in 1984 by Deprins, Simar, and Tulkens. In recent years, research efforts focused on the investigation of the causes of productivity change and its decomposition. Malmquist productivity index (MPI) became the standard approach in productivity measurement over time within nonparametric research. MPI was introduced firstly by Caves et al. (1982). Färe et al. (1994a, 1994b) defined and applied an input-oriented productivity index as the geometric mean of the two MPIs developed by Caves et al. Although it was developed in a consumer context, MPI recently enjoyed widespread use in a production context. MPI can be used to construct indexes of input, output, or productivity, as ratios of input or output distance functions. There are various methods for measuring distance functions, and the most famous one is the linear programming method. MPI allows measuring of total productivity using distance-function calculation, which can be estimated from a solution of mathematical programming problems of the DEA kind.

With respect to the nonparametric approach, it is worth mentioning differences between parametric and nonparametric methods in statistics, especially concerning the fact that we use several descriptive statistics in the paper. Methods are classified by what we know about the population we are studying. Parametric methods are typically the first methods studied in an introductory statistics course. The basic idea is that there is a set of fixed parameters that determine a probability model. Parametric methods are often those for which we know that the population is approximately normal, or we can approximate using a normal distribution after we invoke the central limit theorem. There are two parameters for a normal distribution: mean and standard deviation. To contrast with parametric methods, we define nonparametric methods. These are statistical techniques for which we do not have to make any assumption of parameters for the population we are studying. Indeed, the methods do not have any dependence on the population of interest. The set of parameters is no longer fixed, and neither is the distribution that we use. It is for this reason that nonparametric methods are also referred to as distribution-free methods. Nonparametric methods are growing in popularity and influence for some reasons. The main reason is that we are not constrained as much as when we use a parametric approach. We do not need to make as many assumptions about the population that we are working with as what we have to make with a parametric approach. Many of these nonparametric methods are easy to apply and to understand. It is safe to say that most people who use statistics are more familiar with parametric analyses than nonparametric analyses. What is the comparison of both methods? There are multiple ways to use statistics to find a confidence interval about a mean. The parametric method would involve the calculation of a margin of error with a formula, and the estimation of the population mean with a sample mean. The nonparametric method to calculate confidence mean would involve the use of bootstrapping. Why do we need both parametric and nonparametric methods for this type of problem? Many times, parametric methods are more efficient than the corresponding nonparametric methods. Although this difference in efficiency is typically not that much of an issue, there are instances where we do need to consider which method is more efficient. Concerning statistical error, the difference lies in the fact that nonparametric methods (data envelopment analysis, DEA) use optimization to solve statistical errors, and parametric methods (stochastic frontier analysis, SFA) use econometrics to resolve statistical errors.

As mentioned above, empirical analysis is based on a frontier nonparametric approach and aims to study productivity growth and efficiency. This part of the analysis is based on MPI for measuring the change of technical efficiency and the movement of the frontier in terms of individual DMUs

(Färe et al. 1994a, 1994b). Suppose we have a production function in period t as well as period $t + 1$. MPI calculation requires two single-period and two mixed-period measures. The two single-period measures can be obtained using the CCR CRS model. For simplicity of MPI calculation, it is presented as a basic DEA model based on the assumption of single input/output. With regard to the selected type of DEA model and its assumptions, it is still appropriate to mention here the general way of model selection. The classic input-oriented DEA model can be specified under the condition that the production function has constant returns to scale (CRS). If the production function has variable returns to scale (VRS), there may be returns to scale (RTS) described as increasing (IRTS) or decreasing (DRTS). The selection of the DEA model based on RTS can be assessed according to three methods, as specified Seiford and Zhu (1999), i.e., CCR RTS method, BCC RTS method, and scale efficiency index method. For evaluation of territorial efficiency, DEA in the form of the CRS model is often used, e.g., Lacko and Hajduová (2018), Makridou et al. (2014), Otsuka (2014), or Malhotra and Malhotra (2006).

Suppose each DMU_j (j = 1, 2, … n) produces a vector of output $y_j^t = \left(y_{1j}^t, \ldots, y_{sj}^t\right)$ by using a vector of inputs $x_j^t = \left(x_{1j}^t, \ldots, x_{mj}^t\right)$ at each period t, t = 1, … , T. From time t to time t + 1, DMU_0's efficiency may change and/or the frontier may shift. MPI is calculated via Equation (2) comparing x_0^t to the frontier at time t, i.e., calculating $\theta_0^t\left(x_0^t, y_0^t\right)$ in the following input-oriented IO CCR CRS envelopment model (Zhu 2011):

$$\theta_0^t\left(x_0^t, y_0^t\right) = \min\theta_0, \tag{2}$$

subject to

$$\begin{aligned} \sum_{j=1}^{n} \lambda_j x_j^t &\le \theta_0 x_0^t, \\ \sum_{j=1}^{n} \lambda_j y_j^t &\ge y_0^t, \\ \lambda_j \ge 0,\ j &= 1, \ldots, n, \end{aligned}$$

where θ_0 indicates the efficiency score of observed DMU_0, and $x_0^t = \left(x_{10}^t, \ldots, x_{m0}^t\right)$ and $y_0^t = \left(y_{10}^t, \ldots, y_{s0}^t\right)$ are the input and the output vectors of DMU_0 among others.

MPI is further calculated via Equation (3) comparing x_0^{t+1} to the frontier at time t + 1, i.e., calculating $\theta_0^{t+1}\left(x_0^{t+1}, y_0^{t+1}\right)$ in the following input-oriented CCR CRS envelopment model (Zhu 2011):

$$\theta_0^{t+1}\left(x_0^{t+1}, y_0^{t+1}\right) = \min\theta_0, \tag{3}$$

subject to

$$\begin{aligned} \sum_{j=1}^{n} \lambda_j x_j^{t+1} &\le \theta_0 x_0^{t+1}, \\ \sum_{j=1}^{n} \lambda_j y_j^{t+1} &\ge y_0^{t+1}, \\ \lambda_j \ge 0,\ j &= 1, \ldots, n. \end{aligned}$$

MPI is further calculated via Equation (4) comparing x_0^t to the frontier at time t + 1, i.e., calculating $\theta_0^{t+1}\left(x_0^t, y_0^t\right)$ via the following linear program (Zhu 2011):

$$\theta_0^{t+1}\left(x_0^t, y_0^t\right) = \min\theta_0, \tag{4}$$

subject to

$$\begin{aligned} \sum_{j=1}^{n} \lambda_j x_j^{t+1} &\le \theta_0 x_0^t, \\ \sum_{j=1}^{n} \lambda_j x_j^{t+1} &\ge y_0^t, \\ \lambda_j \ge 0,\ j &= 1, \ldots, n. \end{aligned}$$

MPI is further calculated via Equation (5) comparing x_0^{t+1} to the frontier at time t, i.e., calculating $\theta_0^t\left(x_0^{t+1}, y_0^{t+1}\right)$ via the following linear program (Zhu 2011):

$$\theta_0^t\left(x_0^{t+1}, y_0^{t+1}\right) = \min\theta_0, \tag{5}$$

subject to

$$\sum_{j=1}^{n} \lambda_j x_j^t \leq \theta_0 x_0^{t+1},$$
$$\sum_{j=1}^{n} \lambda_j y_j^t \geq y_0^{t+1},$$
$$\lambda_j \geq 0,\ j = 1, \ldots, n.$$

MPI measuring the efficiency change of production units between successive periods t and $t + 1$, is formulated via Equation (6).

$$M_0(x^{t+1}, y^{t+1}, x^t, y^t) = ECH_0 \cdot FS_0, \tag{6}$$

where ECH_0 is the change in the relative efficiency of DMU_0 about other units (i.e., due to the production possibility frontier) between periods t and $t + 1$. FS_0 describes the change in the production possibility frontier as a result of the technology development between periods t and $t + 1$. The formulation of MPI in Equation (7) makes it possible to measure the change of technical efficiency and the movement of the frontier in terms of a specific DMU_0 (Zhu 2011).

$$M_0 = \frac{\theta_0^t}{\theta_0^{t+1}\left(x_0^{t+1}, y_0^{t+1}\right)}\left[\frac{\theta_0^{t+1}\left(x_0^{t+1}, y_0^{t+1}\right)}{\theta_0^t\left(x_0^{t+1}, y_0^{t+1}\right)} \cdot \frac{\theta_0^{t+1}\left(x_0^t, y_0^t\right)}{\theta_0^t\left(x_0^t, y_0^t\right)}\right]^{\frac{1}{2}}. \tag{7}$$

The first component on the right-hand side measures the magnitude of technical efficiency change between periods t and $t + 1$, indicating that technical efficiency improves, remains, or declines. The second term measures the shift in the possibility frontier, i.e., technology frontier shift, between periods t and $t + 1$. Trends in MPI, ECH, and FS are illustrated in Table 1.

Table 1. Trends in Malmquist productivity index (MPI) and its components (source: Zhu 2011).

MPI	Productivity	ECH	FS
MPI > 1	Improving	Change >1, improving	Change >1, improving
MPI = 1	Unchanging	Change = 1, unchanging	Change = 1, unchanging
MPI < 1	Declining	Change <1, declining	Change <1, declining

MPI—malmquist productivity index; ECH—change in relative efficiency; FS—change in production possibility frontier.

DEA is a popular method for general business management because it has a number of advantages: (1) it can evaluate a DMU's performance with multiple inputs and multiple outputs (fulfilling the criteria of our dataset, i.e., many input and output factors based on the number of numerous initial indicators); (2) it allows the units of input and output variables to be different (again, this criterion meets the paper outline, where the dataset represents various aspects of competitiveness on both side of input and output indicators); and (3) it is not necessary to know the type of production function in advance. However, DEA also has several limitations: (1) the DMUs must be homogeneous (in our case, the criterion of homogeneity represent 28 countries of the EU); (2) to obtain the best results, the number of DMUs must be at least twice the total number of input and output variables (this condition is fulfilled as the following paragraph and equations explain); and (3) isotonicity must exist, that is, the output must not decrease while the input increases (this condition is met as confirmed in the following paragraph).

If a performance measure (input/output) is added or deleted from consideration, it will influence the relative efficiencies. Empirically, when the number of performance measures is high in comparison with the number of DMUs, then most of the DMUs are evaluated efficiently. Hence, the obtained results are not reliable. There is a rule of thumb proposed by Cooper et al. (2007) which expresses the relationship between the number of DMUs and the number of performance measures. Toloo et al. (2015) checked more than 40 papers that contain practical applications and, statistically, they found out that, in nearly all of the cases, the number of inputs and outputs did not exceed six. Suppose there are n DMUs which consume m inputs to produce s outputs. A simple calculation shows that when $m \leq 6$ and $s \leq 6$, then $3\,(m + s) \geq m \times s$. As a result, in this paper, the following formula is applied:

$$n \geq 3(m + s). \tag{8}$$

In the article, this rule is met, i.e., the number of DMUs is three times higher than the sum of inputs and outputs, i.e., $28 \geq 3(6 + 3)$.

In this section, we check the validity of the model in terms of the model specification and the existence of potential outliers in the sample. Firstly, we introduce the isotonicity test for checking the validity of the model specification. Specifically, we checked whether an increase in input indicators brought growth in outputs rather than a decrease in outputs (see Avkiran 2006; Adusei 2016; Hwang et al. 2018; Jiang and He 2018). Input data for the DEA model must meet the isotonicity criteria, i.e., the level of outputs is at least the same, and does not fall when inputs increase. More specifically, the requirement is that the relationship between inputs and outputs is not erratic. Increasing the value of any input while keeping other factors constant should not decrease any output but should instead lead to an increase in the value of at least one output. By calculating the correlations between the input and output variables, we found that, if the pairwise correlation is statistically significant at 5% level of significance, the correlation moves in the range from 0.49 to 0.69 with one exception. Only in the case of input factor 2 (level of infrastructure) and output factor 3 (labor market) was there a correlation (−0.13). These results of the isotonicity test justify the selection of variables.

Secondly, we conducted outlier detection with the idea of a scatter matrix, especially using boxplots and the number of extreme outliers. Based on the assumptions for principal component analysis (PCA), we use standardized variables for the extraction of rotated factors using SPSS Statistics, which recommends determining extreme outliers as component scores with values out of interval (quartile 1 − 3 × IQR; quartile 3 + 3 × IQR). According to Chandola et al. (2009) or Jiang and He (2018), this methodology is simple and widely used. We performed the procedure and calculated the accumulated times that the data of a country are considered to be an outlier with the value of component scores out of interval (quartile 1 − 1.5 × IQR; quartile 3 + 1.5 × IQR). The results show that there are outliers, but they are more or less exceptions. In the case of input factors, we found that Germany and the United Kingdom in factor 2 (infrastructure), Malta in factor 5 (participation in education), and Bulgaria in factor 6 (expenditure on education and civilization diseases) outperformed the other countries during some but not all years of the reference period 2000–2017. In the case of output factors, we found that only Spain in factor 2 (knowledge-based economy) outperformed the other countries during some but not all years of the reference period 2000–2017. In the case of outliers, the DEA method might be inconsistent. Because these countries were outliers and not extreme outliers, present only in some input or output factors and not in all years of the reference period, they were left within the framework of the evaluation.

For the solution of the DEA method, a software tool based on solving linear programming problems is used in the paper—Solver in MS Excel 2016, similar to DEA Frontier.

4. Results

The empirical analysis starts by building a database of indicators that are part of the country competitiveness index (CCI) approach created by Annoni and Kozovska (2010) in 2010, and then updated by Annoni and Dijkstra (2013) and Annoni et al. (2017). CCI also has its dimension in the regional competitiveness index (RCI). The roots of CCI/RCI lay in the most known competitiveness indicator, the global competitiveness index reported by the World Economic Forum. Pillars of CCI/RCI are grouped according to the different dimensions (input versus output aspects) of national competitiveness they describe. The terms "inputs" and "outputs" are meant to classify pillars into those which describe driving forces of competitiveness, in terms of long-term potentiality, and those which are direct or indirect outcomes of a competitive society and economy Annoni and Kozovska (2010).

The CCI/RCI data file consisted of 66 indicators in 2010, 73 indicators in 2013, and 74 indicators in 2016; however, not all indicators are used in the paper because of a lack of data for every country within EU28—15 countries are classified as old EU member states (origin countries from 1957 and countries joining the European community in 1973, 1981, 1986, and 1995), and 13 countries belong to the group of new EU member states (joining the EU in 2004, 2007, and 2013). Some indicators are excluded from analysis because of a lack of data for many of countries and periods; from this point of view, only 61 indicators are used in the paper—37 represent inputs, and 24 represent outputs (see Table 2). Related to the issue of the nature of the dataset and individual indicators, the used database includes quantitative (numerical) indicators with the exact measured values, and not qualitative (categorical) indicators. The data source for downloading these indicators was the European Statistical Office (Eurostat).

Table 2. Country competitiveness index (CCI) indicators in input and output dimensions * (source: own elaboration).

Dimension	Pillar	Indicator of Input
Input	Institution	Political stability (PS), voice and accountability (VA), government effectiveness (GE), regulatory quality (RQ), rule of law (RL), control of corruption (CC)
	Macroeconomic stability	Harmonized index of consumer prices (HICP), gross fixed capital formation (GFCF), income, saving, and net lending/net borrowing (ISLB), total intramural research and development expenditure (GERD), labor productivity per person employed (LPPE)
	Infrastructure	Railway transport—length of tracks (RTLT), air transport of passengers (ATP), volume of passenger transport (VPT), volume of freight transport (VFT), motorway transport—length of motorways (MTLM), air transport of freight (ATF)
	Health	Healthy life expectancy (HLE), infant mortality rate (IMR), cancer disease death rate (CDDR), heart disease death rate (HDDR), suicide death rate (SDR), hospital beds (HB), road fatalities (RF)
	Primary, secondary and tertiary education; training and lifelong learning	Mathematics, science, and technology enrolments and graduates (MSTEG), pupils to teachers ratio (PTR), financial aid to students (FAS), total public expenditure at primary level of education (TPEPLE), total public expenditure at secondary level of education (TPESLE), total public expenditure at tertiary level of education (TPETLE), participants in early education (PEE), participation in higher education (PHE), early leavers from education and training (ELET), accessibility to universities (AU), lifelong learning—participation in education and training (LLPET)
	Indicators for technological readiness	Level of internet access (LIA), E-government availability (EA)

Table 2. *Cont.*

Dimension	Pillar	The Indicator of Output *
Output	Labor market efficiency	Labor productivity (LP), male employment (ME), female employment (FE), male unemployment (MU), female unemployment (FU), Public expenditure on labor market policies (PEoLMP), employment rate (15 to 64 years) (ER15to64), long-term unemployment (LtUR), unemployment rate (UR)
	Market size	Gross domestic product (GDP), compensation of employees (CoE), disposable income (DI)
	Business sophistication	Gross value added in sophisticated sectors (GVA), employment in sophisticated sectors (EiSS)
	Innovation	Human resources in science and technology (HRST), total patent applications (TPAp), employment in technology and knowledge-intensive sectors by education (ETKIedu), employment in technology and knowledge-intensive sectors by gender (ETKIgen), employment in technology and knowledge-intensive sectors by type of occupation (ETKIocc), human resources in science and technology—core (HRSTcore), patent applications to the European Patent Office (EPO), high-tech patent applications to the EPO (HTI), Information and Communication Technologies (ICT) patent applications to EPO (ICT), biotechnology patent applications to the EPO (BioT)

* Due to the extent of the dataset, the authors applied restrictions on data availability.

The reference period consists of years 2000, 2007, 2008, 2011, 2012, and 2017, whereas years are divided into three groups according to the different period of economic cycles they describe. The period of years 2000 to 2007 characterizes a growth period in all evaluated countries and the pre-crisis period; years 2008 to 2011 are part of the period which represents crisis; and years 2012 to 2017 constitute the post-crisis period.

Key Factors of Competitiveness at the EU National Level

What is the background of national competitiveness? What are the key factors having an impact on competitive advantages and disadvantages of nations? What are the crucial factors behind competitive differences and gaps among countries? These are the kinds of questions that motivate the empirical study of aspects of EU member state competitiveness. Especially currently, when governments of countries deal with the impact of the crisis, the policy-makers need a clear sense of its current competitive position, its functioning, and latent factors of competitiveness: the new starting point. By understanding both its position and factors of competitiveness, the policy-makers could better understand the potential development options and also limitations for countries to know which activities are necessary to boost and which ones to limit, followed by plotting a development trajectory toward the desired end state, as mentioned by Martin (2003).

In the following analysis, the key factors of competitiveness for the EU28 member states are described. The first part of FA is devoted to input factors of competitiveness; it means driven forces of competitiveness. Driven forces of competitiveness are divided into factors that are crucial for EU economies. In this paper, six dominating factors for inputs explained 68.098% of the total variability in the reference period (see Table 3), which can be considered as a satisfactory result. For calculation of input factors by FA, principal component analysis was used as the extraction method, and varimax with Kaiser normalization was used as the rotation method.

Table 3. Input factors—total variance explained (source: own calculation and elaboration).

Component	Initial Eigenvalues			Rotation Sums of Squared Loadings		
	Total	% of Variance	Cumulative %	Total	% of Variance	Cumulative %
1	10.540	30.115	30.115	9.112	26.033	26.033
2	5.223	14.923	45.038	5.604	16.011	42.044
3	2.523	7.209	52.247	2.505	7.158	49.203
4	2.163	6.180	58.428	2.436	6.960	56.162
5	1.880	5.372	63.799	2.177	6.220	62.382
6	1.504	4.298	68.098	2.001	5.716	68.098
7	1.362	3.892	71.990			
8	1.233	3.523	75.513			
9	1.061	3.031	78.544			

Table 4 shows 37 indicators (initial FA) and their relevant input factors of competitiveness. Input factors of competitiveness for the EU member states are divided into several areas of the national economy, which are currently key and necessary for an economy based on knowledge and innovation.

Table 4. Input factors—rotated component matrix (source: own calculation and elaboration).

Rotation Converged in 8 Iterations	Component						Group	Factor
	1	2	3	4	5	6		
Zscore(VA)	0.922						(1)	Factor 1 Economic growth and development
Zscore(RL)	0.917						(1)	
Zscore(CC)	0.915						(1)	
Zscore(GE)	0.913						(1)	
Zscore(GERD)	0.873						(2)	
Zscore(LPPE)	0.863						(2)	
Zscore(RQ)	0.851						(1)	
Zscore(PS)	0.765						(1)	
Zscore(GFCF)	0.742					−0.347	(2)	
Zscore(LIA)	0.735			−0.431			(3)	
Zscore(CDDR)	−0.696	−0.315	0.470				(4)	
Zscore(IMR)	−0.695		0.311				(4)	
Zscore(RF)	−0.672		0.306				(4)	
Zscore(LLPET)	0.645					0.373	(5)	
Zscore(TPETLE)	0.553				0.318	0.521	(5)	
Zscore(VFT)	−0.444					−0.392	(6)	
Zscore(ISLB)		0.951					(1)	Factor 2 Level of infrastructure
Zscore(AU)		0.914					(2)	
Zscore(ATP)		0.879					(3)	
Zscore(MTLM)		0.862					(3)	
Zscore(ATF)		0.816					(3)	
Zscore(RTLT)		0.735					(3)	
Zscore(HB)			0.852				(1)	Factor 3 Health phenomena in human life and
Zscore(SDR)			0.530			0.392	(1)	
Zscore(TPEPLE)			−0.505				(2)	
Zscore(PTR)		0.399	0.445				(3)	
Zscore(HICP)			−0.312	−0.732			(1)	Factor 4 Inflation trends, transport, healthy lifestyle, the performance of educational institutions, and public administration
Zscore(VPT)				0.665			(2)	
Zscore(HLE)				0.511			(3)	
Zscore(ELET)				0.509	−0.433		(4)	
Zscore(FAS)				−0.457	0.334		(4)	
Zscore(EA)		0.369		0.423			(5)	
Zscore(PEE)	0.350				−0.663		(1)	Factor 5 Participation in education
Zscore(PHE)	−0.326				0.627		(1)	
Zscore(MSTEG)		0.330			0.614		(1)	
Zscore(TPESLE)						0.811	(1)	Factor 6 Expenditure on education and civilization diseases
Zscore(HDDR)	−0.308					−0.466	(2)	

Factor 1 (economic growth and development) is composed of indicators in the following groups: (1) institutional environment, (2) macroeconomic stability, (3) technological readiness, (4) health, (5) education, and (6) infrastructure. (1) Effective institutions improve the delivery of public goods and services, address market failures, reduce transaction costs, promote transparency of entrepreneurship, and facilitate the functioning of the labor market. (2) Macroeconomic stability ensures confidence in the markets and leads to higher long-term investment and is essential for maintaining competitiveness. (3) ICT fundamentally changed the organizational structure of society, facilitating the adoption of new and more efficient ways of working and working practices, changing lifestyle, increasing productivity, and accelerating business processes. (4) Indicators of health describe human capital in terms of health status, with a particular focus on the workforce. A healthy workforce is a key factor in increasing labor market participation and labor productivity, and it strengthens competitiveness. (5) An economy based on knowledge and innovation requires educated human capital, which can adapt to changing the economic and social situation, and educational systems that successfully create key skills and abilities. (6) Transport, regardless of its type, is fully dependent on the needs of the economy and society, both in freight and passenger traffic. The functioning of the transport market is influenced much more than in other areas of government economic and social policy.

Factor 2 (level of infrastructure) is composed of indicators in the following categories: (1) macroeconomic stability, (2) training, and (3) infrastructure. (1) An indicator of income, saving, and net lending and borrowing signals the behavior of fundamental institutional, economic sectors. The relationship between income, savings, and gross capital formation determines the ability or need to finance various sectors (net lending/borrowing), which significantly affect the macroeconomic sector and, thus, the national economy. (2) Participation in education and the accessibility of higher education are considered essential for the continuous updating of skills and competencies of people that are needed for coping with the challenges of a continually evolving society based on knowledge, innovation, and ICT. (3) Modern and efficient infrastructure contributes to both economic efficiency and improving territorial equality, as it allows for maximizing local economic potential and optimum utilization of resources.

Factor 3 (health phenomena in human life and cultivation) is composed of the following indicators: (1) health, (2) education, and (3) training. (1) An indicator of hospital beds indicates the availability of healthcare in hospitals, i.e., the possibility of being admitted to treatment in hospital for some time. There is a rising trend in numbers of suicides related not only to personal problems but also to the considerable amount of hopelessness associated with the political situation in many countries or economic crisis. Economic downturn strongly tolls on the mental health of the population, because people living in uncertainty suffer from depression and psychological problems, which may subsequently result in suicides. (2) Primary education provides the basis for lifelong learning, forming relationships to education, responsible for the further motivation of children and attenuating the inequality of the social and cultural environment of the family. (3) Smaller classes are beneficial for all pupils because they are dedicated to individual attention from teachers, reflected in their ability to learn with a significant impact on their participation in further higher education.

Factor 4 (inflation trends, transport, healthy lifestyle, the performance of educational institutions, and public administration) is composed of the following indicators: (1) macroeconomic stability, (2) infrastructure, (3) health, (4) education, and (5) technological readiness. (1) The harmonized index of consumer prices (HICP) was introduced to establish a comparable index of consumer prices, so as to measure inflation trends in all EU countries as a criterion for entry into the monetary union. (2) Transport is one of the basic needs of humanity, mainly due to the different potential landscapes of the world. Transport routes can be used to move and transport people, matter, goods, energy, etc. (3) An indicator of healthy lifestyle is used to monitor health as a factor affecting productivity, to measure the employability of workers, to monitor progress in the field of accessibility, and to monitor the quality and sustainability of healthcare. (4) EU applies strategies against early school leaving; at the same time, however, it should try to widen access to higher education and improve its quality. If we manage to provide young people with the right skills and professional qualifications, it helps the economy in the fight against youth unemployment. The issue of inequality in financial resources in access to higher education is a key topic in recent years. Today's system of financial support for students in higher education is insufficient. Universities must be genuinely open to all who have sufficient skills to cope with studies. (5) The E-government deals with computerization of public administration. The E-government is a tool for using modern technology to simplify the lives of public administration customers while saving state funds.

Factor 5 (participation in education) is composed of indicators in one category: (1) education. An educated population is a fundamental prerequisite for the economic and social development of each country, whether currently or in the future. Governments, therefore, have an interest in broad population access to education and a wide range of educational opportunities for children and adults, which has an impact on future access to universities and a subsequent educated labor force.

Factor 6 (expenditure on education and civilization diseases) is composed of the following indicators: (1) education and (2) health. (1) Secondary schools provide education and vocational training for nearly the entire population of young people who completed their compulsory education and pre-employment or before entering college. (2) Heart disease falls into the category of lifestyle diseases, which is a group of diseases in which a significant contributor is the lifestyle and environment of industrial society. A crucial prerequisite for an economically, socially, and personally successful company is a healthy population.

The second part of FA is devoted to output factors of competitiveness representing direct or indirect outcomes of a competitive society and economy. In this paper, three dominating factors for outputs explained 70.258% of the total variability in the reference period (see Table 5), which can also be considered as a very satisfactory result. For calculation of output factors by FA, principal component analysis was used as the extraction method, and varimax with Kaiser normalization was used as the rotation method.

Table 5. Output factors—total variance explained (Source: own calculation and elaboration).

Component	Initial Eigenvalues			Rotation Sums of Squared Loadings		
	Total	% of Variance	Cumulative %	Total	% of Variance	Cumulative %
1	11.807	45.412	45.412	6.547	25.182	25.182
2	3.517	13.526	58.939	6.088	23.415	48.597
3	2.943	11.320	70.258	5.632	21.662	70.258
4	2.314	8.899	79.157			
5	1.874	7.210	86.367			

Table 6 shows 24 indicators and their relevant output factors of competitiveness. Output factors of competitiveness for the EU member states are divided into three areas which are currently considered as the main output of the knowledge-based economy.

Table 6. Output factors—rotated component matrix (source: own calculation and elaboration).

Rotation Converged in 5 Iterations	Component			Group	Factor
	1	2	3		
Zscore(EPO)	0.871			(1)	Factor 1 Economic performance and innovative potential
Zscore(DI)	0.821		0.305	(2)	
Zscore(HTI)	0.803			(1)	
Zscore(ICT)	0.802			(1)	
Zscore(HRSTcore)	0.801			(1)	
Zscore(GDP)	0.778			(2)	
Zscore(HRST)	0.776			(1)	
Zscore(PEoLMP)	0.734			(3)	
Zscore(LP)	0.726			(3)	
Zscore(BioT)	0.683			(1)	
Zscore(FE)	0.578		0.382	(3)	
Zscore(GVA)	0.519			(4)	

Table 6. *Cont.*

Rotation Converged in 5 Iterations	Component			Group	Factor
	1	2	3		
Zscore(ETKIedu)		0.982		(1)	Factor 2 Knowledge-based economy
Zscore(EiSS)		0.982		(2)	
Zscore(ETKIocc)		0.982		(1)	
Zscore(ETKIgen)		0.982		(1)	
Zscore(TPAp)		0.852		(1)	
Zscore(CoE)		0.843		(3)	
Zscore(UR)			−0.966	(1)	Factor 3 Labor Market
Zscore(MU)			−0.937	(1)	
Zscore(LtUR)			−0.898	(1)	
Zscore(FU)			−0.890	(1)	
Zscore(ME)	0.392		0.760	(1)	
Zscore(ER15to64)	0.578		0.617	(1)	

Factor 1 (economic performance and innovative potential) is composed of indicators in the following groups: (1) innovation, (2) market size, (3) labor market efficiency, and (4) business sophistication. Factor 2 (knowledge-based economy) is composed of indicators in the following categories: (1) innovation, (2) business sophistication, and (3) market size. Factor 3 (the labor market) is composed of one indicator: (1) labor market efficiency. Based on output factors on competitiveness, it is clear that the most economically advanced countries in the world offer excellent conditions for business, with a long-term focus on supporting research and development. Substantial funding from both public budgets and business budgets is oriented to promote new ideas and a creative approach to economic activities. Domestic companies know that the future belongs to prepared companies offering something extra to their customers, i.e., the added value. In the coming years, economic growth belongs to countries experiencing "creative" companies. The profitability of large and small companies mainly depends on new ideas and thoughts. Promoting education and learning of residents is very important for the future of countries. Innovative employees determine the success of companies. The driving force is the ideas. The greatest asset of prosperous companies does not involve material things, but employees who can create new values, to respond flexibly to changing market needs and to bring constantly new ideas.

The database of factors of competitiveness (six factors for inputs and three factors for outputs) was used for the efficiency analysis by the DEA method, representing the values of input and output factors for each EU28 member state in the years of the reference periods, i.e., 2000, 2007, 2008, 2011, 2012, and 2017. Because of the DEA requirement on positive values, it was necessary to correct the initial values of input and output factors (several countries showed negative values in some factors). The conventional DEA method assumes that inputs and outputs are non-negative data. In our case, the use of standardized input or output factors from factor analysis showed that not all values met the non-negativity assumption. Thus, a data transformation was used by adding a given constant (as explained below), transforming the distribution of inputs and outputs as non-negative data; in other words, negative data cannot be directly used under any CRS DEA model. Assuming normal distribution, this distribution is transferred to non-negative data; for more information, see, e.g., Tung et al. (2018) who explored the properties of the efficiency measures for a variant of radial measure (VRM) and proposed new efficiency measures for input-oriented and output-oriented VRM models. However, there are other ways to work with negative data; e.g., Bansal and Mehra (2018) proposed a DEA efficiency model that possesses the requisite features of translation invariance and unit independence, obligatory when dealing with negative values in the original dataset coming into the analysis. Izadikhah et al. (2018) proposed a new type of DEA model for measuring and assessing the sustainability of suppliers in the presence of negative data and volume discounts. For more information about comparing different types of transformation methods, see, e.g., Chortirat et al. (2011)

or Shu et al. (2002). Generally, data transformation is the process of converting data (in the original set of indicators and values) from one format into another format. Data transformation is, thus, both critical and essential for activities such as data integration and data management, i.e., for solving such types of problem appearing in this paper. Depending on the needs of the issues, data are transformed to make them compatible with other data, move them to another system, join them with other data, or aggregate information in the data. However, the methods of data transformation are influenced not only by the nature of the problem being solved and the purpose of the measurement for which the data are to be used, but also by the methods that will be used to solve the problem. Thus, the DEA method is also an option. As Barnum et al. (2017) explained, there are some methodological hazards associated with the use of DEA that are especially relevant to managerial decisions, but which are largely ignored in the literature, especially the problem of economic assumptions regarding input substitutions and output transformations.

For all EU28 member states across all reference years, the correction by adding a given constant was made as follows: minimum values were calculated for input factors F1–F6, where min was equal to −3.882; and the minimum values were calculated for output factors F1–F3, where min was equal to −3.387. Based on these minimum values, the value 4.000 was added to the initial factor values; all factors gained positive values from this correction, as required for DEA. The range of values (among input factors and among output factors, as well as the range of values among input and output factors) was not changed. Therefore, only the level of values for all factors was shifted to the same extent as positive (non-negative) values for all factors. Therefore, all data indicators, in this case, input and output factors, had positive (non-negative) values. The range among values of all indicators was the same after the change as before making it. Values from negative to positive, as well as from positive to positive, were moved in the same way, i.e., differences among all values were not lost.

5. Discussion

According to the efficiency analysis and derived results from the solution of MPI, it emerges that the 2000–2007 efficiency ratios of the EU28 countries ranged from 0.785 to 1.653. In the case of 2008–2011, the efficiency ratios of the EU28 countries ranged from 0.396 to 1.240. In the case of 2012–2017, the efficiency ratios of the EU28 countries ranged from 0.869 to 1.033. From the main descriptive results for all MPI parts, i.e., MPI, ECH, and FS (see Table 7), it was possible to see that the level of efficiency measured by MPI increased among the three reference periods. However, what do these values mean concerning the MPI definition or any of its elements? If MPI is less than one, it signifies productivity is getting worse, while, if MPI is equal to one, it indicates unchanging productivity, and, if MPI is higher than one, it means productivity is getting better (Zhu 2011). From this point of view, it is necessary to say that the increasing trend of MPI seems to be positive information, but, in fact (based on mean values), it means that, in a comparison of periods 2000–2007, 2008–2011, and 2012–2017, the overall productivity of evaluated countries recorded a decreasing (negative) trend. This result is not surprising because of the nature of compared periods. Period 2000–2007 was characterized by economic growth and improving living standards in all EU member states and with the convergence process of EU12 member states to the EU15 member states. For period 2008–2011, all evaluated European countries suffered from impacts of the financial and economic crisis. Finally, in the period 2012–2017, most of these countries solved these economic problems, but this period was also characterized as a post-crisis period with a slow increasing trend of the main macroeconomic indicators.

Table 7. MPI descriptive statistics (source: own calculation and elaboration).

Statistics		Period								
		2000–2007			2008–2011			2012–2017		
		MPI	ECH	FS	MPI	ECH	FS	MPI	ECH	FS
N	Valid	28	28	28	28	28	28	28	28	28
0	Missing	0	0	0	0	0	0	0	0	0
Mean		0.97235	0.99416	0.97789	0.99377	1.00394	0.98987	0.99961	0.99965	0.99996
SD		0.159261	0.027815	0.155983	0.135679	0.013288	0.135008	0.027900	0.005487	0.027283
Variance		0.025	0.001	0.024	0.018	0.000	0.018	0.001	0.000	0.001
Range		0.867	0.156	0.867	0.844	0.070	0.844	0.165	0.028	0.165
Minimum		0.785	0.885	0.785	0.396	0.991	0.396	0.869	0.986	0.869
Maximum		1.653	1.041	1.653	1.240	1.061	1.240	1.033	1.014	1.033

In Tables 8–10, the MPI results for periods 2000–2007, 2008–2011, and 2012–2017 are outlined, including information about the number of evaluated DMUs (the first column), codes of EU28 member states (the second column), efficiency scores of MPI (the third column), scores of efficiency change (the fourth column), scores of frontier shift (the fifth column), rank of EU28 member states based on MPI (the sixth, seventh, and eighth columns), and groups of countries (the ninth column). In Tables 8–10, results of the MPI and its dimensions are highlighted using the traffic light method. The range of colors of this method changes from dark to light shades of gray. Countries with the highest values of the MPI, catch-up, and frontier shift suggest a better level of efficiency and, thus, competitiveness; they are highlighted by dark shades of gray—the higher the value is, the darker the shade of gray is. On the contrary, countries with the lowest values of the MPI and its two dimensions (catch-up and frontier shift) suggest a worse level of efficiency; they are highlighted by light shades of gray—the lower the value is, the lighter the shade of gray is. Countries with values of the MPI falling between efficient (dark shades of gray) and inefficient (light shades of grey color) are highlighted by medium shades of gray.

Table 8. MPI results for period 2000–2007 (source: own calculation and elaboration).

No.	DMUs	IO CRS MPI	Efficiency Change	Frontier Shift	Rank			Group of Countries
1	BE	0.972	1.000	0.972	1.	MT	1.653	1st (3 EU15, 5 EU13)
2	BG	0.785	1.000	0.785	2.	HR	1.138	
3	CZ	0.903	0.994	0.908	3.	PT	1.109	
4	DK	0.939	1.000	0.939	4.	RO	1.097	
5	DE	0.880	1.000	0.880	5.	IE	1.055	
6	EE	0.928	1.013	0.915	6.	LT	1.049	
7	IE	1.055	1.000	1.055	7.	FI	1.036	
8	EL	0.948	0.978	0.970	8.	SK	1.010	
9	ES	0.858	1.000	0.858	9.	AT	0.979	2nd (7 EU15, 6 EU13)
10	FR	0.888	1.000	0.888	10.	BE	0.972	
11	IT	0.892	1.000	0.892	11.	LU	0.970	
12	CY	0.907	1.000	0.907	12.	EL	0.948	
13	LV	0.904	0.996	0.907	13.	DK	0.939	
14	LT	1.049	1.000	1.049	14.	EE	0.928	
15	LU	0.970	1.000	0.970	15.	HU	0.927	
16	HU	0.927	1.000	0.927	16.	PL	0.920	
17	MT	1.653	1.000	1.653	17.	SE	0.919	
18	NL	0.906	1.000	0.906	18.	CY	0.907	
19	AT	0.979	1.041	0.940	19.	NL	0.906	
20	PL	0.920	0.885	1.040	20.	LV	0.904	
21	PT	1.109	1.030	1.077	21.	CZ	0.903	

Table 8. *Cont.*

No.	DMUs	IO CRS MPI	Efficiency Change	Frontier Shift	Rank			Group of Countries
22	RO	1.097	1.000	1.097	22.	IT	0.892	3rd (5 EU15, 1 EU13)
23	SI	0.826	0.940	0.879	23	FR	0.888	
24	SK	1.010	1.000	1.010	24.	DE	0.880	
25	FI	1.036	1.000	1.036	25.	ES	0.858	
26	SE	0.919	1.000	0.919	26.	UK	0.827	
27	UK	0.827	0.959	0.863	27.	SI	0.826	
28	HR	1.138	1.000	1.138	28.	BG	0.785	4th (1 EU13)

Note: Belgium (BE), Bulgaria (BG), Czech Republic (CZ), Denmark (DK), Germany (DE), Estonia (EE), Ireland (IE), Greece (EL), Spain (ES), France (FR), Italy (IT), Cyprus (CY), Latvia (LV), Lithuania (LT), Luxembourg (LU), Hungary (HU), Malta (MT), Netherlands (NL), Austria (AT), Poland (PL), Portugal (PT), Romania (RO), Slovenia (SI), Slovakia (SK), Finland (FI), Sweden (SE), United Kingdom (UK), Croatia (CR).

Table 9. MPI results for period 2008–2011 (source: own calculation and elaboration).

No.	DMUs	IO CRS MPI	Efficiency Change	Frontier Shift	Rank			Group of Countries
1	BE	0.989	1.000	0.989	1.	MT	1.240	1st (1 EU13)
2	BG	0.396	1.000	0.396	2.	CY	1.120	2nd (1 EU13)
3	CZ	1.034	1.000	1.034	3.	PT	1.075	3rd (8 EU15, 8 EU13)
4	DK	0.987	1.000	0.987	4.	NL	1.065	
5	DE	1.021	1.000	1.021	5.	LU	1.065	
6	EE	1.013	1.061	0.954	6.	AT	1.062	
7	IE	0.905	1.000	0.905	7.	LT	1.042	
8	EL	0.942	1.000	0.942	8.	SI	1.039	
9	ES	1.035	1.000	1.035	9.	ES	1.035	
10	FR	0.975	1.000	0.975	10.	CZ	1.034	
11	IT	1.002	1.000	1.002	11.	RO	1.029	
12	CY	1.120	1.000	1.120	12.	PL	1.021	
13	LV	0.948	1.000	0.948	13.	DE	1.021	
14	LT	1.042	1.000	1.042	14.	HR	1.014	
15	LU	1.065	1.000	1.065	15.	EE	1.013	
16	HU	0.875	1.000	0.875	16.	SK	1.010	
17	MT	1.240	1.000	1.240	17.	FI	1.003	
18	NL	1.065	1.000	1.065	18.	IT	1.002	
19	AT	1.062	1.000	1.062	19.	BE	0.989	4th (7 EU15, 1 EU13)
20	PL	1.021	1.008	1.013	20.	DK	0.987	
21	PT	1.075	1.030	1.044	21.	SE	0.982	
22	RO	1.029	1.000	1.029	22.	FR	0.975	
23	SI	1.039	1.000	1.039	23	LV	0.948	
24	SK	1.010	1.000	1.010	24.	EL	0.942	
25	FI	1.003	1.000	1.003	25.	UK	0.938	
26	SE	0.982	1.000	0.982	26.	IE	0.905	
27	UK	0.938	0.991	0.947	27.	HU	0.875	5th (1 EU13)
28	HR	1.014	1.020	0.993	28.	BG	0.396	6th (1 EU13)

Table 10. MPI results for period 2012–2017 (source: own calculation and elaboration).

No.	DMUs	IO CRS MPI	Efficiency Change	Frontier Shift			Rank	Group of Countries
1	BE	1.005	1.000	1.005	1.	EL	1.033	1st (12 EU15, 7 EU13)
2	BG	0.869	1.000	0.869	2.	EE	1.020	
3	CZ	0.993	1.000	0.993	3.	RO	1.019	
4	DK	1.004	1.000	1.004	4.	UK	1.016	
5	DE	0.996	1.000	0.996	5.	IE	1.015	
6	EE	1.020	1.014	1.007	6.	PL	1.015	
7	IE	1.015	1.000	1.015	7.	ES	1.012	
8	EL	1.033	1.000	1.033	8.	LU	1.011	
9	ES	1.012	1.000	1.012	9.	FI	1.009	
10	FR	1.002	1.000	1.002	10.	HU	1.008	
11	IT	1.002	1.000	1.002	11.	BE	1.005	
12	CY	0.988	0.986	1.002	12.	SK	1.005	
13	LV	0.989	1.000	0.989	13.	SE	1.004	
14	LT	1.001	1.000	1.001	14.	DK	1.004	
15	LU	1.011	1.000	1.011	15.	MT	1.004	
16	HU	1.008	1.000	1.008	16.	NL	1.003	
17	MT	1.004	1.000	1.004	17.	FR	1.002	
18	NL	1.003	1.000	1.003	18.	IT	1.002	
19	AT	0.997	1.000	0.997	19.	LT	1.001	
20	PL	1.015	1.014	1.001	20.	AT	0.997	2nd (3 EU15, 5 EU13)
21	PT	0.985	0.988	0.997	21.	DE	0.996	
22	RO	1.019	1.000	1.019	22.	HR	0.996	
23	SI	0.991	1.000	0.991	23	CZ	0.993	
24	SK	1.005	1.000	1.005	24.	SI	0.991	
25	FI	1.009	1.000	1.009	25.	LV	0.989	
26	SE	1.004	0.999	1.005	26.	CY	0.988	
27	UK	1.016	1.000	1.016	27.	PT	0.985	
28	HR	0.996	0.991	1.006	28.	BG	0.869	3rd (1 EU13)

Broader aspects enter the overall evaluation of economics, and these aspects are unnoticeable for DEA, i.e., parts of the qualitative assessment in line with the evaluation of overall performance. Performance is linked concerning competitiveness; a good performance in the innovation group is expected to also be a good performance in the efficiency and the basic groups as they are instrumental in increasing levels of competitiveness. As countries move along the path of development, their socio-economic conditions change, and different determinants become more important for the national level of competitiveness. As a result, the best way to improve the competitiveness of more developed countries will not necessarily coincide with the way to improve less developed countries. Consistent with the theory of economic growth and economic development, CCI results confirm that the most competitive countries are those with the highest level of economic development (for more information, see Annoni and Kozovska 2010; Annoni and Dijkstra 2013; or Annoni et al. 2017). It is striking that several of the top competitors are traditionally economically strong countries. At the end of the competitiveness scale, it is possible to find some countries which are unfortunately steadily the worst performers. These differences in CCI editions indicate that the EU moved far from a homogeneous entity in terms of competitiveness, but CCI results show a more polycentric pattern. Therefore, part of the explanation of inequalities among the EU member states has to do with differences in competitiveness.

An economic entity with a low level of competitiveness may not have similar opportunities as a highly competitive economic entity. This fact remains and is confirmed. However, what does it mean for efficiency in competitiveness? In the case of efficiency analysis of competitiveness and in the time comparison analysis of change, the results are just a little bit different. Why? The concept of competitiveness may then be necessary not only to evaluate why some countries grow faster than others, but also why some countries have a better and more efficient distribution of competitiveness over time than others. Is a high level of competitiveness necessarily associated with a high level of efficiency, and vice versa? It may not always be the case because evaluated countries have a lower level of input; these countries were able to achieve competitiveness at the level of CCI. While the CCI value may not be high in the less competitive countries, it is necessary to compare the values of inputs and outputs. In DEA efficiency analysis, although the IO CRS MPI value is not so high, overall, it is possible to state that the country operates more efficiently at the end than at the beginning of the reference period. Such a conclusion is relevant by comparing values of inputs and outputs, and the fact that outputs are achieved with given inputs.

More specifically, based on MPI results in periods 2000–2007, 2008–2011, and 2012–2017, it is important to notice that many European countries achieved a value of MPI higher than 1.000 and, thus, productivity is increasing. As mentioned above, part of the explanation of the large inequalities within EU countries is linked with the differences in competitiveness. Finally, Tables 8–10 show reordered countries, from best to worst, their MPI score, and the corresponding rank. The results state positive trends within the community of EU member states. Based on the MPI results, it is clear that the best efficiency changes in competitiveness comparing reference years were achieved by countries belonging to the group of EU13 countries, i.e., new EU member states, than in the case of countries belonging to the group of EU15 countries, i.e., the old EU member states. This fact is not surprising, because it has the following key political implications with several reasons/factors:

- The new EU member states constantly fall into the category of less developed and competitive states based on gross domestic product (GDP) per head in Purchasing Parity Standard (PPS), which is the reason for their inclusion in the appropriate categorization stage of development (see Annoni and Kozovska 2010; Annoni and Dijkstra 2013; or Annoni et al. 2017);
- The association of each country with the relevant stage of development testifies to its competitive advantages and disadvantages and determines its weaknesses. A medium stage of development is associated with economies primarily driven by factors such as lower skilled labor and basic infrastructures. Aspects related to good governance and quality of public health are considered basic inputs in this framework. An intermediate stage of development is characterized by labor market efficiency, quality of higher education, and market size, factors which contribute to a more sophisticated economy and more significant potential for competitiveness. In the high stage of development, factors related to innovation, business sophistication, and technological readiness are necessary inputs for innovation-driven economies (Annoni and Dijkstra 2013);
- The threshold defining the level of GDP as a percentage of EU average was taken as a reference as it is the criterion for identifying countries and their regions eligible for funding under the established criteria of the EU regional policy framework. European funds are an essential tool for regional development and reducing economic, social, and territorial disparities among European countries and their regions. Reducing disparities have a significant impact on competitiveness, and these two concepts are, thus, the EU complementary objectives. Of the total budget allocated to regional policy, a substantial part goes just to the NUTS 2 regions of EU13 countries (i.e., the basic regions for the application of regional policies classify based on the EU Nomenclature of Territorial Units for Statistics), where development is significantly supported;
- New EU member states are often considerably dependent on exports into the old EU member states and on the flow of money for this exchange shift.

The above facts can raise the question of whether the results automatically provide the prerequisites for improving the development of the new EU member states. This is the question of the convergence process de jure and de facto. For the Baltic, Balkan, and central and eastern European countries, joining the EU held the implicit promise of economic convergence to Western European standards of living represented by the old EU member states. As officially stated by the European Commission (2019), this was true for both the first wave of eastern enlargement in 2004 and the subsequent accession of Bulgaria and Romania in 2007 and finally Croatia in 2013. As of the 15th anniversary of the 2004 accession, this expectation was largely met; access to the European single market (i.e., internal market) created new business opportunities, triggered vast capital flowed to the new EU member states, and facilitated their integration into global supply chains. The catch-up process, thus, gained additional impetus during the accession talks and negotiation and again upon joining the EU. Although a significant gap remains today, it is shrinking at a rapid pace, highlighting central improvements among the new EU member states, as well as convergence of the group of EU13 countries to the group of EU15 countries in the following areas: income convergence; convergence in labor productivity; convergence in workforce; convergence in participation rates; convergence in educational attainment; convergence in competitiveness; convergence in quality of governance; convergence in research, development, and innovation; convergence in digital connectivity; convergence in openness to trade and integration into European supply chains; and convergence in openness to foreign direct investment.

Figure 2 constitute the box plots of all parts of MPI, i.e., MPI, ECH, and FS. Box plots of each MPI part show data skewness and kurtosis to mean values, reflected by the equal location of the median (X_{50}) between the upper (X_{75}) and lower (X_{25}) quartiles. In the cases of MPI, ECH, and FS, data are skewed to the upper levels—the median is shifted to the upper quartile (X_{75}). The shapes of box plots also indicate the symmetrical layout. Each box plot represents data from the normal distribution, not only due to its symmetry but also due to the position of the median, which lies almost in the middle of the rectangle. In the context of efficiency analysis, the outliers and extreme values are interesting, i.e., the highest or lowest values of MPI in comparison to values of MPI of other countries in the evaluated sample within the reference period. The current version of the EU has 28 member states and, therefore, we aim to have relevant analysis for all EU countries and not only the selected sample. Therefore, DMUs present the EU countries in the form of outliers, and extreme values are not excluded from our empirical analysis. Our analysis aims to have comprehensible results for the entire sample of countries and not a partial sample; we are concerned about the diversity that the EU is characterized by, as highlighted by its motto "unity in diversity".

The classification of EU15 and EU13 member states concerning the nature of technical and technological change is illustrated in Figure 3. In all reference periods, the location of all European countries is recorded concerning results of ECH and FS. Evaluated countries are divided into two groups (the EU15 member states and the EU13 member states) for a better comparison of common features and differences. It is convenient to remind the reader that ECH and FS values of 1.000 mean no productivity change, values higher than 1.000 mean that productivity is improving, and values lower than 1.000 mean that productivity is deteriorating. From this point of view, it is possible to divide European countries into four categories or quadrants. Via the illustration of Figure 2, information about differences in efficiency recorded by MPI among three reference periods is confirmed. Across the reference periods, most European countries are located in quadrants with a low level of FS, and a higher or lower level of ECH. It means that efficiency change is especially caused by the difference in the production possibility frontier because of the technology development between reference years, i.e., technology frontier shift. This fact is positive information concerning factors of competitiveness; it signifies that countries can utilize their internal factor endowment efficiently and can apply technological progress for boosting their competitive advantages, i.e., they contribute to qualitative-based economic growth, allowing raising the steady state. On the other side, some European countries are located in quadrants with a high level of FS, and a more upper or lower level of ECH. It means that efficiency change is due to a change in the relative efficiency of the evaluated country with respect to other countries, due to the production possibility frontier between reference years, i.e., technical efficiency change. This fact is not such positive information because it means that countries extract their efficiency based on shifts in sources of competitiveness, i.e., they make changes in composition and quantity of sources based on their exchange business with other countries. The characteristic of technical efficiency change, thus, contributes only to quantitative-based economic growth, which has its limits; this is disconcerting concerning limited sources, utilization of sources, and possibility/impossibility of their recovery.

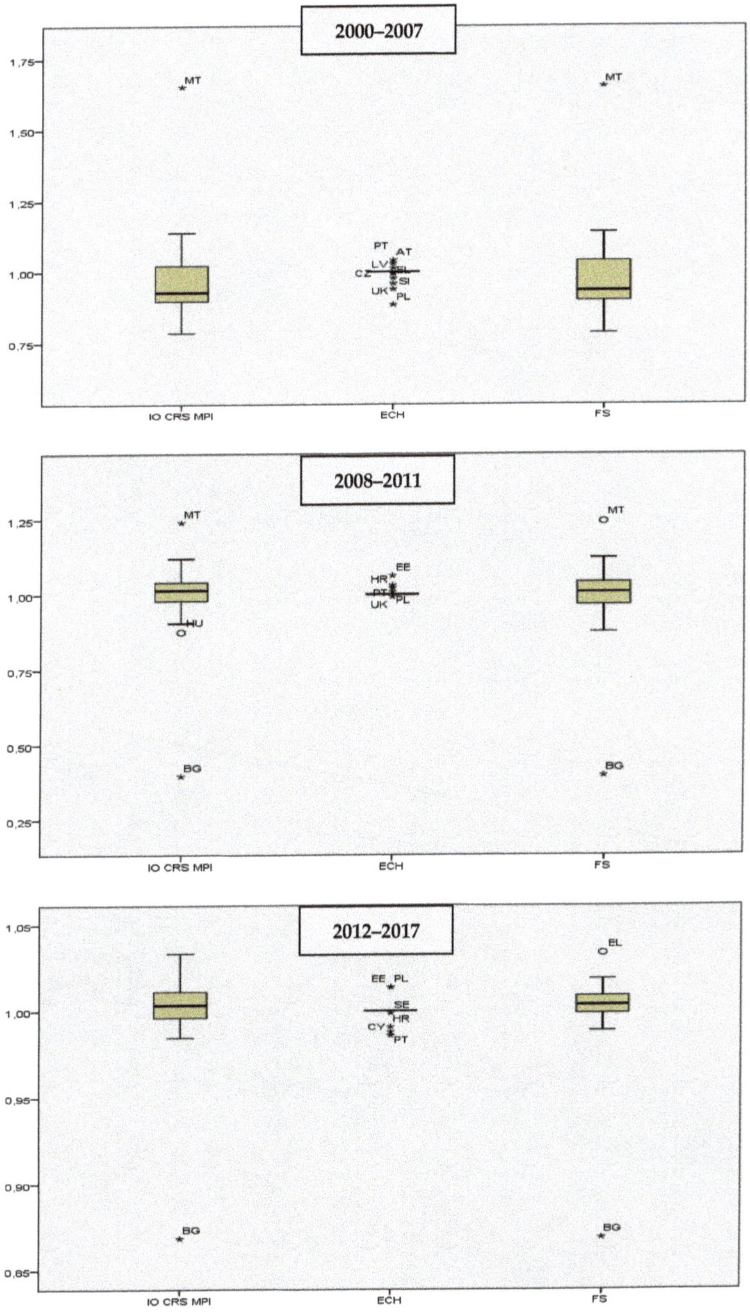

Figure 2. Box plots of Malmquist productivity index (MPI), change in relative efficiency (ECH), and change in production possibility frontier (FS)—outliers (source: own calculation and elaboration).

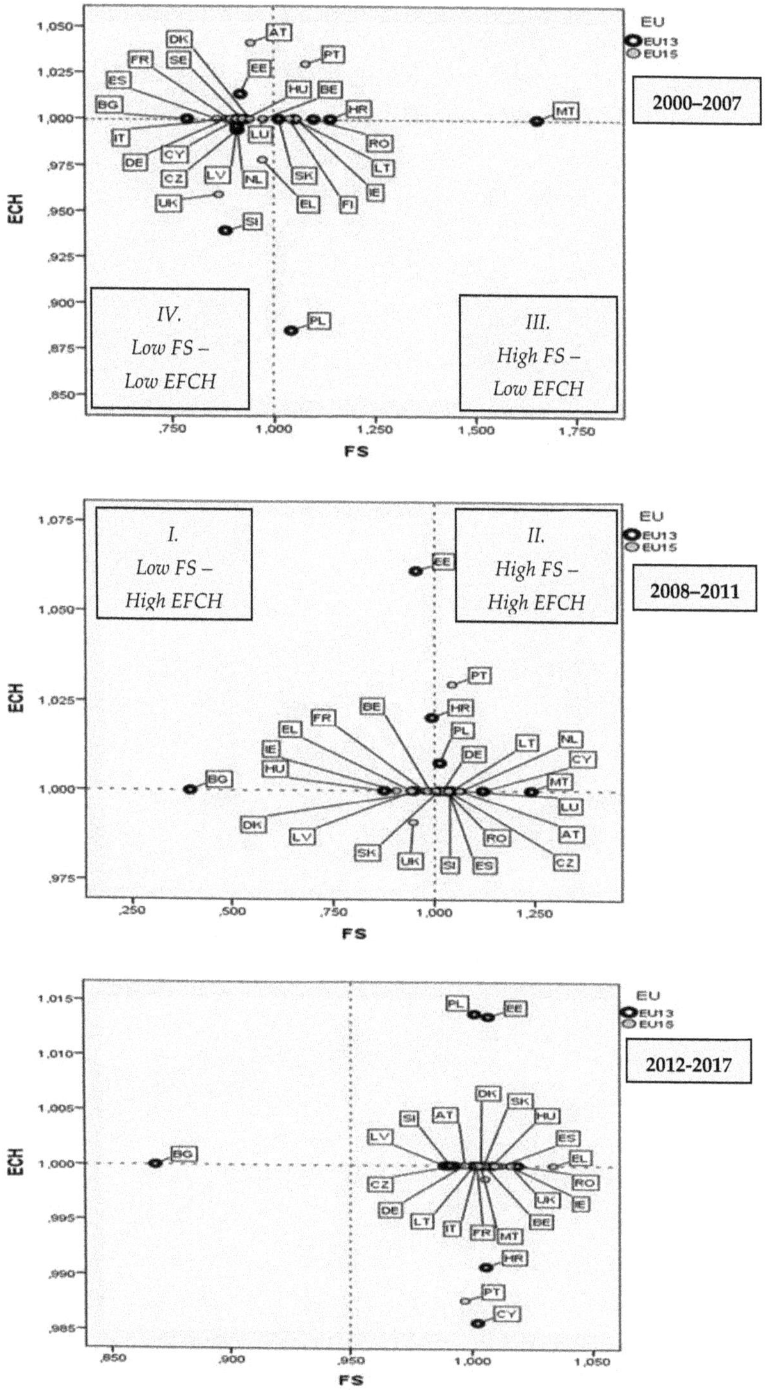

Figure 3. Comparison of EU15 and EU13 distances in ECH and FCH (source: own calculation and elaboration).

The practicality or applicability of these results in terms of economic policy is, however, limiting because the results only refer to relative efficiency. What does it mean? In the framework of the evaluation, it is necessary to move from efficiency to effectiveness, i.e., instead of conducting economic policy activities based on their setting and objectives; however, this cannot be done using the DEA method. For future research, it is necessary to rely on the evaluation of the relationship between output and outcome (effectiveness) and not input and output (efficiency), which the DEA method evaluates. The reconstructed or newly built technical and transport infrastructure, the reconstruction of buildings and companies, and buying new technical tools, i.e., factual or physical re-modernization should be taken in account, as well as the possibilities of proper use in activities generating added value for the economy, i.e., qualitative, competitive advantage, which is key for the knowledge economy. This should be the topic of future research, i.e., how the factor endowment of the given economy contributes to its growth and how the economy can use not only its quantitative but also its qualitative competitive advantages. To this end, however, it is necessary to find suitable methods used in the evaluation of effectiveness. The quality and utility of assessment could be improved further by developing a more integrated and ongoing approach to evaluation.

All these factors affect the convergence trend of the new EU member states and their regions to the old EU member states, and the growth in the old EU member states has an implicative impact on growth in the new EU member states. This growth may have the same degree in EU13 countries as in EU15 countries or may be higher. Many of the differences in economic growth and quality of life within a country may be explained by the differences in competitiveness. Countries with more paved roads, with better institutions, with better business environment, and with better human capital, for example, may experience faster economic growth and a clearer reduction in poverty levels (Charles and Zegarra 2014). All these trends and facts have very significant effects on the competitiveness of all EU member states, changing the efficiency/inefficiency development. The internal variation and heterogeneity also underline the inevitable steps needed at the national level. Policies oriented to solve the main economic and social problems of citizens may then not only focus on the improvement of the aggregate or average indicators of competitiveness, but also on the reduction of the regional differences in competitiveness. Effective thematic policies and efficient use of public spending on the established aims will help the overall efficiency of the whole system, ensuring desired outcomes—effectiveness that has a significant impact on reducing disparities and improving competitiveness.

The White Paper on the Future of Europe makes a powerful statement about the current precarious state of European integration and its uncertain future. The continuing effects of the financial, economic, and migration crises are associated with reduced confidence and trust in democratic institutions and politicians, and a rise in populism, threatening the unity of the EU. A significant cause is the unequal impact of globalization and technological change on different parts of the EU. Thus, the EU not only needs to accelerate sustainable growth but also to resume convergence so that all parts of the EU can exploit the opportunities from the globalization of trade and technological change. The past three decades were characterized by trade liberalization, the rise of global value chains, and global production networks. The integration of emerging countries challenged the EU's attractiveness as a production location, because of import competition and off-shoring.

Furthermore, technological change and digital transformation (the fourth production revolution) is associated with jobless growth and concerns that the EU is falling behind technologically. Europe generally has a strong position concerning advances in technology, value added, productivity, profitability, and profits, but there are significant questions about its technological leadership. There are significant opportunities from the structural change that the EU is well placed to exploit. The cost advantages of some emerging economies are eroding, labor costs are becoming a less critical factor in location decisions, and some supply chains are being shortened to ensure greater control. These trends do not guarantee the renewed competitiveness of developed economies but depend on the ability of developed economies to effect the necessary structural transformation. Structural change across the EU requires a different policy and institutional focus on "ecosystems" of open, interconnected networks of stakeholders, cooperating through strategic partnerships able to respond rapidly and flexibly to technological, market, and social changes. Disruptive innovation and creativity require multidisciplinary and open models of collaboration. The support of an environment for such ecosystems will unavoidably need to be tailored to specific national, regional, or even local contexts. Policy packages need to be integrated and coordinated, delivered at a national, regional, and local level, while being adapted to the needs of different territories (Bachtler et al. 2017).

Many observers believe that Europe is at the beginning of a new industrial revolution, considered to be the fourth such leap forward labeled Industry 4.0. The ubiquitous use of sensors, the expansion of wireless communication and networks, the deployment of increasingly intelligent robots and machines, as well as increased computing power at a lower cost and the development of "big data" analytics, have the potential to transform the way goods are manufactured in Europe. This new digital industrial revolution holds the promise of increased flexibility in manufacturing, mass customization, increased speed, better quality, and improved productivity. However, to capture these benefits, enterprises will need to invest in equipment, information and communication technologies (ICT), and data analysis, as well as the integration of data flow throughout the global value chain. The EU supports industrial change through its industrial policy and research and infrastructure funding. Member states are also sponsoring national initiatives such as Industrie 4.0 in Germany, the Factory of the Future in France and Italy, and Catapult centers in the United Kingdom (UK). However, challenges remain. The need for investment, changing business models, data issues, legal questions of liability and intellectual property, standards, and skill mismatches are among the challenges that must be met if benefits are to be gained from new manufacturing and industrial technologies. If these obstacles can be overcome, Industry 4.0 may help reverse the past decline in industrialization and increase total value added from manufacturing to a targeted 20% of all value added by strategy Europe 2020.

Based on the facts mentioned in the two paragraphs above, the issue of reducing disparities among the EU member states and improving internal and external competitiveness can be solved by the current technical and digital revolution (Industry 4.0), especially via the EU cohesion policy instruments, e.g., in the form of Cohesion Policy 4.0 and through the European Structural and Investment Funds for current programming period 2014–2020. The challenge for the EU as a whole and the individual member state policy-makers is to develop or adopt policy frameworks and strategies that will stimulate sustainable growth, in a manner that ensures greater inclusiveness, especially in access to employment and capacity for entrepreneurship. This demands a more granular approach to structural policy, tailored better to the specific conditions of the different types of regions and communities across the EU. Different strategies are needed for frontier regions, intermediate regions (some catching up but others only keeping pace), and lagging regions. Existing EU strategies—from Lisbon strategy for period 2000–2010 to current strategy Europe 2020 for period 2010–2020—are only partially successful, with limited results about the scale of the challenge.

Notwithstanding specific achievements, strategies were over-ambitious about the resources available, the deficits in governance (especially on coherence and the coordination of policies), and the performance of interventions. Importantly, policy responses gave inadequate recognition of the spatial unevenness of current and development needs and challenges for economic growth and development in the EU. Looking forward, any new EU strategic approach needs to recognize the lessons from the past and be realistic about what can be achieved. With relatively limited budgetary resources at the EU level, the EU will need to establish some principles for a new EU strategy. The critical requirement is a coherent, consistent, and mutually enforcing policy framework. Sectoral policies cannot deliver on a new EU agenda without integrated territorial policy packages. Equally, integrated territorial policy approaches cannot achieve prosperity and inclusive growth in the EU without well-designed sectoral and structural policies and reforms.

The EU model of integration delivered unmatched long-term growth and economic and social convergence. However, the model is threatened by the effects of the financial and economic crises on employment opportunities and living standards. The EU needs both to accelerate sustainable growth and ensure that all parts of the EU can exploit the growing globalization of trade and technological change. Structural transformation should be central to renewed policy priorities, requiring a new balance between policies for competitiveness and cohesion. The pursuit of economic and social cohesion is a collective task of both national and EU policies. Member states have the primary responsibility for the conduct and coordination of their economic policies to meet cohesion objectives. The same obligation applies to all EU policies and actions, including the implementation of the internal market. The agenda for Cohesion 4.0 is, thus, a much broader task than for cohesion policy alone. It requires the EU member states to demonstrate that they implemented structural reforms to support growth and cohesion before uploading domestic interests to the European level. It also underscores the necessity of an integrated approach to structural transformation and cohesion under all EU regulatory and investment policies (Bachtler et al. 2017).

The informative ability of the results depends on the methods used; the results, as such, are dependent on the selected measurement methods that affect their limits and usage assumptions. Generally, the results of each analysis and method depend on the data used, i.e., they depend on data quality. There exist different assumptions that your data must meet for the method used to give a valid result. In the case of our analysis, the limitations are lined primarily with using principal component analysis (PCA). When we chose to analyze our data using PCA, part of the process involved checking to make sure that the data we wanted to examine could be analyzed using PCA. In practice, checking for these assumptions required using SPSS Statistics to carry out a few more tests, as well as to think a little bit more about our data. When analyzing our data using SPSS Statistics, one or more of these assumptions may be violated (i.e., not met). This is not uncommon when working with real-world data rather than textbook examples. However, even when our data fail certain assumptions, there is often a solution to try and overcome this. The particulars that we had to deal with in our analysis mainly concerned that data should be suitable for data reduction and there should be no significant outliers. Involving DEA assumptions, we had to deal with the homogeneity of units, sampling adequacy, i.e., comparison of the number of units and the number of input and output variables, and last but not least isotonicity. All of these limitations were addressed, tested, and explained in the article.

6. Conclusions

Currently, the EU consists of 28 member states and is continually expanding to include new countries. The considerable geographic, demographic, and cultural diversity of the EU also brings differences in the socio-economic position of the EU member states. Different results in economic performance and living standards of the population indicate the status of the competitiveness of every country. Each country should know its competitive advantages and disadvantages and aim to strengthen advantages and reduce disadvantages, i.e., key factors of competitiveness. One of the main aims of the paper was to define the main factors of socio-economic development that determine the competitiveness level of EU member states. Based on FA results, it is possible to state that, in most of the cases, the old EU member states reflect the best results in driven forces of competitiveness (inputs aspects) as an assumption for better outcomes of economic activities and functioning of society (outputs aspects). The competitiveness of territory resides not only in the competitiveness of its constituent firms and their interactions, but also in the broader assets and social, economic, institutional, and public attributes of the country itself. The notion of competitiveness is as much about qualitative factors and conditions (such as untraded networks of informal knowledge, trust, social capital, and the like) as it is about quantifiable attributes and processes (such as inter-firm trading, patenting rates, labor supply, and so on). Furthermore, the causes of competitiveness are usually attributed to the effects of an aggregate of factors rather than the impact of any individual factor. The sources of competitiveness may also originate at a variety of geographical scales, from the local through to the regional, national, and even international. Therefore, the possibility of isolating the precise effects of any individual factor is limited, as mentioned by Martin (2003). The emergence of new perspectives in creating competitive advantages at the national level clearly emphasizes the role of local factors and economic initiatives in the general economic development of a country through conceptual constructions such as industrial clusters or districts, innovation networks, or competence centers.

From efficiency analysis, it is evident that there are significant economic development disparities between European countries. For smoothing of these disparities, the EU authorities are developing various strategies to further the economic growth of all EU member states and especially their regions both in the old and new EU member states. The pace of convergence also has an impact on the level of economic growth of the EU as such. Catch-up of less developed economies (the EU13 countries) can occur through several different channels. As these effects occur simultaneously, they can cause feedback to other economic developments, meaning that many of the dynamics can be mutually reinforcing, thus having a positive impact not only on the group of EU13 countries but also on the group of EU15 countries. From efficiency analysis, the five channels can be distinguished in the EU context, i.e., intensification of trade, increases in investment in human and physical capital, financial integration, improvements in institutional quality, and innovation and technological progress. As the European Commission (2019) explained, the nature of the convergence process is in line with enlargement process, and any transition from a centrally planned economy to a market-based one is bound to produce a rise in productivity, economic growth, and per capita income. The main channels through which this occurs is through greater allocative efficiency and, perhaps less clear-cut, higher capital investment rates and more effortless technology transfer.

When the Baltic, Balkan, and central and eastern European countries joined the EU in 2004–2007–2013, they became part of the European single market, i.e., one territory without any internal borders or other regulatory obstacles to the four free movements (movement of goods, services, persons, and capital). Membership of the European single market raised their integration with the rest of the EU, stimulated macroeconomic competitiveness, as well as market competition and trade, improved efficiency, raised quality, and reduced prices. It boosted trade with the old EU member states of the EU15 countries, as well as among each other. It also had a large impact on incomes and welfare of citizens in the EU as a whole. Not only access to the European single market but also the EU cohesion policy had a significant impact on the convergence pace, i.e., the EU cohesion policy supports the catch-up process in Europe's regions. The Baltic, Balkan, and central and eastern European countries joining the EU became eligible for this support from the EU cohesion policy programs. The results of DEA analysis, thus, confirm the potential benefits of the EU cohesion policy with significant output gains in the long-run period due to sizeable productivity improvements. As officially stated by the European Commission (2019) concerning the impact of the EU cohesion policy, in the medium-run period, the productivity-enhancing effects of infrastructure investment, research and development-promoting policies, and human capital investments become gradually stronger and generate large output effects in the long-run period; therefore, there are permanent positive output gains in the EU as a whole.

Many European countries, even those with an acceptable level of economic growth, are developing new strategic plans aiming at keeping up in the "rat race" of international and interregional competition to attract the best investments. A policy focusing on improving the physical and social environment may be one of the essential tools to attract the natural territorial sources of economic growth. This competition may be seen as the result of an increasing variety of production opportunities in a growing number of regions across the EU (Lambooy and Boschma 2001). The new variety evolved with the development of new technologies and new organizational structures. Many countries feel the threat of being outperformed by other countries and, therefore, they have to utilize their competitive advantages efficiently. Bringing together different development factors which illustrate single aspects of competitiveness gives a first impression of the overall international competitiveness of European countries and shows the diversity that exists within the EU territory. Among the essential driving forces influencing future territorial development are demographic development (including migration), economic integration, transport, energy, agriculture and rural development, climate change, further EU enlargements, and territorial governance. A significant role is played by exogenous factors having an impact on regional competitiveness, as mentioned. Current theories of regional competitiveness emphasize the significance of "soft" factors such as human, cultural (knowledge and creativity), and socio-institutional capital, environmental quality, etc. A wide range of soft location factors is, thus, of increasing importance. "Soft" factors like governance, culture, and natural environment are part of territorial potentials and offer synergies for jobs and the growth agenda. The potentials for these "soft factors" differ widely between areas. Quality living environments and access to environmental and cultural amenities are among factors that attract investment and people to a location, which is very important for competitiveness for each country and its competitive advantage and factor endowment. Currently, hazards do not undermine the competitiveness of a region. Only a few places have shallow exposure to the main natural and technological hazards in Europe, and climate change is expected to increase the risk of hazards in the future. To gaze into the future, it is necessary to understand the driving forces that shape territorial development and various possible future developments and interrelations with the territory each driving force might bring. Bringing them together into integrated prospective scenarios is then the final challenge.

Author Contributions: Conceptualization, L.M., M.S., and J.H.; methodology, M.S. and J.H.; software, M.S. and J.H.; validation, L.M. and M.S.; formal analysis, L.M. and M.S.; investigation, L.M.; resources, L.M.; data curation, M.S.; writing—original draft preparation, L.M. and M.S.

Funding: This research received no external funding.

Acknowledgments: The paper was supported by grant No. 17-23411Y of the Czech Science Agency, the Operational Program Education for Competitiveness—Project No. CZ.1.07/2.3.00/20.0296, and the SGS project (SP2014/111) of the Faculty of Economics, VŠB Technical University of Ostrava.

Conflicts of Interest: The authors declare no conflicts of interest. The funders had no role in the design of the study; in the collection, analyses, or interpretation of data; in the writing of the manuscript, and in the decision to publish the results.

Appendix A

Table A1. DEA method in countries' macroeconomy and KBE studies (source: own review and elaboration).

Authors	Datasets	Inputs and Outputs Used in DEA	Key Results
Cheng Chen 2017	20 Taiwan counties/cities in the period 1999–2013	Inputs and outputs: variables for the department of economic development, variables for the department of public security, variables for the department of social welfare, variables for the department of education	The police security department is the most efficient in most counties/cities in the period 1999–2013, and the economic development department is the second most efficient one in 2002–2005 and after 2009. There exist urban–rural gaps in the efficiency scores between counties and cities, between service-type and non-service type counties/cities, and among different regions.
Nurboja and Košak 2017	11 southeast European countries; 82 banks from EU member countries and 157 banks from non-EU countries; period 1999–2013	Inputs: borrowed funds, labor, and physical Capital Outputs: loans, securities, and other earning assets, ratio of equity	Statistically significant cost efficiency gap between EU and non-EU banking systems in the region, where on average EU banking systems tend to be more cost efficient than their non-EU counterparts.
Wu et al. 2014	21 Organisation for Economic Co-Operation and Development (OECD) countries	Inputs: real physical capital per worker, real knowledge capital per worker Outputs: Real income per worker, real income per worker over unemployment rate, real income per worker over air pollutants	Research and development expenditures, the proxy variable for knowledge capital, can indeed improve countries' efficiency scores, implying that the endogenous growth theory is supported in OECD countries. Whether the undesirable outputs are included in the DEA models and are properly treated is crucial in the evaluation of efficiency values.
Foddi and Usai 2013	271 regions in 29 European countries	Inputs: Total intramural R&D expenditure, Economically active population with tertiary education attainment Outputs: Number of the European Patent Office (EPO) patent applications per priority year and residence region of inventors	Malmquist index shows extremely differences in productivity dynamics across regions, important differences are between the core and periphery of Europe.
Rabar 2013	Croatian regions, three-year period 2005–2007	Inputs: registered unemployment rate, number of support allowance users Outputs: share of the secondary sector in Gross Valued Added (GVA), gross fixed capital formation in fixed assets, level of import coverage by export, number of graduate students, Gross Domestic Product (GDP)	Among 63 observed entities, 15 turned out to be efficient. The highest efficiency results were achieved in 2007 toward both orientations. None of the 21 counties was efficient during the entire period. The worst efficiency results were achieved in 2006, while the lowest average efficiency was achieved in 2005. Average efficiency scores for all three periods are greater in output orientation than in input orientation.

Table A1. *Cont.*

Authors	Datasets	Inputs and Outputs Used in DEA	Key Results
Goryushina and Mesropyan 2013	Russian regional economy performance for the period from 2008 to 2010	Inputs: number of cattle, organizations acreage under crops, average number of employees, power capacity, equipment parks Outputs: gross grain yield, production of milk, production of livestock and poultry	Agrarian production of the south of Russia shows the reserve of stability, and the southern regions belong to Pareto-efficient set of Russian regions. Only 4 regions among 13 of the south are estimated as having the stable decline. The economic development opportunities of this regions are significant, nevertheless, the considerable potential of regions is not used.
Afzal and Lawrey 2012	Association of southeast Asian nations (ASEAN) in two years 1995 and 2010, World Development Indicators (WDI) and World Competitiveness Yearbook (WCY)	Inputs: Export/GDP, import/GDP, Foreign Direct Investment (FDI) inward flows, R&D expenditure, intellectual property rights, education expenditure, net enrolment ratio at secondary school, knowledge transfer rate (university to industry), FDI inflows Outputs: Real GDP growth, scientific and technical publications per 1000 population, computer users per 1000 population, high-tech export	Indonesia in knowledge acquisition; Singapore, South Korea and Thailand in knowledge production; Singapore in knowledge distribution; the Philippines, and South Korea in knowledge utilization are the most productive and 100% efficient countries in either one or both of the years investigated.
Deliktas and Balcilar 2005	25 transition economies (east European, Baltic, and other former Soviet Union countries)	Inputs: total labor force, gross capital formation Outputs: real GDP	No technological progress, but over the whole period 1991–2000 there was a technological regress, and also decline in the average annual total factor productivity. Results suggest that, on average, chance in technical efficiency is outweighed by the technical regress.
Tan et al. 2008	WDI-2001 dataset for 54 developing countries	Inputs: Research and Development (R&D) expenditure, labor productivity, average schooling Outputs: mobile phone users, internet users, Personal Computer (PC) penetration, high-tech exports	India, Indonesia, Thailand, and China are inefficient countries due to the outflow of human resources.
Christopoulos 2007	Selected OECD and non-OECD countries	Inputs: human capital, openness Output: real GDP	Movements towards openness increase the efficiency performance of non-OECD countries.
Mohammad 2007	Selected Asia–Pacific countries. Datasets collected in 1996, 2000, and 2003	Inputs: government expenditure as % of GDP Outputs: real GDP growth, real employment rate, inflation rate	Only seven of 25 selected countries are efficient.

Table A1. *Cont.*

Authors	Datasets	Inputs and Outputs Used in DEA	Key Results
Ramanathan 2006	Selected Middle Eastern and north African countries, WDI-1999	Inputs and outputs: ratio of labour to population, life expectancy, primary education teachers, GNP per capita, literacy rate, mortality rate, etc.	Bahrain, Jordan, Kuwait, and the United Arab Emirates (UAE) are the most efficient while Yemen is the least efficient country.
Malhotra and Malhotra 2006	European Union (EU15) nations against one another from 1993 to 2006	Seven economic variables: current account as % of GDP, current account as % of exports, GDP per head of population, inflation, international liquidity, real GDP growth, exchange rate stability	All the participating nations were not equally efficient at the beginning of the economic integration in 1993. Economic integration did help in achieving convergence in economic performance of EU15 nations because 13 of the 15 nations were efficient in 1998. After 1998, there is lack of convergence in the performance of EU 15 nations and some nations performed more efficiently in contrast to other nations.
Halkos and Tzeremes 2005	51 Greek prefectures, three decades (1980, 1990, 2000)	Inputs: Number of hospital beds per 1000 citizens, number of doctors per 1000 citizens, number of public schools per 1000 students, number of public buses per 1000 citizens Outputs: GDP as a percentage of the mean GDP of the country, difference of urban–rural population, number of new houses per 1000 citizens	Results of effect of fiscal policies on the Greek prefectures: the resources of a prefecture do not necessarily ensure the efficiency of this prefecture.
Hsu et al. 2008	World Competitiveness Yearbook 2004	WCY-2004 pillars used as input and output variables for OECD and non-OECD countries	Indonesia and Argentina outperform in all the efficiency scores and Turkey, Poland, and Mexico appear to have stable efficiencies. Twenty-nine countries are shown to be efficient.
Hseu and Shang 2005	OECD countries, 1991-2000	Inputs: wood pulp capacity, paper and paperboard capacity, number of employees Outputs: wood pulp, paper and paperboard	The productivity change of pulp and paper industry in OECD countries ranged from Switzerland's 0.9% to Japan's 2.4% over the sampled period. The Nordic nations (Finland, Norway, and Sweden) recorded 1.2–1.5% improvement in their performance. The productivity of the Canadian pulp and paper industry increased by 2%, while that of its United States counterpart increased only by 0.8%. The results also showed that the last decade's productivity growth was attributed more to the technical change than efficiency change.

Table A1. *Cont.*

Authors	Datasets	Inputs and Outputs Used in DEA	Key Results
Breuss et al. 2000	Central and eastern European candidate countries to the EU	Three Copenhagen criteria: (i) political criteria—i.e., the establishment of democracy and the protection of human rights and minorities; (ii) economic criteria—the building up of a functioning market economy able to withstand the competition on the single market; (iii) acquis criterion—i.e., the complete takeover of the legal status of the Union plus the acceptance of its targets (meaning monetary and political union)	Macroeconomic performance of most of the Central and Eastern European countries (CEEC) lies far behind the EU standards, in foreign trade some of the CEECs already perform better than some EU countries. Interestingly, authors find out that some CEECs were already better prepared for the European Monetary Union (EMU) than many EU member states.
Golany and Thore 1997	Statistical department of 72 developed and developing countries in 1970–1985	Inputs: real investment as % of GDP, real government consumption as % of GDP, education expenditure as % of GDP Outputs: real GDP growth, infant mortality, enrolment ratio for secondary schools, welfare payments	Japan, the United States of America (USA), Canada and the Asian tigers show increasing returns to scale (IRS); Scandinavian and very poor developing countries show decreasing returns to scale (DRS).

References

Adusei, Michael. 2016. Modelling the efficiency of universal banks in Ghana. *Quantitative Finance Letters* 4: 60–70. [CrossRef]

Afzal, Munshi Naser Ibne, and Roger Lawrey. 2012. Evaluating the Comparative Performance of Technical and Scale Efficiencies in Knowledge-Based Economies (KBEs) in ASEAN: A Data Envelopment Analysis (DEA) Application. *European Journal of Economics, Finance and Administrative Sciences* 51: 81–95.

Annoni, Paola, and Lewis Dijkstra. 2013. *EU Regional Competitiveness Index 2013*. Luxembourg: Publication Office of the European Union.

Annoni, Paola, and Kornelia Kozovska. 2010. *EU Regional Competitiveness Index 2010*. Luxembourg: Publication Office of the European Union.

Annoni, Paola, Lewis Dijkstra, and Nadia Gargano. 2017. *EU Regional Competitiveness Index 2016*. Working Paper WP 02/2017. Brussels: European Commission.

Avkiran, Necmi K. 2006. *Productivity Analysis in the Service Sector with Data Envelopment Analysis*. SSRN Working Paper 2006. Brisbane: The University of Queensland.

Bachtler, John, Joaquim Oliveira Martins, Peter Wostner, and Piotr Zuber. 2017. *Towards Cohesion Policy 4.0: Structural Transformation and Inclusive Growth*. Brussels: Regional Studies Association.

Balcerowicz, Leszek, Andrzej Rzónca, Lech Kalina, and Aleksander Łaszek. 2013. *Economic Growth in the European Union*. Brussels: Lisbon Council asbl.

Bansal, Pooja, and Aparna Mehra. 2018. Multi-period additive efficiency measurement in data envelopment analysis with non-positive and undesirable data. *OPSEARCH* 55: 642–61. [CrossRef]

Barnum, Darold, Jason Coupet, John Gleason, Abagail McWilliams, and Annaleena Parhankangas. 2017. Impact of input substitution and output transformation on data envelopment analysis decisions. *Applied Economics* 49: 1543–56. [CrossRef]

Breuss, Fritz, Mikulás Luptácik, and Bernhard Mahlberg. 2000. How far away are the CEECs from the EU economic standards? A data envelopment analysis of the economic performance of the CEECs. In *EI Working Papers/Europainstitut, 35*. Vienna: Vienna University of Economics and Business.

Caves, Douglas W., Laurits R. Christensen, and W. Erwin Diewert. 1982. The Economic Theory of Index Numbers and the Measurement of Input, Output, and Productivity. *Econometrica* 50: 1393–414. [CrossRef]

Chandola, Varun, Banerjee Arindam, and Vipin Kumar. 2009. Anomaly detection: A survey. *ACM Computing Surveys* 41: 1–58. [CrossRef]

Charles, Vincent, and Luis Felipe Zegarra. 2014. Measuring regional competitiveness through Data Envelopment Analysis: A Peruvian case. *Expert Systems with Applications* 41: 5371–81. [CrossRef]

Charnes, Abraham, William W. Cooper, and Edwardo L. Rhodes. 1978. Measuring the efficiency of decision making units. *European Journal of Operational Research* 2: 429–44. [CrossRef]

Cheng Chen, Chih. 2017. Measuring departmental and overall regional performance: Applying the multi-activity DEA model to Taiwan's cities/counties. *Omega* 67: 60–80. [CrossRef]

Christopoulos, Dimitris K. 2007. Explaining country's efficiency performance. *Economic Modelling* 24: 224–35. [CrossRef]

Chortirat, Thunyaporn, Boonorm Chomtee, and Juthaphorn Sinsomboonthong. 2011. Comparison of four data transformation methods for weibull distributed data. *Kasetsart Journal-Natural Science* 45: 366–83.

Conte, Andrea, Philip Schweizer, Adriaan Dierx, and Fabienne Ilzkovitz. 2009. *An Analysis of the Efficiency of Public Spending and National Policies in the Area of R&D*. European Economy—Occassional Papers 54. Brussels: European Commission.

Cooper, William W., Lawrence M. Seiford, and Kaoru Tone. 2007. Data Envelopment Analysis: A Comprehensive Text with Models, Applications, References and DEA-Solver Software. New York: Springer.

Deliktas, Ertugrul, and Mehmet Balcilar. 2005. A Comparative Analysis of Productivity Growth, Catch-Up, and Convergence in Transition Economies. *Emerging Markets Finance and Trade* 41: 6–28. [CrossRef]

Drucker, Peter. 2001. *The Efficiency of the Decision Makers*. Bucharest: Editura Destin.

Easterly, William, and Ross Levine. 2012. *The European Origins of Economic Development*. NBER Working Paper Series 18162; Cambridge: National Bureau of Economic Research.

Esser, Klaus, Wolfgang Hillebrand, Dirk Messner, and Jörg Meyer-Stamer. 1995. *Systemic Competitiveness. New Governance Patterns for Industrial Development*. London: Frank Cass.

European Commission. 2019. 11 Trends for 11 Countries on EU Convergence: The EU Enlargement Countries in the Baltics, Balkans and Central and Eastern Europe. Available online: https://ec.europa.eu/info/conference-15th-anniversary-2004-eu-enlargement-looking-back-looking-forward/edited-volume_en (accessed on 1 April 2019).

Färe, Rolf, Shawna Grosskopf, and C. A. Knox Lovell. 1994a. *Production Frontiers*. Cambridge: Cambridge University Press.

Färe, Rolf, Shawna Grosskopf, Marry Norris, and Zhongyang Zhang. 1994b. Productivity Growth, Technical Progress and Efficiency Change in Industrialized Countries. *The American Economic Review* 84: 66–83.

Farrell, Michael James. 1957. The measurement of productivity efficiency. *Journal of the Royal Statistical Society* 120: 253–90. [CrossRef]

Foddi, Marta, and Stefano Usai. 2013. *Technological catching up among European regions. Lessons from Data Envelopment Analysis*. WP4/02 Search Working Paper. Brussels: European Commission.

Gardiner, Ben, Ron Martin, and Peter Tyler. 2004. Competitiveness, Productivity and Economic Growth across the European Regions. *Journal of Regional Studies* 38: 1045–67. [CrossRef]

Ghosh, Jayati, Peter Havlik, Marcos Poplawski-Ribeiro, and Waltraut Urban. 2009. *Models of BRICs' Economic Development and Challenges for EU Competitiveness*. Vienna: The Vienna Institute for International Economics Studies.

Golany, Boaz, and Sten Thore. 1997. Restricted best practice selection in DEA: An overview with a case study evaluating the socio-economic performance of nations. *Annals of Operations Research* 73: 117–40. [CrossRef]

Goryushina, Evgenija, and Karine Mesropyan. 2013. Economic Inequality and Political Instability Measuring by DEA and Alternative Indices: State of the Art and Research Perspectives for Cross-Regional Studies. *Der Donauraum* 52: 445–64. [CrossRef]

Hair, Joseph F., William C. Black, Barry J. Babin, and Roplh E. Anderson. 2009. *Multivariate Data Analysis*. Upper Saddle River: Prentice Hall.

Halkos, George, and Nickolaos Tzeremes. 2005. A DEA Approach to Regional Development. MPRA Paper 3992. Available online: https://mpra.ub.uni-muenchen.de/id/eprint/3992 (accessed on 1 July 2007).

Hseu, Jiing-Shyang, and Jui-Kou Shang. 2005. Productivity Changes of Pulp and Paper Industry in OECD Countries, 1991–2000: A Non-Parametric Malmquist Approach. *Forest Policy and Economics* 7: 411–22. [CrossRef]

Hsu, Maxwell, Xueming Luo, and Gary H. Chao. 2008. The Fog of OECD and Non-OECD Country Efficiency: A Data Envelopment Analysis Approach. *The Journal of Developing Areas* 42: 81–93.

Hwang, Yun-Gi, Soohyun Park, and Daecheol Kim. 2018. Efficiency Analysis of Official Development Assistance Provided by Korea. *Sustainability* 10: 2697. [CrossRef]

Izadikhah, Mohammad, Reza Farzipoor Saen, and Razieh Roostaee. 2018. How to assess sustainability of suppliers in the presence of volume discount and negative data in data envelopment analysis? *Annals of Operations Research* 269: 241–67. [CrossRef]

Jiang, Huichen, and Yifan He. 2018. Applying Data Envelopment Analysis in Measuring the Efficiency of Chinese Listed Banks in the Context of Macroprudential Framework. *Mathematics* 6: 184. [CrossRef]

Lacko, Roman, and Zuzana Hajduová. 2018. Determinants of Environmental Efficiency of the EU Countries Using Two-Step DEA Approach. *Sustainability* 10: 3525. [CrossRef]

Lambooy, Jan G., and Ron A. Boschma. 2001. Evolutionary economics and regional policy. *The Annals of Regional Science* 35: 113–31. [CrossRef]

Lukovics, Miklos. 2009. Measuring Regional Disparities on Competitiveness Basis. In *Regional Competitiveness, Innovation and Environment*. Edited by Zoltán Bajmócy and Imre Lengyel. Szeged: JATE Press, pp. 39–53.

MacGregor Pelikánová, Radka. 2017. European myriad of approaches to parasitic commercial practices. *Oeconomia Copernicana* 8: 167–80. [CrossRef]

Makridou, Georgia, Kostas Andriosopoulos, Michael Doumpos, and Constantin Zopounidis. 2014. *An Integrated Approach for Energy Efficiency Analysis in European Union Countries*. Working Paper 2014.02. Chania: Technical University of Crete.

Malhotra, Rashmi, and Davinder K. Malhotra. 2006. Evaluating the efficiency of European Union integration. *International Journal of Commerce and Management* 19: 233–52. [CrossRef]

Mandl, Ulrike, Adriaan Dierx, and Fabienne Ilzkovitz. 2008. *The Effectiveness and Efficiency of Public Spending*. Brussels: European Commission-Directorate General for Economic and Financial Affairs.

Martin, Ron. 2003. A Study on the Factors of Regional Competitiveness. Available online: http://ec.europa.eu/regional_policy/sources/docgener/studies/pdf/3cr/competitiveness.pdf (accessed on 1 September 2003).

Melecký, Lukáš. 2018. The main achievements of the EU structural funds 2007–2013 in the EU member states: efficiency analysis of transport sector. *Equilibrium. Quarterly Journal of Economics and Economic Policy* 13: 285–306. [CrossRef]

Mihaiu, Diana Marieta, Alin Opreana, and Marian Pompiliu Cristescu. 2010. Efficiency, effectiveness and performance of the public sector. *Romanian Journal of Economic Forecasting* 1: 132–47.

Mohammad, Nordin. 2007. A Linear Programming Formulation of Macroeconomic Performance: The Case of Asia Pacific. *Matematika* 23: 29–40.

Nurboja, Bashkim, and Marko Košak. 2017. Banking efficiency in South East Europe: Evidence for financial crises and the gap between new EU members and candidate countries. *Economic Systems* 41: 122–38. [CrossRef]

Ocubo, Toshihiro. 2012. Antiagglomeration subsidies with heterogeneous firms. *Journal of Regional Science* 52: 285–87. [CrossRef]

Otsuka, Akihiro. 2014. Analysis of Productive Efficiency in Japanese Regional Economies. *Studies in Regional Science* 44: 453–65. [CrossRef]

Rabar, Danijela. 2013. Assessment of Regional Efficiency in Croatia using Data Envelopment Analysis. *Croatian Operational Research Review* 4: 76–88.

Ramanathan, Ramakrishnan. 2006. Evaluating the comparative performance of countries of the Middle East and North Africa: A DEA Application. *Socio-Economic Planning Sciences* 40: 156–67. [CrossRef]

Seiford, Lawrence M., and Joe Zhu. 1999. An investigation of returns to scale in data envelopment analysis. *Omega* 27: 1–11. [CrossRef]

Shu, Guoping, Beiyan Zeng, Deanne Wright, and Oscar Smith. 2002. Impact of Data Transformation on the Performance of Different Clustering Methods and Cluster Number Determination Statistics for Analyzing Gene Expression Profile Data. Paper presented at 14th Annual Conference on Applied Statistics in Agriculture, Manhattan, Kansas, April 28–30; pp. 94–110.

Staníčková, Michaela. 2017. Can the implementation of the Europe 2020 Strategy goals be efficient? The challenge for achieving social equality in the European Union. *Equilibrium. Quarterly Journal of Economics and Economic Policy* 12: 383–98.

Stevens, James P. 1986. *Applied Multivariate Statistics for the Social Sciences*. Mahwah: Lawrence Erlbaum Associates.

Tan, Hui-Boon, Chee-Wooi Hooy, Sardar M.N. Islam, and Alex Manzoni. 2008. Relative efficiency measures for the knowledge economies in the Asia Pacific region. *Journal of Modelling in Management* 3: 111–24.

Toloo, Mehdi, Mona Barat, and Atefeh Masoumzadeh. 2015. Selective measures in data envelopment analysis. *Annals of Operations Research* 226: 523–642. [CrossRef]

Tung, Shiue-Jen, Guo-Ya Gan, and Wen-Li Chyr. 2018. Efficiency Measures for VRM Models Dealing with Negative Data in DEA. *Journal of Marine Science and Technology-Taiwan* 26: 180–84.

Watt, Andrew, and Andreas Botsch. 2010. *After the Crisis: Towards a Sustainable Growth Model*. Brussels: European Trade Union Institute.

Wu, Po-Chin, Tzu-Hsien Huang, and Sheng-Chieh Pan. 2014. Country Performance Evaluation: The DEA Model Approach. *Social Indicators Research* 118: 835–49. [CrossRef]

Zhu, Joe. 2011. Manual DEA Frontier—DEA Add-In for Microsoft Excel. Available online: http://www.deafrontier.net (accessed on 1 May 2011).

MDPI
St. Alban-Anlage 66
4052 Basel
Switzerland
Tel. +41 61 683 77 34
Fax +41 61 302 89 18
www.mdpi.com

Journal of Risk and Financial Management Editorial Office
E-mail: jrfm@mdpi.com
www.mdpi.com/journal/jrfm

www.ingramcontent.com/pod-product-compliance
Lightning Source LLC
Chambersburg PA
CBHW051841210326
41597CB00033B/5732
9783038979647